W Juliet

Volume 7

Story & Art by Emura

W Juliet
Volume 7

Story and Art by Emura

Translation & English Adaptation/William Flanagan, Naomi Kokubo & Jeff Carlson
Touch-up Art & Lettering/Mark McMurray
Graphic Design/Hidemi Sahara
Editor/Carrie Shepherd

Managing Editor/Annette Roman
Director of Production/Noboru Watanabe
Vice President of Publishing/Alvin Lu
Sr. Director of Acquisitions/Rika Inouye
Vice President of Sales & Marketing/Liza Coppola
Publisher/Hyoe Narita

W Juliet by Emura © Emura 1998. All rights reserved.
First published in Japan in 2001 by HAKUSENSHA, Inc., Tokyo. English language translation rights in America and Canada arranged with HAKUSENSHA, Inc., Tokyo.
The W JULIET logo is a trademark of VIZ Media, LLC. All rights reserved.
The stories, characters and incidents mentioned in this publication are entirely fictional.

Printed in Canada.

Published by VIZ Media, LLC
P.O. Box 77010
San Francisco, CA 94107

10 9 8 7 6 5 4 3 2 1
First printing, October 2005

T 251555

www.viz.com
store.viz.com

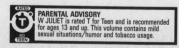

PARENTAL ADVISORY
W JULIET is rated T for Teen and is recommended for ages 13 and up. This volume contains mild sexual situations/humor and tobacco usage.

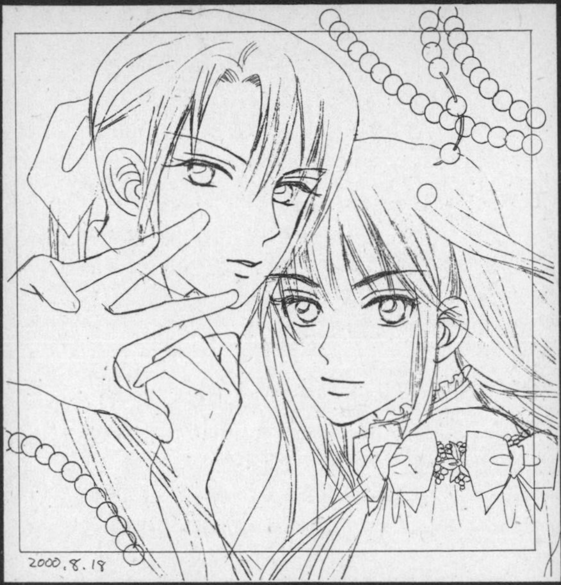
2000.8.18

The CD jacket! ↑Cover ↓Back cover

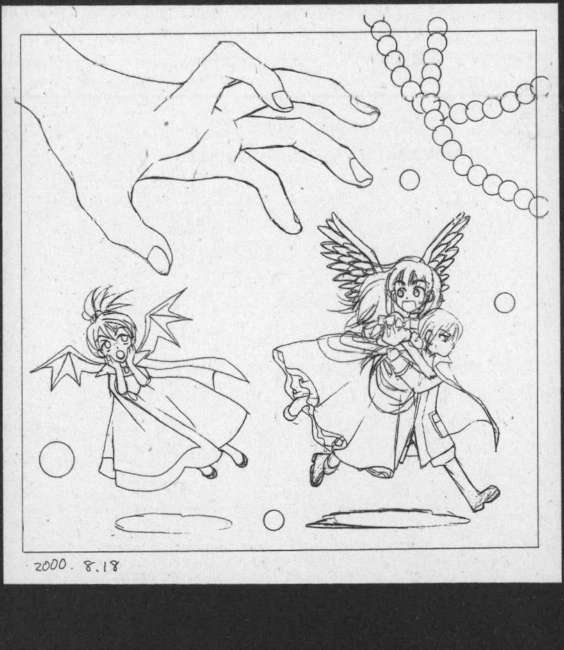
2000.8.18

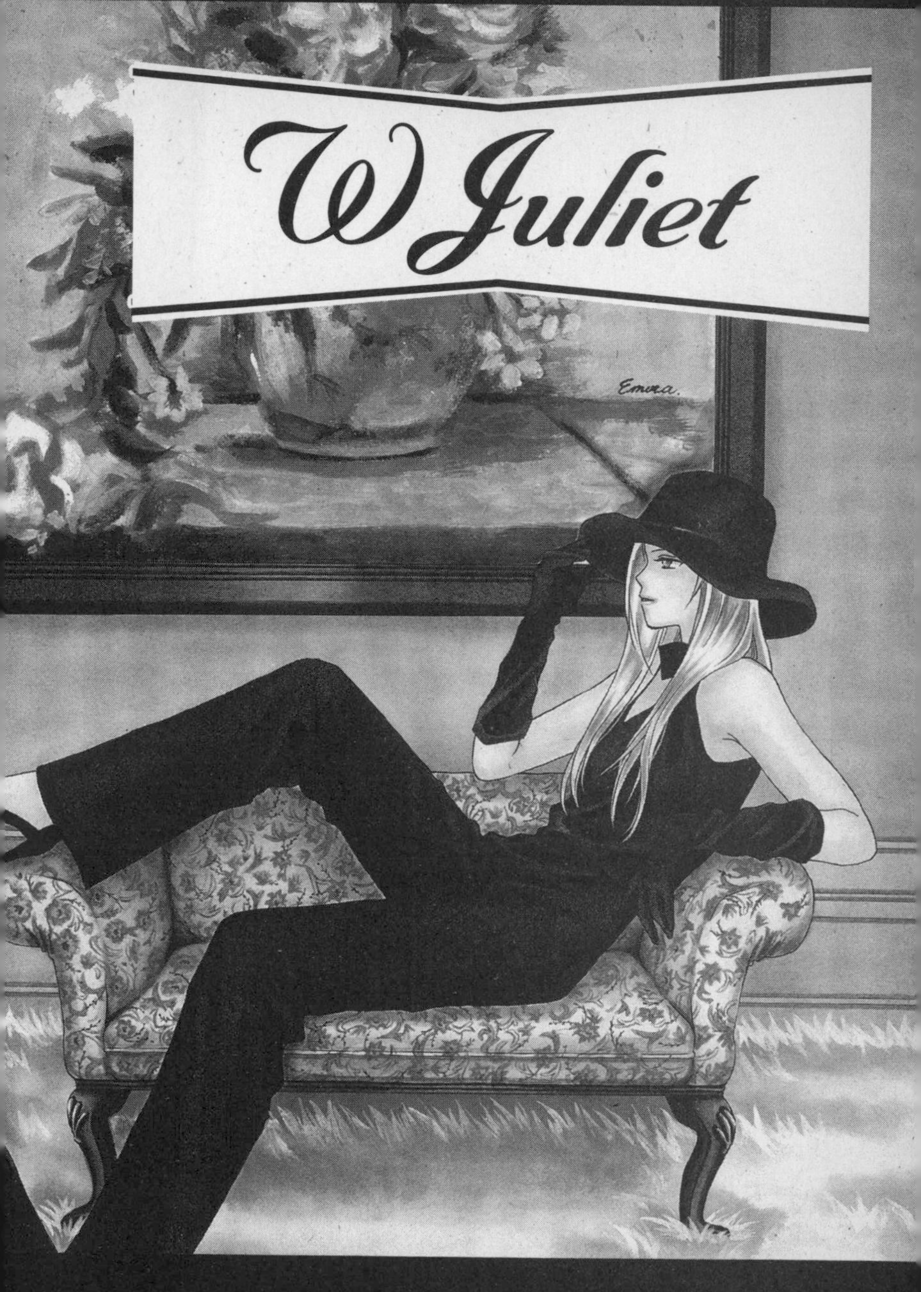
W Juliet
Emura.

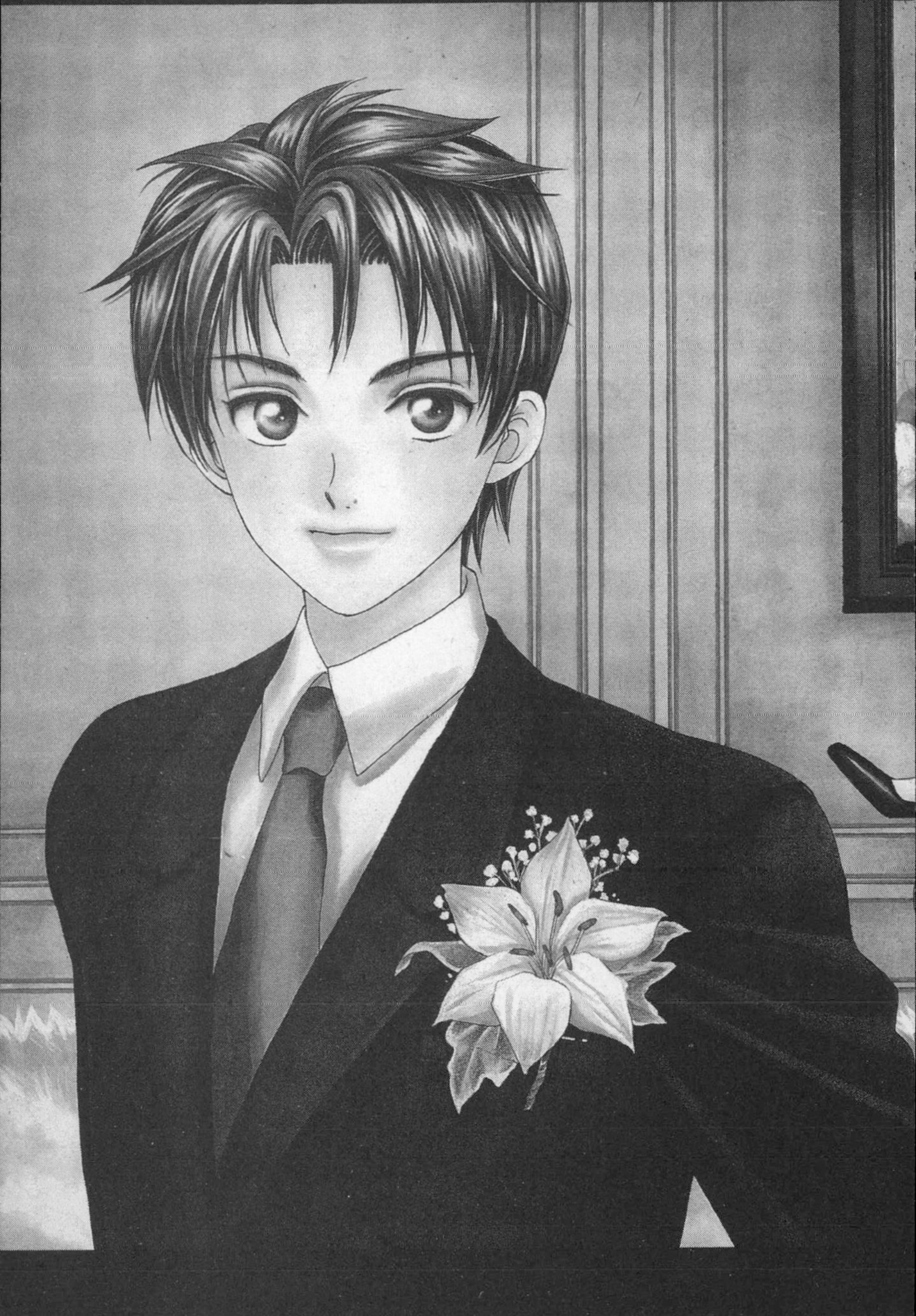

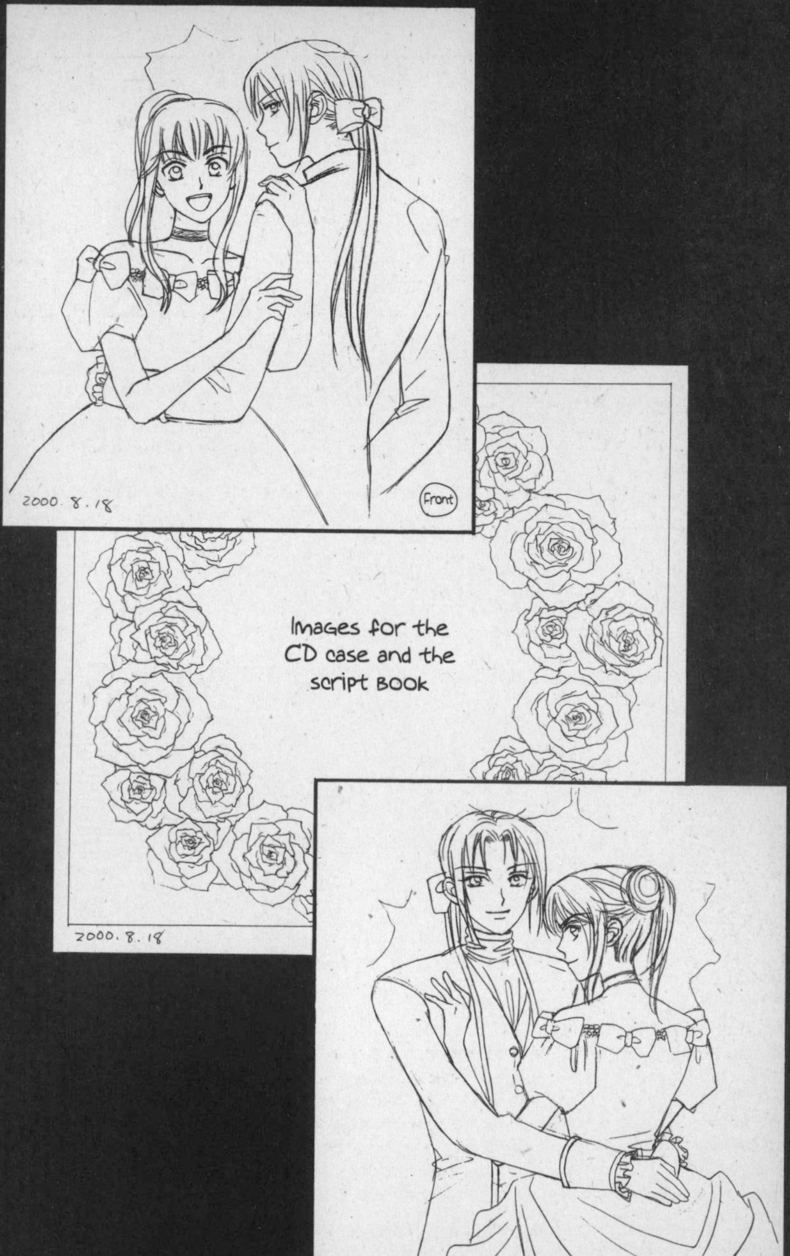
2000. 8. 18
Front
Images for the CD case and the script book
2000. 8. 18
2000. 8. 18
Back

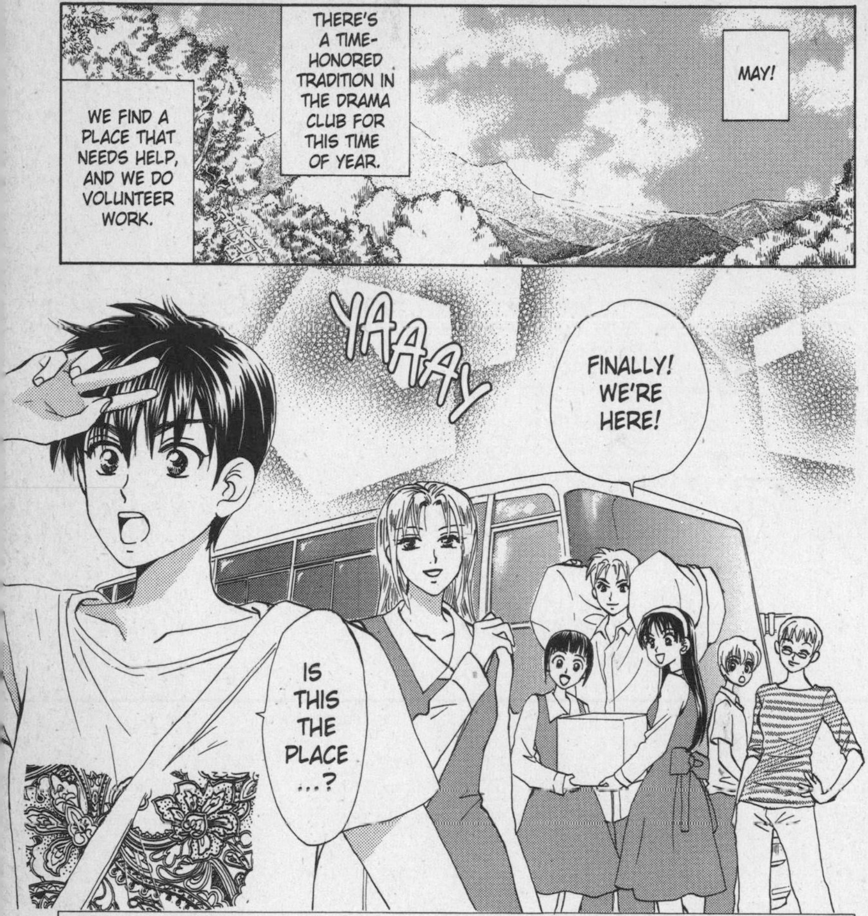

MAY!
THERE'S A TIME-HONORED TRADITION IN THE DRAMA CLUB FOR THIS TIME OF YEAR.
WE FIND A PLACE THAT NEEDS HELP, AND WE DO VOLUNTEER WORK.
FINALLY! WE'RE HERE!
YAAAY
IS THIS THE PLACE ...?

-Behind the Scenes Story- ①

At first, I wanted Tsubaki's name to be "Mai." But I wanted so much for her to be based on *La Traviata* (in Japanese it's called *Tsubaki Hime* or "Camellia Princess"), I changed it to Tsubaki. But when Ito gets splashed with tea (that was tea, you know!), the readers resented her doing it a little. On the title page, I got to draw Ito as a guy after so long, so I'm happy! ♥ Just once in a while! But one sharp-eyed reader remarked that the pollen hadn't been removed from the corsage on her jacket. Aww... I should have learned my lesson about that in school!

Am I really a graduate of flower arranging school?!

Pollen sticks to clothes, so you must remove the stamens before making a corsage!

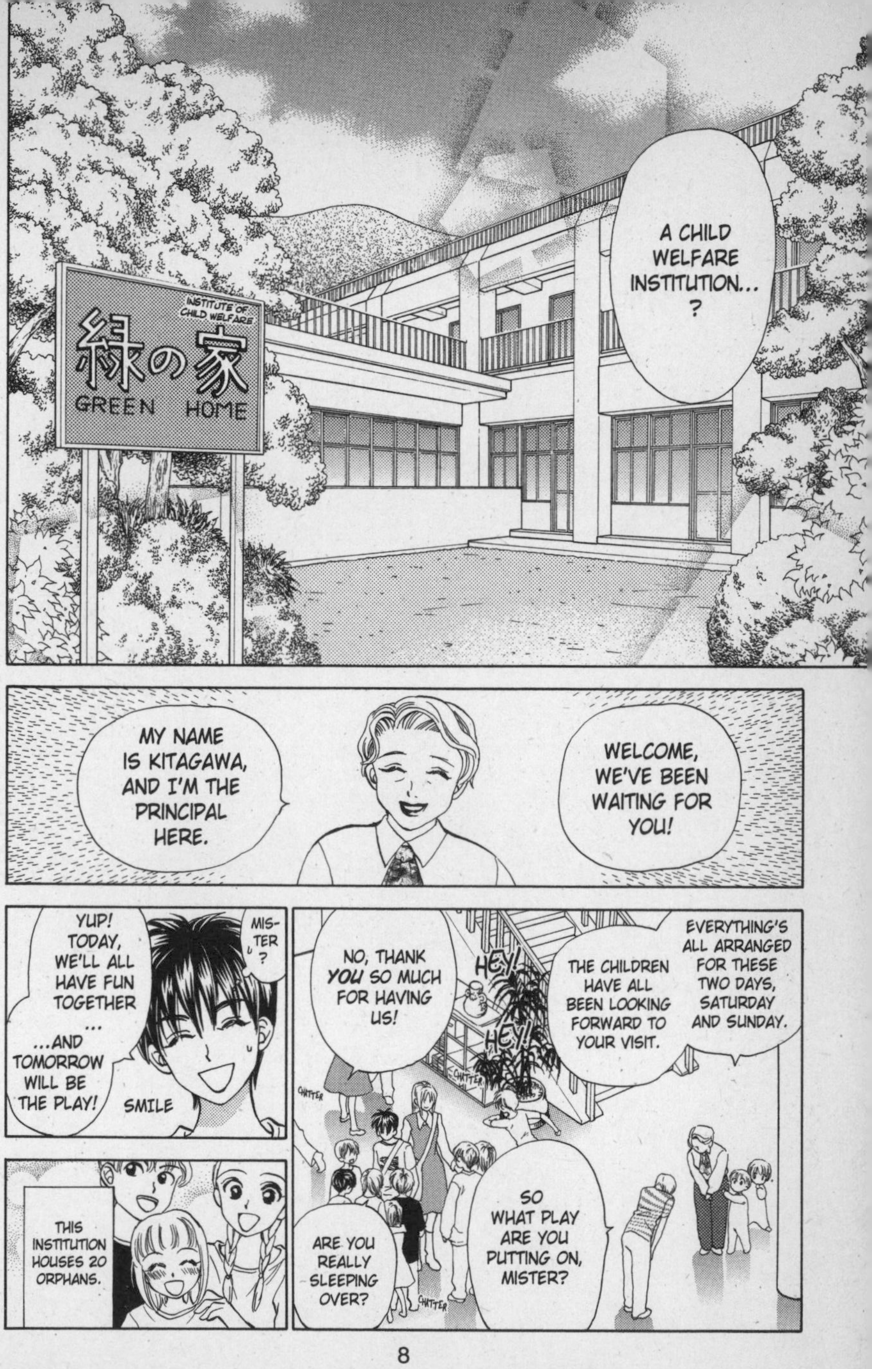
INSTITUTE OF CHILD WELFARE
緑の家
GREEN HOME
A CHILD WELFARE INSTITUTION... ?
WELCOME, WE'VE BEEN WAITING FOR YOU!
MY NAME IS KITAGAWA, AND I'M THE PRINCIPAL HERE.
EVERYTHING'S ALL ARRANGED FOR THESE TWO DAYS, SATURDAY AND SUNDAY.
THE CHILDREN HAVE ALL BEEN LOOKING FORWARD TO YOUR VISIT.
HEY!
HEY!
NO, THANK *YOU* SO MUCH FOR HAVING US!
CHATTER
CHATTER
SO WHAT PLAY ARE YOU PUTTING ON, MISTER?
ARE YOU REALLY SLEEPING OVER?
CHATTER
MIS-TER?
YUP! TODAY, WE'LL ALL HAVE FUN TOGETHER ...
...AND TOMORROW WILL BE THE PLAY!
SMILE
THIS INSTITUTION HOUSES 20 ORPHANS.

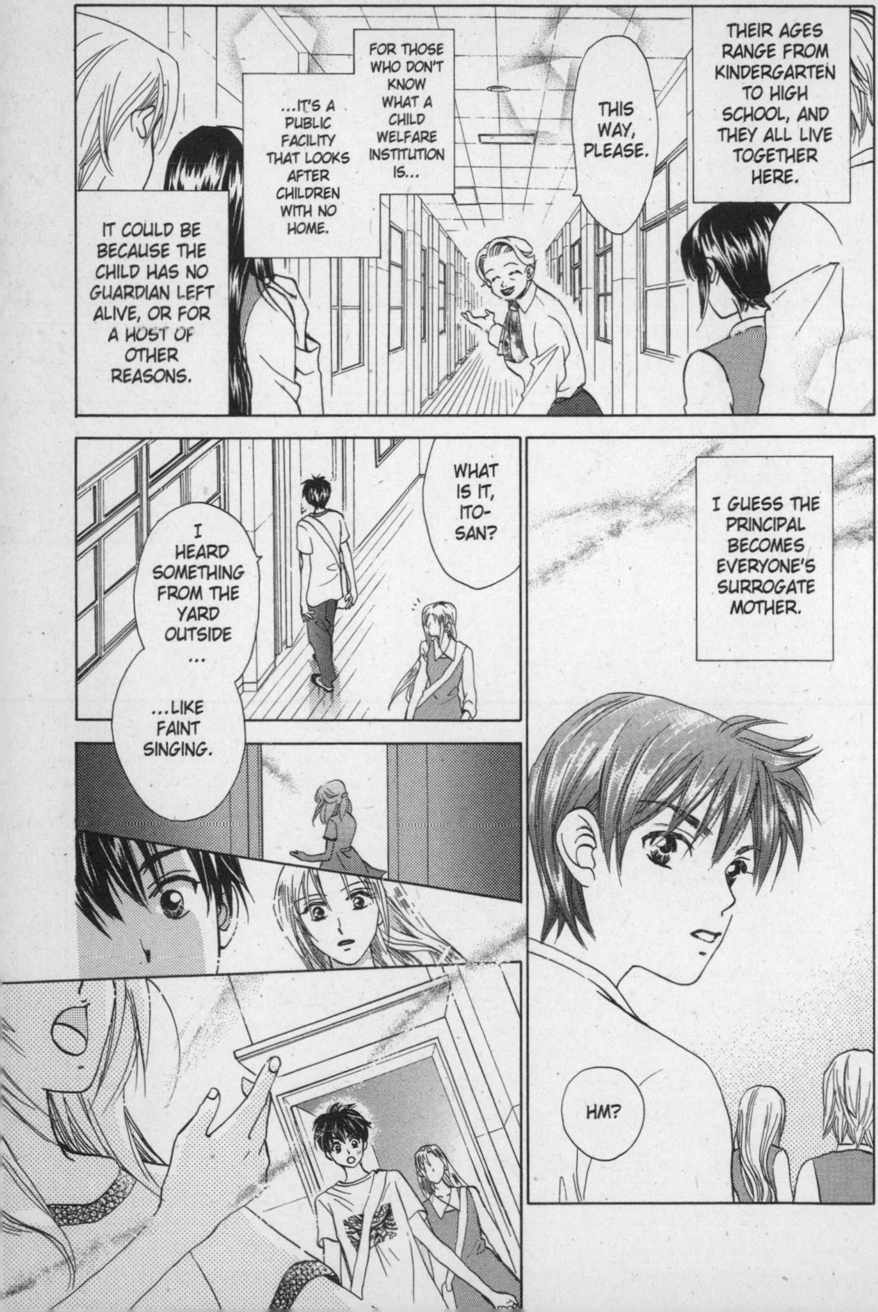
THEIR AGES RANGE FROM KINDERGARTEN TO HIGH SCHOOL, AND THEY ALL LIVE TOGETHER HERE.
THIS WAY, PLEASE.
FOR THOSE WHO DON'T KNOW WHAT A CHILD WELFARE INSTITUTION IS...
...IT'S A PUBLIC FACILITY THAT LOOKS AFTER CHILDREN WITH NO HOME.
IT COULD BE BECAUSE THE CHILD HAS NO GUARDIAN LEFT ALIVE, OR FOR A HOST OF OTHER REASONS.
I GUESS THE PRINCIPAL BECOMES EVERYONE'S SURROGATE MOTHER.
HM?
WHAT IS IT, ITO-SAN?
I HEARD SOMETHING FROM THE YARD OUTSIDE...
...LIKE FAINT SINGING.

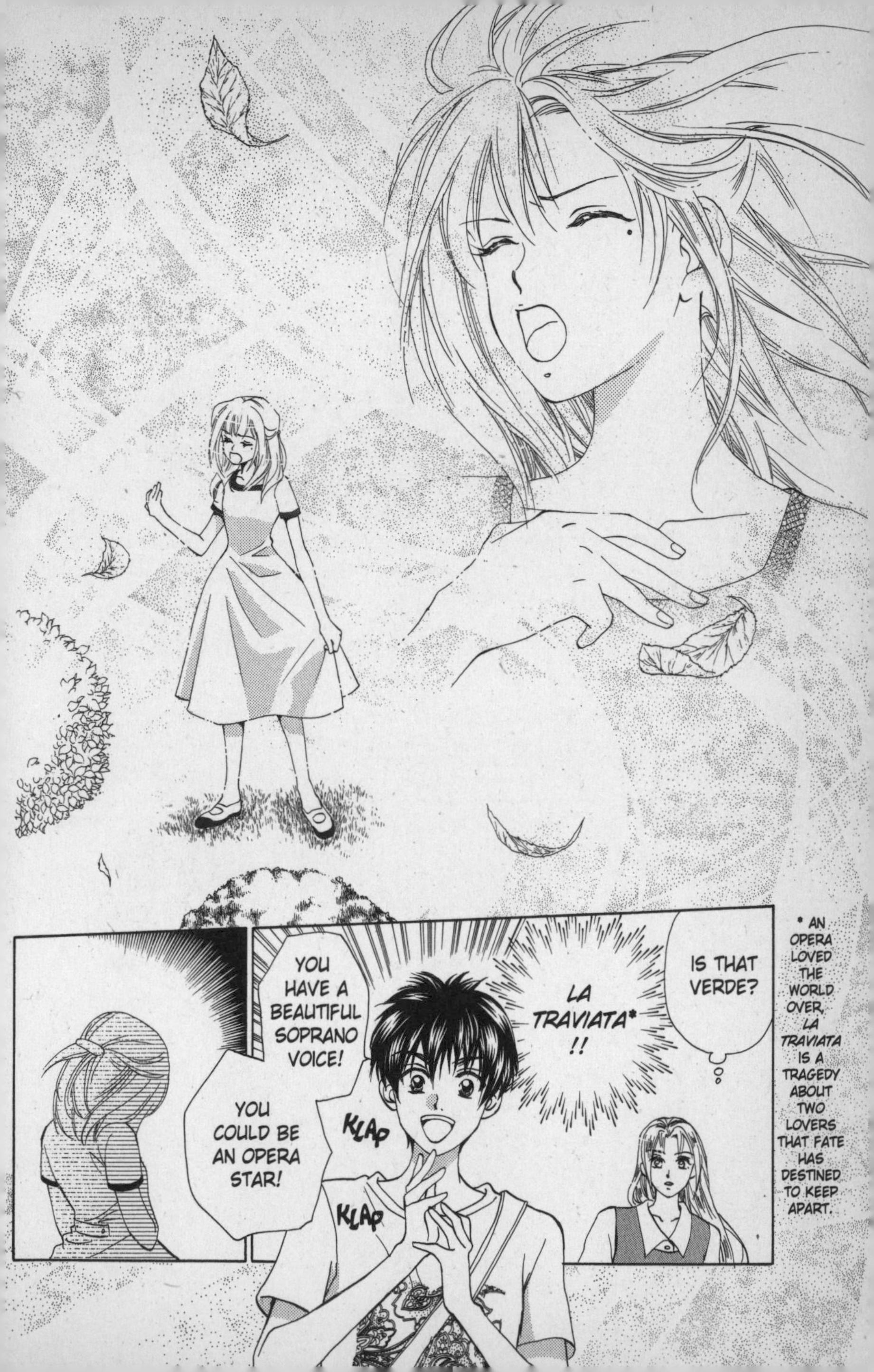
IS THAT VERDE?
LA TRAVIATA* !!
YOU HAVE A BEAUTIFUL SOPRANO VOICE!
KLAP
KLAP
YOU COULD BE AN OPERA STAR!
* AN OPERA LOVED THE WORLD OVER, LA TRAVIATA IS A TRAGEDY ABOUT TWO LOVERS THAT FATE HAS DESTINED TO KEEP APART.

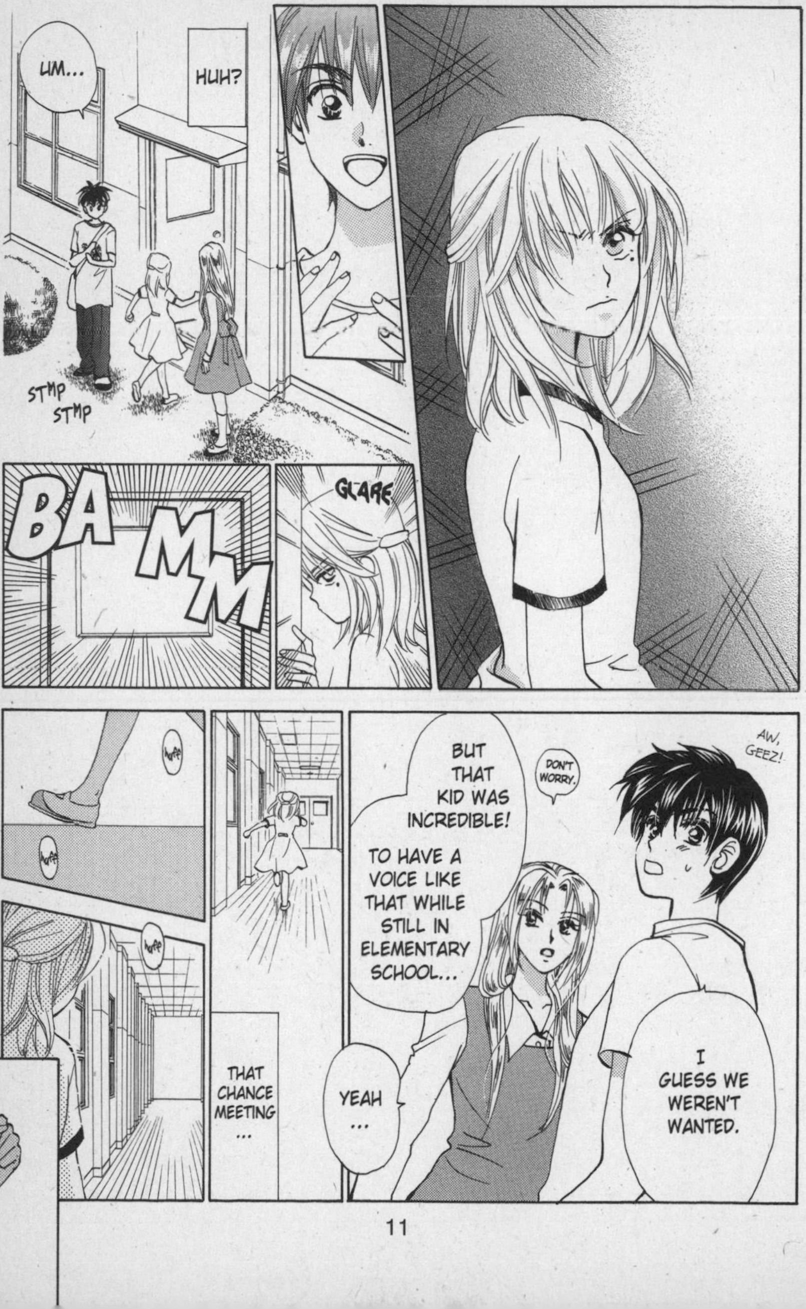
HUH?
UM...
STMP STMP
GLARE
BAMM
AW, GEEZ!
DON'T WORRY.
BUT THAT KID WAS INCREDIBLE!
TO HAVE A VOICE LIKE THAT WHILE STILL IN ELEMENTARY SCHOOL...
I GUESS WE WEREN'T WANTED.
YEAH...
THAT CHANCE MEETING...
huff
huff
huff

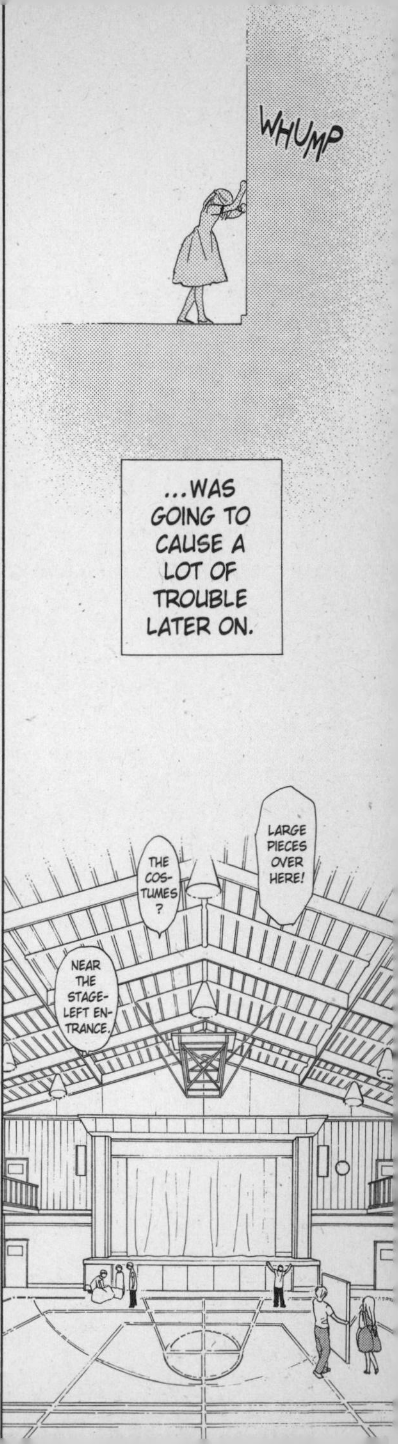
WHUMP
...WAS GOING TO CAUSE A LOT OF TROUBLE LATER ON.
LARGE PIECES OVER HERE!
THE COSTUMES?
NEAR THE STAGE-LEFT ENTRANCE.

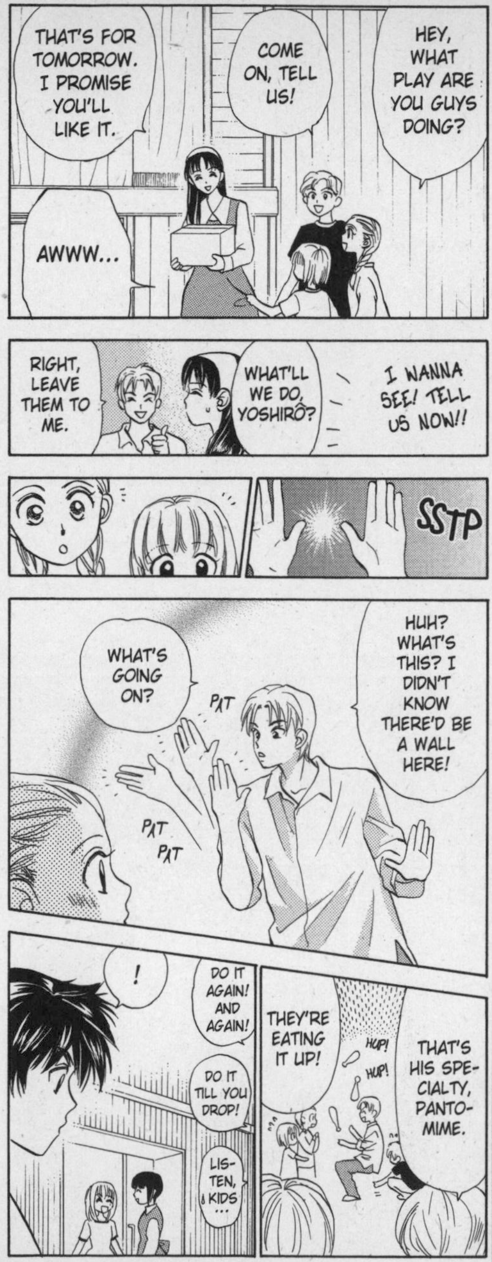
HEY, WHAT PLAY ARE YOU GUYS DOING?
COME ON, TELL US!
THAT'S FOR TOMORROW. I PROMISE YOU'LL LIKE IT.
AWWW...
I WANNA SEE! TELL US NOW!!
WHAT'LL WE DO, YOSHIRÔ?
RIGHT, LEAVE THEM TO ME.
SSTP
HUH? WHAT'S THIS? I DIDN'T KNOW THERE'D BE A WALL HERE!
PAT
WHAT'S GOING ON?
PAT
PAT
THAT'S HIS SPECIALTY, PANTOMIME.
HUP!
HUP!
THEY'RE EATING IT UP!
DO IT AGAIN! AND AGAIN!
!
DO IT TILL YOU DROP!
LISTEN, KIDS...

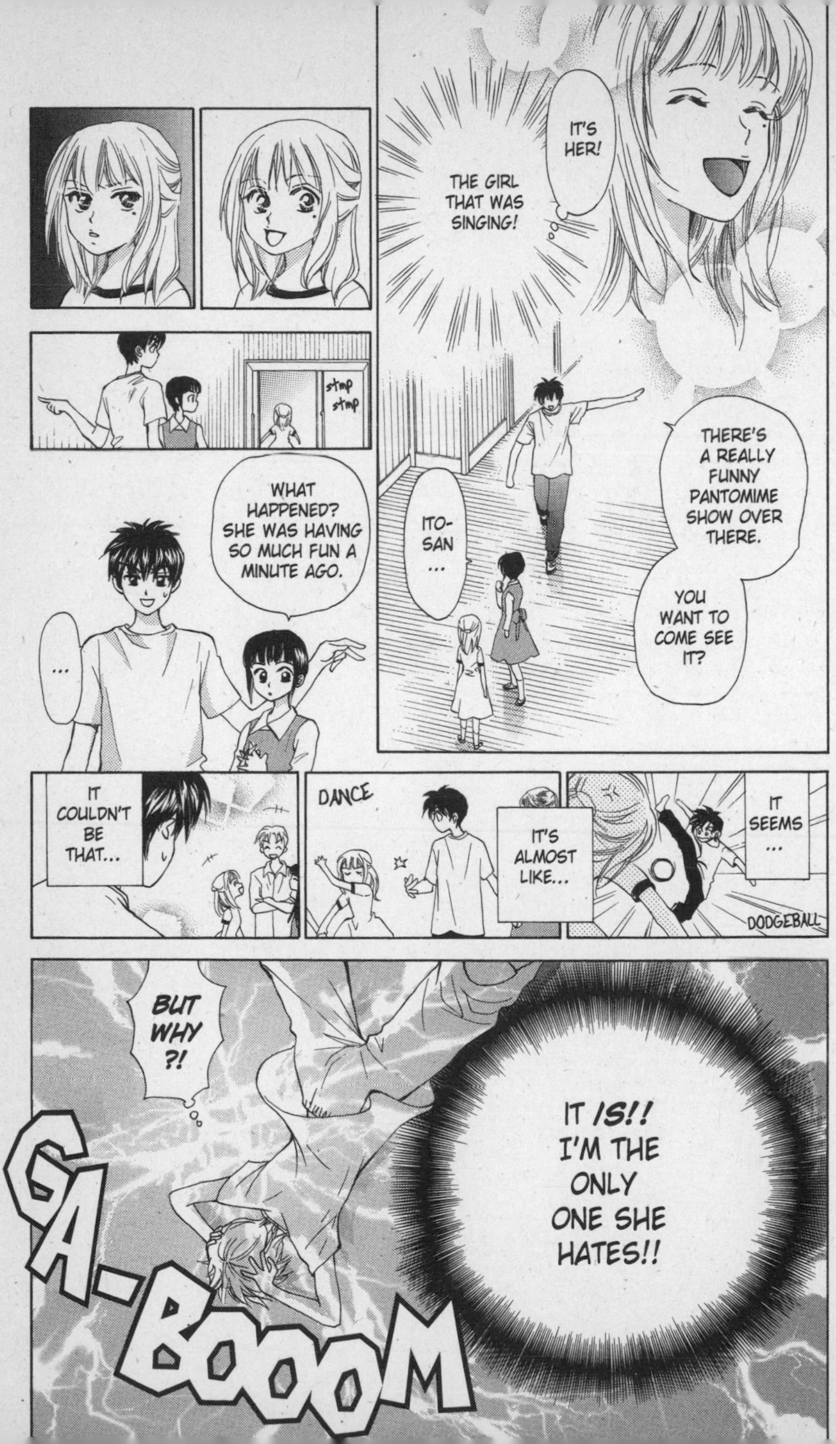
IT'S HER!
THE GIRL THAT WAS SINGING!
THERE'S A REALLY FUNNY PANTOMIME SHOW OVER THERE.
YOU WANT TO COME SEE IT?
ITO-SAN ...
stmp stmp
WHAT HAPPENED? SHE WAS HAVING SO MUCH FUN A MINUTE AGO.
...
IT SEEMS ...
DODGEBALL
IT'S ALMOST LIKE...
DANCE
IT COULDN'T BE THAT...
BUT WHY?!
IT *IS*!! I'M THE ONLY ONE SHE HATES!!
GA-BOOOM

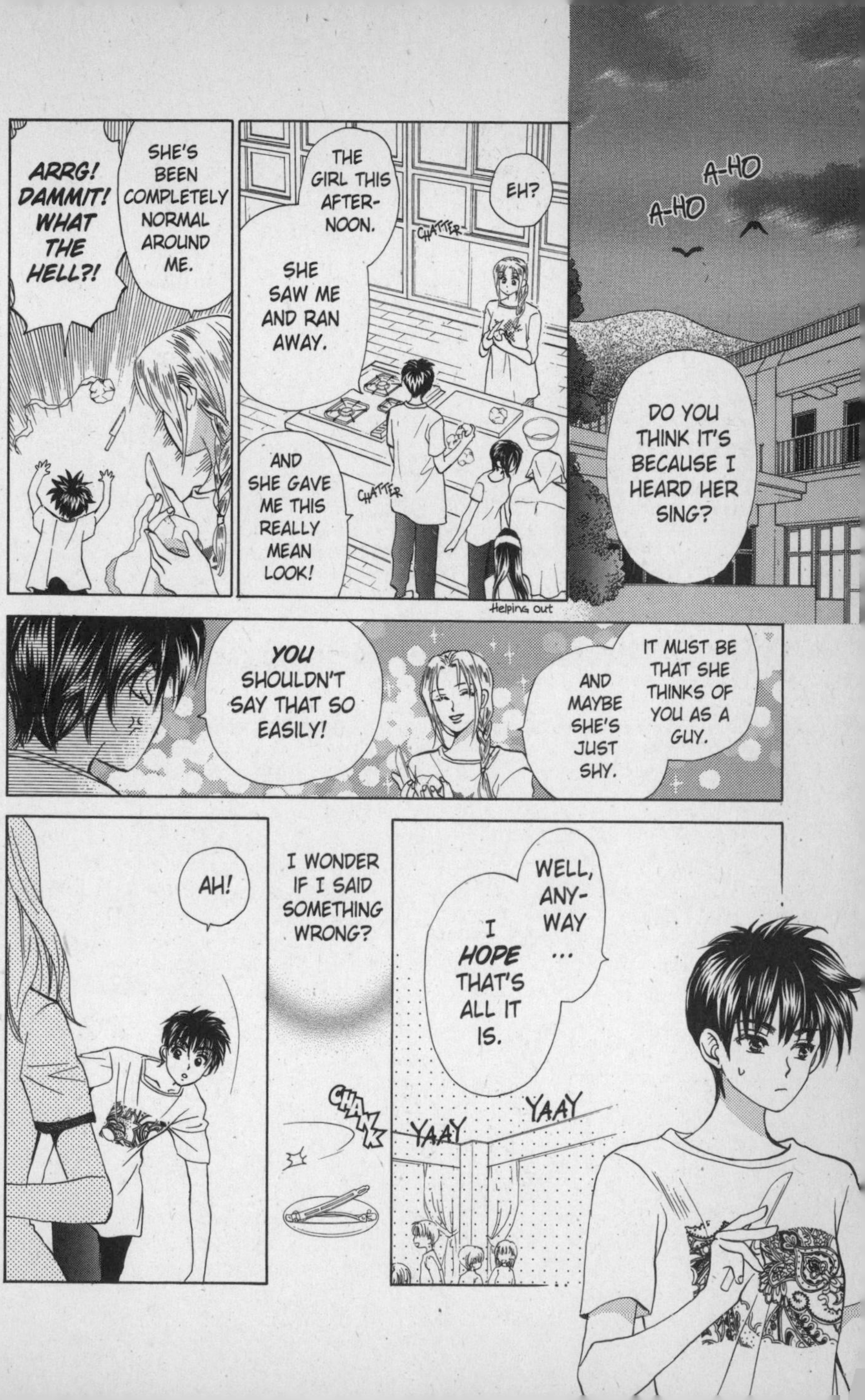
A-HO
A-HO
DO YOU THINK IT'S BECAUSE I HEARD HER SING?
EH?
THE GIRL THIS AFTERNOON.
SHE SAW ME AND RAN AWAY.
CHATTER
AND SHE GAVE ME THIS REALLY MEAN LOOK!
CHATTER
Helping out
SHE'S BEEN COMPLETELY NORMAL AROUND ME.
ARRG! DAMMIT! WHAT THE HELL?!
IT MUST BE THAT SHE THINKS OF YOU AS A GUY.
AND MAYBE SHE'S JUST SHY.
YOU SHOULDN'T SAY THAT SO EASILY!
WELL, ANYWAY ...
I HOPE THAT'S ALL IT IS.
YAAY
YAAY
CHANK
I WONDER IF I SAID SOMETHING WRONG?
AH!

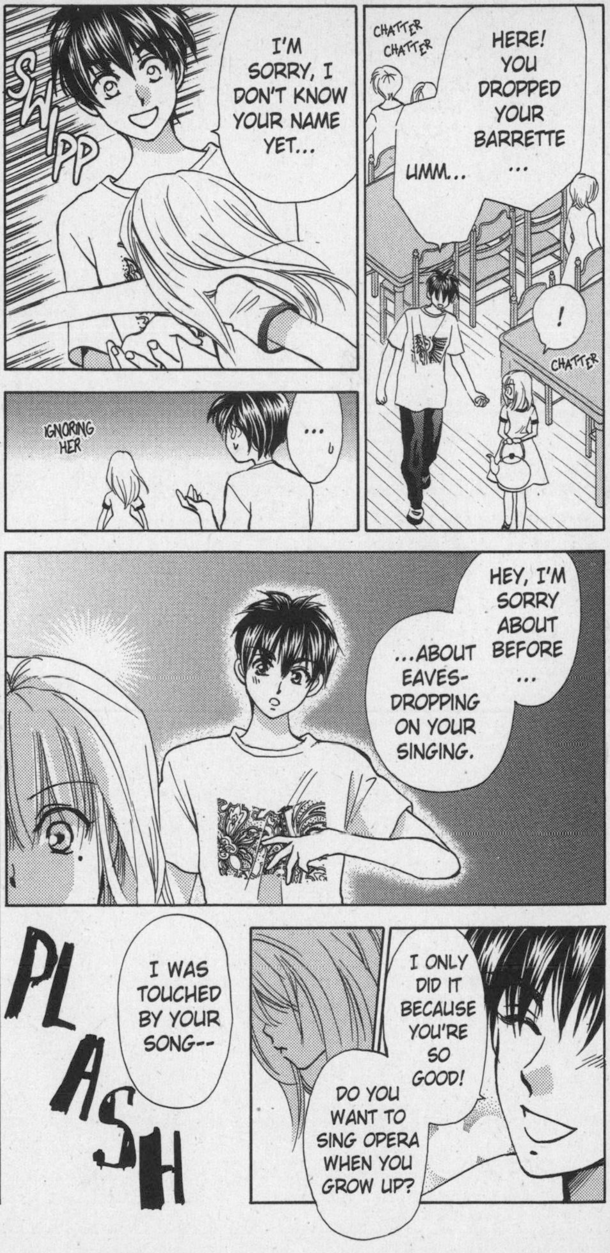
CHATTER CHATTER
HERE! YOU DROPPED YOUR BARRETTE...
UMM...
!
CHATTER
I'M SORRY, I DON'T KNOW YOUR NAME YET...
SWIPP
IGNORING HER
...
HEY, I'M SORRY ABOUT BEFORE...
...ABOUT EAVES-DROPPING ON YOUR SINGING.
I ONLY DID IT BECAUSE YOU'RE SO GOOD!
DO YOU WANT TO SING OPERA WHEN YOU GROW UP?
I WAS TOUCHED BY YOUR SONG--
PLASH

GREETINGS!

Hello, it's me, Emura! I write this every time, but we've finally arrived at Volume 7! This one has a lot of love scenes and talking about dreams. And there's the Summer Training Camp story you've all been waiting for in the back of the book! Please read it and enjoy it! ♥ It's a 46-page story, so this volume wound up a little thicker than the normal volumes did. Call it a bonus!

The Summer Training Camp story is the opposite of the normal story. In this, Ito gets to rescue Makoto! The early stories had the same pattern pretty often, but in this story, it is reversed quite naturally. ♥ Ito, who is always being looked out for by Makoto, this time looks out for Mako and rescues him! Well, they save each other, huh? But Mako is just better at it.

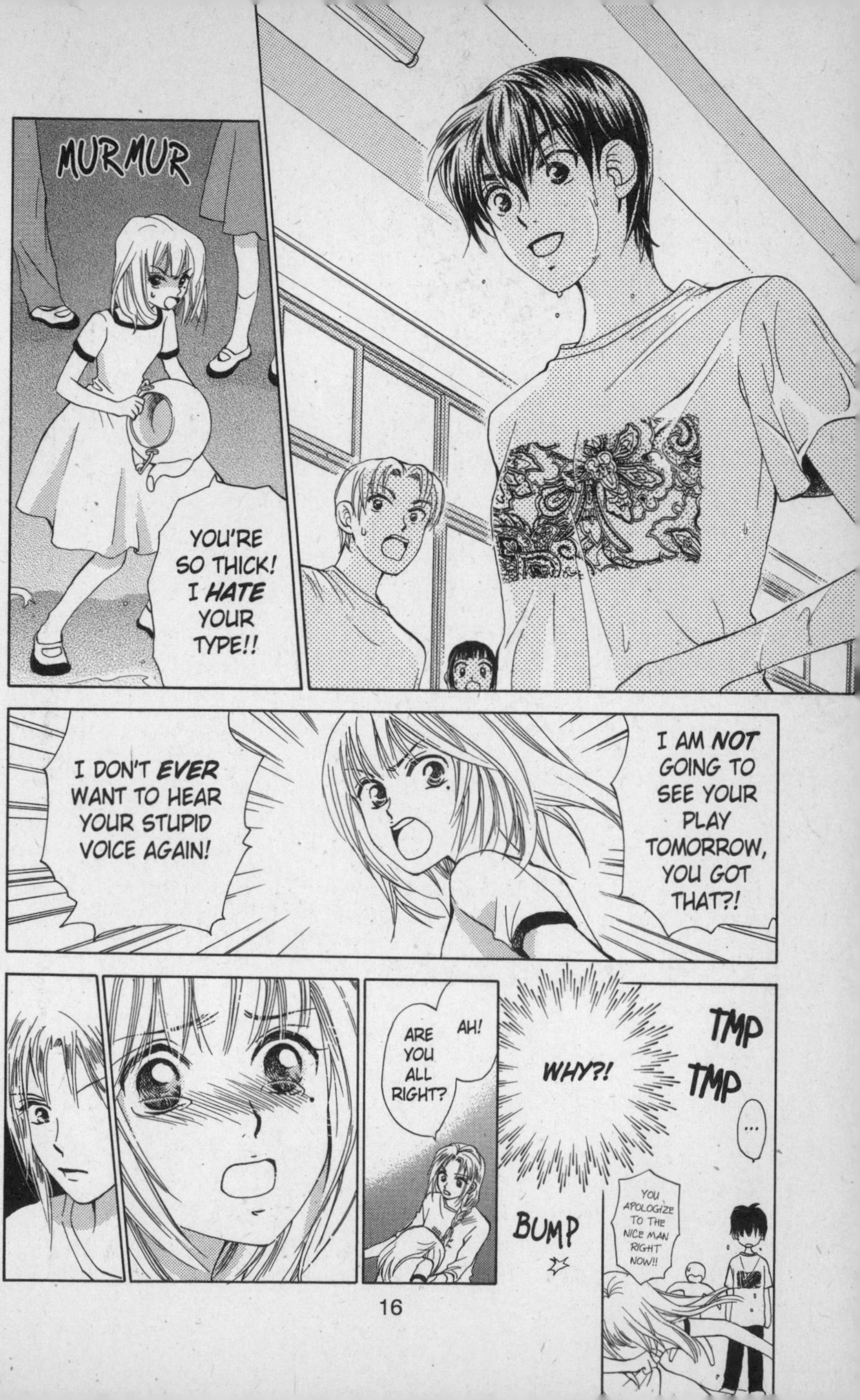
MURMUR
YOU'RE SO THICK! I *HATE* YOUR TYPE!!
I AM *NOT* GOING TO SEE YOUR PLAY TOMORROW, YOU GOT THAT?!
I DON'T *EVER* WANT TO HEAR YOUR STUPID VOICE AGAIN!
TMP TMP
WHY?!
...
YOU APOLOGIZE TO THE NICE MAN RIGHT NOW!!
BUMP
AH!
ARE YOU ALL RIGHT?

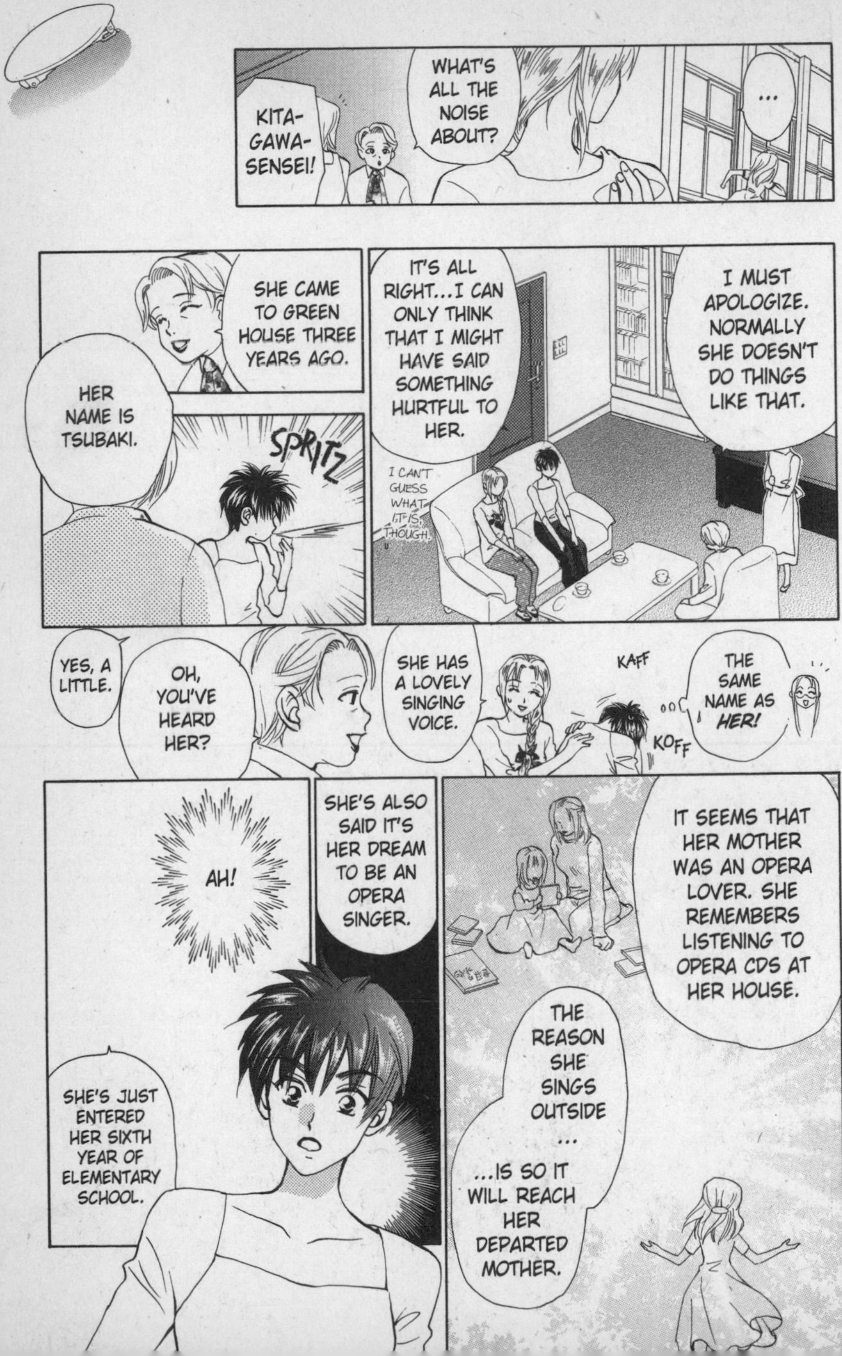
...
WHAT'S ALL THE NOISE ABOUT?
KITA-GAWA-SENSEI!
I MUST APOLOGIZE. NORMALLY SHE DOESN'T DO THINGS LIKE THAT.
IT'S ALL RIGHT...I CAN ONLY THINK THAT I MIGHT HAVE SAID SOMETHING HURTFUL TO HER.
I CAN'T GUESS WHAT IT IS, THOUGH.
SHE CAME TO GREEN HOUSE THREE YEARS AGO.
HER NAME IS TSUBAKI.
SPRITZ
THE SAME NAME AS HER!
KAFF
KOFF
SHE HAS A LOVELY SINGING VOICE.
OH, YOU'VE HEARD HER?
YES, A LITTLE.
IT SEEMS THAT HER MOTHER WAS AN OPERA LOVER. SHE REMEMBERS LISTENING TO OPERA CDS AT HER HOUSE.
THE REASON SHE SINGS OUTSIDE...
...IS SO IT WILL REACH HER DEPARTED MOTHER.
SHE'S ALSO SAID IT'S HER DREAM TO BE AN OPERA SINGER.
AH!
SHE'S JUST ENTERED HER SIXTH YEAR OF ELEMENTARY SCHOOL.

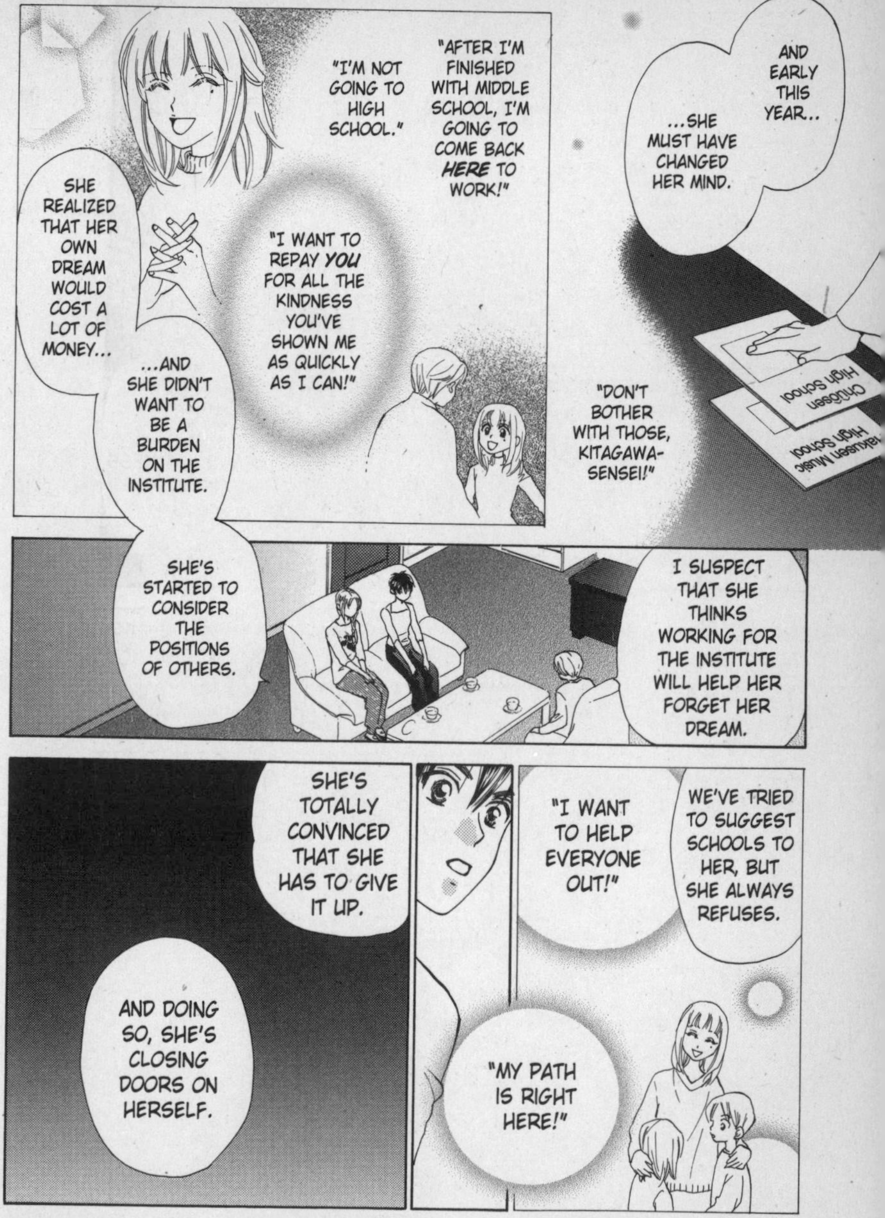
AND EARLY THIS YEAR...
...SHE MUST HAVE CHANGED HER MIND.
"DON'T BOTHER WITH THOSE, KITAGAWA-SENSEI!"
"AFTER I'M FINISHED WITH MIDDLE SCHOOL, I'M GOING TO COME BACK *HERE* TO WORK!"
"I'M NOT GOING TO HIGH SCHOOL."
"I WANT TO REPAY *YOU* FOR ALL THE KINDNESS YOU'VE SHOWN ME AS QUICKLY AS I CAN!"
SHE REALIZED THAT HER OWN DREAM WOULD COST A LOT OF MONEY...
...AND SHE DIDN'T WANT TO BE A BURDEN ON THE INSTITUTE.
I SUSPECT THAT SHE THINKS WORKING FOR THE INSTITUTE WILL HELP HER FORGET HER DREAM.
SHE'S STARTED TO CONSIDER THE POSITIONS OF OTHERS.
WE'VE TRIED TO SUGGEST SCHOOLS TO HER, BUT SHE ALWAYS REFUSES.
"I WANT TO HELP EVERYONE OUT!"
"MY PATH IS RIGHT HERE!"
SHE'S TOTALLY CONVINCED THAT SHE HAS TO GIVE IT UP.
AND DOING SO, SHE'S CLOSING DOORS ON HERSELF.

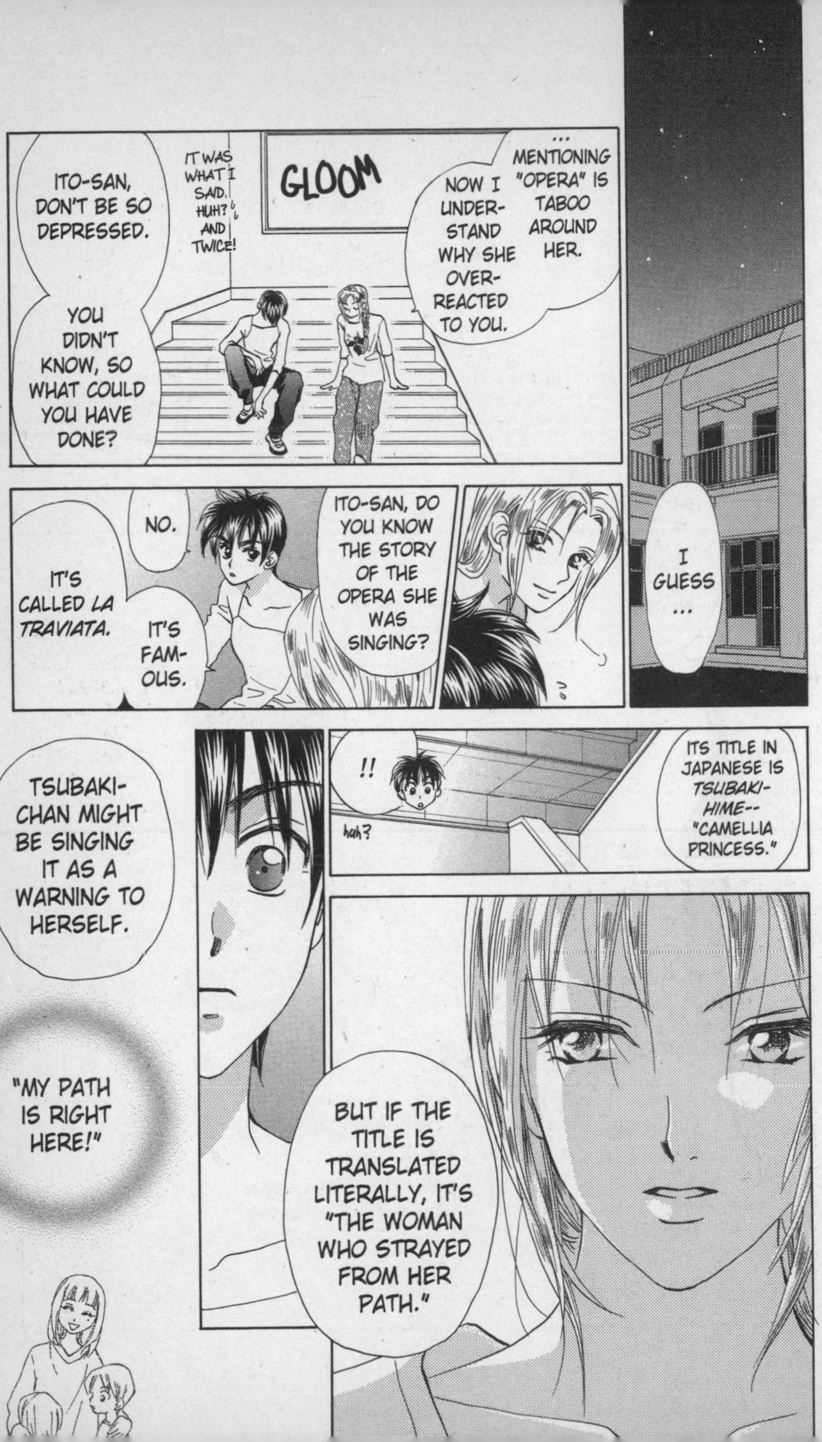
I GUESS ...
... MENTIONING "OPERA" IS TABOO AROUND HER.
NOW I UNDERSTAND WHY SHE OVER-REACTED TO YOU.
GLOOM
IT WAS WHAT I SAID, HUH? AND TWICE!
ITO-SAN, DON'T BE SO DEPRESSED.
YOU DIDN'T KNOW, SO WHAT COULD YOU HAVE DONE?
ITO-SAN, DO YOU KNOW THE STORY OF THE OPERA SHE WAS SINGING?
NO.
IT'S FAM-OUS.
IT'S CALLED *LA TRAVIATA.*
ITS TITLE IN JAPANESE IS *TSUBAKI-HIME*-- "CAMELLIA PRINCESS."
!!
huh?
BUT IF THE TITLE IS TRANSLATED LITERALLY, IT'S "THE WOMAN WHO STRAYED FROM HER PATH."
TSUBAKI-CHAN MIGHT BE SINGING IT AS A WARNING TO HERSELF.
"MY PATH IS RIGHT HERE!"

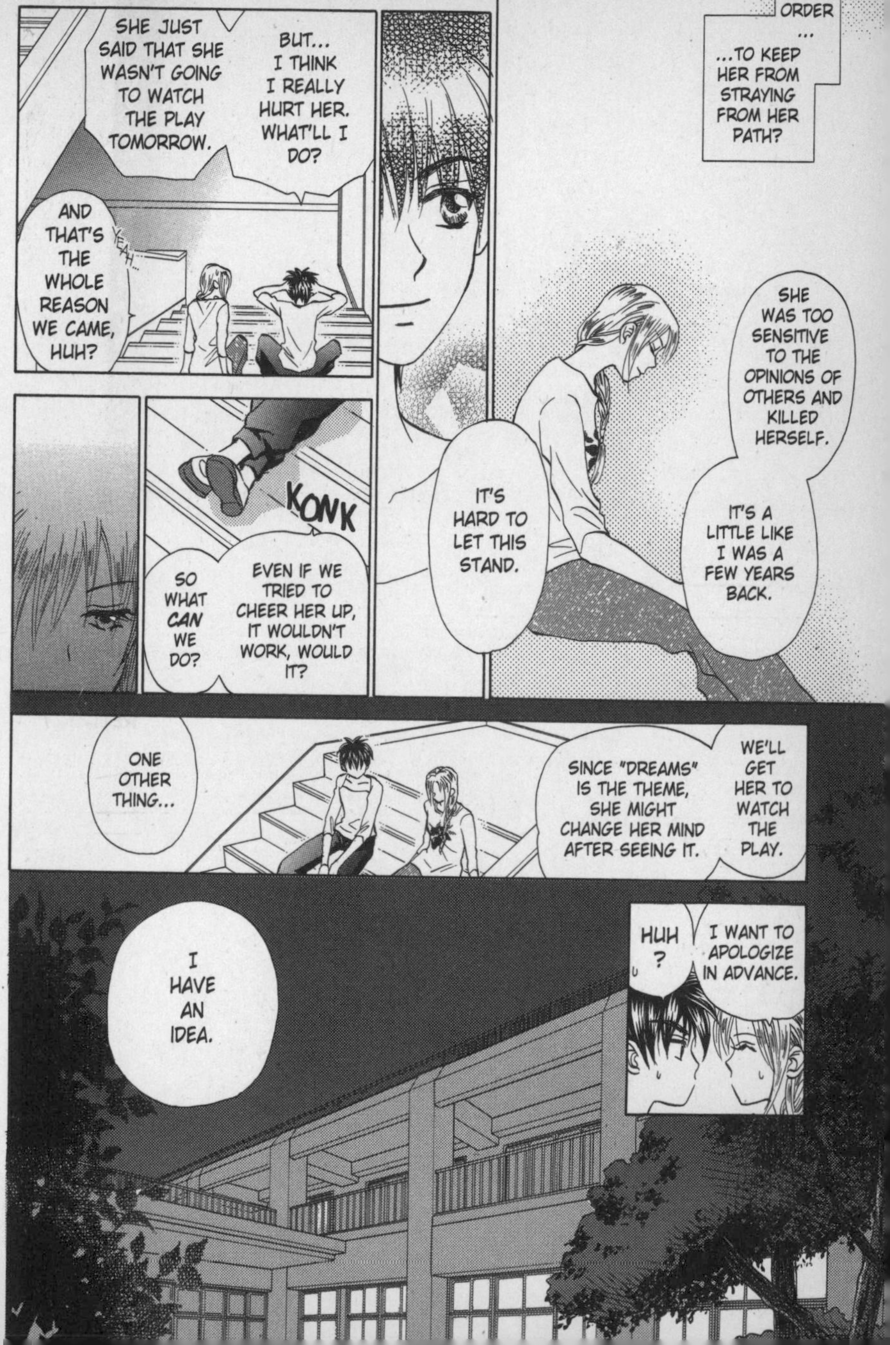
IN ORDER ...
...TO KEEP HER FROM STRAYING FROM HER PATH?
SHE WAS TOO SENSITIVE TO THE OPINIONS OF OTHERS AND KILLED HERSELF.
IT'S A LITTLE LIKE I WAS A FEW YEARS BACK.
IT'S HARD TO LET THIS STAND.
SHE JUST SAID THAT SHE WASN'T GOING TO WATCH THE PLAY TOMORROW.
BUT... I THINK I REALLY HURT HER. WHAT'LL I DO?
AND THAT'S THE WHOLE REASON WE CAME, HUH?
YEAH...
KONK
EVEN IF WE TRIED TO CHEER HER UP, IT WOULDN'T WORK, WOULD IT?
SO WHAT CAN WE DO?
WE'LL GET HER TO WATCH THE PLAY.
SINCE "DREAMS" IS THE THEME, SHE MIGHT CHANGE HER MIND AFTER SEEING IT.
ONE OTHER THING...
I WANT TO APOLOGIZE IN ADVANCE.
HUH?
I HAVE AN IDEA.

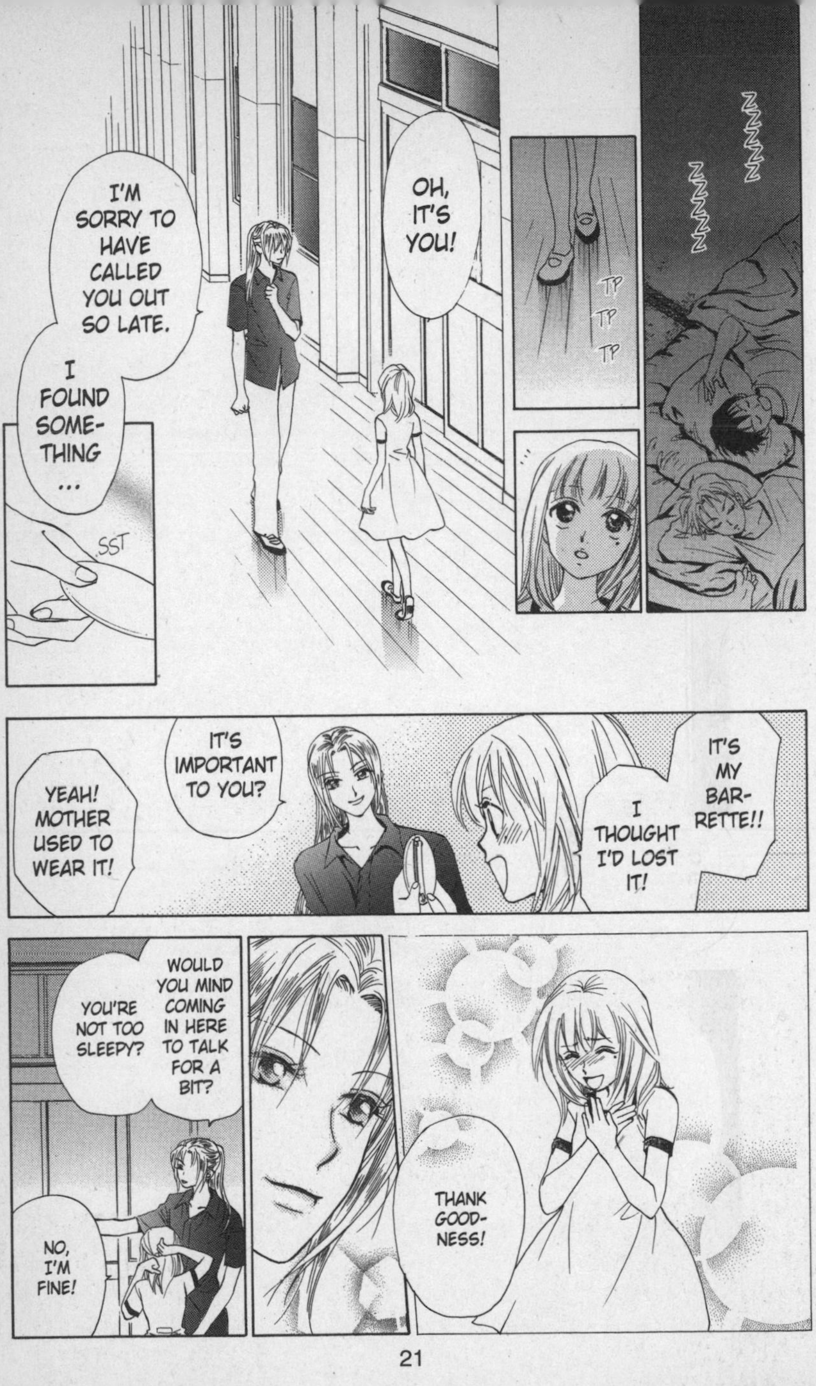
ZZZZZ
ZZZZZ
TP TP TP
OH, IT'S YOU!
I'M SORRY TO HAVE CALLED YOU OUT SO LATE.
I FOUND SOME-THING ...
SST
IT'S MY BAR-RETTE!!
I THOUGHT I'D LOST IT!
IT'S IMPORTANT TO YOU?
YEAH! MOTHER USED TO WEAR IT!
THANK GOOD-NESS!
WOULD YOU MIND COMING IN HERE TO TALK FOR A BIT?
YOU'RE NOT TOO SLEEPY?
NO, I'M FINE!

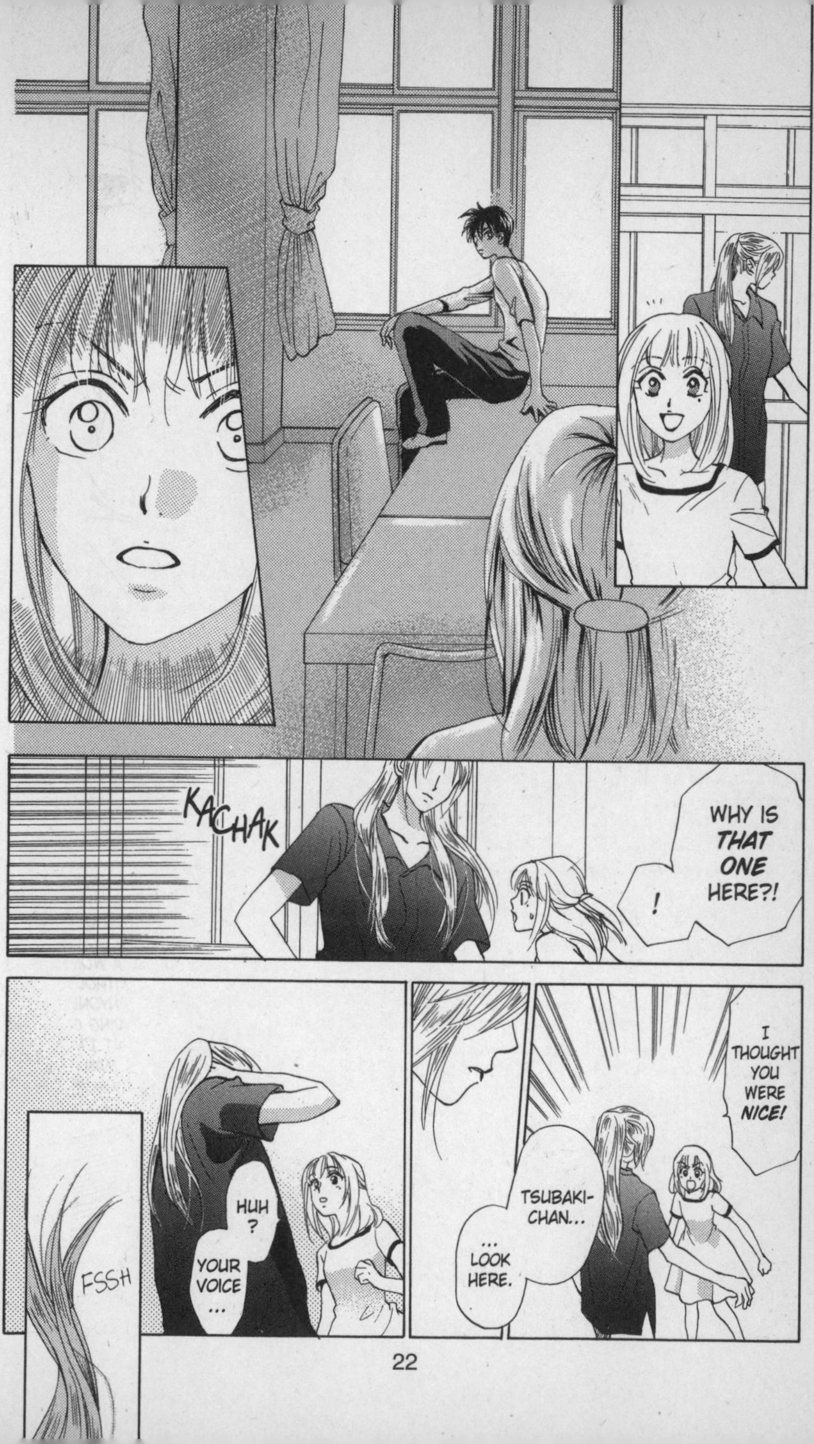
WHY IS *THAT ONE* HERE?!
!
KACHAK
I THOUGHT YOU WERE *NICE!*
TSUBAKI-CHAN...
... LOOK HERE.
HUH?
YOUR VOICE ...
FSSH

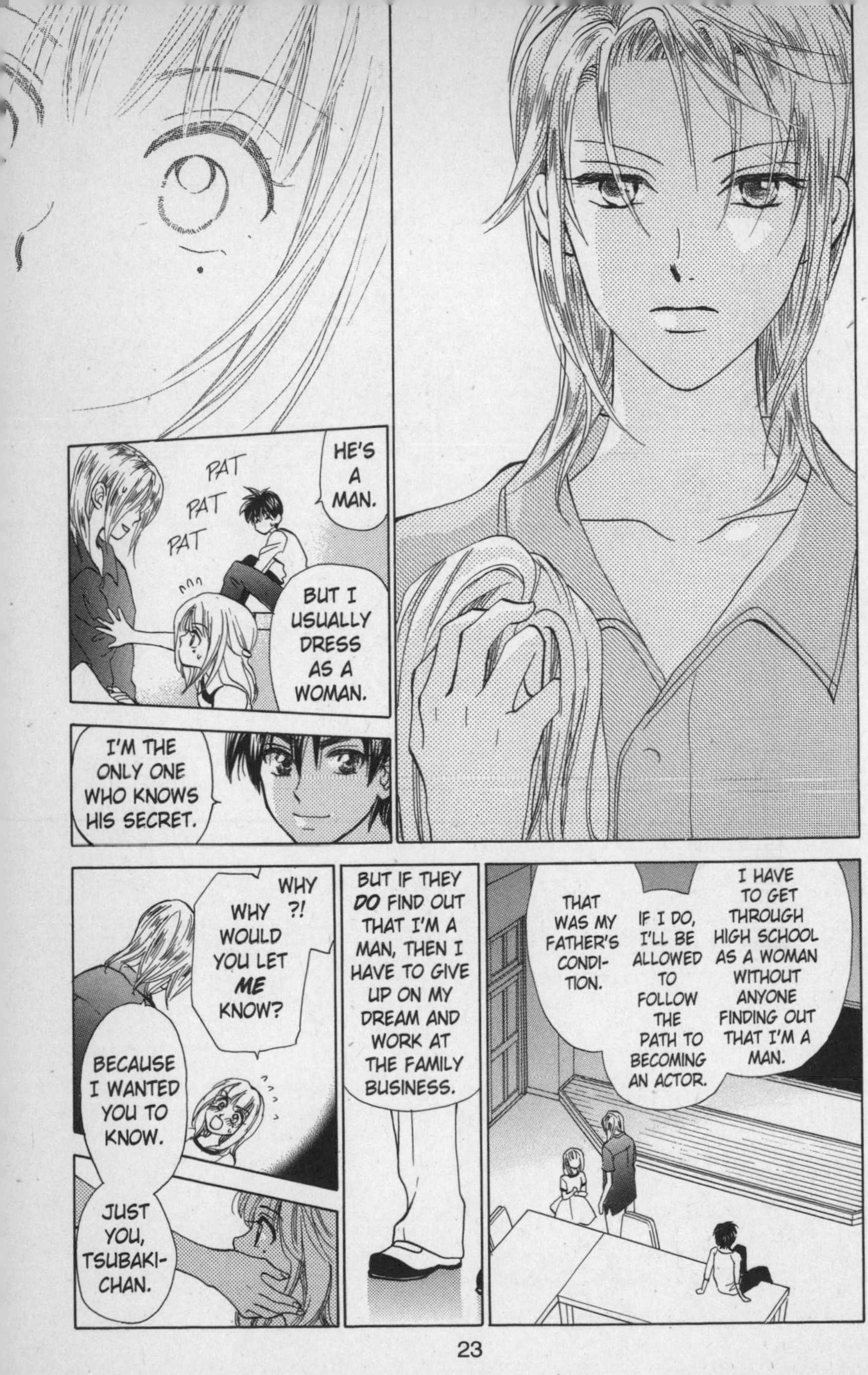
HE'S A MAN.
PAT PAT PAT
BUT I USUALLY DRESS AS A WOMAN.
I'M THE ONLY ONE WHO KNOWS HIS SECRET.
I HAVE TO GET THROUGH HIGH SCHOOL AS A WOMAN WITHOUT ANYONE FINDING OUT THAT I'M A MAN.
IF I DO, I'LL BE ALLOWED TO FOLLOW THE PATH TO BECOMING AN ACTOR.
THAT WAS MY FATHER'S CONDITION.
BUT IF THEY *DO* FIND OUT THAT I'M A MAN, THEN I HAVE TO GIVE UP ON MY DREAM AND WORK AT THE FAMILY BUSINESS.
WHY ?!
WHY WOULD YOU LET *ME* KNOW?
BECAUSE I WANTED YOU TO KNOW.
JUST YOU, TSUBAKI-CHAN.

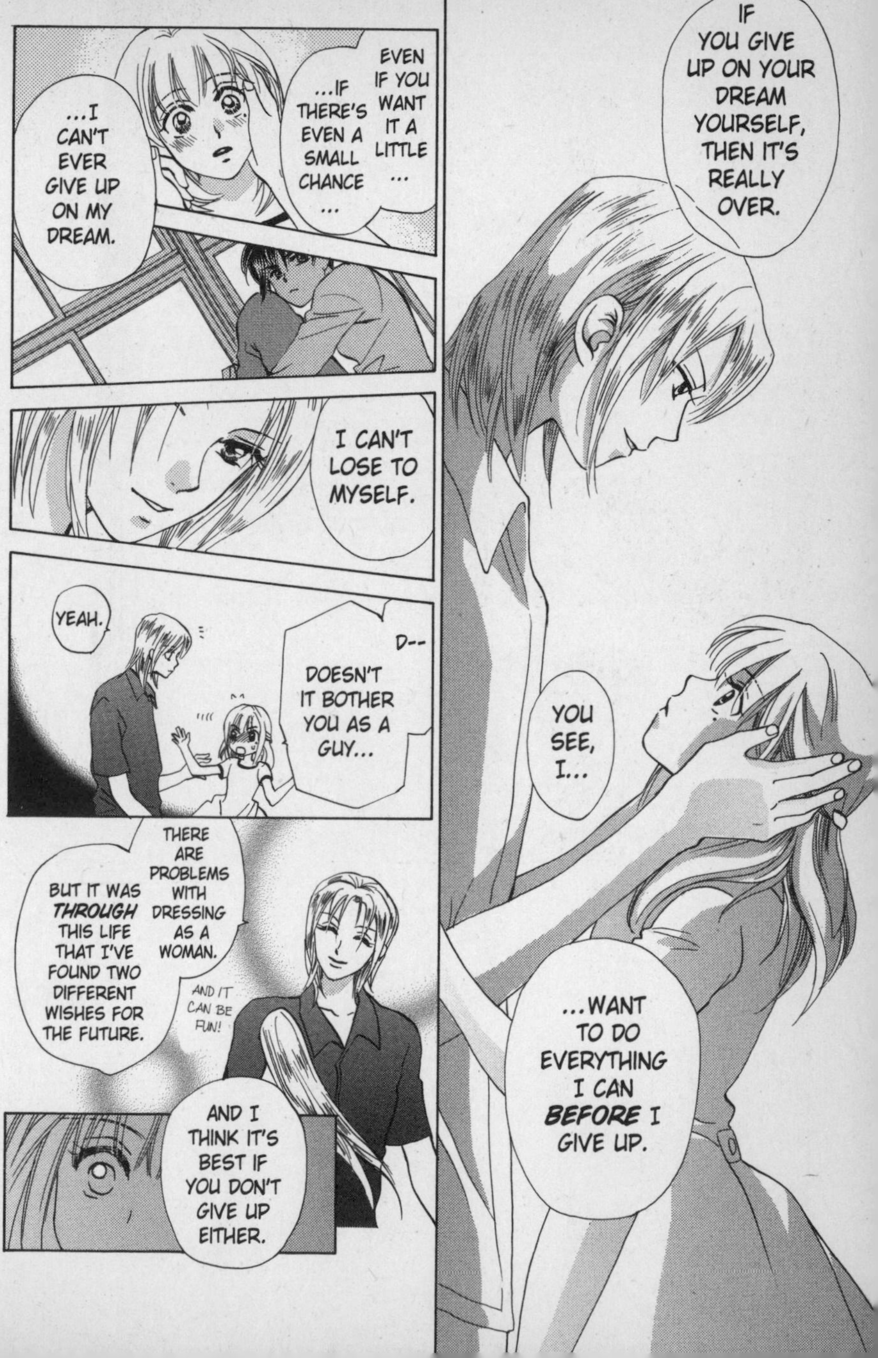
IF YOU GIVE UP ON YOUR DREAM YOURSELF, THEN IT'S REALLY OVER.
YOU SEE, I...
...WANT TO DO EVERYTHING I CAN *BEFORE* I GIVE UP.
EVEN IF YOU WANT IT A LITTLE ...
...IF THERE'S EVEN A SMALL CHANCE ...
...I CAN'T EVER GIVE UP ON MY DREAM.
I CAN'T LOSE TO MYSELF.
D-- DOESN'T IT BOTHER YOU AS A GUY...
YEAH.
THERE ARE PROBLEMS WITH DRESSING AS A WOMAN.
BUT IT WAS *THROUGH* THIS LIFE THAT I'VE FOUND TWO DIFFERENT WISHES FOR THE FUTURE.
AND IT CAN BE FUN!
AND I THINK IT'S BEST IF YOU DON'T GIVE UP EITHER.

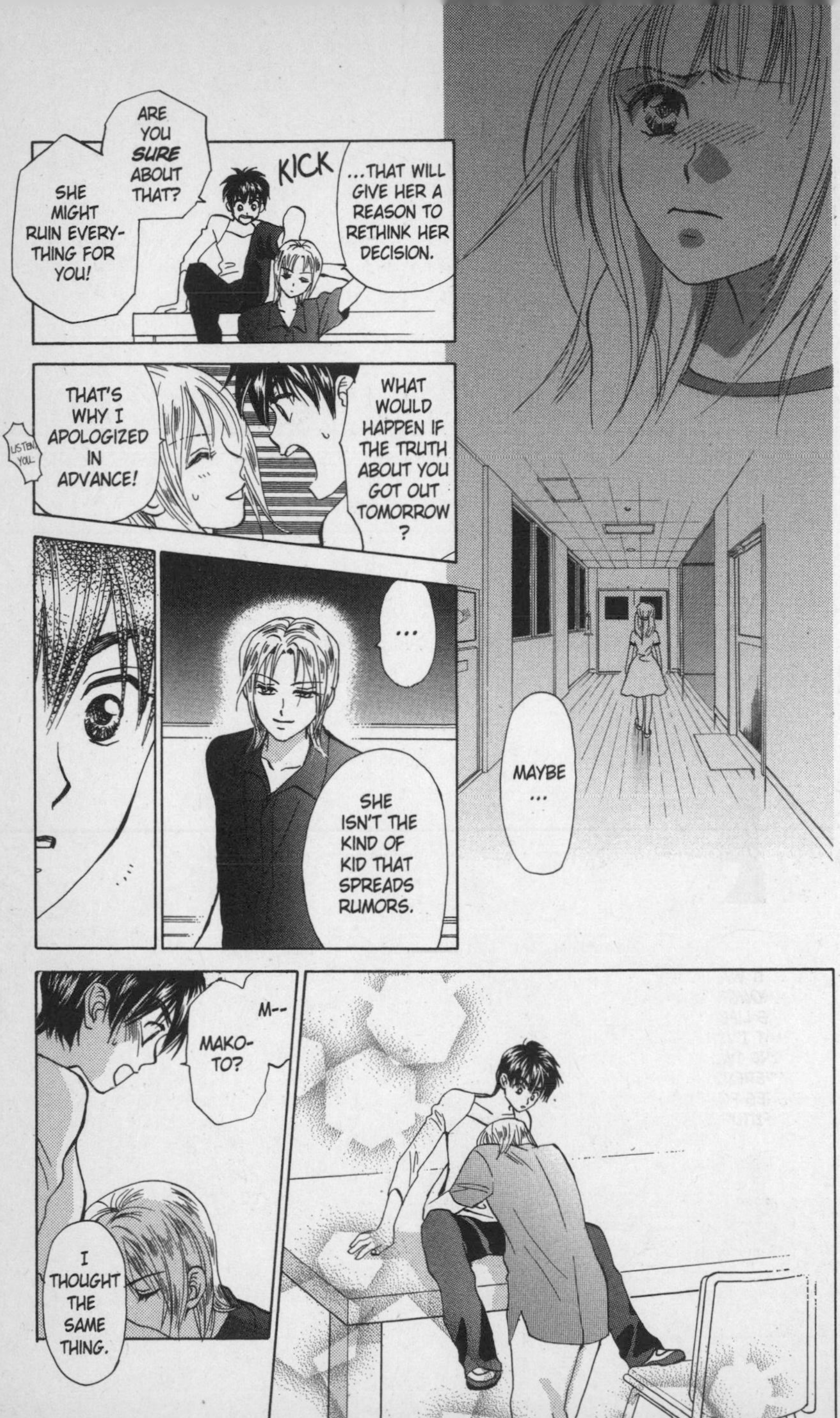
MAYBE ...
...THAT WILL GIVE HER A REASON TO RETHINK HER DECISION.
KICK
ARE YOU *SURE* ABOUT THAT?
SHE MIGHT RUIN EVERY-THING FOR YOU!
WHAT WOULD HAPPEN IF THE TRUTH ABOUT YOU GOT OUT TOMORROW?
THAT'S WHY I APOLOGIZED IN ADVANCE!
LISTEN YOU...
...
SHE ISN'T THE KIND OF KID THAT SPREADS RUMORS.
M-- MAKO-TO?
I THOUGHT THE SAME THING.

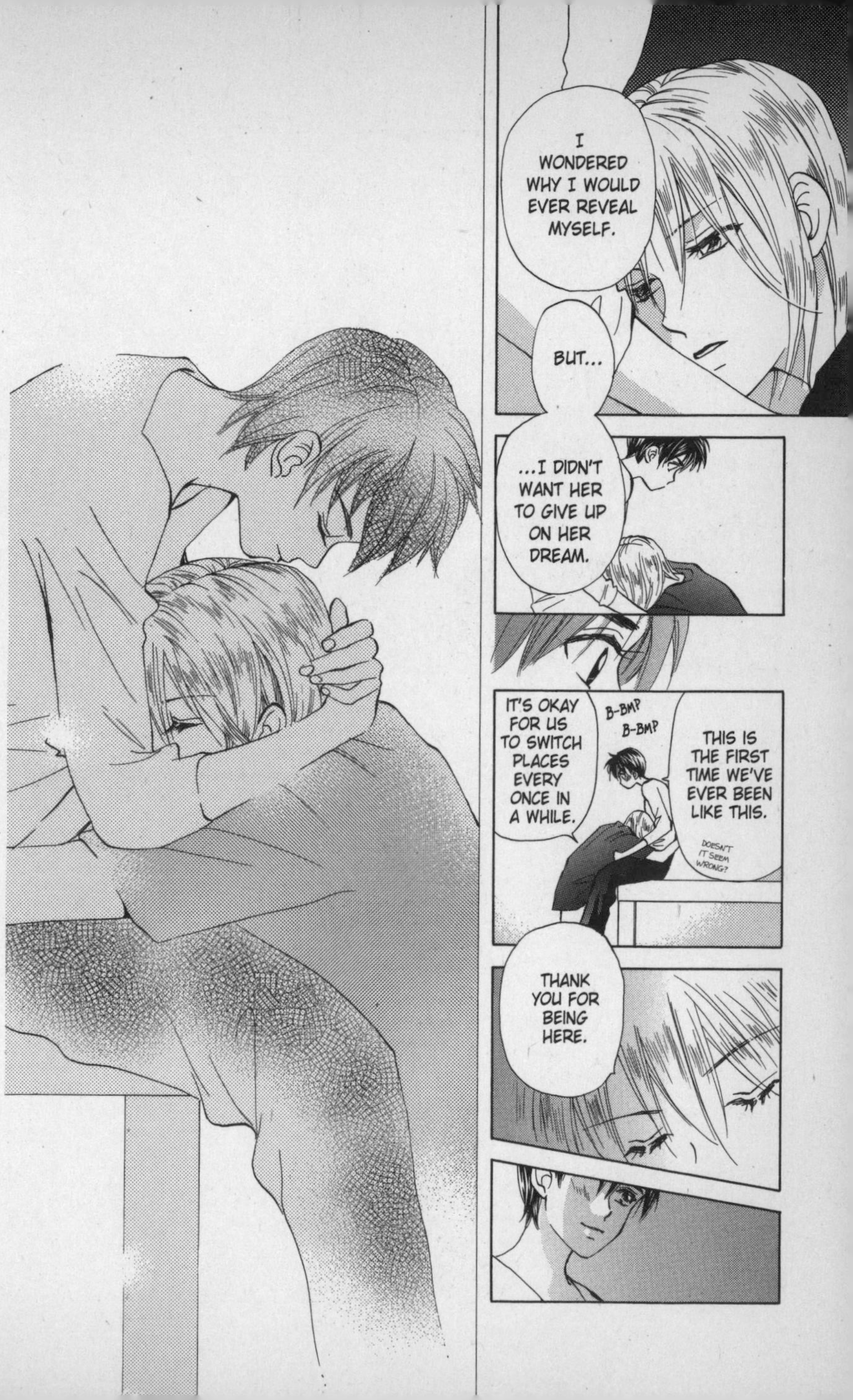
I WONDERED WHY I WOULD EVER REVEAL MYSELF.
BUT...
...I DIDN'T WANT HER TO GIVE UP ON HER DREAM.
THIS IS THE FIRST TIME WE'VE EVER BEEN LIKE THIS.
DOESN'T IT SEEM WRONG?
B-BMP
B-BMP
IT'S OKAY FOR US TO SWITCH PLACES EVERY ONCE IN A WHILE.
THANK YOU FOR BEING HERE.

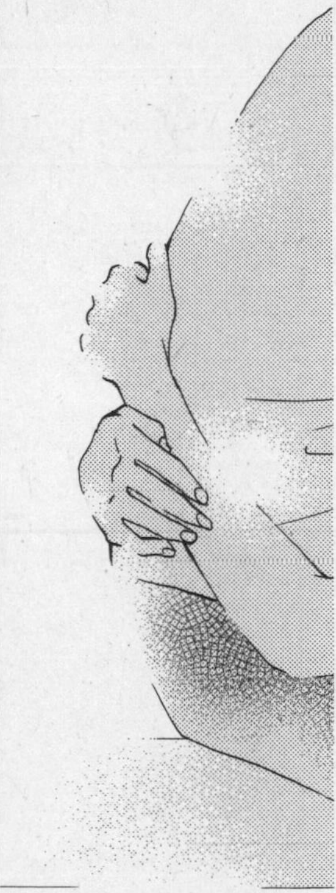

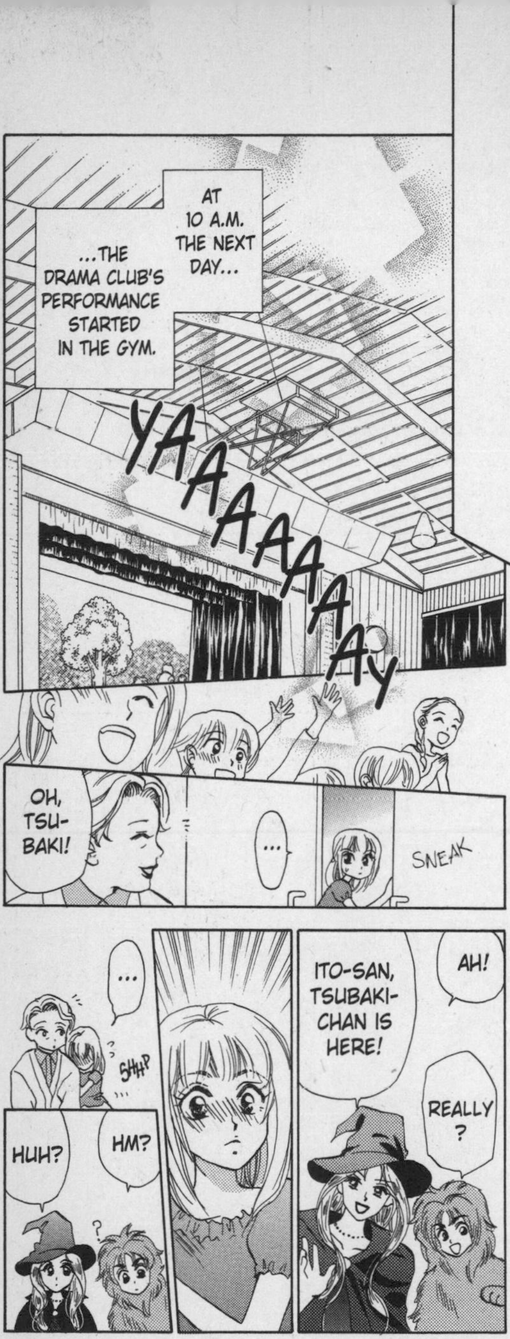
AT 10 A.M. THE NEXT DAY...
...THE DRAMA CLUB'S PERFORMANCE STARTED IN THE GYM.
YAAAAAAAY
SNEAK
...
OH, TSUBAKI!
AH!
ITO-SAN, TSUBAKI-CHAN IS HERE!
REALLY?
...
SHHP
HM?
HUH?

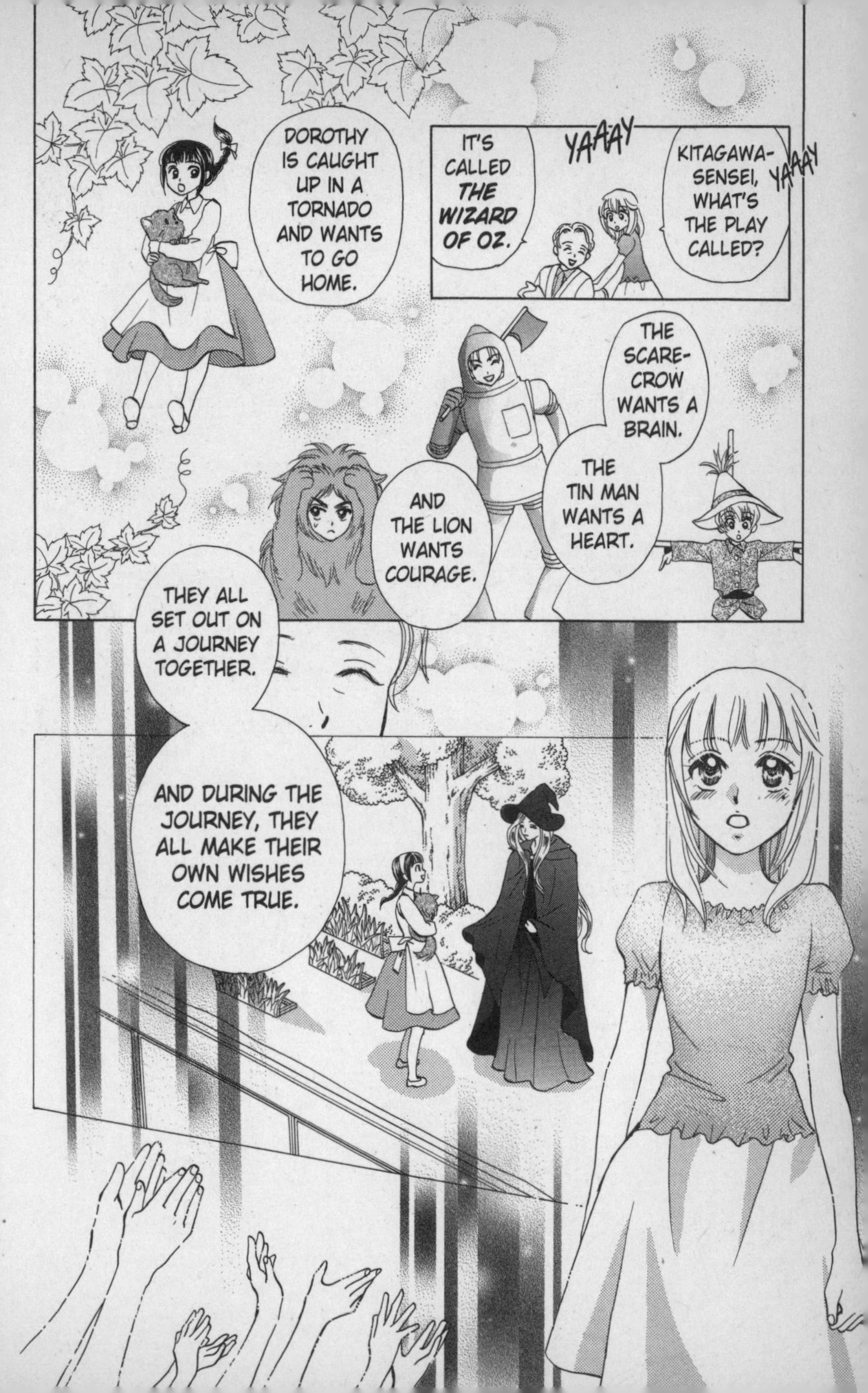
KITAGAWA-SENSEI, WHAT'S THE PLAY CALLED?
YAAAY
YAAAY
IT'S CALLED *THE WIZARD OF OZ.*
DOROTHY IS CAUGHT UP IN A TORNADO AND WANTS TO GO HOME.
THE SCARE-CROW WANTS A BRAIN.
THE TIN MAN WANTS A HEART.
AND THE LION WANTS COURAGE.
THEY ALL SET OUT ON A JOURNEY TOGETHER.
AND DURING THE JOURNEY, THEY ALL MAKE THEIR OWN WISHES COME TRUE.

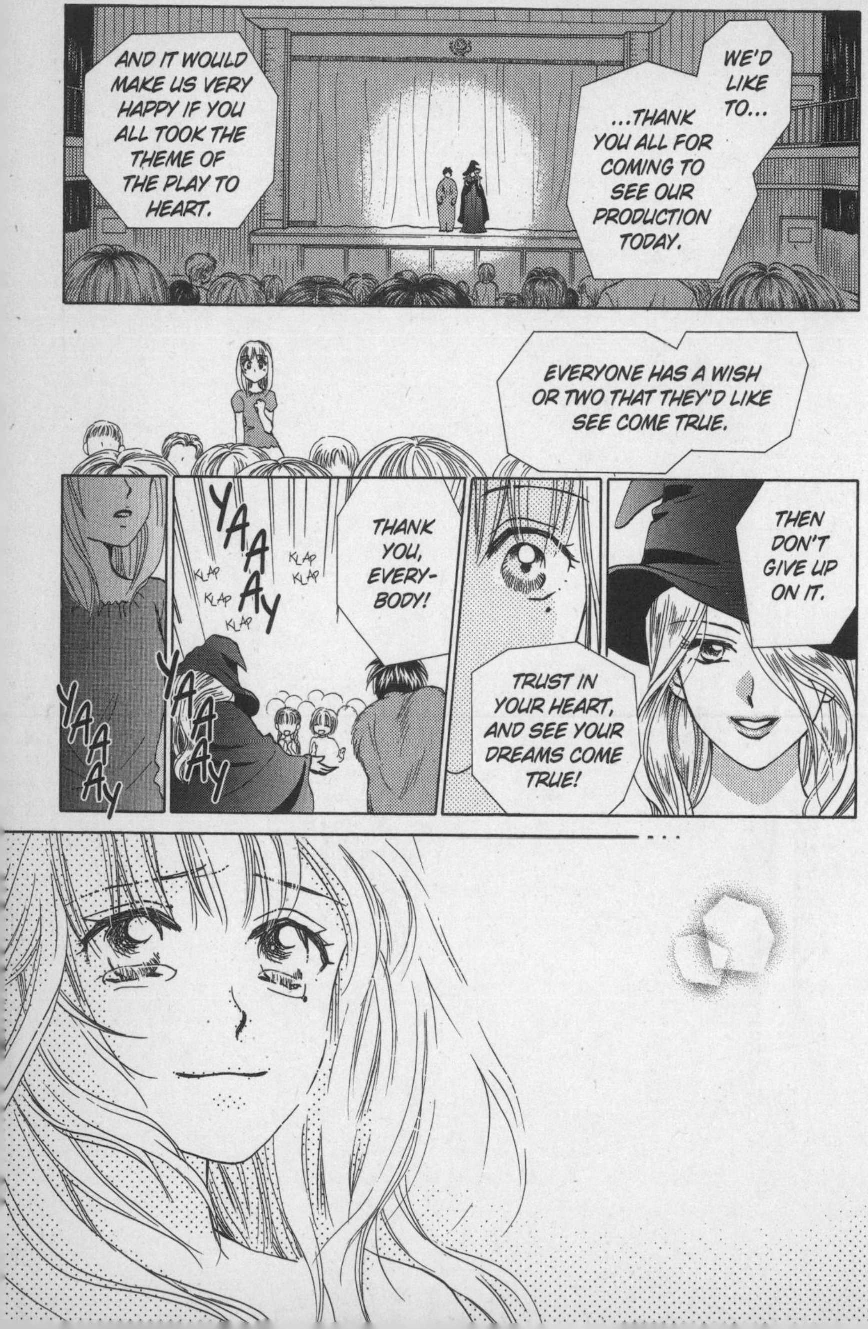
WE'D LIKE TO...
...THANK YOU ALL FOR COMING TO SEE OUR PRODUCTION TODAY.
AND IT WOULD MAKE US VERY HAPPY IF YOU ALL TOOK THE THEME OF THE PLAY TO HEART.
EVERYONE HAS A WISH OR TWO THAT THEY'D LIKE SEE COME TRUE.
THEN DON'T GIVE UP ON IT.
TRUST IN YOUR HEART, AND SEE YOUR DREAMS COME TRUE!
THANK YOU, EVERY-BODY!
YAAAAY
KLAP KLAP
KLAP KLAP KLAP
YAAAAY
YAAAAY

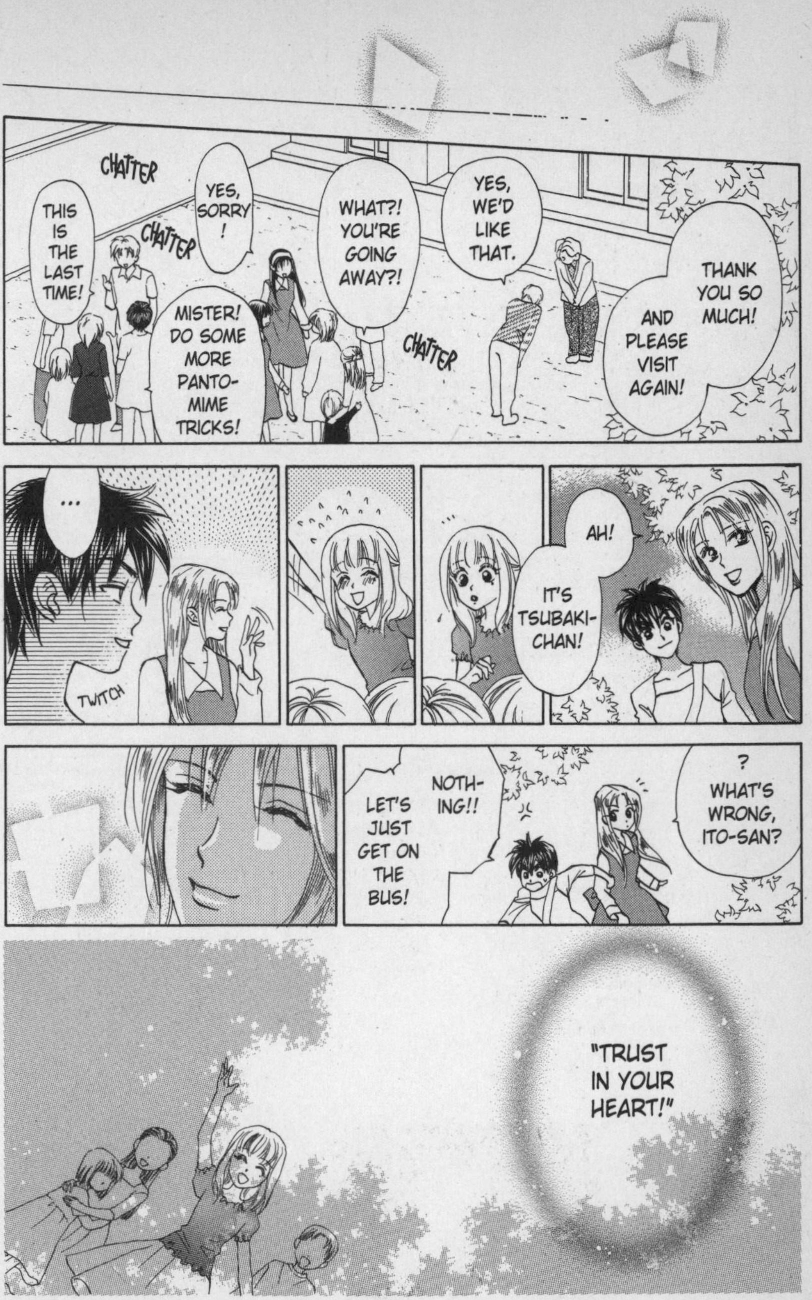
THANK YOU SO MUCH!
AND PLEASE VISIT AGAIN!
YES, WE'D LIKE THAT.
CHATTER
WHAT?! YOU'RE GOING AWAY?!
YES, SORRY!
CHATTER
CHATTER
THIS IS THE LAST TIME!
MISTER! DO SOME MORE PANTOMIME TRICKS!
AH!
IT'S TSUBAKI-CHAN!
...
...
TWITCH
? WHAT'S WRONG, ITO-SAN?
NOTHING!!
LET'S JUST GET ON THE BUS!
"TRUST IN YOUR HEART!"

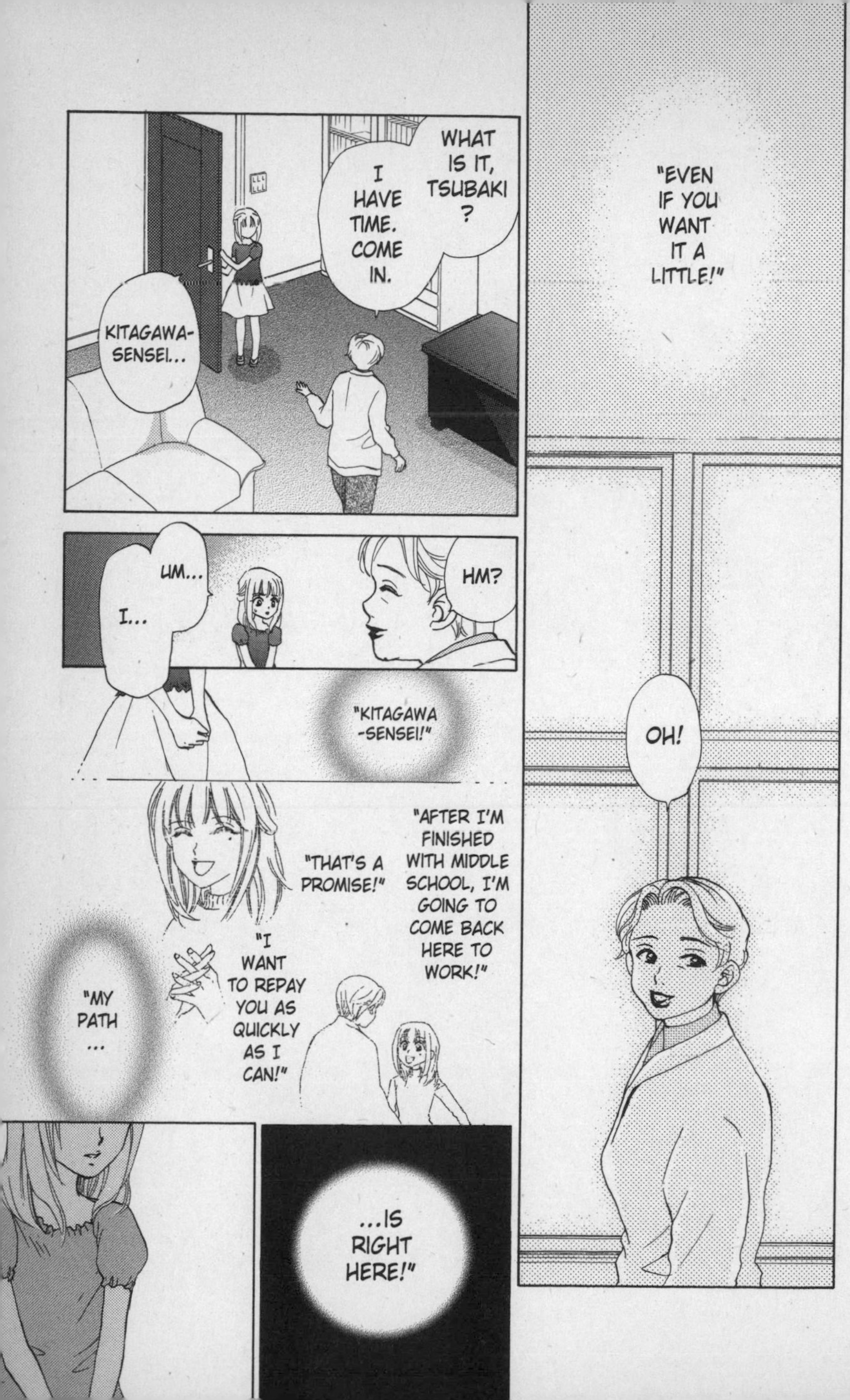
"EVEN IF YOU WANT IT A LITTLE!"
OH!
WHAT IS IT, TSUBAKI?
I HAVE TIME. COME IN.
KITAGAWA-SENSEI...
HM?
UM...
I...
"KITAGAWA-SENSEI!"
"AFTER I'M FINISHED WITH MIDDLE SCHOOL, I'M GOING TO COME BACK HERE TO WORK!"
"THAT'S A PROMISE!"
"I WANT TO REPAY YOU AS QUICKLY AS I CAN!"
"MY PATH ...
...IS RIGHT HERE!"

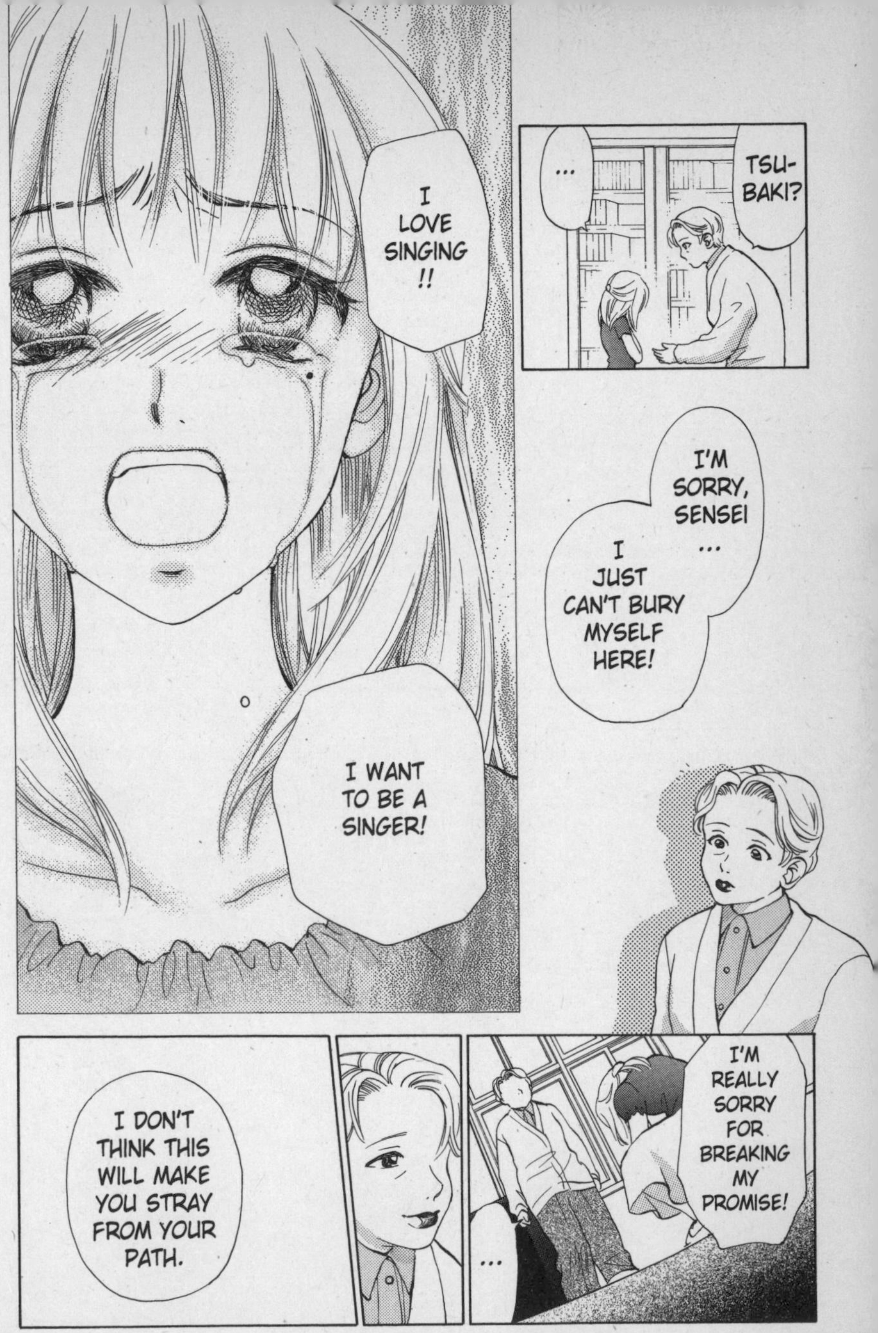
TSU-BAKI?
...
I'M SORRY, SENSEI ...
I JUST CAN'T BURY MYSELF HERE!
I LOVE SINGING !!
I WANT TO BE A SINGER!
I'M REALLY SORRY FOR BREAKING MY PROMISE!
...
I DON'T THINK THIS WILL MAKE YOU STRAY FROM YOUR PATH.

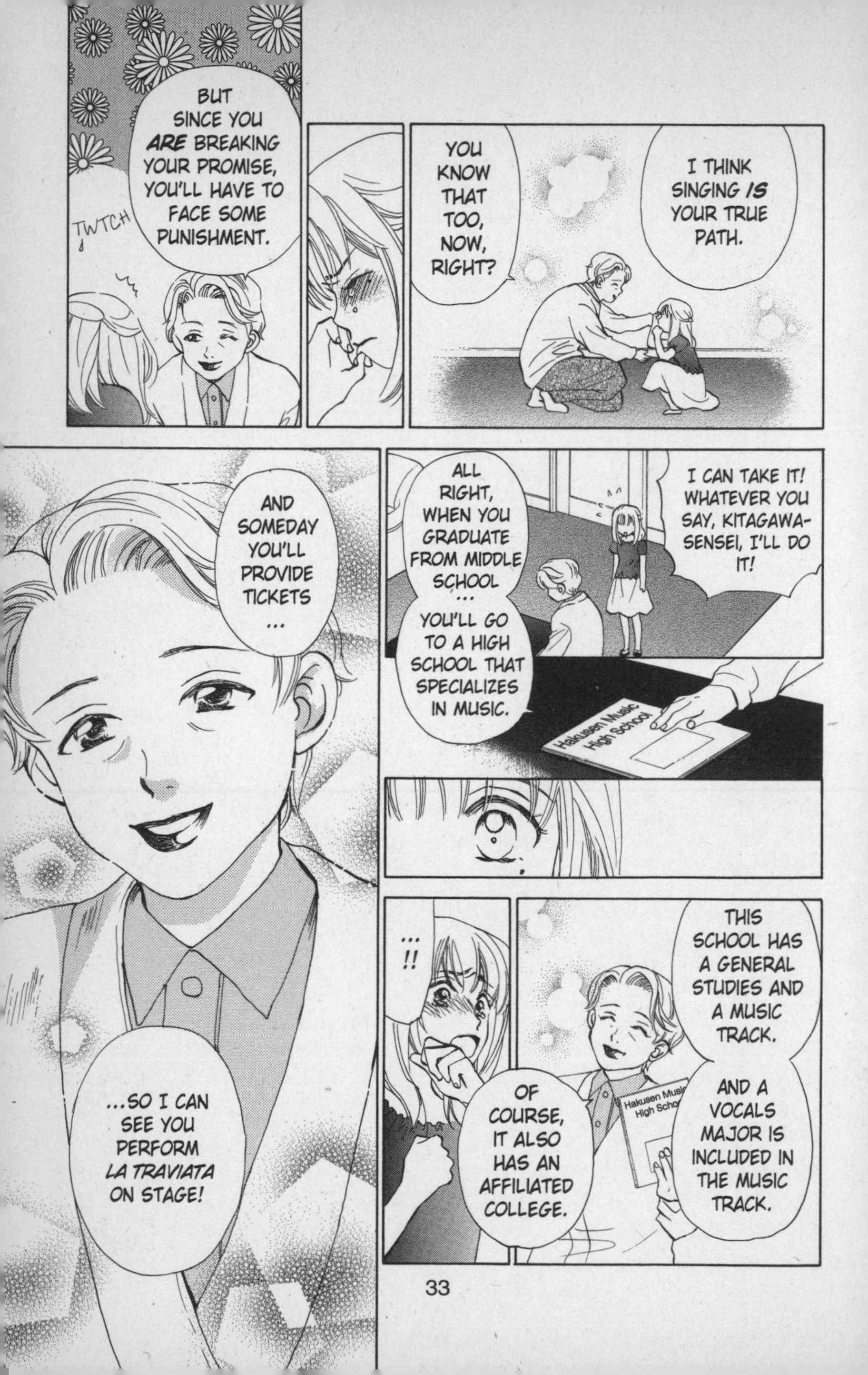
I THINK SINGING *IS* YOUR TRUE PATH.
YOU KNOW THAT TOO, NOW, RIGHT?
BUT SINCE YOU *ARE* BREAKING YOUR PROMISE, YOU'LL HAVE TO FACE SOME PUNISHMENT.
TWTCH
I CAN TAKE IT! WHATEVER YOU SAY, KITAGAWA-SENSEI, I'LL DO IT!
ALL RIGHT, WHEN YOU GRADUATE FROM MIDDLE SCHOOL...
YOU'LL GO TO A HIGH SCHOOL THAT SPECIALIZES IN MUSIC.
Hakusen Music High School
THIS SCHOOL HAS A GENERAL STUDIES AND A MUSIC TRACK.
AND A VOCALS MAJOR IS INCLUDED IN THE MUSIC TRACK.
OF COURSE, IT ALSO HAS AN AFFILIATED COLLEGE.
...!!
AND SOMEDAY YOU'LL PROVIDE TICKETS...
...SO I CAN SEE YOU PERFORM *LA TRAVIATA* ON STAGE!

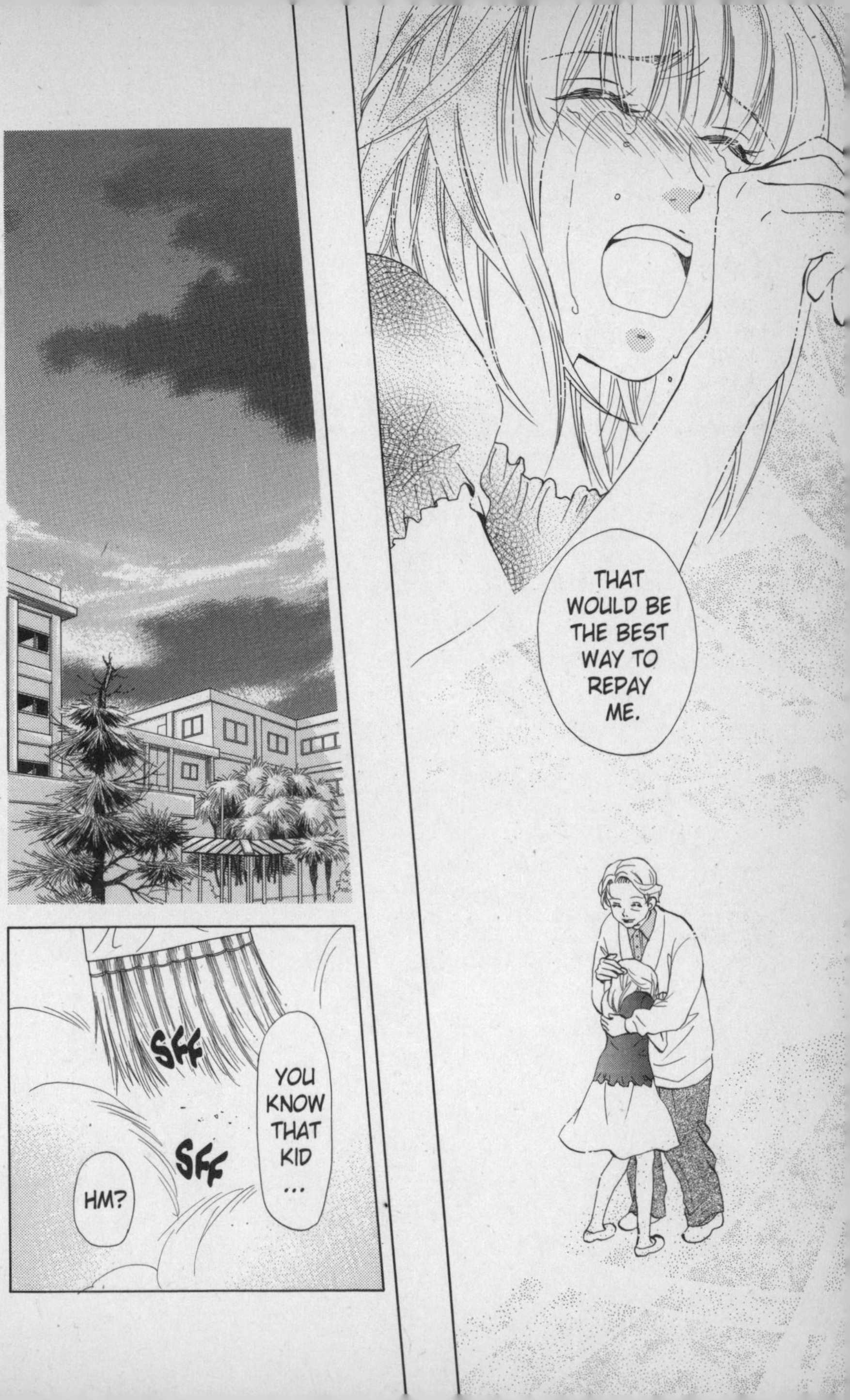
THAT WOULD BE THE BEST WAY TO REPAY ME.
SFF
YOU KNOW THAT KID ...
SFF
HM?

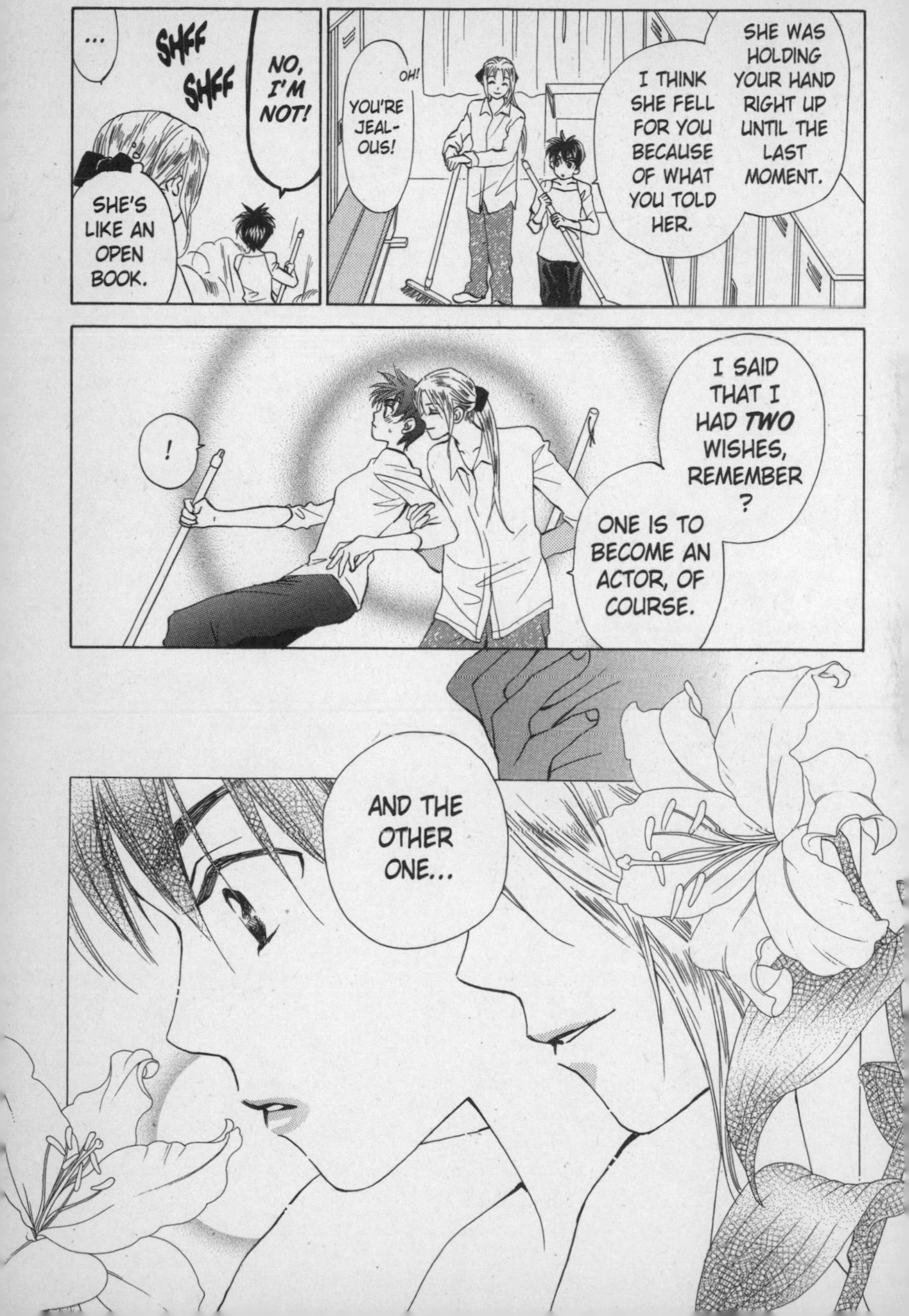
SHE WAS HOLDING YOUR HAND RIGHT UP UNTIL THE LAST MOMENT.
I THINK SHE FELL FOR YOU BECAUSE OF WHAT YOU TOLD HER.
OH!
YOU'RE JEAL-OUS!
NO, I'M NOT!
SHFF
SHFF
...
SHE'S LIKE AN OPEN BOOK.
I SAID THAT I HAD TWO WISHES, REMEMBER?
ONE IS TO BECOME AN ACTOR, OF COURSE.
!
AND THE OTHER ONE...

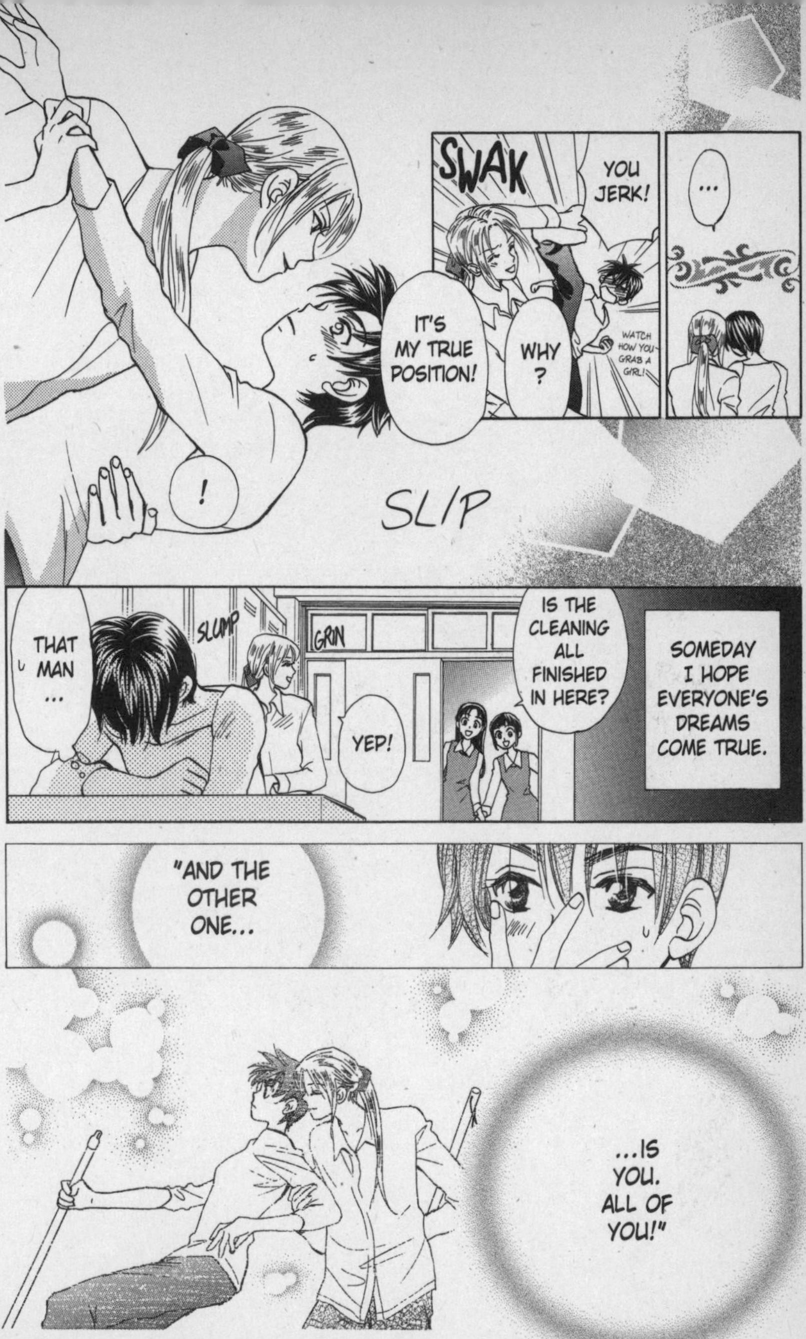
...
SWAK
YOU JERK!
WATCH HOW YOU GRAB A GIRL!
WHY ?
IT'S MY TRUE POSITION!
SLIP
!
SOMEDAY I HOPE EVERYONE'S DREAMS COME TRUE.
IS THE CLEANING ALL FINISHED IN HERE?
YEP!
GRIN
SLUMP
THAT MAN ...
"AND THE OTHER ONE...
...IS YOU. ALL OF YOU!"

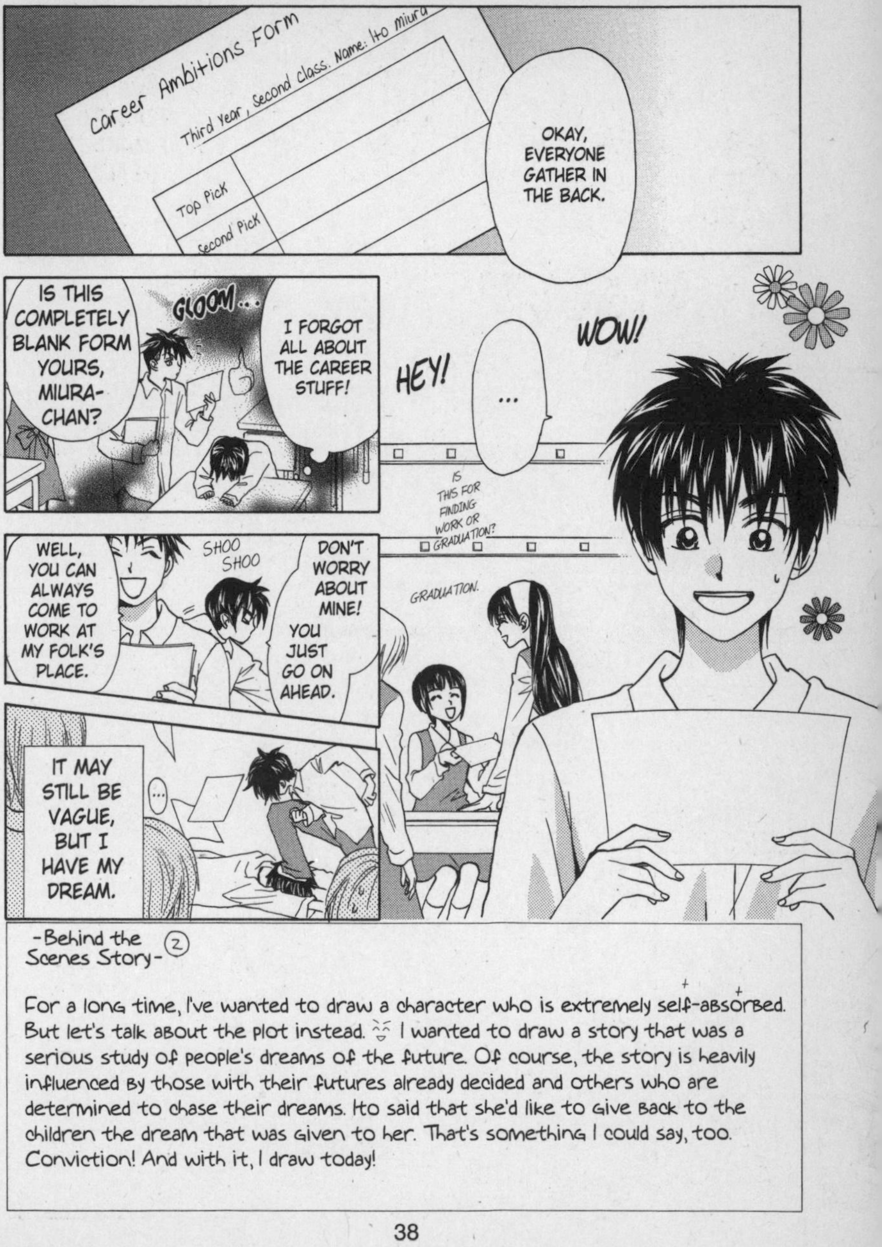
OKAY, EVERYONE GATHER IN THE BACK.
Career Ambitions Form
Third Year, Second class. Name: Ito Miura
Top Pick
Second Pick
WOW!
HEY!
...
IS THIS FOR FINDING WORK OR GRADUATION?
GRADUATION.
IS THIS COMPLETELY BLANK FORM YOURS, MIURA-CHAN?
I FORGOT ALL ABOUT THE CAREER STUFF!
GLOOM...
DON'T WORRY ABOUT MINE! YOU JUST GO ON AHEAD.
SHOO SHOO
WELL, YOU CAN ALWAYS COME TO WORK AT MY FOLK'S PLACE.
...
IT MAY STILL BE VAGUE, BUT I HAVE MY DREAM.

-Behind the Scenes Story- ②

For a long time, I've wanted to draw a character who is extremely self-absorbed. But let's talk about the plot instead. I wanted to draw a story that was a serious study of people's dreams of the future. Of course, the story is heavily influenced by those with their futures already decided and others who are determined to chase their dreams. Ito said that she'd like to give back to the children the dream that was given to her. That's something I could say, too. Conviction! And with it, I draw today!

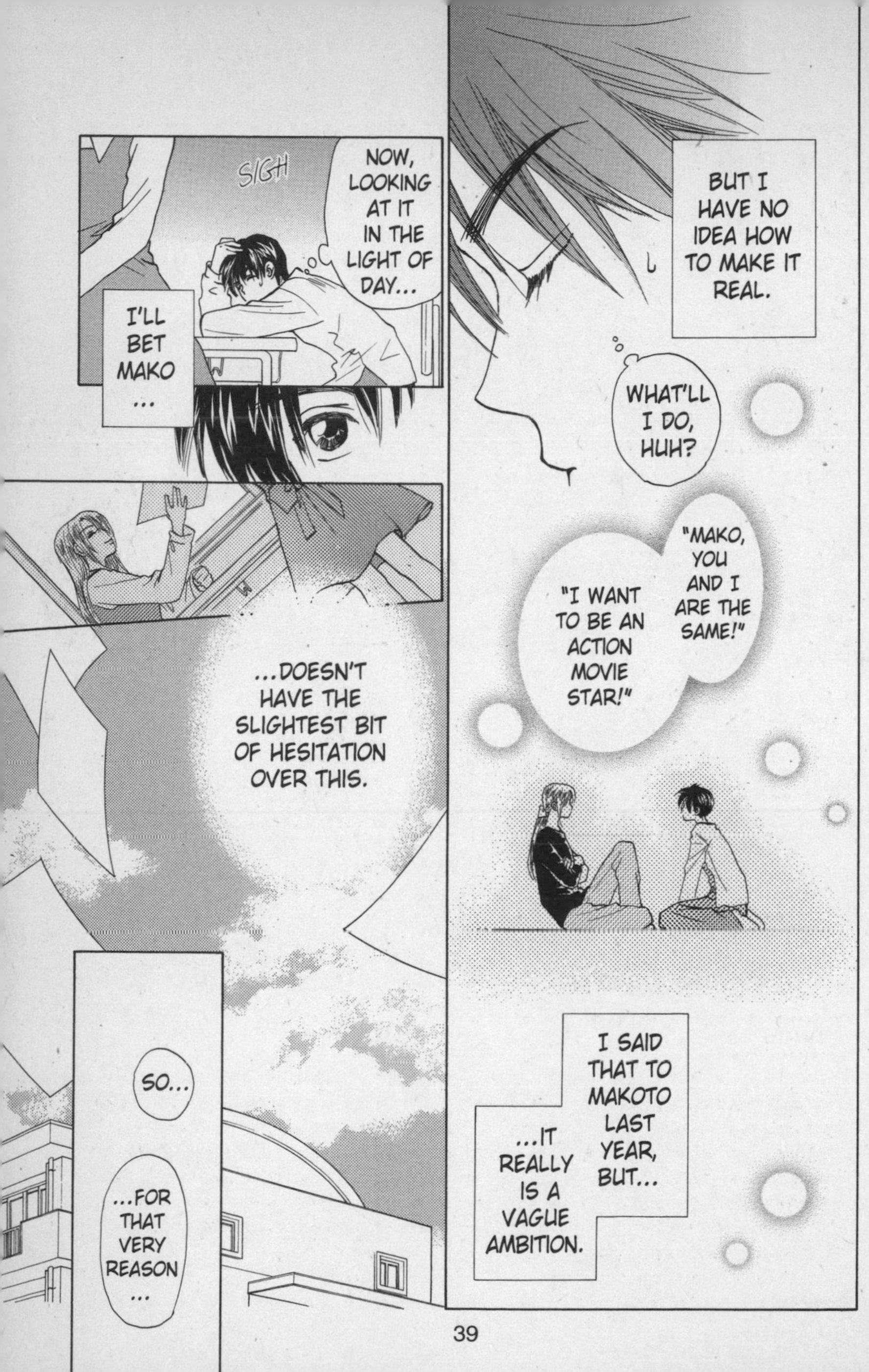
BUT I HAVE NO IDEA HOW TO MAKE IT REAL.
WHAT'LL I DO, HUH?
"MAKO, YOU AND I ARE THE SAME!"
"I WANT TO BE AN ACTION MOVIE STAR!"
I SAID THAT TO MAKOTO LAST YEAR, BUT...
...IT REALLY IS A VAGUE AMBITION.
NOW, LOOKING AT IT IN THE LIGHT OF DAY...
SIGH
I'LL BET MAKO...
...DOESN'T HAVE THE SLIGHTEST BIT OF HESITATION OVER THIS.
SO...
...FOR THAT VERY REASON...

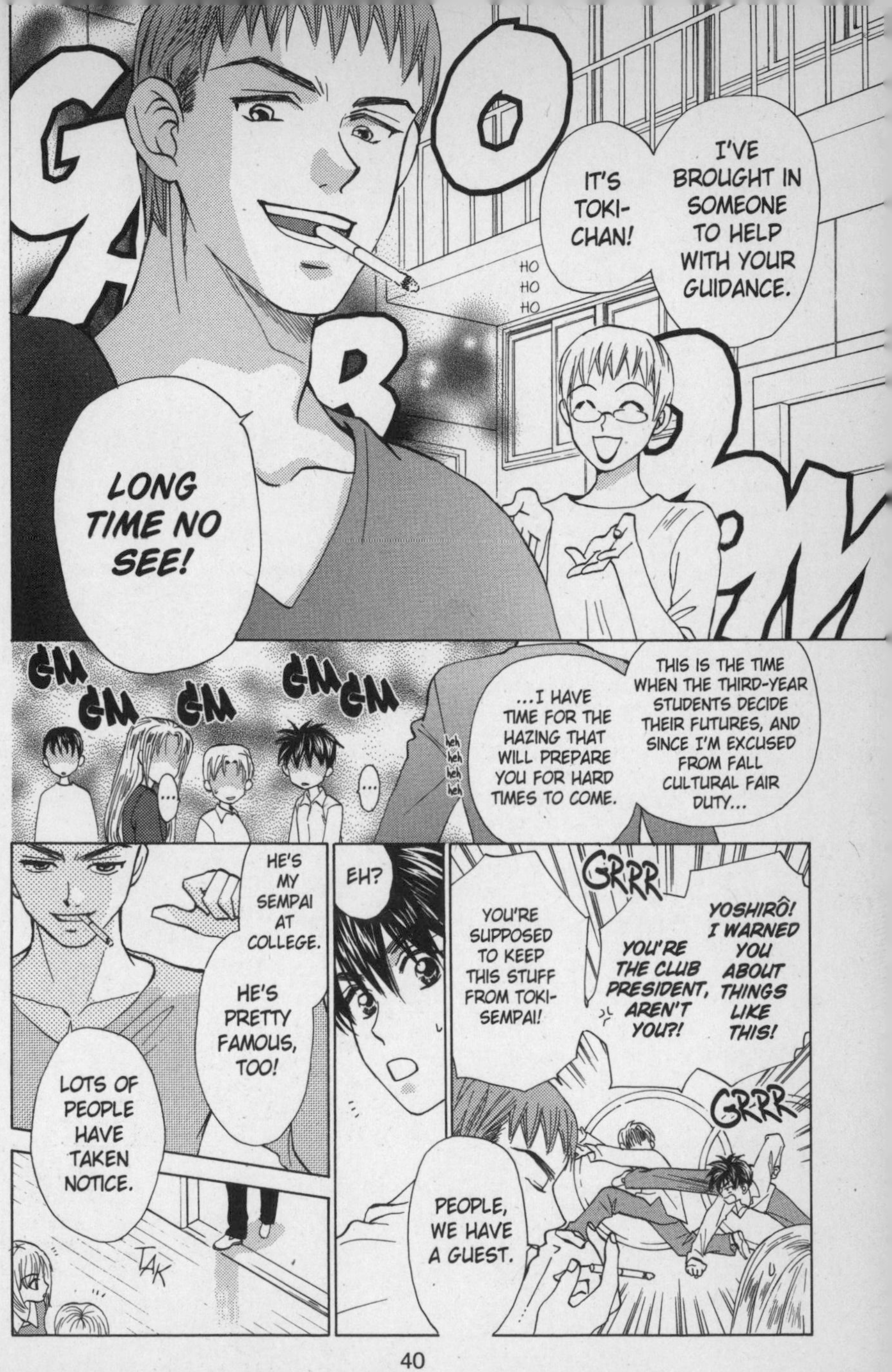
I'VE BROUGHT IN SOMEONE TO HELP WITH YOUR GUIDANCE.
IT'S TOKI-CHAN!
HO HO HO
LONG TIME NO SEE!
THIS IS THE TIME WHEN THE THIRD-YEAR STUDENTS DECIDE THEIR FUTURES, AND SINCE I'M EXCUSED FROM FALL CULTURAL FAIR DUTY...
...I HAVE TIME FOR THE HAZING THAT WILL PREPARE YOU FOR HARD TIMES TO COME.
heh heh heh heh
GMGM
GM
GM
GM
...
...
GRRR
YOSHIRÔ! I WARNED YOU ABOUT THINGS LIKE THIS!
YOU'RE THE CLUB PRESIDENT, AREN'T YOU?!
YOU'RE SUPPOSED TO KEEP THIS STUFF FROM TOKI-SEMPAI!
GRRR
PEOPLE, WE HAVE A GUEST.
EH?
HE'S MY SEMPAI AT COLLEGE.
HE'S PRETTY FAMOUS, TOO!
LOTS OF PEOPLE HAVE TAKEN NOTICE.
TAK

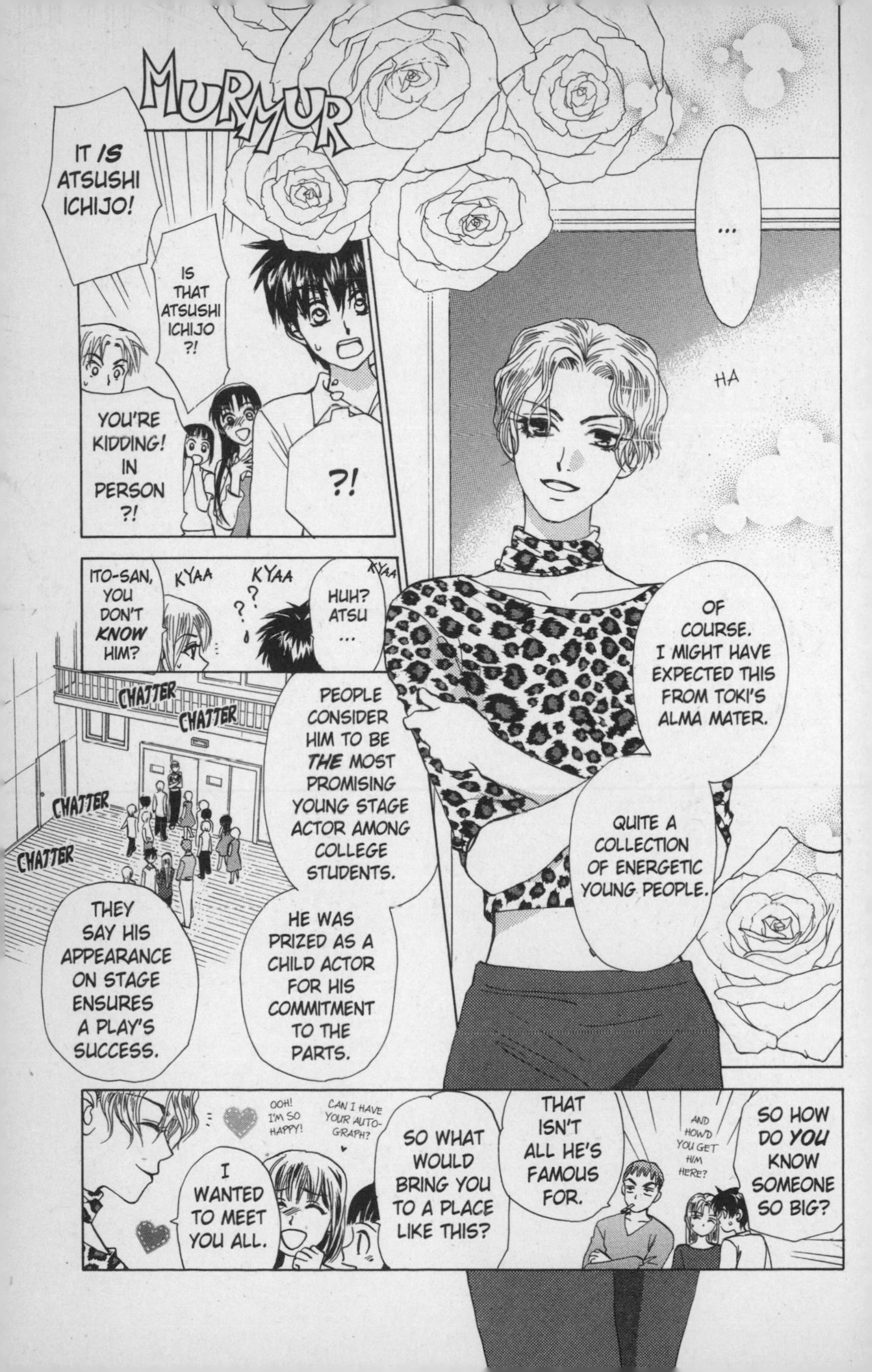
...
HA
OF COURSE. I MIGHT HAVE EXPECTED THIS FROM TOKI'S ALMA MATER.
QUITE A COLLECTION OF ENERGETIC YOUNG PEOPLE.
MURMUR
IT IS ATSUSHI ICHIJO!
IS THAT ATSUSHI ICHIJO ?!
?!
YOU'RE KIDDING! IN PERSON ?!
KYAA
HUH? ATSU ...
KYAA
KYAA
ITO-SAN, YOU DON'T KNOW HIM?
PEOPLE CONSIDER HIM TO BE THE MOST PROMISING YOUNG STAGE ACTOR AMONG COLLEGE STUDENTS.
HE WAS PRIZED AS A CHILD ACTOR FOR HIS COMMITMENT TO THE PARTS.
THEY SAY HIS APPEARANCE ON STAGE ENSURES A PLAY'S SUCCESS.
CHATTER
CHATTER
CHATTER
CHATTER
SO HOW DO YOU KNOW SOMEONE SO BIG?
AND HOW'D YOU GET HIM HERE?
THAT ISN'T ALL HE'S FAMOUS FOR.
SO WHAT WOULD BRING YOU TO A PLACE LIKE THIS?
CAN I HAVE YOUR AUTO-GRAPH?
OOH! I'M SO HAPPY!
I WANTED TO MEET YOU ALL.

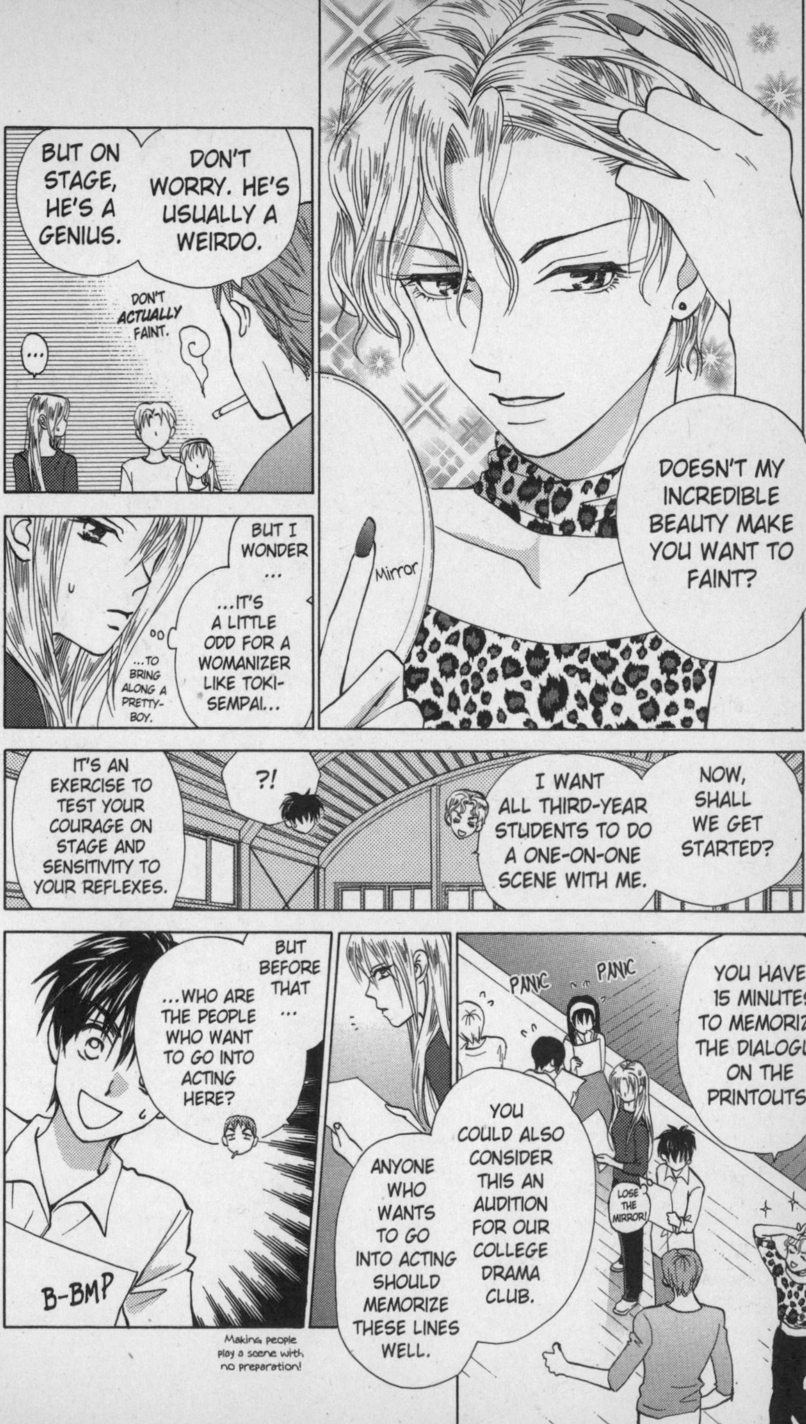
Mirror
DOESN'T MY INCREDIBLE BEAUTY MAKE YOU WANT TO FAINT?
DON'T WORRY. HE'S USUALLY A WEIRDO.
BUT ON STAGE, HE'S A GENIUS.
DON'T ACTUALLY FAINT.
...
BUT I WONDER ...
...IT'S A LITTLE ODD FOR A WOMANIZER LIKE TOKI-SEMPAI...
...TO BRING ALONG A PRETTY-BOY.
NOW, SHALL WE GET STARTED?
I WANT ALL THIRD-YEAR STUDENTS TO DO A ONE-ON-ONE SCENE WITH ME.
?!
IT'S AN EXERCISE TO TEST YOUR COURAGE ON STAGE AND SENSITIVITY TO YOUR REFLEXES.
YOU HAVE 15 MINUTES TO MEMORIZE THE DIALOGUE ON THE PRINTOUTS.
PANIC
PANIC
LOSE THE MIRROR!
YOU COULD ALSO CONSIDER THIS AN AUDITION FOR OUR COLLEGE DRAMA CLUB.
ANYONE WHO WANTS TO GO INTO ACTING SHOULD MEMORIZE THESE LINES WELL.
BUT BEFORE THAT ...
...WHO ARE THE PEOPLE WHO WANT TO GO INTO ACTING HERE?
B-BMP
Making people play a scene with no preparation!

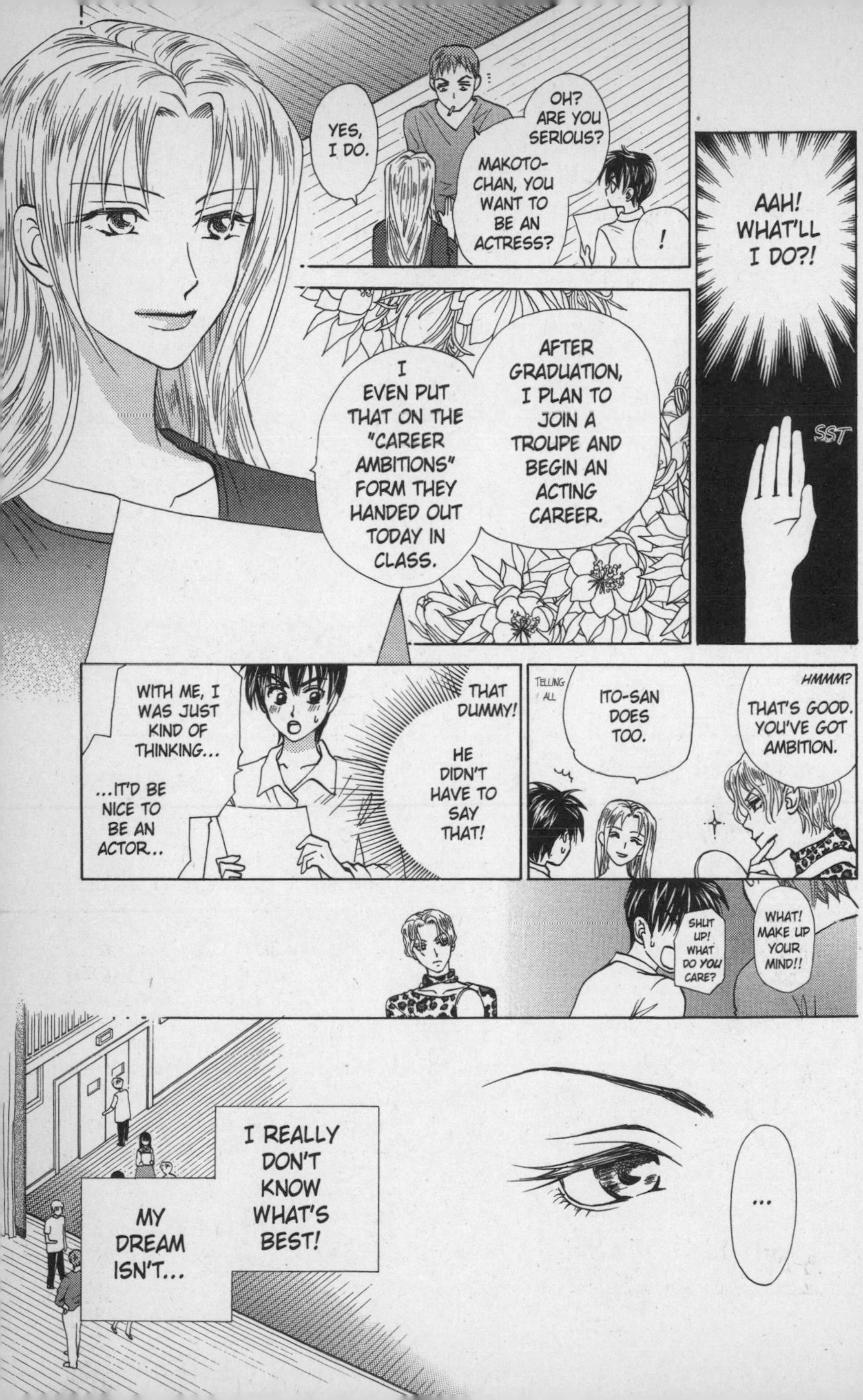

AAH! WHAT'LL I DO?!
SST
OH? ARE YOU SERIOUS?
MAKOTO-CHAN, YOU WANT TO BE AN ACTRESS?
!
YES, I DO.
AFTER GRADUATION, I PLAN TO JOIN A TROUPE AND BEGIN AN ACTING CAREER.
I EVEN PUT THAT ON THE "CAREER AMBITIONS" FORM THEY HANDED OUT TODAY IN CLASS.
HMMM?
THAT'S GOOD. YOU'VE GOT AMBITION.
ITO-SAN DOES TOO.
TELLING ALL
THAT DUMMY!
HE DIDN'T HAVE TO SAY THAT!
WITH ME, I WAS JUST KIND OF THINKING...
...IT'D BE NICE TO BE AN ACTOR...
WHAT! MAKE UP YOUR MIND!!
SHUT UP! WHAT DO YOU CARE?
...
I REALLY DON'T KNOW WHAT'S BEST!
MY DREAM ISN'T...

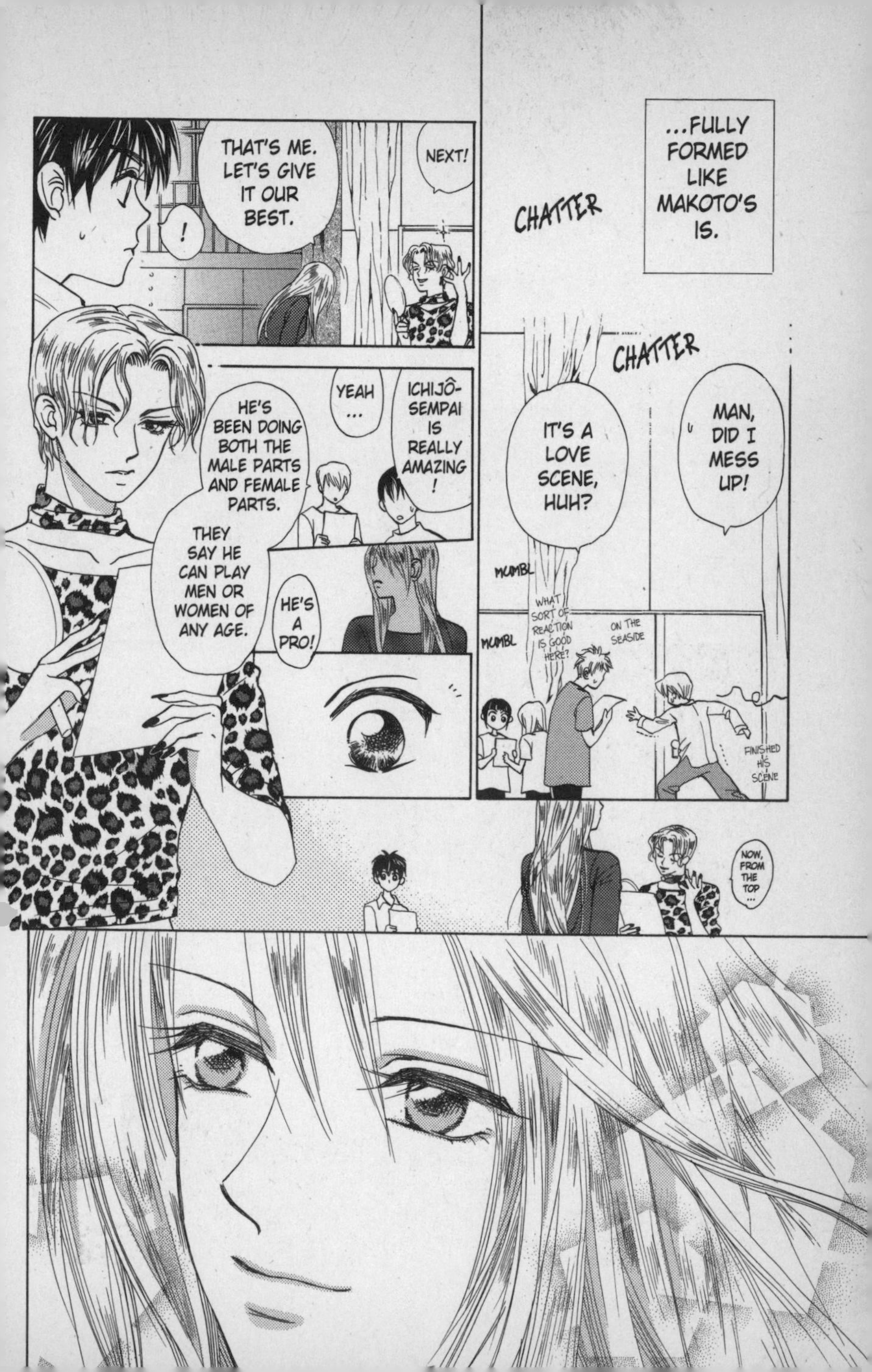
...FULLY FORMED LIKE MAKOTO'S IS.
CHATTER
NEXT!
THAT'S ME. LET'S GIVE IT OUR BEST.
!
CHATTER
MAN, DID I MESS UP!
IT'S A LOVE SCENE, HUH?
MUMBL
MUMBL
WHAT SORT OF REACTION IS GOOD HERE?
ON THE SEASIDE
FINISHED HIS SCENE
ICHIJÔ-SEMPAI IS REALLY AMAZING!
YEAH...
HE'S BEEN DOING BOTH THE MALE PARTS AND FEMALE PARTS.
THEY SAY HE CAN PLAY MEN OR WOMEN OF ANY AGE.
HE'S A PRO!
NOW, FROM THE TOP...

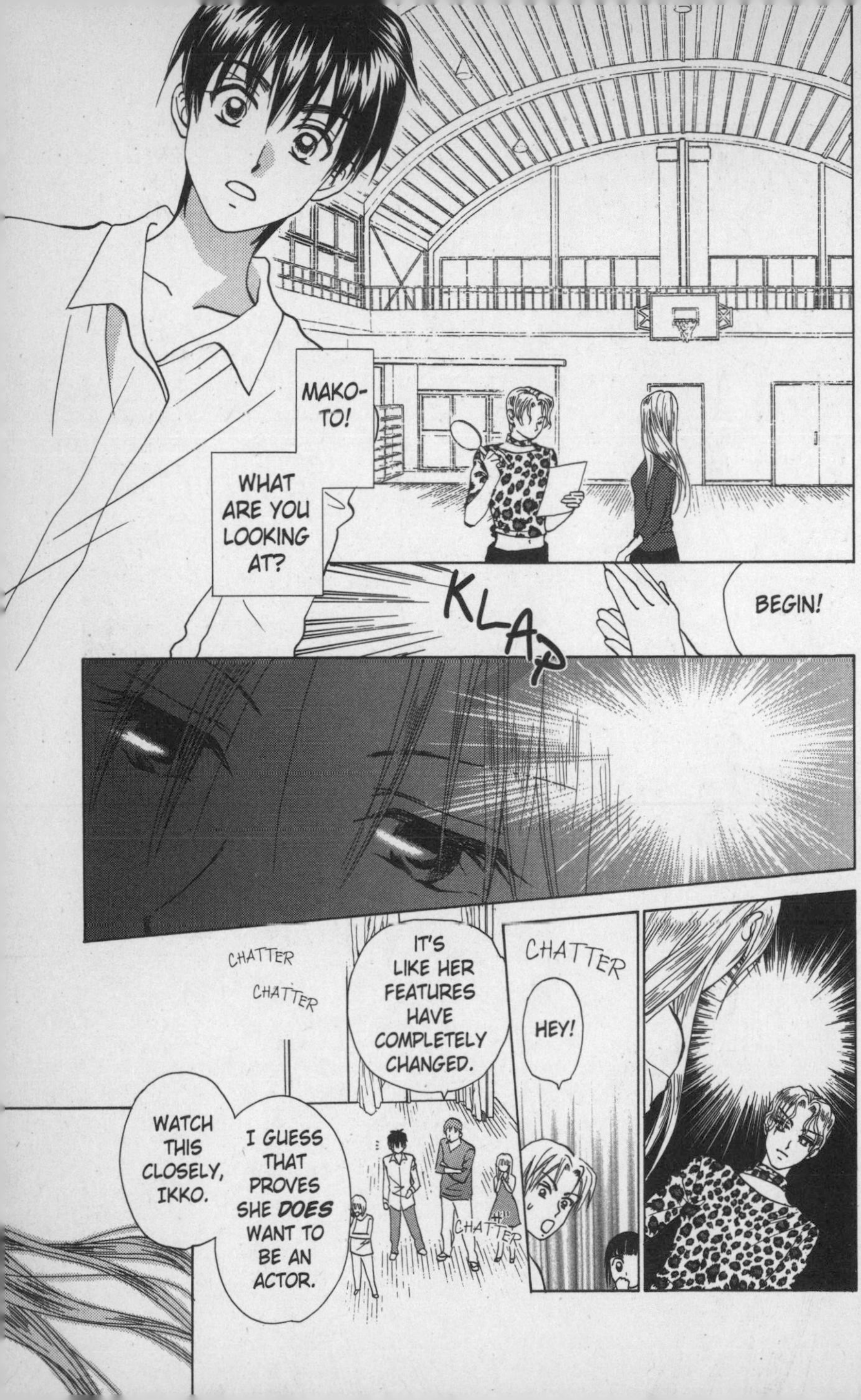
MAKO-TO!
WHAT ARE YOU LOOKING AT?
BEGIN!
KLAP
CHATTER
HEY!
IT'S LIKE HER FEATURES HAVE COMPLETELY CHANGED.
CHATTER
CHATTER
I GUESS THAT PROVES SHE **DOES** WANT TO BE AN ACTOR.
WATCH THIS CLOSELY, IKKO.
CHATTER

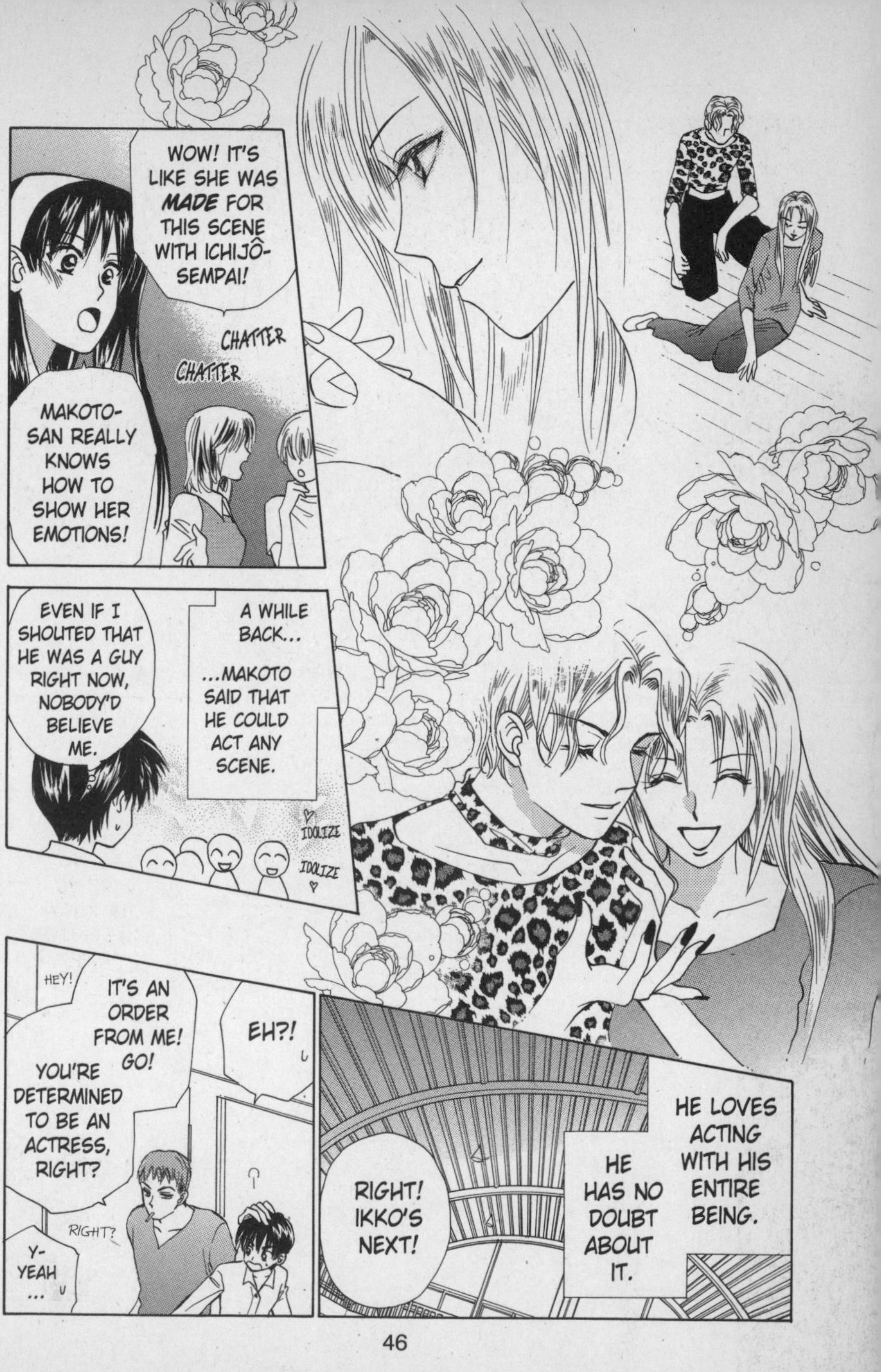
WOW! IT'S LIKE SHE WAS MADE FOR THIS SCENE WITH ICHIJÔ-SEMPAI!
CHATTER
CHATTER
MAKOTO-SAN REALLY KNOWS HOW TO SHOW HER EMOTIONS!
A WHILE BACK...
...MAKOTO SAID THAT HE COULD ACT ANY SCENE.
EVEN IF I SHOUTED THAT HE WAS A GUY RIGHT NOW, NOBODY'D BELIEVE ME.
IDOLIZE
IDOLIZE
HE LOVES ACTING WITH HIS ENTIRE BEING.
HE HAS NO DOUBT ABOUT IT.
RIGHT! IKKO'S NEXT!
EH?!
IT'S AN ORDER FROM ME! GO!
HEY!
YOU'RE DETERMINED TO BE AN ACTRESS, RIGHT?
RIGHT?
Y-YEAH...

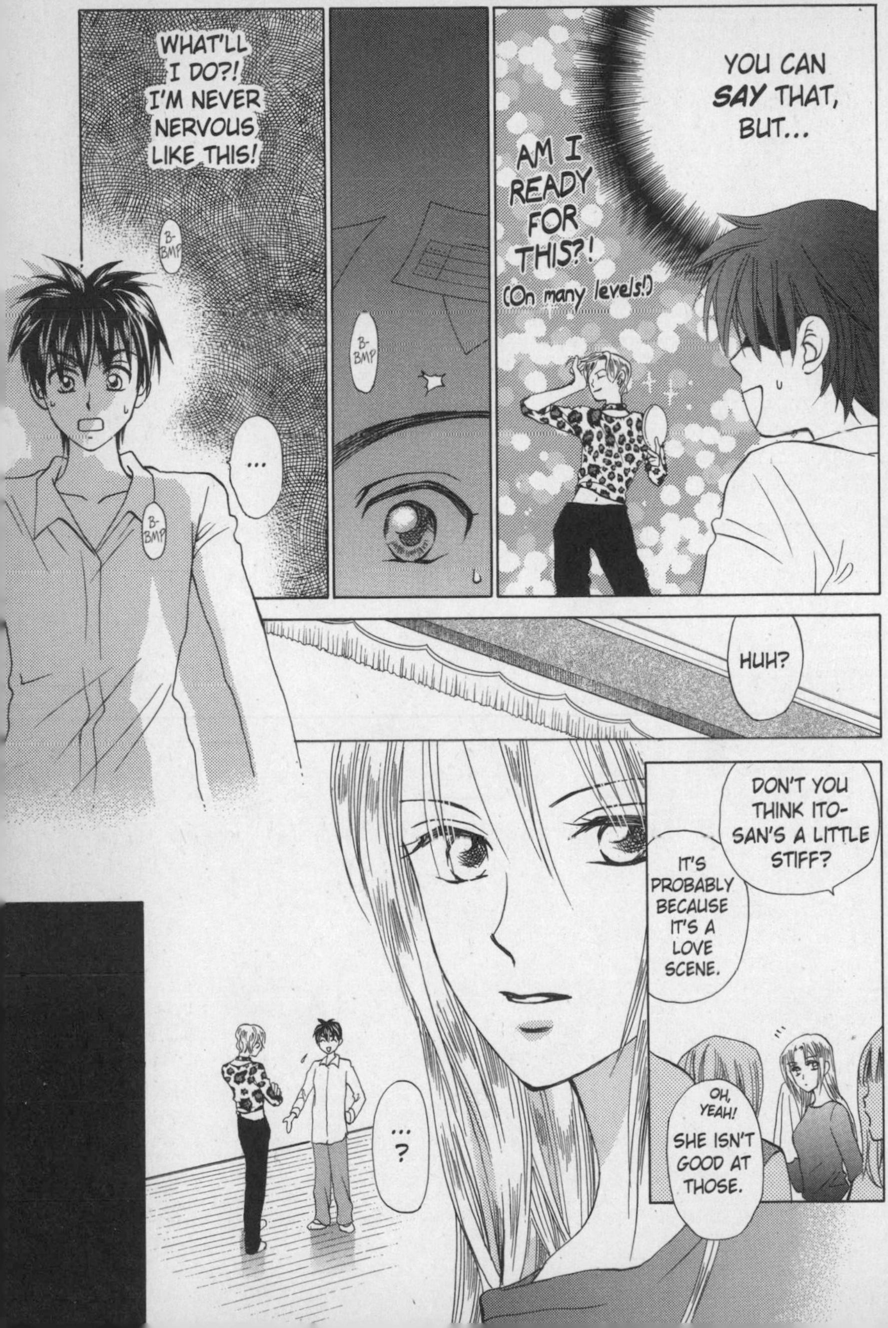
YOU CAN SAY THAT, BUT...
AM I READY FOR THIS?!
(On many levels!)
B-BMP
WHAT'LL I DO?! I'M NEVER NERVOUS LIKE THIS!
B-BMP
...
B-BMP
HUH?
DON'T YOU THINK ITO-SAN'S A LITTLE STIFF?
IT'S PROBABLY BECAUSE IT'S A LOVE SCENE.
OH, YEAH! SHE ISN'T GOOD AT THOSE.
...?

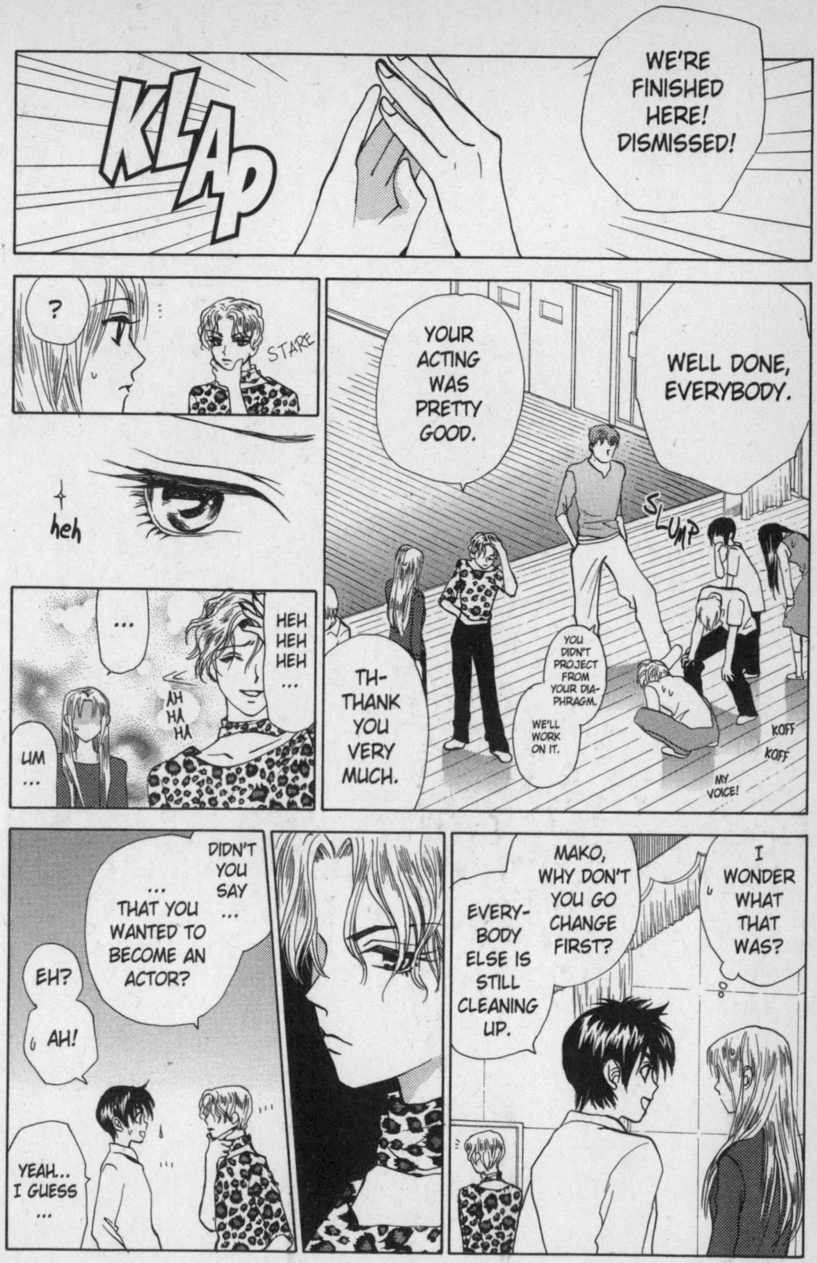
WE'RE FINISHED HERE! DISMISSED!
KLAP
WELL DONE, EVERYBODY.
YOUR ACTING WAS PRETTY GOOD.
SLUMP
YOU DIDN'T PROJECT FROM YOUR DIAPHRAGM.
WE'LL WORK ON IT.
TH-THANK YOU VERY MUCH.
KOFF
KOFF
MY VOICE!
?
STARE
heh
HEH HEH HEH ...
...
AH HA HA
UM ...
I WONDER WHAT THAT WAS?
MAKO, WHY DON'T YOU GO CHANGE FIRST?
EVERYBODY ELSE IS STILL CLEANING UP.
DIDN'T YOU SAY ...
... THAT YOU WANTED TO BECOME AN ACTOR?
EH?
AH!
YEAH... I GUESS ...

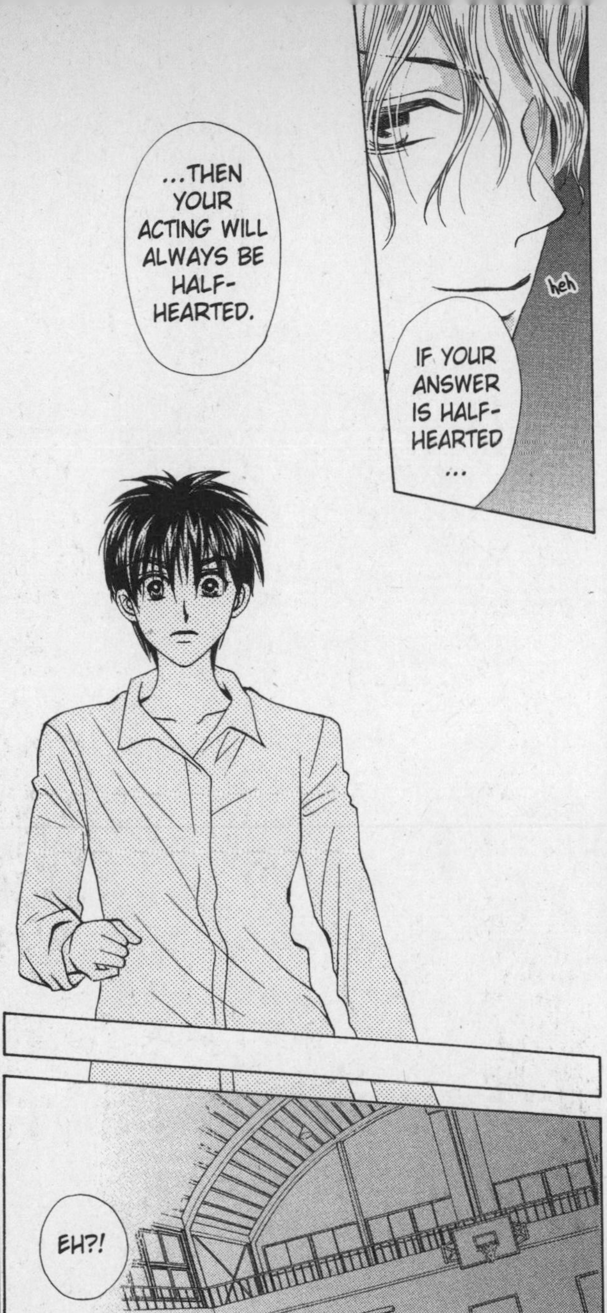
heh
IF YOUR ANSWER IS HALF-HEARTED...
...THEN YOUR ACTING WILL ALWAYS BE HALF-HEARTED.
EH?!

W·J NOW A CD!

Nov. or Dec 2000
Um... As a thank you to all the loyal fans who read the magazine, they're putting out a *W-J* drama CD! There will be three installments including the *Swan Lake* story I drew last spring and an original short drama. It's more than 70 minutes of drama! I received a letter asking, "Is there a way to purchase the CD at my local store?" Sorry! This CD set is only available to those who subscribe by December 2000. And since it's only available to subscribers, there is no way to find these at any retail establishment. It won't be at any CD stores. I have to apologize to the fans who only read the story in the graphic novels.

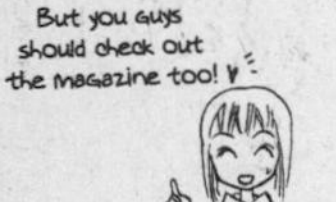
But you guys should check out the magazine too!

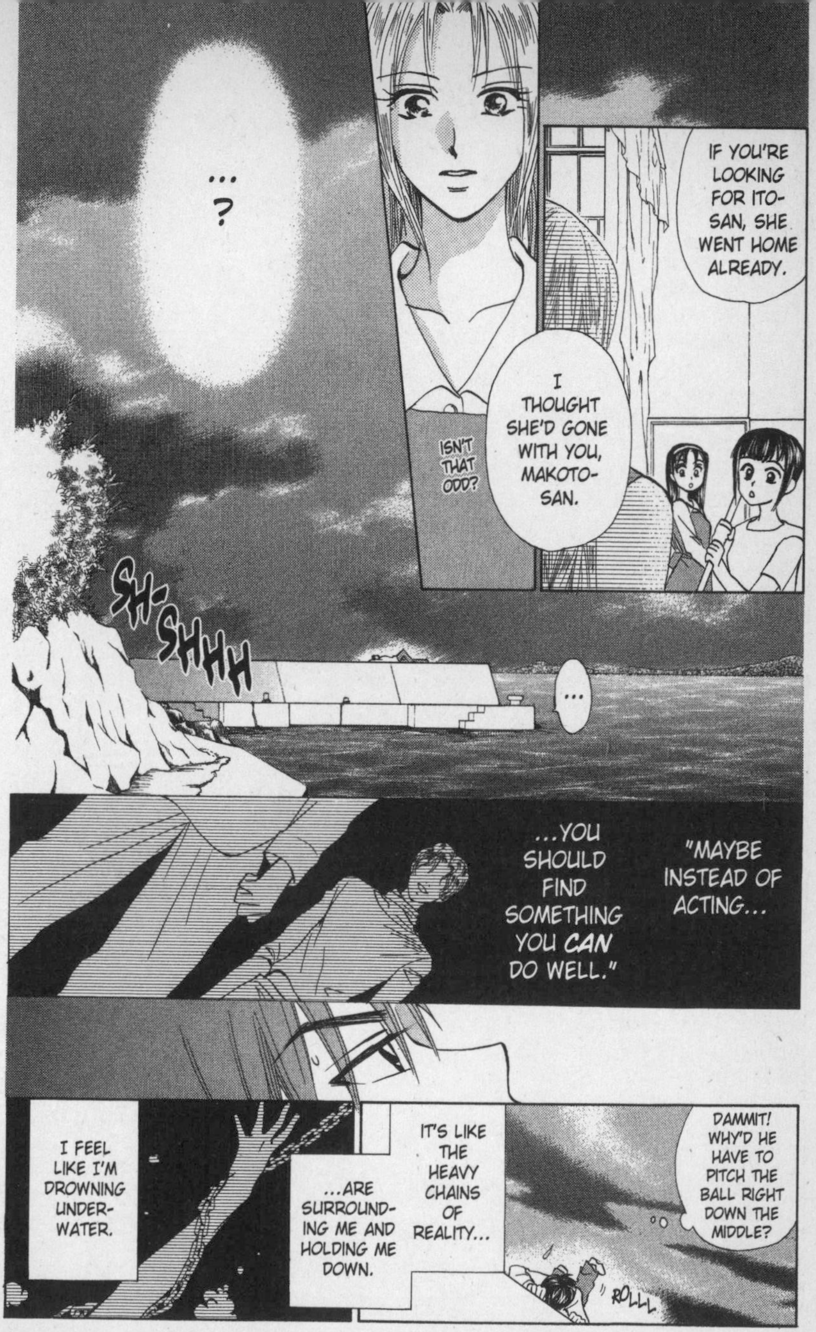
IF YOU'RE LOOKING FOR ITO-SAN, SHE WENT HOME ALREADY.
I THOUGHT SHE'D GONE WITH YOU, MAKOTO-SAN.
ISN'T THAT ODD?
...?
SH-SHHH
...
"MAYBE INSTEAD OF ACTING...
...YOU SHOULD FIND SOMETHING YOU CAN DO WELL."
DAMMIT! WHY'D HE HAVE TO PITCH THE BALL RIGHT DOWN THE MIDDLE?
ROLLL
IT'S LIKE THE HEAVY CHAINS OF REALITY...
...ARE SURROUNDING ME AND HOLDING ME DOWN.
I FEEL LIKE I'M DROWNING UNDERWATER.

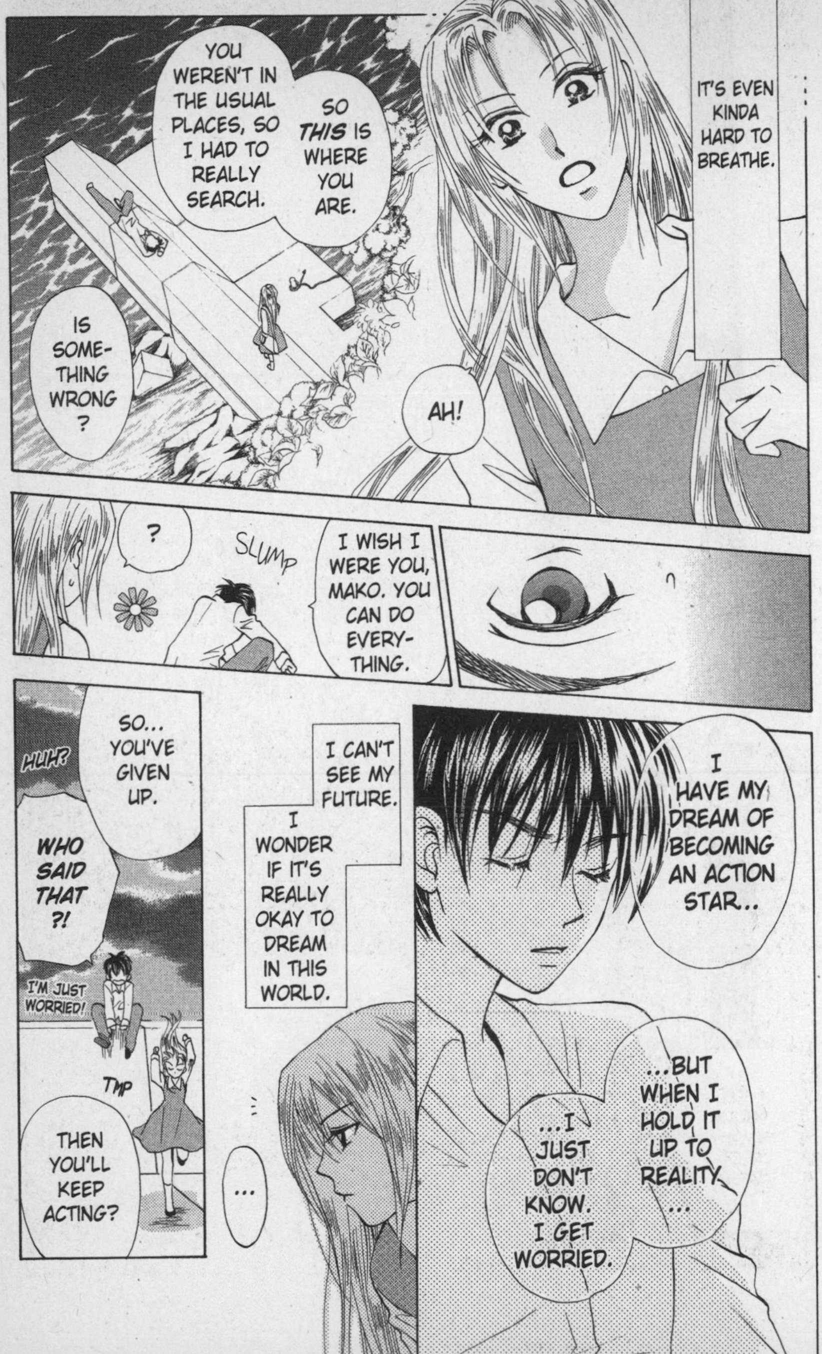
IT'S EVEN KINDA HARD TO BREATHE.
SO THIS IS WHERE YOU ARE.
YOU WEREN'T IN THE USUAL PLACES, SO I HAD TO REALLY SEARCH.
AH!
IS SOMETHING WRONG?
I WISH I WERE YOU, MAKO. YOU CAN DO EVERYTHING.
SLUMP
?
I HAVE MY DREAM OF BECOMING AN ACTION STAR...
...BUT WHEN I HOLD IT UP TO REALITY...
...I JUST DON'T KNOW. I GET WORRIED.
...
I CAN'T SEE MY FUTURE.
I WONDER IF IT'S REALLY OKAY TO DREAM IN THIS WORLD.
SO... YOU'VE GIVEN UP.
HUH?
WHO SAID THAT?!
I'M JUST WORRIED!
TMP
THEN YOU'LL KEEP ACTING?

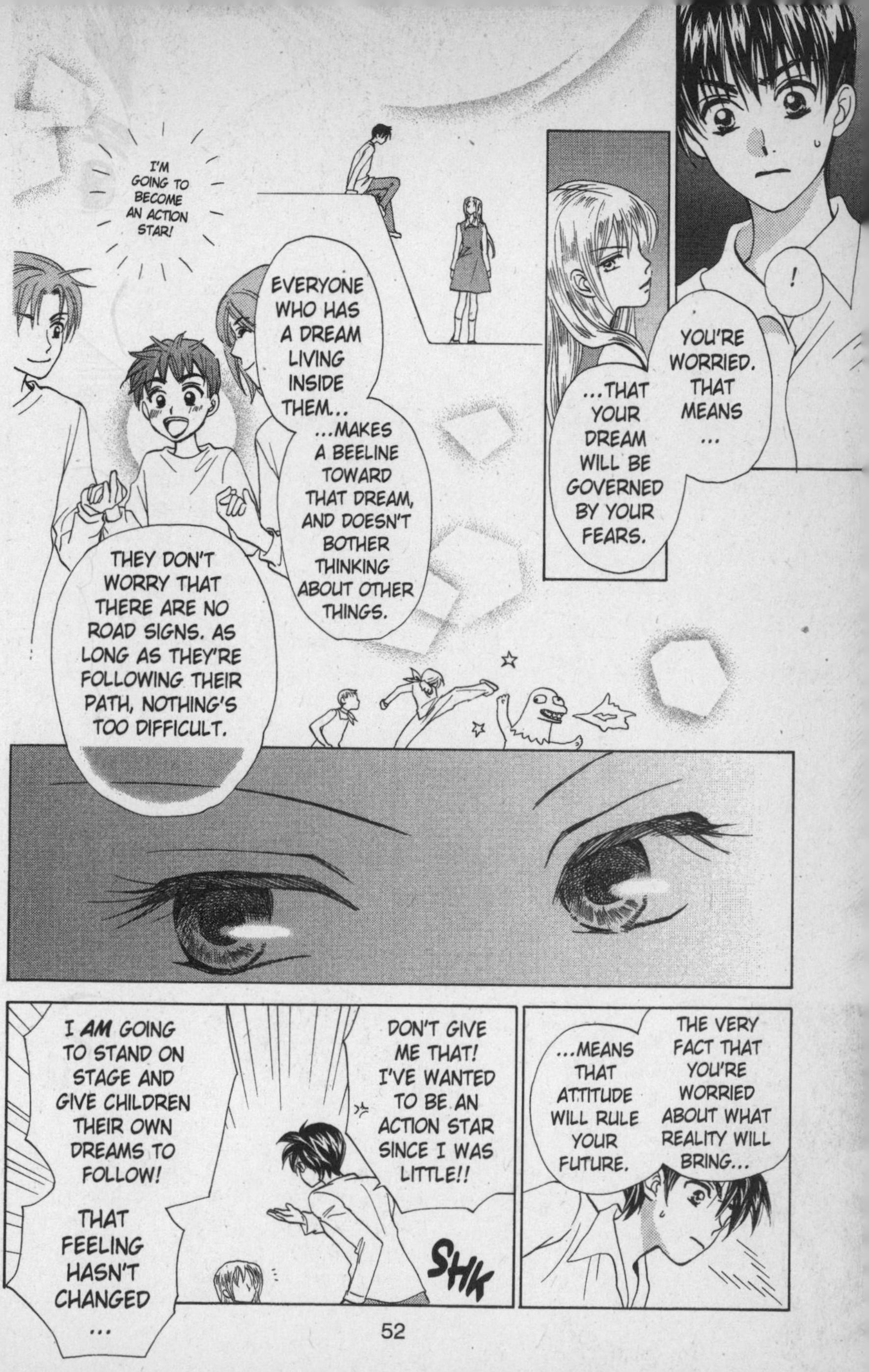
!
YOU'RE WORRIED. THAT MEANS ...
...THAT YOUR DREAM WILL BE GOVERNED BY YOUR FEARS.
I'M GOING TO BECOME AN ACTION STAR!
EVERYONE WHO HAS A DREAM LIVING INSIDE THEM...
...MAKES A BEELINE TOWARD THAT DREAM, AND DOESN'T BOTHER THINKING ABOUT OTHER THINGS.
THEY DON'T WORRY THAT THERE ARE NO ROAD SIGNS. AS LONG AS THEY'RE FOLLOWING THEIR PATH, NOTHING'S TOO DIFFICULT.
THE VERY FACT THAT YOU'RE WORRIED ABOUT WHAT REALITY WILL BRING...
...MEANS THAT ATTITUDE WILL RULE YOUR FUTURE.
DON'T GIVE ME THAT! I'VE WANTED TO BE AN ACTION STAR SINCE I WAS LITTLE!!
SHK
I *AM* GOING TO STAND ON STAGE AND GIVE CHILDREN THEIR OWN DREAMS TO FOLLOW!
THAT FEELING HASN'T CHANGED ...

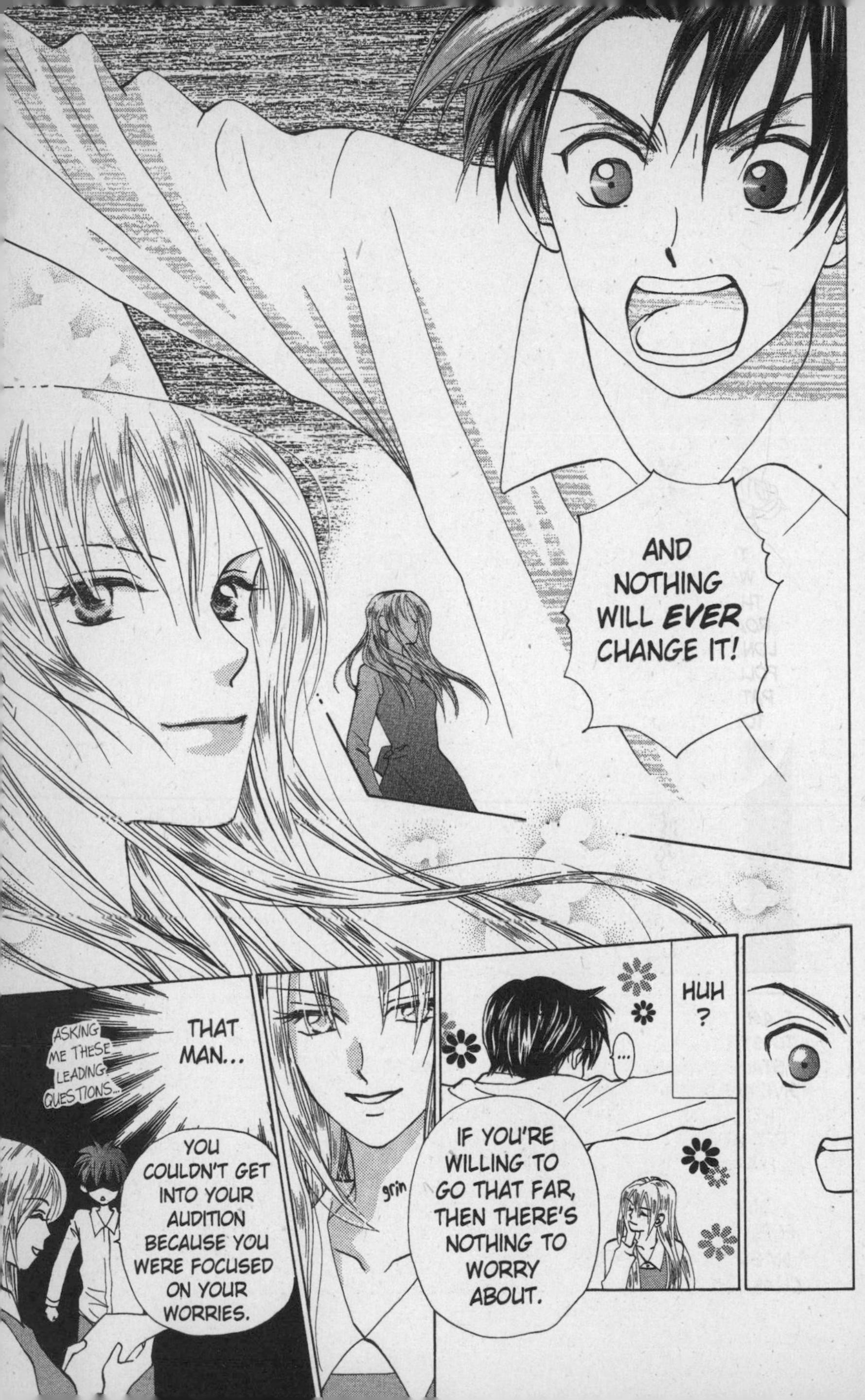
AND NOTHING WILL EVER CHANGE IT!
HUH ?
...
IF YOU'RE WILLING TO GO THAT FAR, THEN THERE'S NOTHING TO WORRY ABOUT.
grin
THAT MAN...
ASKING ME THESE LEADING QUESTIONS...
YOU COULDN'T GET INTO YOUR AUDITION BECAUSE YOU WERE FOCUSED ON YOUR WORRIES.

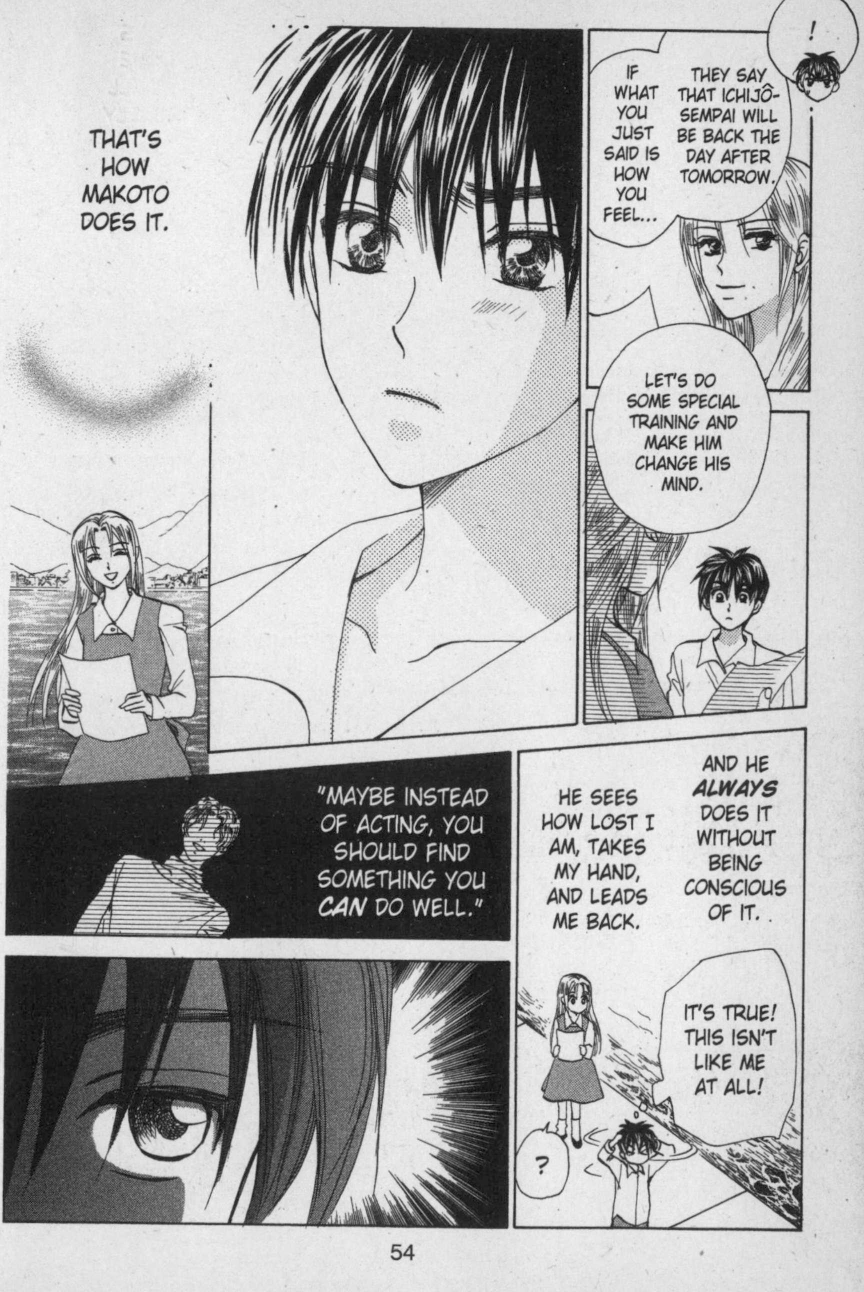
!
THEY SAY THAT ICHIJÔ-SEMPAI WILL BE BACK THE DAY AFTER TOMORROW.
IF WHAT YOU JUST SAID IS HOW YOU FEEL...
LET'S DO SOME SPECIAL TRAINING AND MAKE HIM CHANGE HIS MIND.
...
THAT'S HOW MAKOTO DOES IT.
HE SEES HOW LOST I AM, TAKES MY HAND, AND LEADS ME BACK.
AND HE ALWAYS DOES IT WITHOUT BEING CONSCIOUS OF IT.
IT'S TRUE! THIS ISN'T LIKE ME AT ALL!
?
"MAYBE INSTEAD OF ACTING, YOU SHOULD FIND SOMETHING YOU CAN DO WELL."

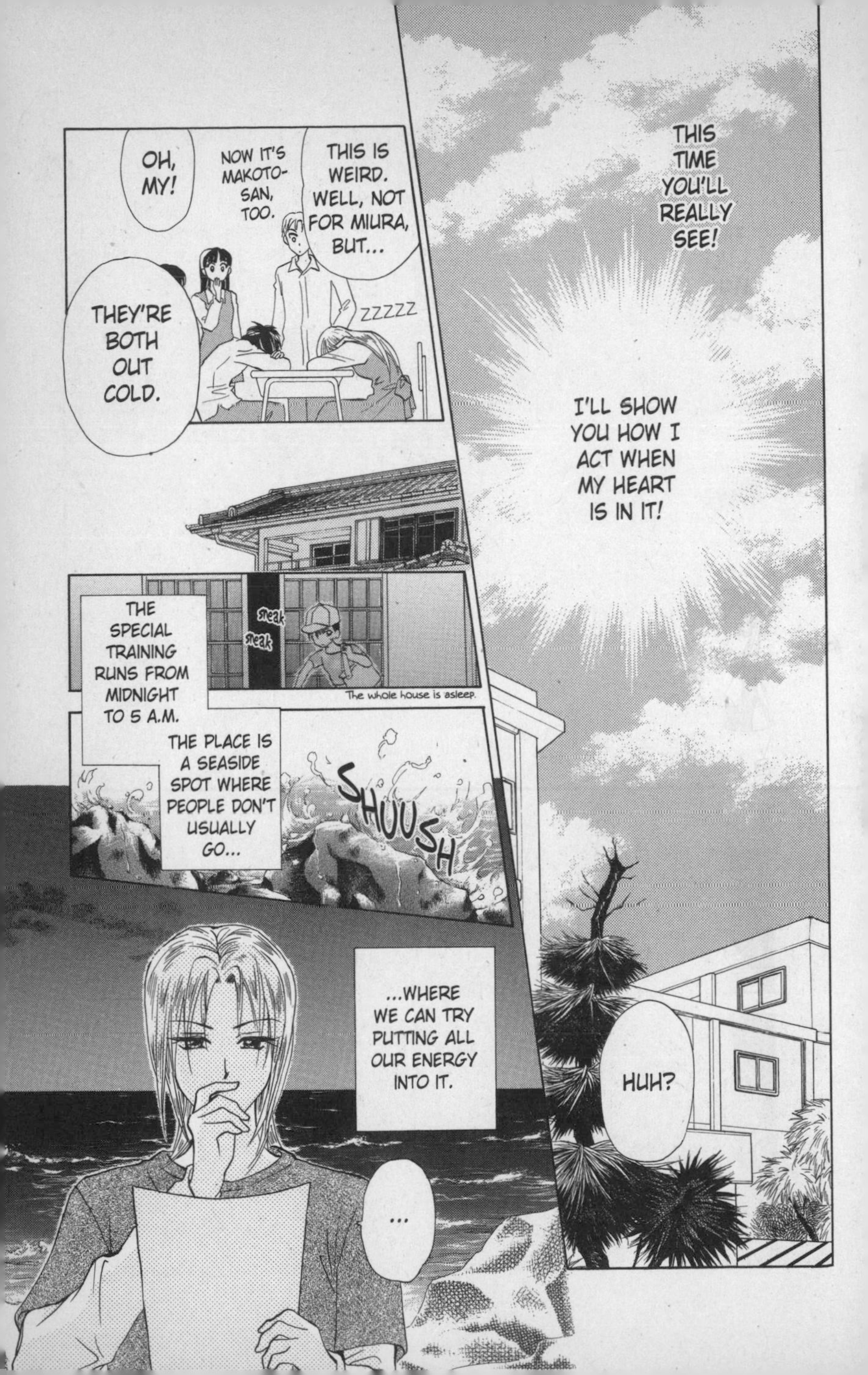
THIS TIME YOU'LL REALLY SEE!
I'LL SHOW YOU HOW I ACT WHEN MY HEART IS IN IT!
HUH?
THIS IS WEIRD. WELL, NOT FOR MIURA, BUT...
NOW IT'S MAKOTO-SAN, TOO.
OH, MY!
ZZZZZ
THEY'RE BOTH OUT COLD.
sneak
sneak
The whole house is asleep.
THE SPECIAL TRAINING RUNS FROM MIDNIGHT TO 5 A.M.
SHUUSH
THE PLACE IS A SEASIDE SPOT WHERE PEOPLE DON'T USUALLY GO...
...WHERE WE CAN TRY PUTTING ALL OUR ENERGY INTO IT.
...

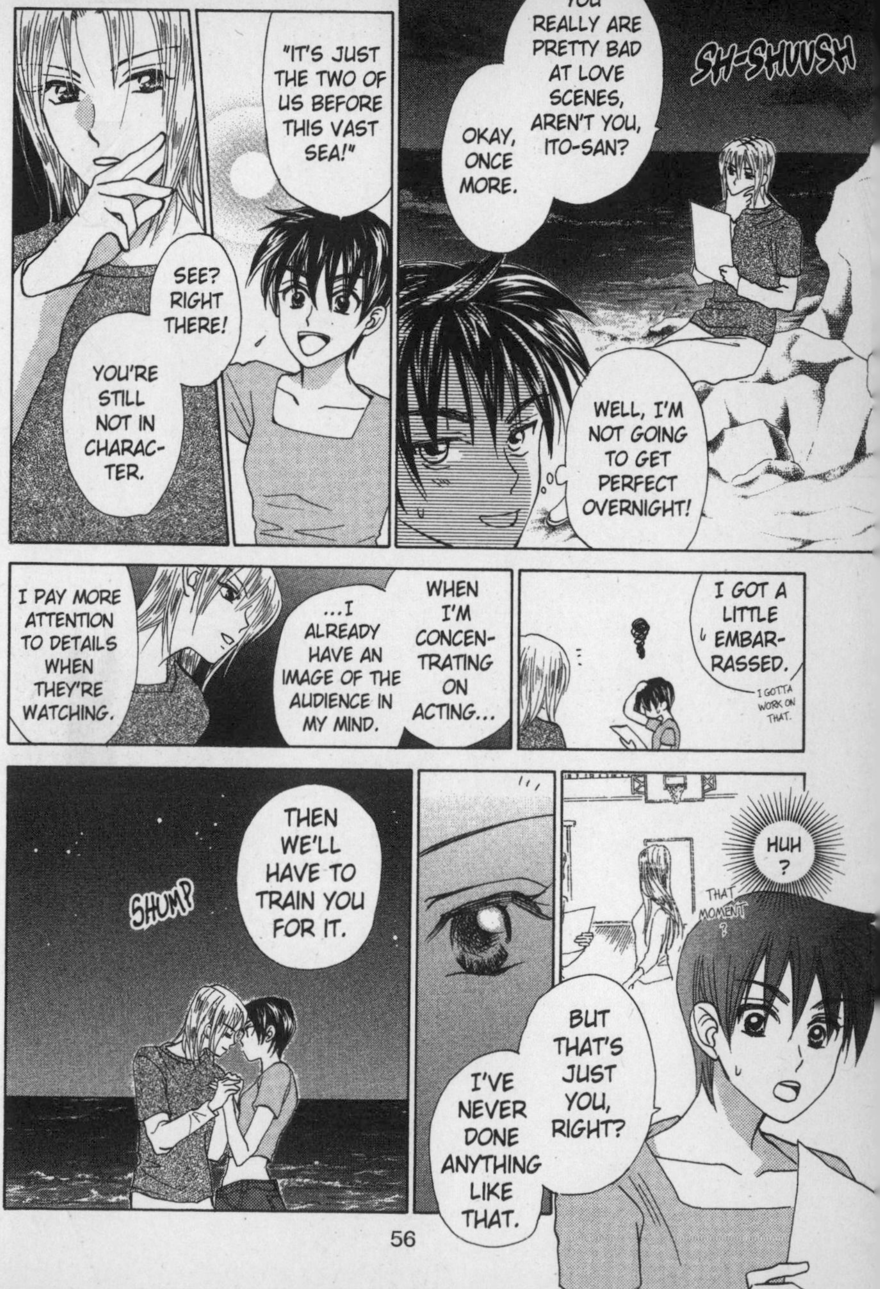
SH-SHUUSH
YOU REALLY ARE PRETTY BAD AT LOVE SCENES, AREN'T YOU, ITO-SAN?
OKAY, ONCE MORE.
WELL, I'M NOT GOING TO GET PERFECT OVERNIGHT!
"IT'S JUST THE TWO OF US BEFORE THIS VAST SEA!"
SEE? RIGHT THERE!
YOU'RE STILL NOT IN CHARAC-TER.
I GOT A LITTLE EMBAR-RASSED.
I GOTTA WORK ON THAT.
WHEN I'M CONCEN-TRATING ON ACTING...
...I ALREADY HAVE AN IMAGE OF THE AUDIENCE IN MY MIND.
I PAY MORE ATTENTION TO DETAILS WHEN THEY'RE WATCHING.
HUH?
THAT MOMENT?
BUT THAT'S JUST YOU, RIGHT?
I'VE NEVER DONE ANYTHING LIKE THAT.
THEN WE'LL HAVE TO TRAIN YOU FOR IT.
SHUMP

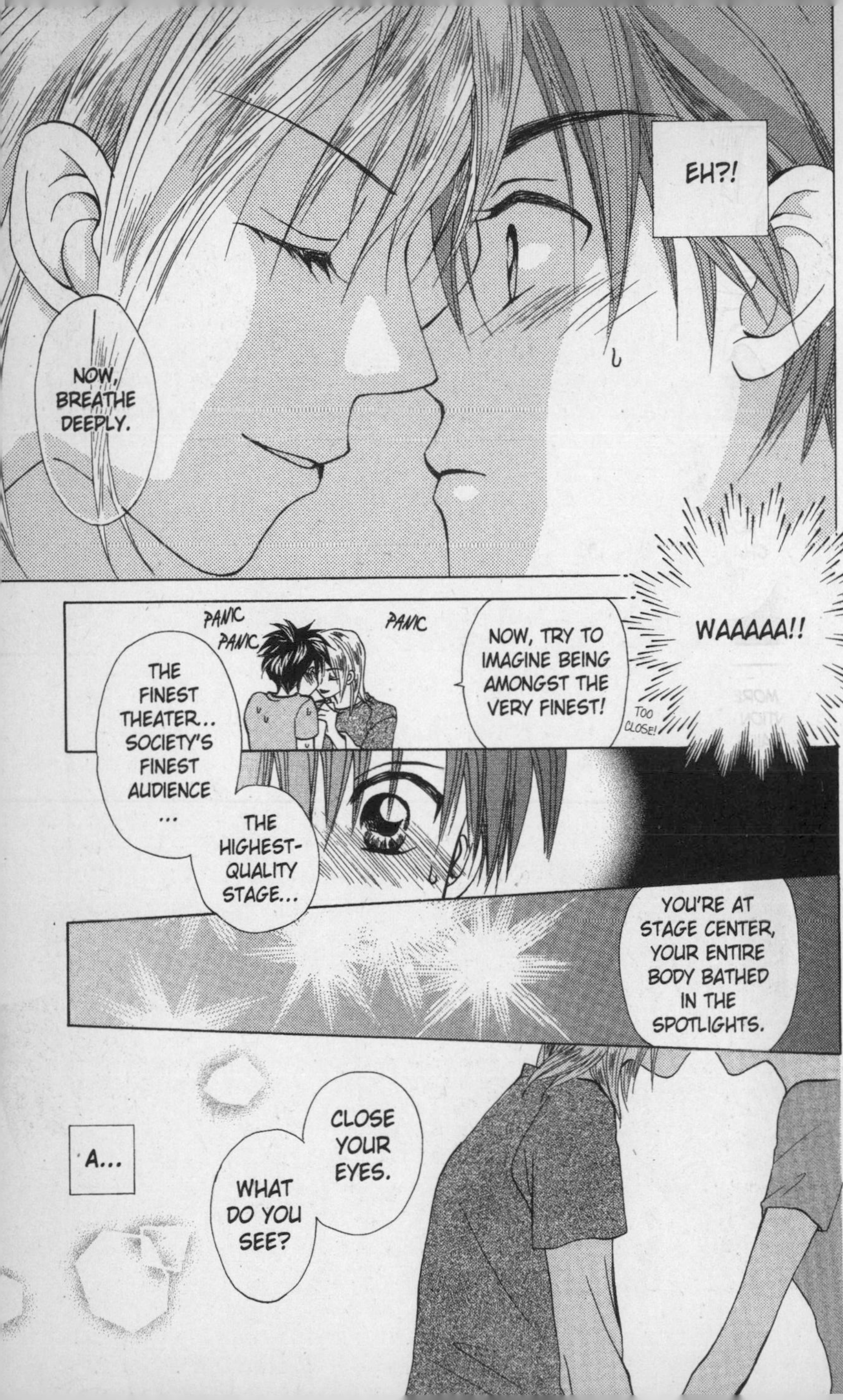
EH?!
NOW, BREATHE DEEPLY.
WAAAAA!!
TOO CLOSE!
NOW, TRY TO IMAGINE BEING AMONGST THE VERY FINEST!
PANIC
PANIC PANIC
THE FINEST THEATER... SOCIETY'S FINEST AUDIENCE ...
THE HIGHEST-QUALITY STAGE...
YOU'RE AT STAGE CENTER, YOUR ENTIRE BODY BATHED IN THE SPOTLIGHTS.
CLOSE YOUR EYES.
WHAT DO YOU SEE?
A...

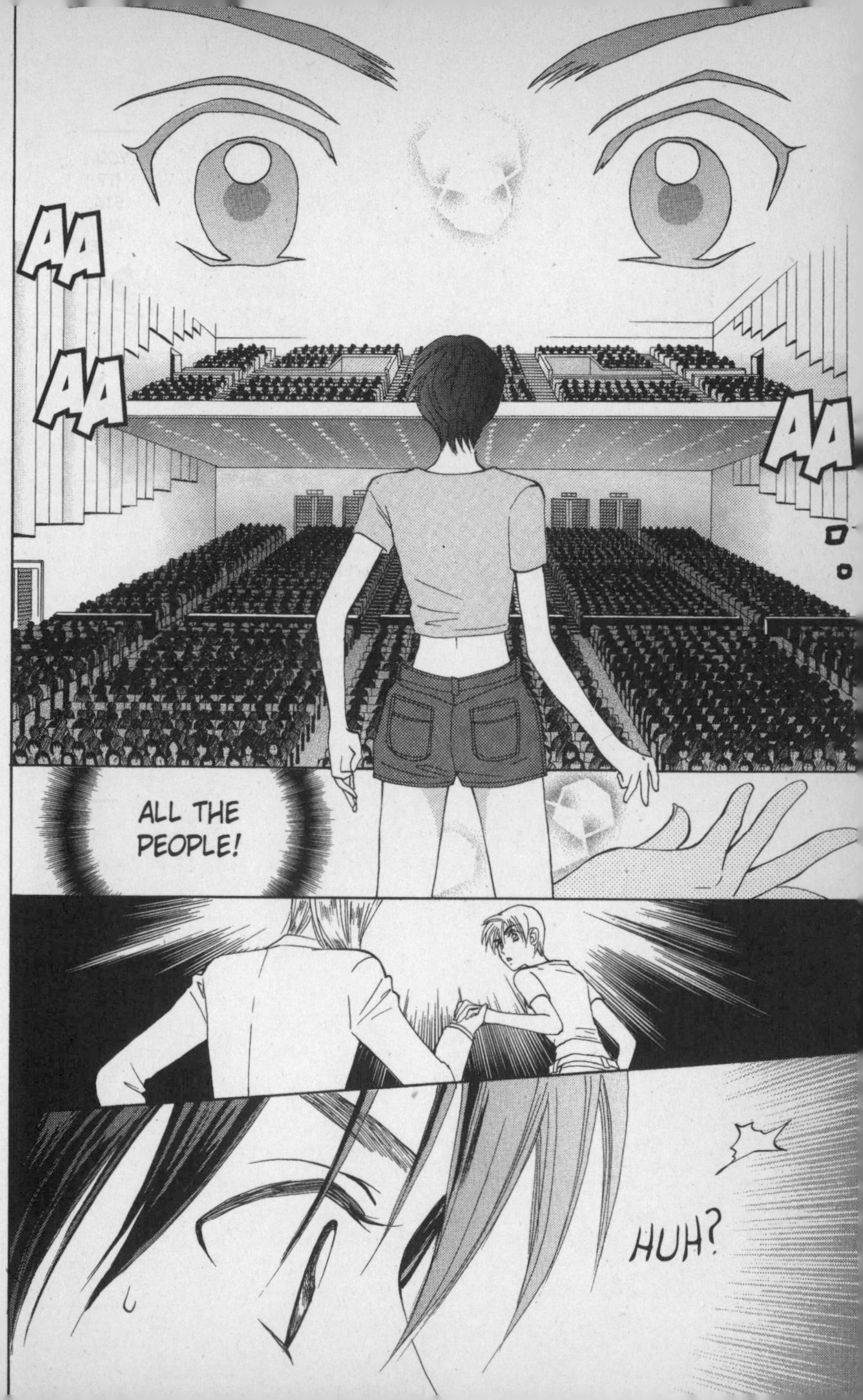
AA
AA
AA
ALL THE PEOPLE!
HUH?

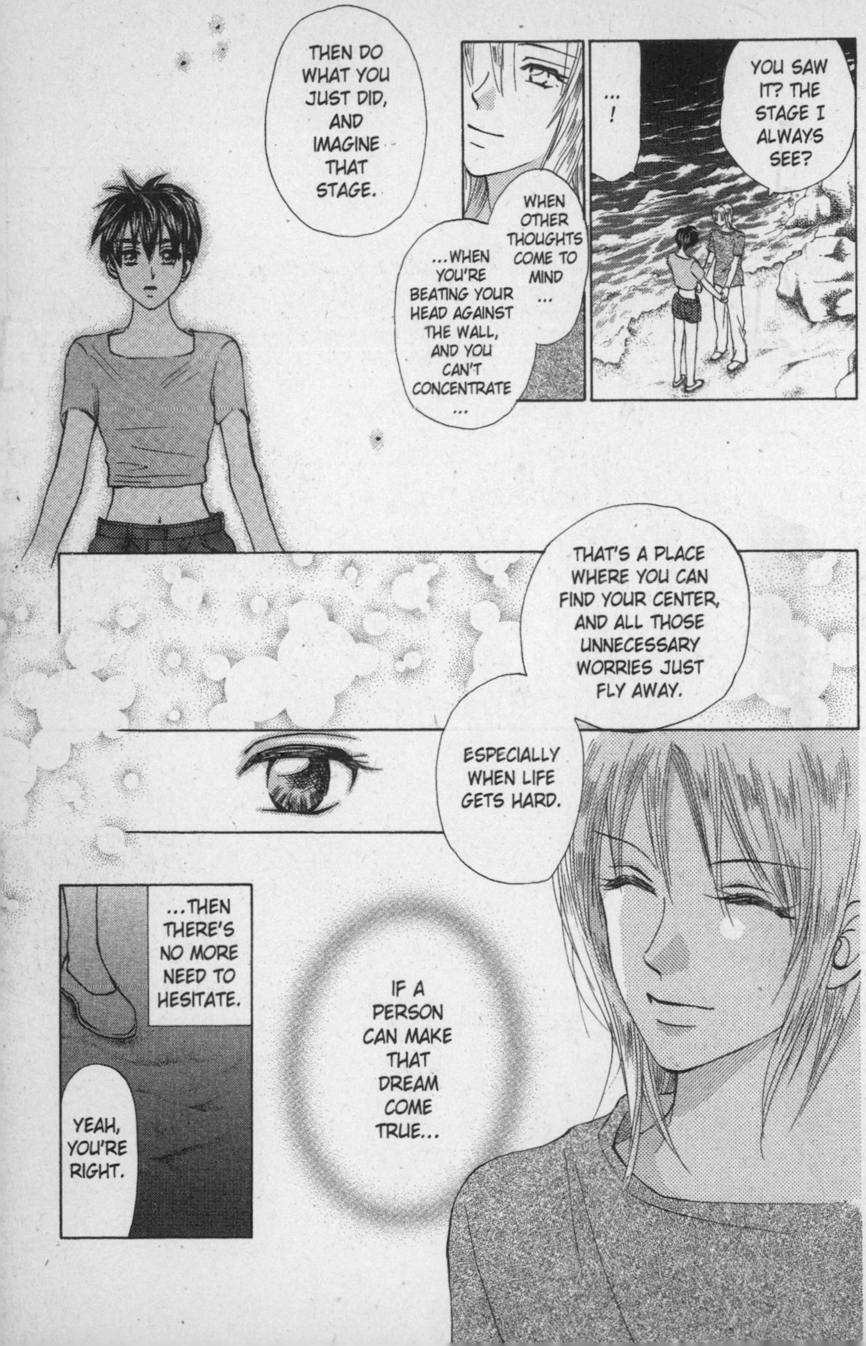
YOU SAW IT? THE STAGE I ALWAYS SEE?
...!
WHEN OTHER THOUGHTS COME TO MIND...
...WHEN YOU'RE BEATING YOUR HEAD AGAINST THE WALL, AND YOU CAN'T CONCENTRATE...
THEN DO WHAT YOU JUST DID, AND IMAGINE THAT STAGE.
THAT'S A PLACE WHERE YOU CAN FIND YOUR CENTER, AND ALL THOSE UNNECESSARY WORRIES JUST FLY AWAY.
ESPECIALLY WHEN LIFE GETS HARD.
IF A PERSON CAN MAKE THAT DREAM COME TRUE...
...THEN THERE'S NO MORE NEED TO HESITATE.
YEAH, YOU'RE RIGHT.

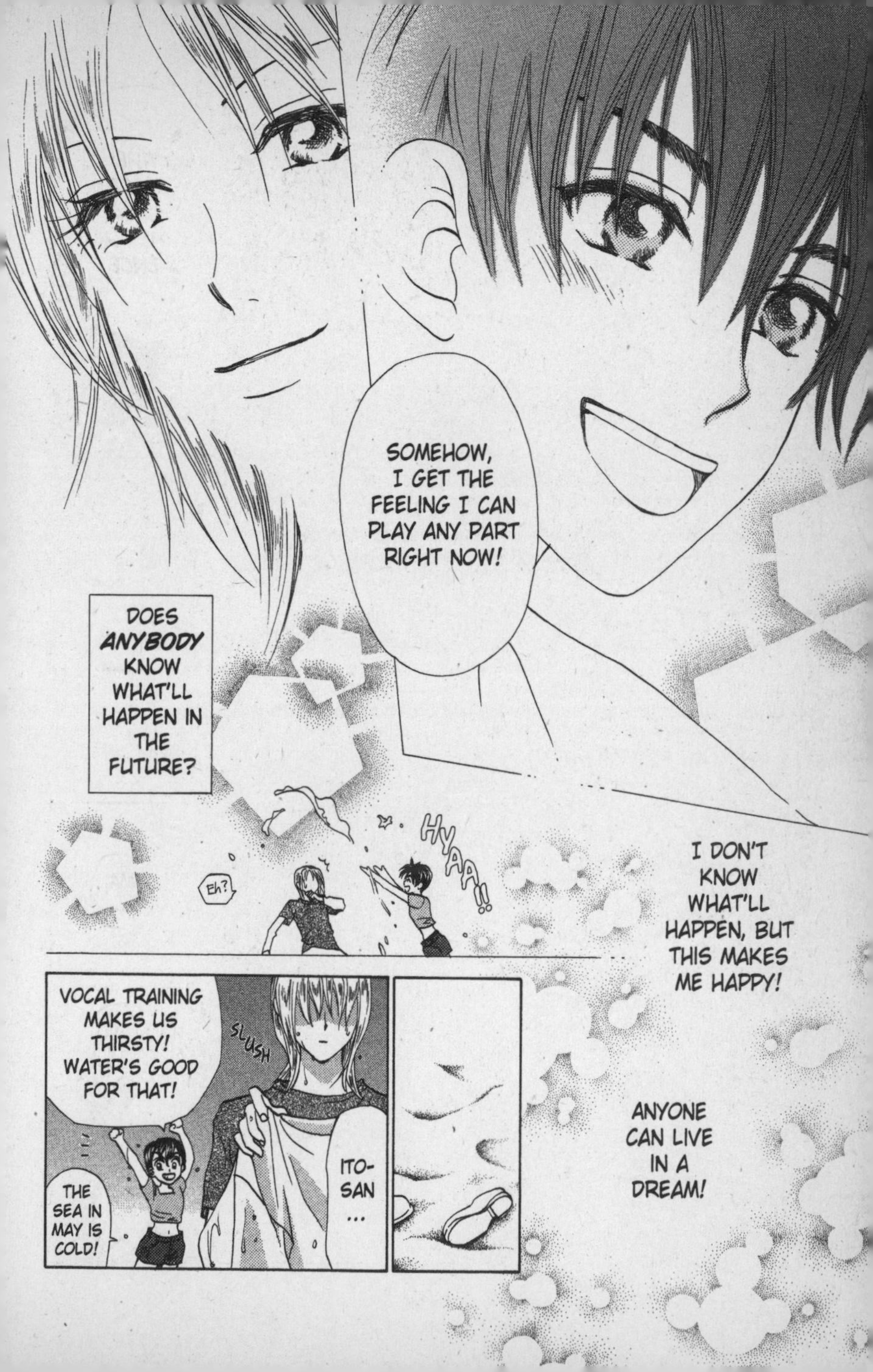

SOMEHOW, I GET THE FEELING I CAN PLAY ANY PART RIGHT NOW!
DOES *ANYBODY* KNOW WHAT'LL HAPPEN IN THE FUTURE?
HYAAA!!
Eh?
I DON'T KNOW WHAT'LL HAPPEN, BUT THIS MAKES ME HAPPY!
ANYONE CAN LIVE IN A DREAM!
ITO-SAN...
VOCAL TRAINING MAKES US THIRSTY! WATER'S GOOD FOR THAT!
SLUSH
THE SEA IN MAY IS COLD!

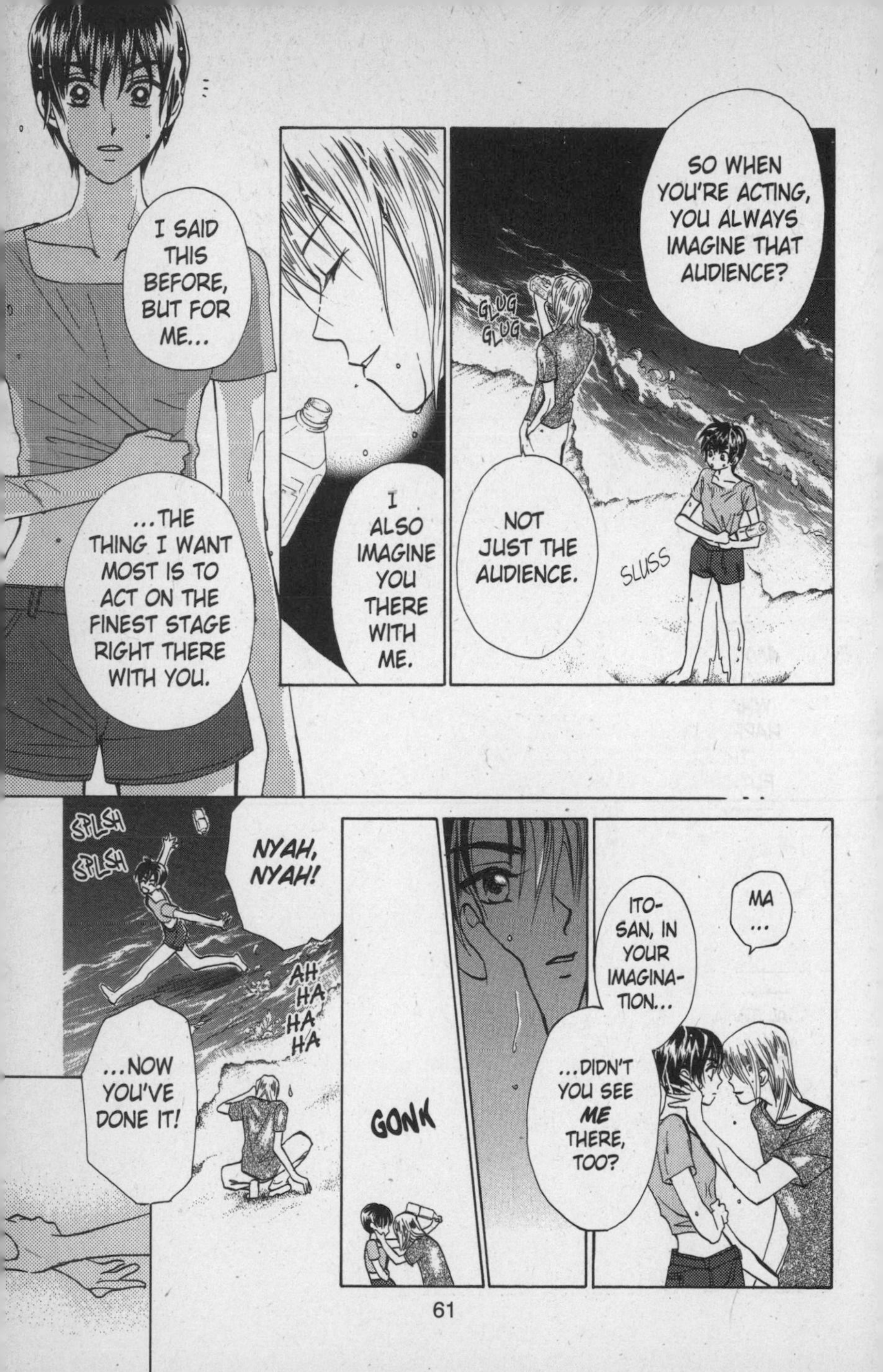
SO WHEN YOU'RE ACTING, YOU ALWAYS IMAGINE THAT AUDIENCE?
GLUG GLUG
NOT JUST THE AUDIENCE.
SLUSS
I ALSO IMAGINE YOU THERE WITH ME.
I SAID THIS BEFORE, BUT FOR ME...
...THE THING I WANT MOST IS TO ACT ON THE FINEST STAGE RIGHT THERE WITH YOU.
MA ...
ITO-SAN, IN YOUR IMAGINATION...
...DIDN'T YOU SEE ME THERE, TOO?
GONK
SPLSH SPLSH
NYAH, NYAH!
AH HA HA HA
...NOW YOU'VE DONE IT!

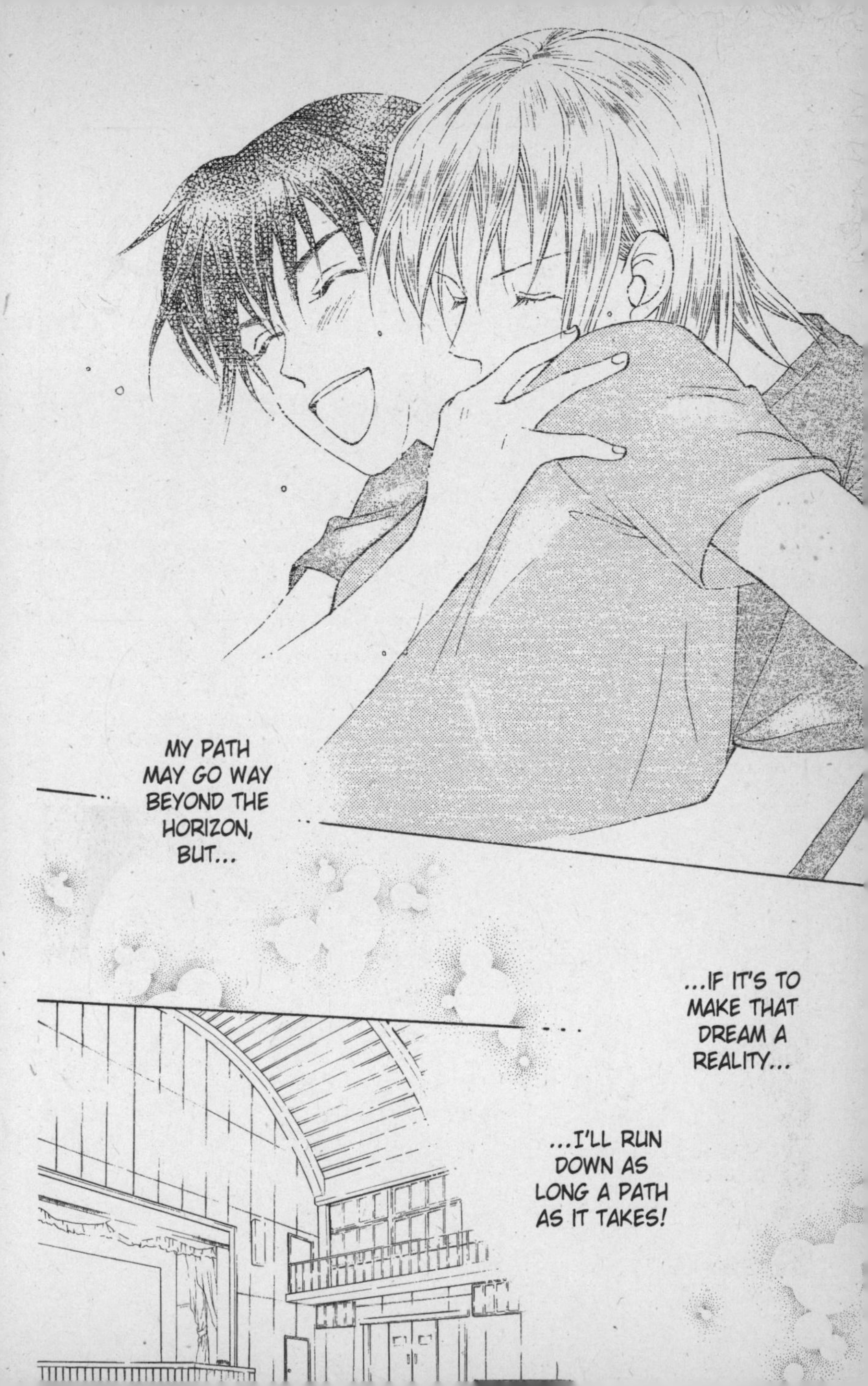
MY PATH MAY GO WAY BEYOND THE HORIZON, BUT...
...IF IT'S TO MAKE THAT DREAM A REALITY...
...I'LL RUN DOWN AS LONG A PATH AS IT TAKES!

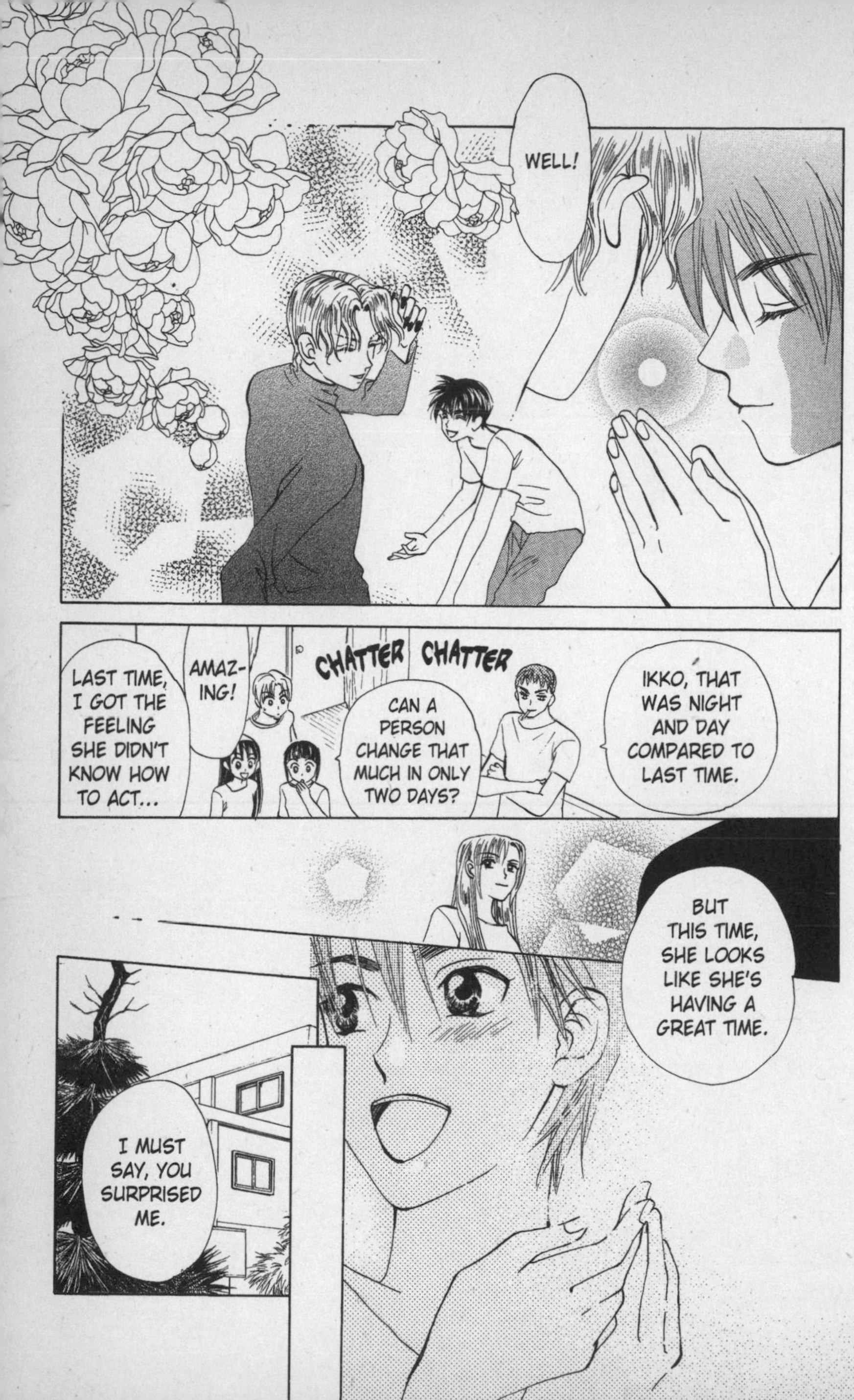
WELL!
IKKO, THAT WAS NIGHT AND DAY COMPARED TO LAST TIME.
CHATTER CHATTER
CAN A PERSON CHANGE THAT MUCH IN ONLY TWO DAYS?
AMAZ-ING!
LAST TIME, I GOT THE FEELING SHE DIDN'T KNOW HOW TO ACT...
BUT THIS TIME, SHE LOOKS LIKE SHE'S HAVING A GREAT TIME.
I MUST SAY, YOU SURPRISED ME.

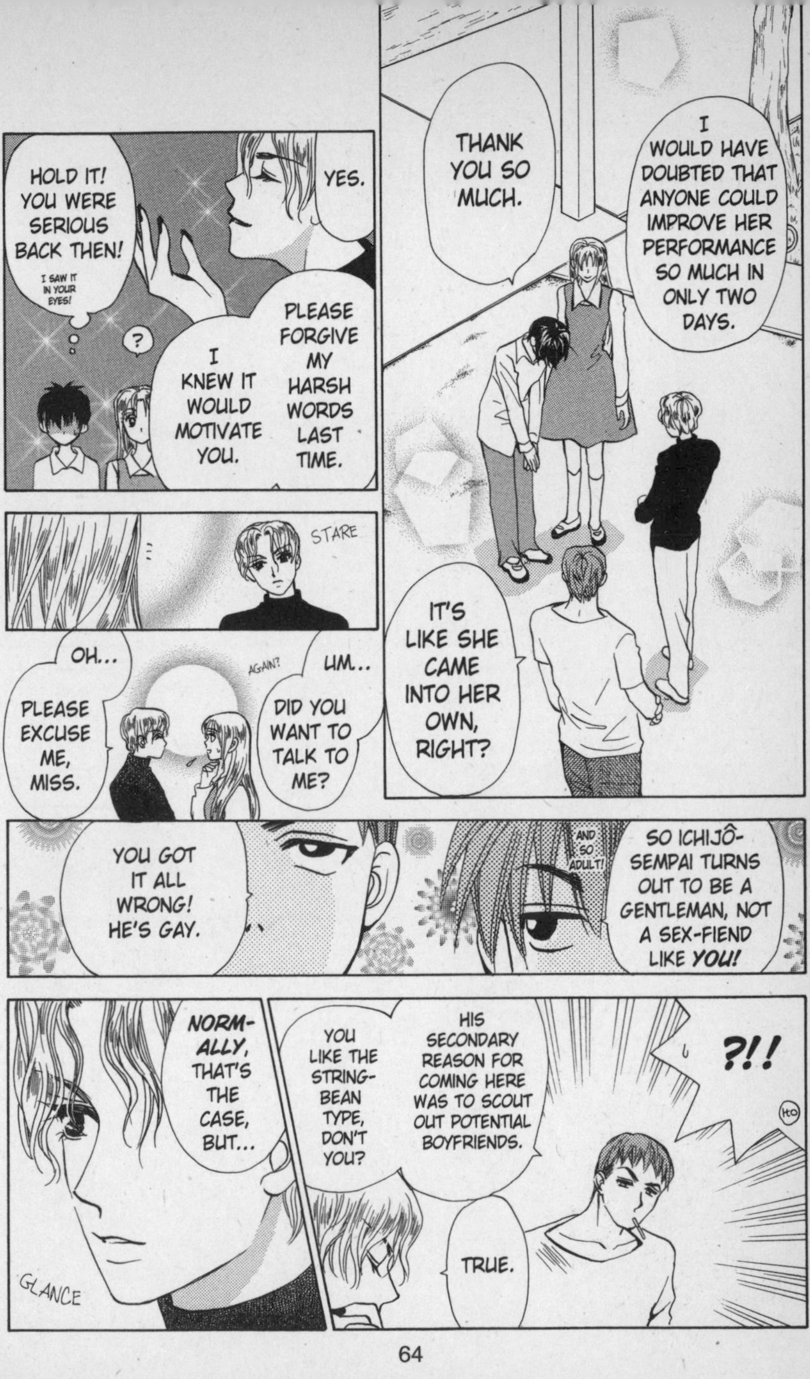
I WOULD HAVE DOUBTED THAT ANYONE COULD IMPROVE HER PERFORMANCE SO MUCH IN ONLY TWO DAYS.
THANK YOU SO MUCH.
IT'S LIKE SHE CAME INTO HER OWN, RIGHT?
YES.
HOLD IT! YOU WERE SERIOUS BACK THEN!
I SAW IT IN YOUR EYES!
PLEASE FORGIVE MY HARSH WORDS LAST TIME.
I KNEW IT WOULD MOTIVATE YOU.
?
STARE
UM...
DID YOU WANT TO TALK TO ME?
AGAIN?
OH...
PLEASE EXCUSE ME, MISS.
SO ICHIJÔ-SEMPAI TURNS OUT TO BE A GENTLEMAN, NOT A SEX-FIEND LIKE ***YOU!***
AND SO ADULT!
YOU GOT IT ALL WRONG! HE'S GAY.
?!!
HIS SECONDARY REASON FOR COMING HERE WAS TO SCOUT OUT POTENTIAL BOYFRIENDS.
YOU LIKE THE STRING-BEAN TYPE, DON'T YOU?
TRUE.
NORM-ALLY, THAT'S THE CASE, BUT...
GLANCE

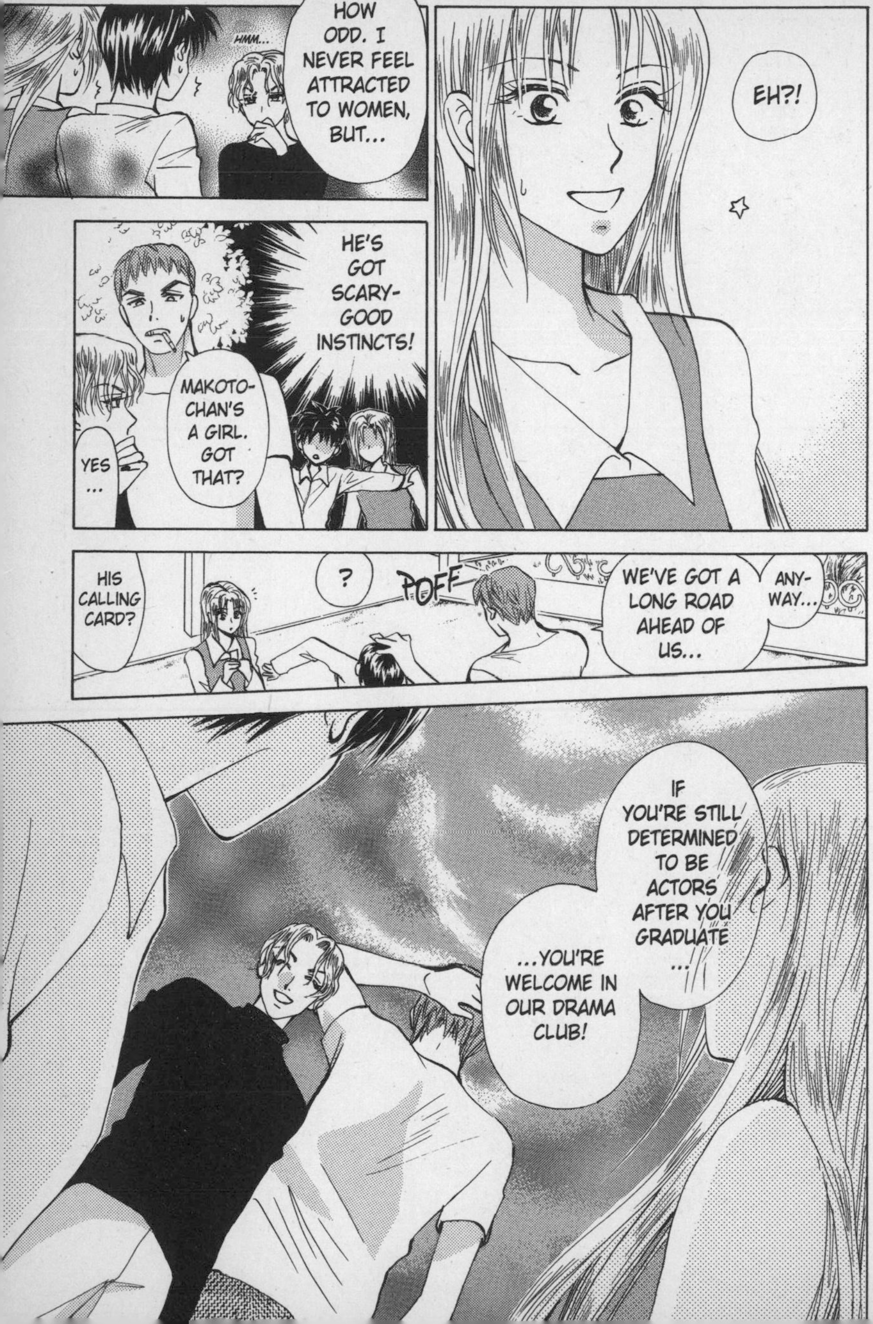
EH?!
HMM...
HOW ODD. I NEVER FEEL ATTRACTED TO WOMEN, BUT...
HE'S GOT SCARY-GOOD INSTINCTS!
MAKOTO-CHAN'S A GIRL. GOT THAT?
YES...
ANY-WAY...
WE'VE GOT A LONG ROAD AHEAD OF US...
POFF
?
HIS CALLING CARD?
IF YOU'RE STILL DETERMINED TO BE ACTORS AFTER YOU GRADUATE...
...YOU'RE WELCOME IN OUR DRAMA CLUB!

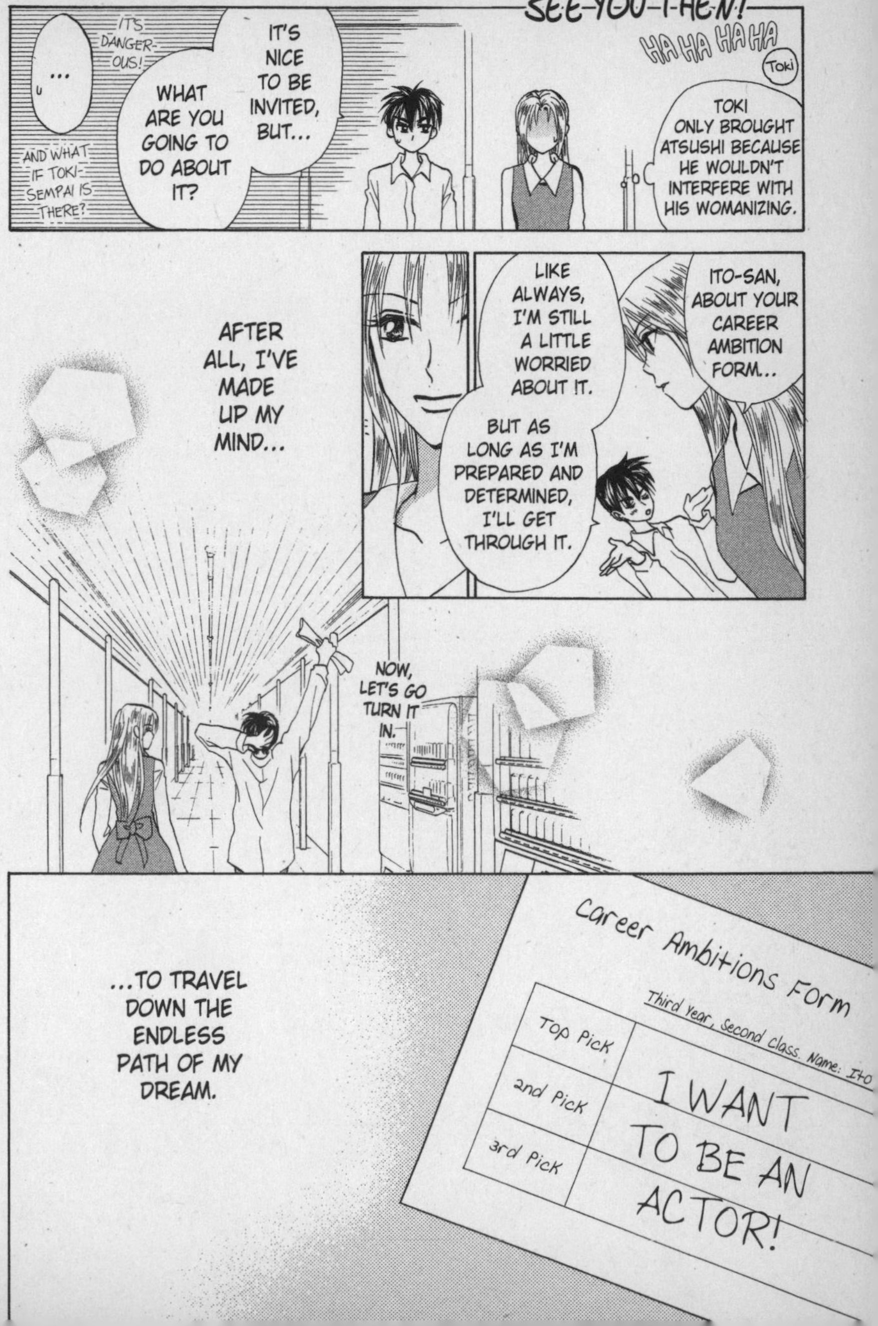
SEE-YOU-T-HE-N!
HA HA HA HA
Toki
TOKI ONLY BROUGHT ATSUSHI BECAUSE HE WOULDN'T INTERFERE WITH HIS WOMANIZING.
IT'S NICE TO BE INVITED, BUT...
WHAT ARE YOU GOING TO DO ABOUT IT?
IT'S DANGER-OUS!
...
AND WHAT IF TOKI-SEMPAI IS THERE?
ITO-SAN, ABOUT YOUR CAREER AMBITION FORM...
LIKE ALWAYS, I'M STILL A LITTLE WORRIED ABOUT IT.
BUT AS LONG AS I'M PREPARED AND DETERMINED, I'LL GET THROUGH IT.
AFTER ALL, I'VE MADE UP MY MIND...
NOW, LET'S GO TURN IT IN.
Career Ambitions Form
Third Year, Second class. Name: Ito
Top Pick
2nd Pick
3rd Pick
I WANT TO BE AN ACTOR!
...TO TRAVEL DOWN THE ENDLESS PATH OF MY DREAM.

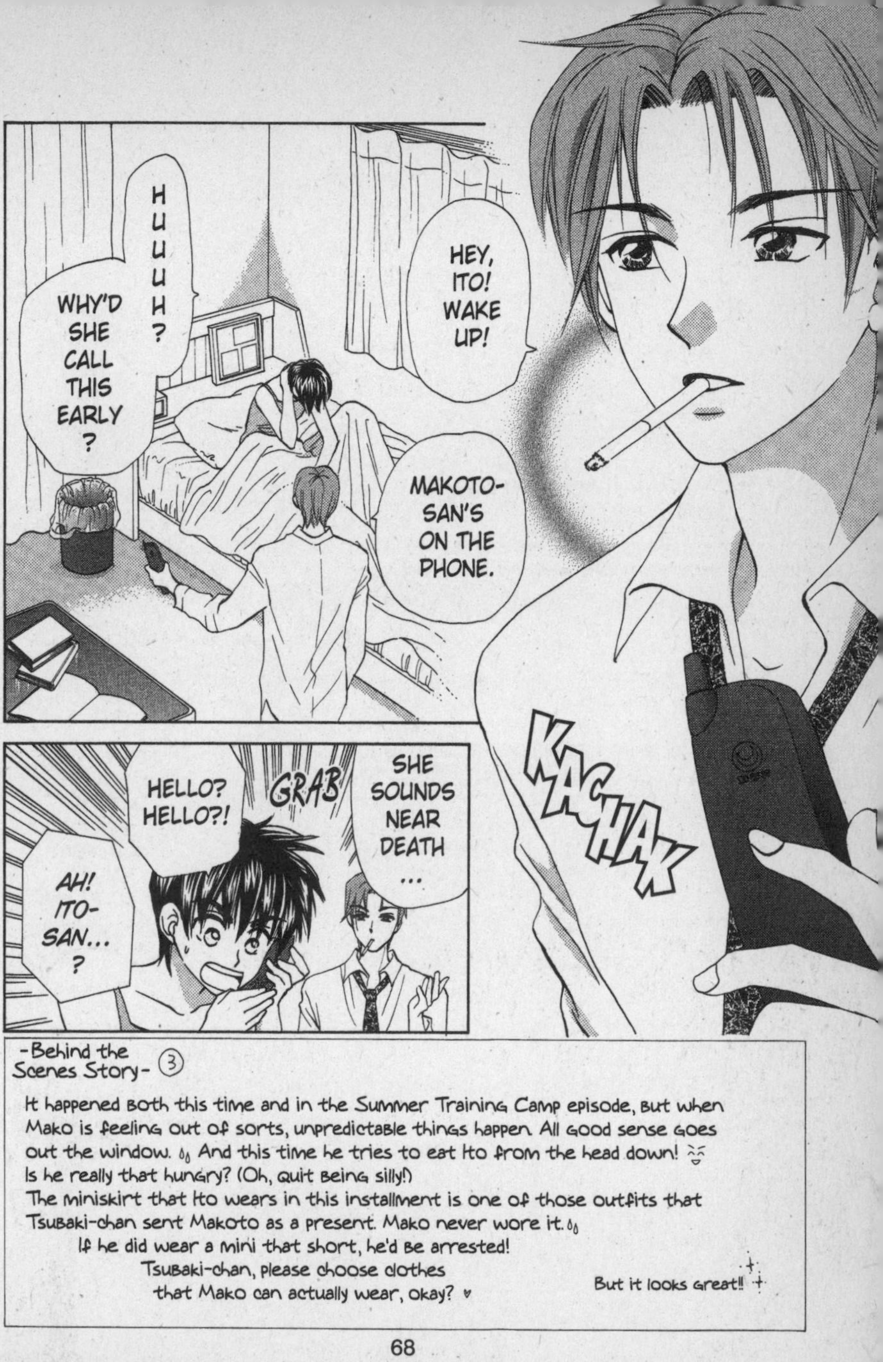
KACHAK
HEY, ITO! WAKE UP!
MAKOTO-SAN'S ON THE PHONE.
HUUUUH?
WHY'D SHE CALL THIS EARLY?
SHE SOUNDS NEAR DEATH ...
GRAB
HELLO? HELLO?!
AH! ITO-SAN...?

-Behind the Scenes Story- ③

It happened both this time and in the Summer Training Camp episode, but when Mako is feeling out of sorts, unpredictable things happen. All good sense goes out the window. And this time he tries to eat Ito from the head down! Is he really that hungry? (Oh, quit being silly!)
The miniskirt that Ito wears in this installment is one of those outfits that Tsubaki-chan sent Makoto as a present. Mako never wore it.
If he did wear a mini that short, he'd be arrested!
Tsubaki-chan, please choose clothes that Mako can actually wear, okay? ♥

But it looks great!!

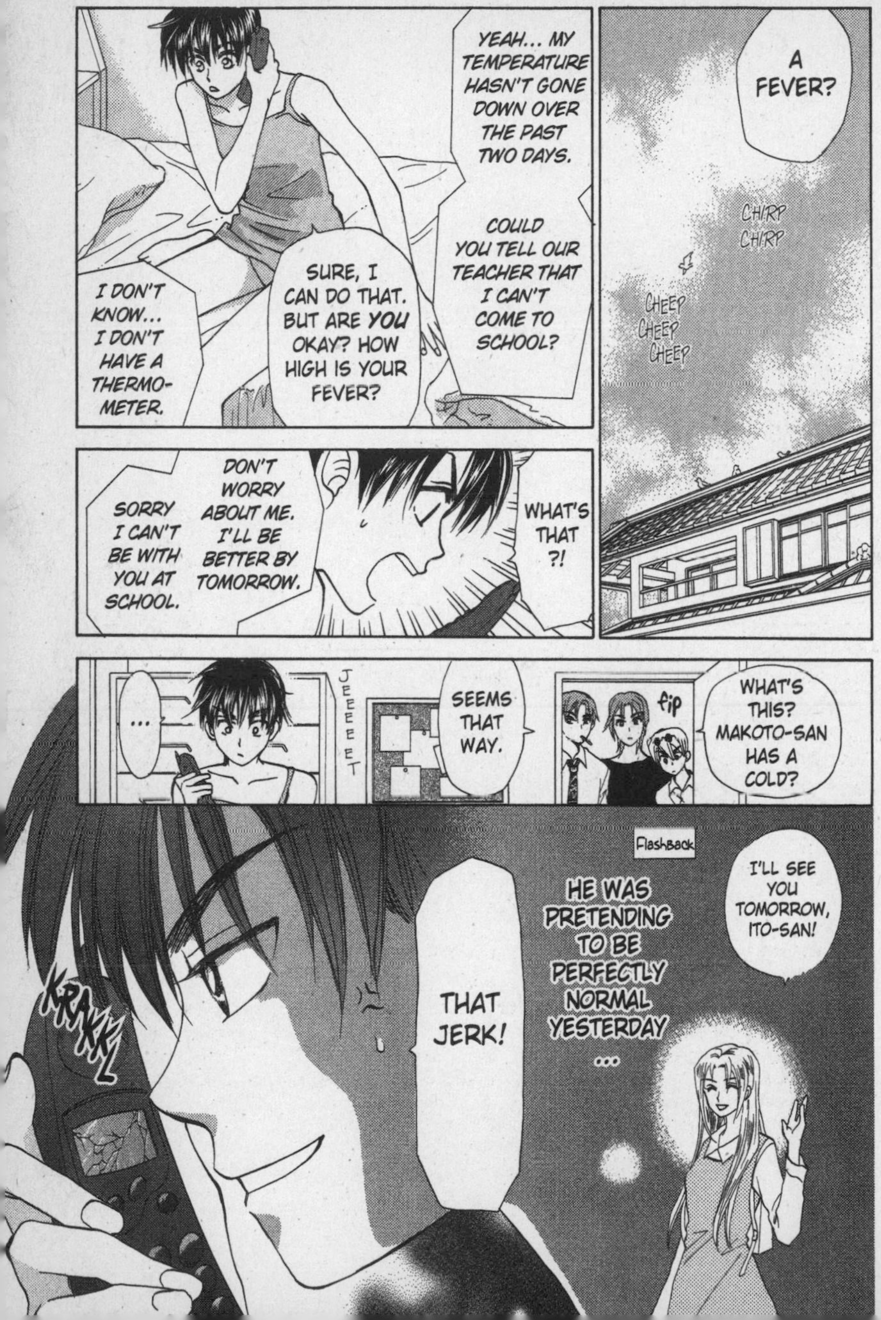
A FEVER?
CHIRP CHIRP
CHEEP CHEEP CHEEP
YEAH... MY TEMPERATURE HASN'T GONE DOWN OVER THE PAST TWO DAYS.
COULD YOU TELL OUR TEACHER THAT I CAN'T COME TO SCHOOL?
SURE, I CAN DO THAT. BUT ARE YOU OKAY? HOW HIGH IS YOUR FEVER?
I DON'T KNOW... I DON'T HAVE A THERMO-METER.
WHAT'S THAT ?!
DON'T WORRY ABOUT ME. I'LL BE BETTER BY TOMORROW.
SORRY I CAN'T BE WITH YOU AT SCHOOL.
WHAT'S THIS? MAKOTO-SAN HAS A COLD?
fip
SEEMS THAT WAY.
JEEEEET
...
Flashback
I'LL SEE YOU TOMORROW, ITO-SAN!
HE WAS PRETENDING TO BE PERFECTLY NORMAL YESTERDAY...
THAT JERK!
KRAKKL

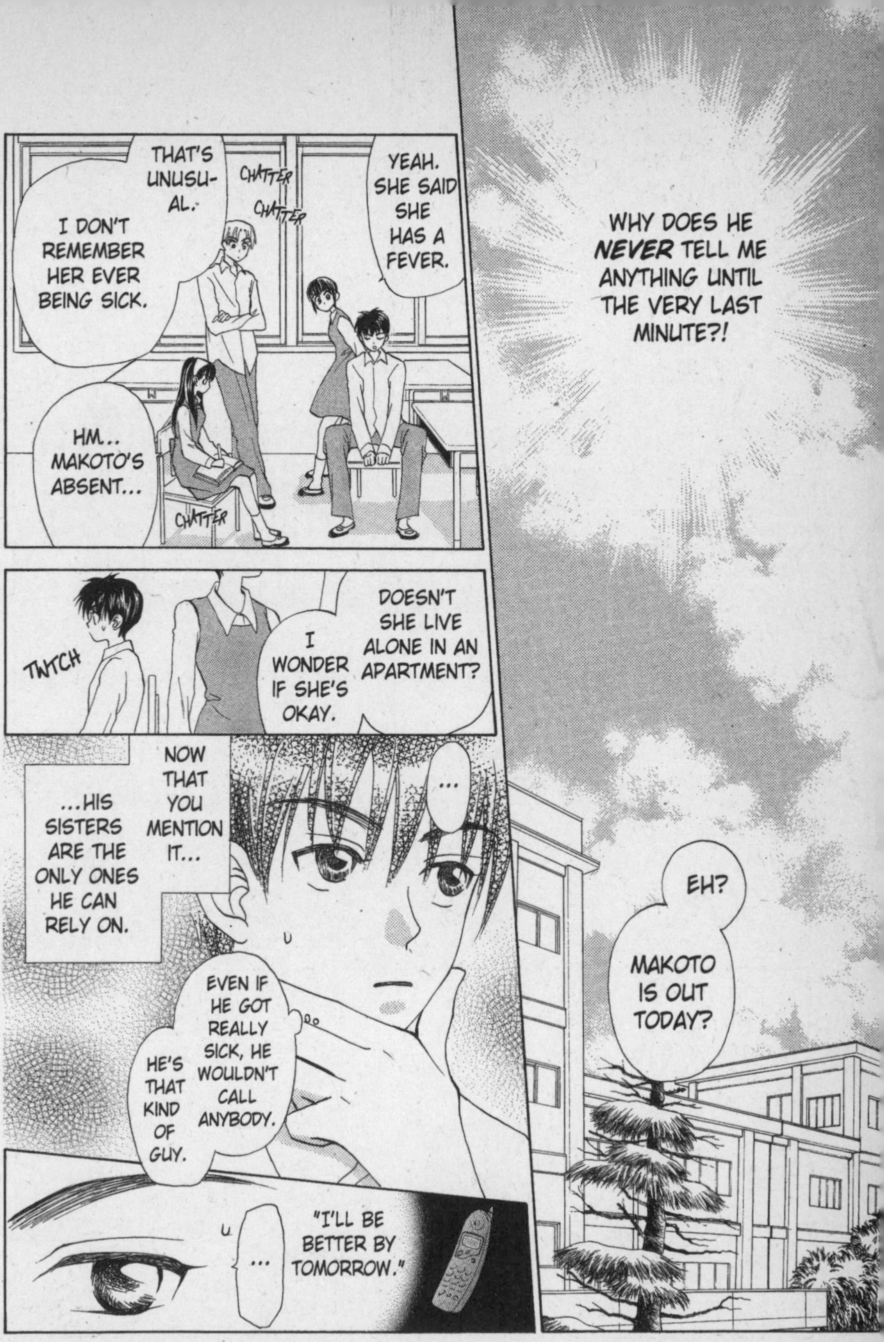
WHY DOES HE **NEVER** TELL ME ANYTHING UNTIL THE VERY LAST MINUTE?!
EH?
MAKOTO IS OUT TODAY?
YEAH. SHE SAID SHE HAS A FEVER.
THAT'S UNUSU-AL.
CHATTER
CHATTER
I DON'T REMEMBER HER EVER BEING SICK.
HM... MAKOTO'S ABSENT...
CHATTER
DOESN'T SHE LIVE ALONE IN AN APARTMENT?
I WONDER IF SHE'S OKAY.
TWITCH
...
NOW THAT YOU MENTION IT...
...HIS SISTERS ARE THE ONLY ONES HE CAN RELY ON.
EVEN IF HE GOT REALLY SICK, HE WOULDN'T CALL ANYBODY.
HE'S THAT KIND OF GUY.
"I'LL BE BETTER BY TOMORROW."
...

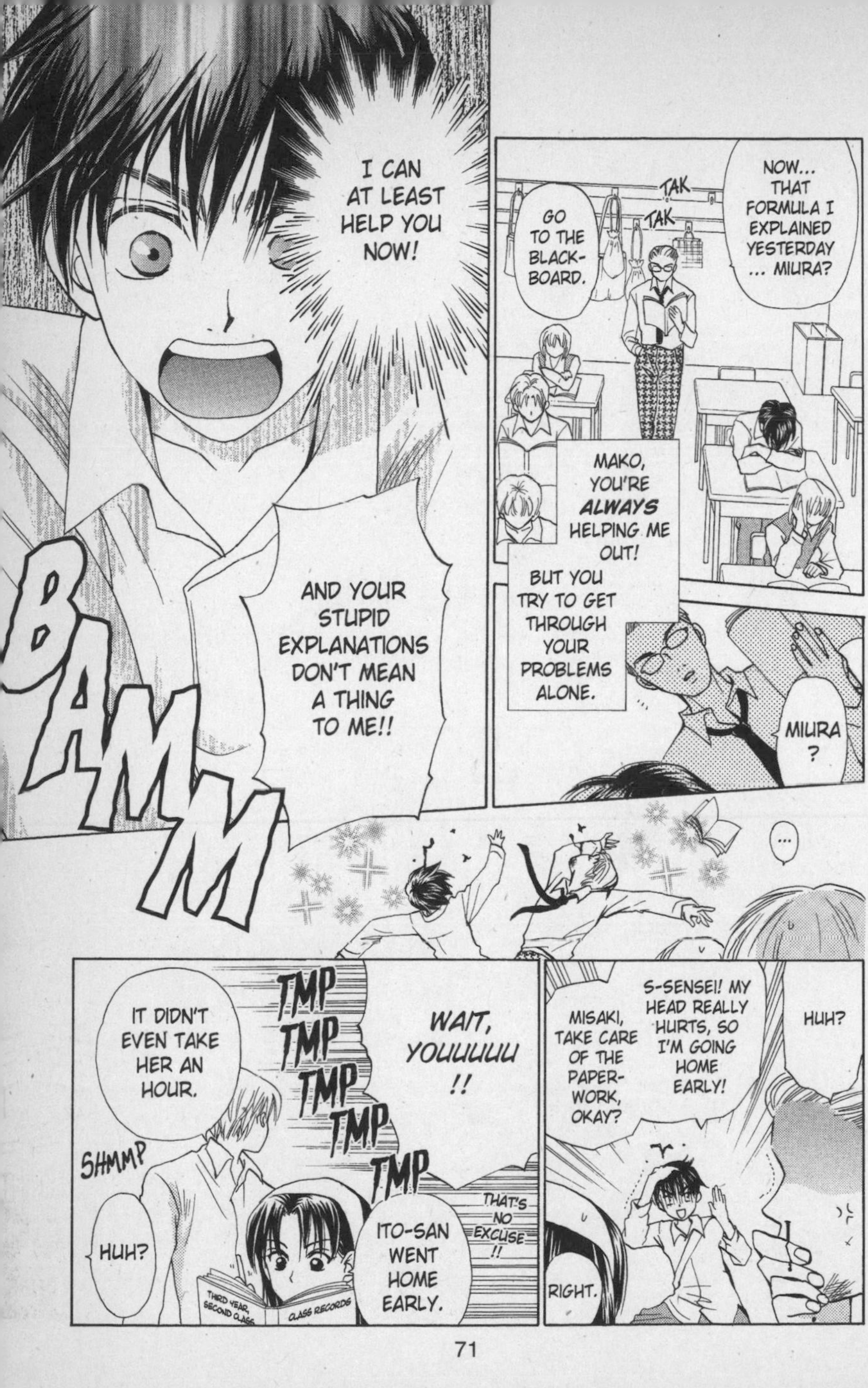
NOW... THAT FORMULA I EXPLAINED YESTERDAY ... MIURA?
TAK
TAK
GO TO THE BLACK-BOARD.
MAKO, YOU'RE *ALWAYS* HELPING ME OUT!
BUT YOU TRY TO GET THROUGH YOUR PROBLEMS ALONE.
MIURA ?
I CAN AT LEAST HELP YOU NOW!
AND YOUR STUPID EXPLANATIONS DON'T MEAN A THING TO ME!!
BAMM
...
HUH?
S-SENSEI! MY HEAD REALLY HURTS, SO I'M GOING HOME EARLY!
MISAKI, TAKE CARE OF THE PAPER-WORK, OKAY?
RIGHT.
WAIT, YOUUUUU !!
TMP TMP TMP TMP TMP
THAT'S NO EXCUSE !!
ITO-SAN WENT HOME EARLY.
IT DIDN'T EVEN TAKE HER AN HOUR.
SHMMP
HUH?
THIRD YEAR, SECOND CLASS
CLASS RECORDS

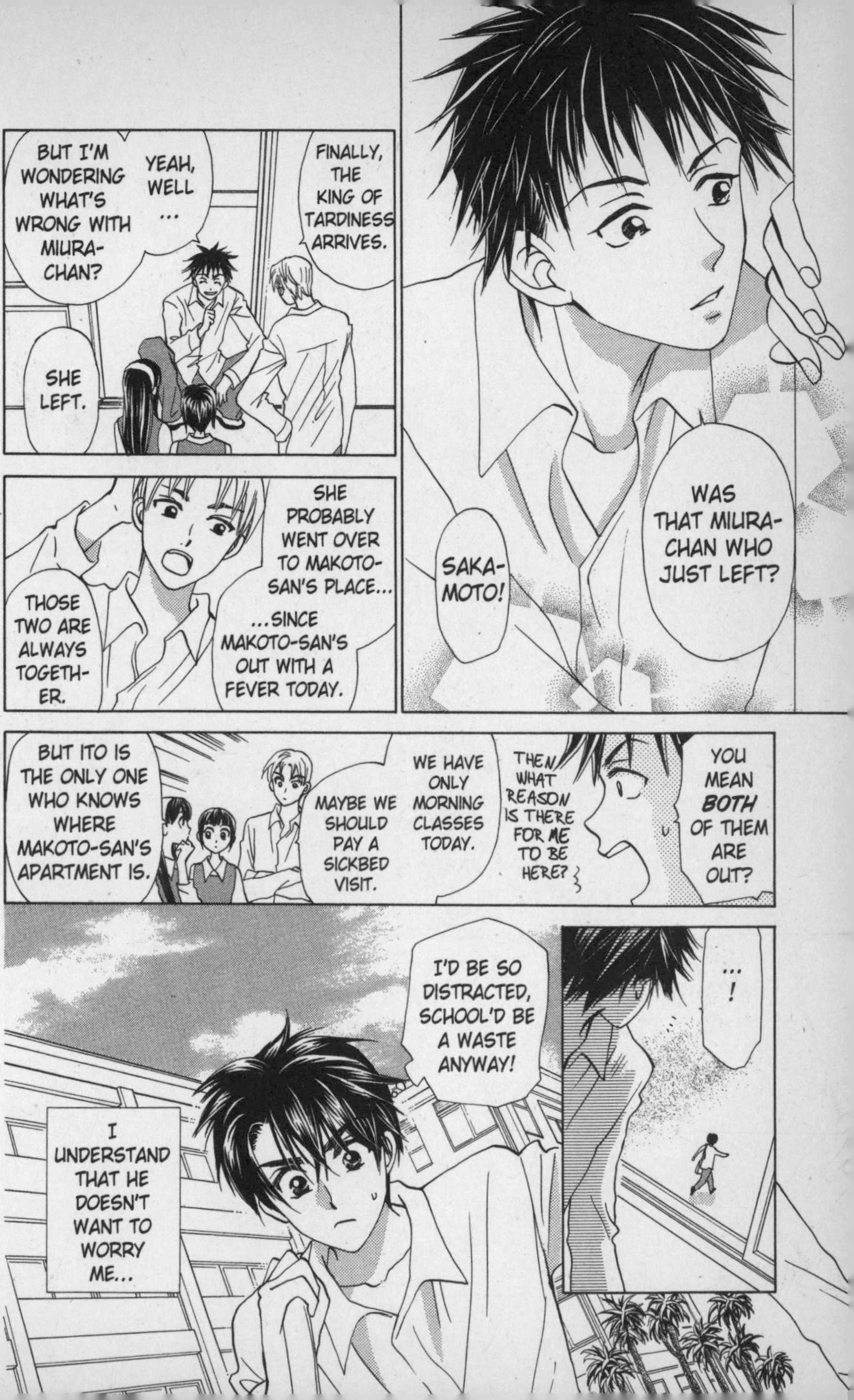
WAS THAT MIURA-CHAN WHO JUST LEFT?
SAKA-MOTO!
FINALLY, THE KING OF TARDINESS ARRIVES.
YEAH, WELL ...
BUT I'M WONDERING WHAT'S WRONG WITH MIURA-CHAN?
SHE LEFT.
SHE PROBABLY WENT OVER TO MAKOTO-SAN'S PLACE...
...SINCE MAKOTO-SAN'S OUT WITH A FEVER TODAY.
THOSE TWO ARE ALWAYS TOGETH-ER.
YOU MEAN BOTH OF THEM ARE OUT?
THEN WHAT REASON IS THERE FOR ME TO BE HERE?
WE HAVE ONLY MORNING CLASSES TODAY.
MAYBE WE SHOULD PAY A SICKBED VISIT.
BUT ITO IS THE ONLY ONE WHO KNOWS WHERE MAKOTO-SAN'S APARTMENT IS.
...!
I'D BE SO DISTRACTED, SCHOOL'D BE A WASTE ANYWAY!
I UNDERSTAND THAT HE DOESN'T WANT TO WORRY ME...

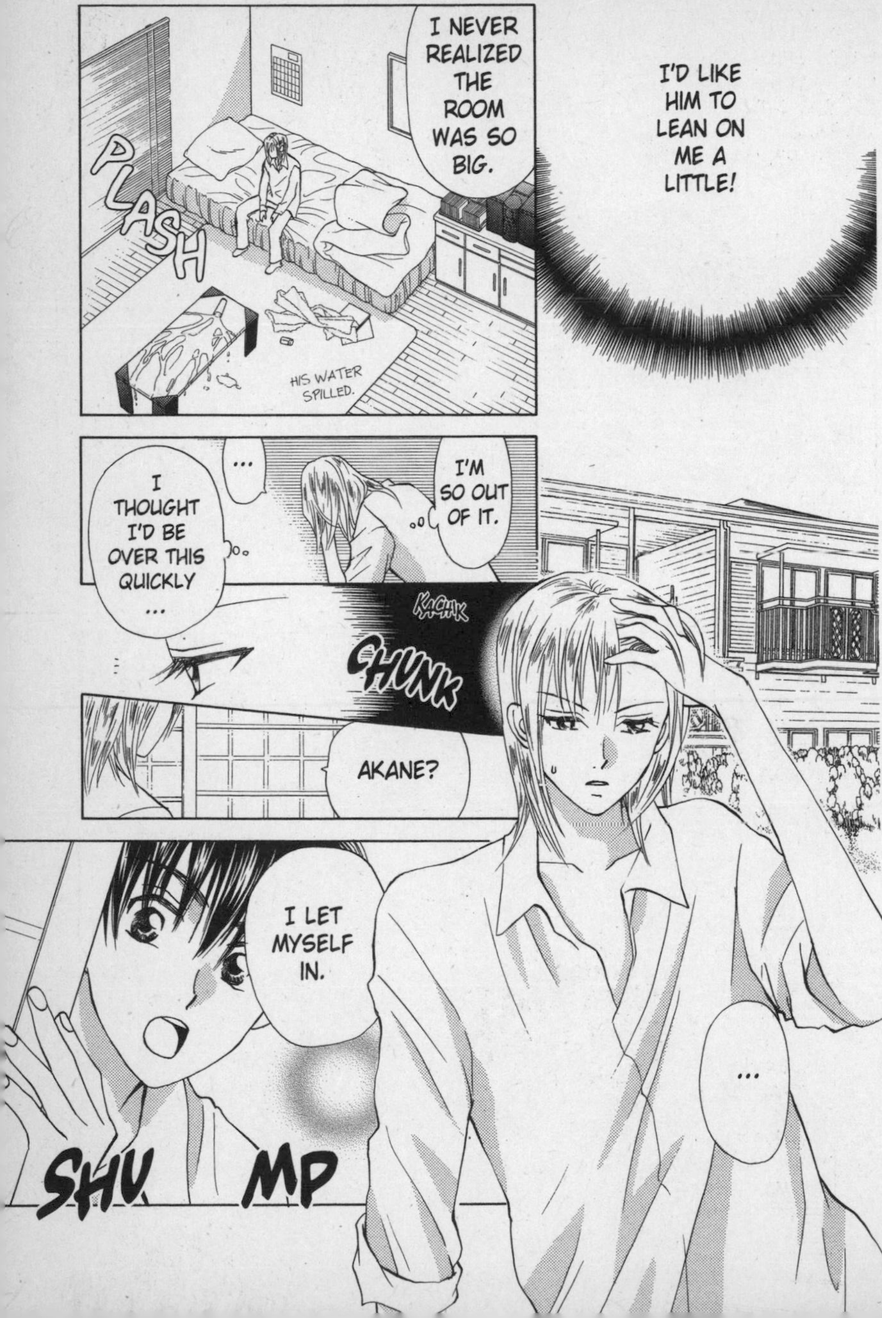
I'D LIKE HIM TO LEAN ON ME A LITTLE!
I NEVER REALIZED THE ROOM WAS SO BIG.
PLASH
HIS WATER SPILLED.
I'M SO OUT OF IT.
...
I THOUGHT I'D BE OVER THIS QUICKLY ...
KACHAK
CHUNK
AKANE?
...
I LET MYSELF IN.
SHU MP

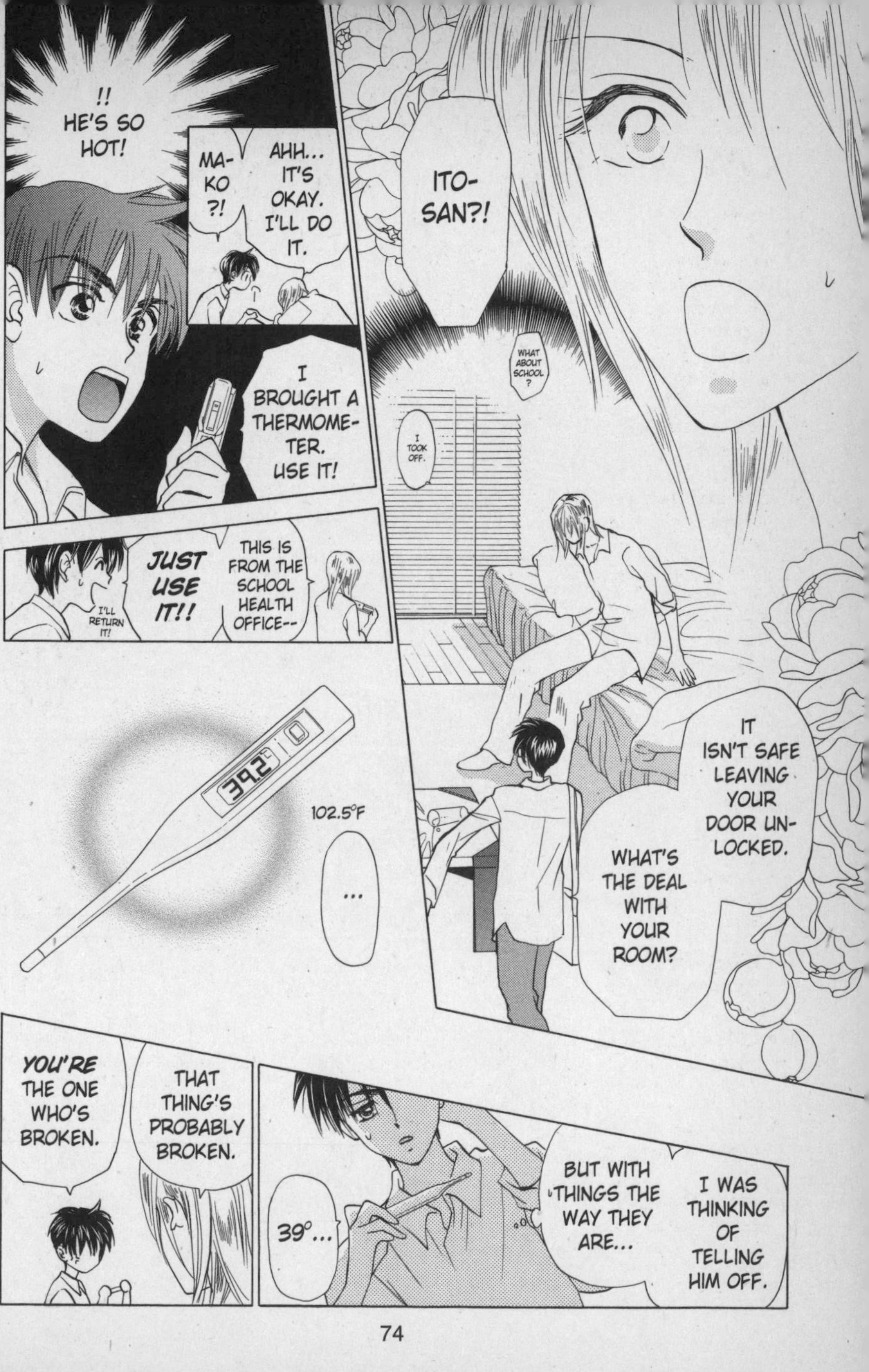
ITO-SAN?!
WHAT ABOUT SCHOOL?
I TOOK OFF.
IT ISN'T SAFE LEAVING YOUR DOOR UNLOCKED.
WHAT'S THE DEAL WITH YOUR ROOM?
AHH... IT'S OKAY. I'LL DO IT.
MA-KO?!
!! HE'S SO HOT!
I BROUGHT A THERMOMETER. USE IT!
THIS IS FROM THE SCHOOL HEALTH OFFICE--
JUST USE IT!!
I'LL RETURN IT!
39.2
102.5°F
...
I WAS THINKING OF TELLING HIM OFF.
BUT WITH THINGS THE WAY THEY ARE...
39°...
THAT THING'S PROBABLY BROKEN.
YOU'RE THE ONE WHO'S BROKEN.

CASTING!

I have a great respect for all of the actors who play the parts of my characters. More than that, I respect the very job of voice acting! As the voice recording proceeded, I was so moved! ♥ Before this happened, I didn't know much about voice actors, but because of this CD, I've learned a few more details. This is how the casting turned out.

With all my respect!

- Ito Miura (Minami Takayama)
- Makoto Amano (Urara Takano)
- Ryûya Miura (Nobutoshi Canna)
- Yûto Miura (Susumu Chiba)
- Tatsuyoshi Miura (Kenji Nojima)
- Hideo Toki (Isshin Chiba)

← Continued...

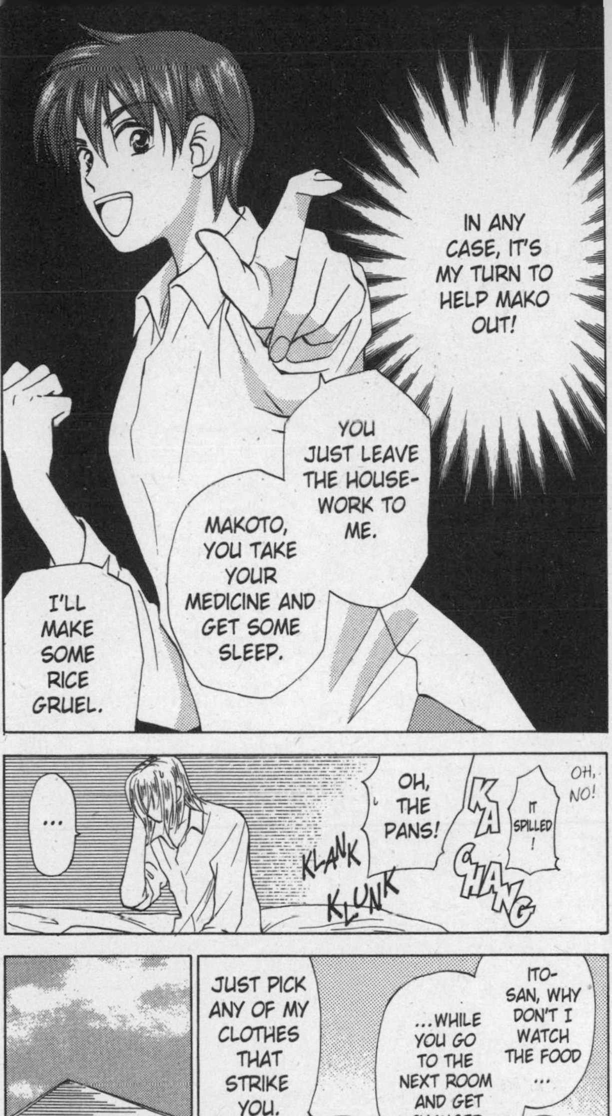
IN ANY CASE, IT'S MY TURN TO HELP MAKO OUT!
YOU JUST LEAVE THE HOUSE-WORK TO ME.
MAKOTO, YOU TAKE YOUR MEDICINE AND GET SOME SLEEP.
I'LL MAKE SOME RICE GRUEL.
OH, NO!
IT SPILLED!
KA CHANG
OH, THE PANS!
KLANK
KLUNK
...
ITO-SAN, WHY DON'T I WATCH THE FOOD ...
...WHILE YOU GO TO THE NEXT ROOM AND GET CHANGED.
JUST PICK ANY OF MY CLOTHES THAT STRIKE YOU.
GLUP GLUP
EH?
GLUP GLUP

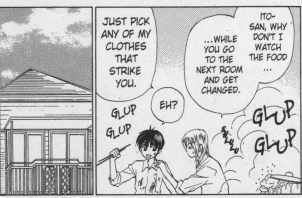

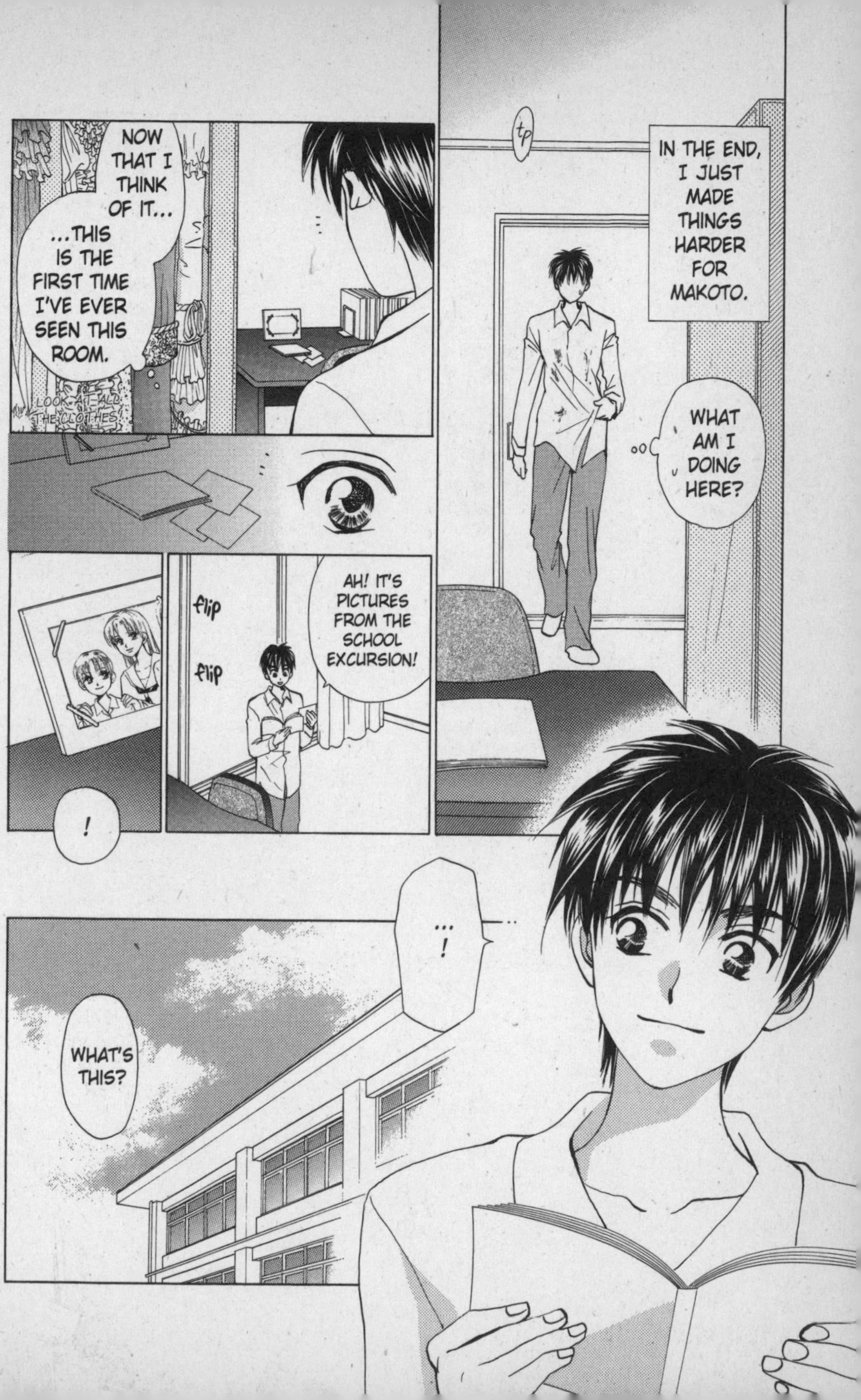
tp
IN THE END, I JUST MADE THINGS HARDER FOR MAKOTO.
WHAT AM I DOING HERE?
NOW THAT I THINK OF IT...
...THIS IS THE FIRST TIME I'VE EVER SEEN THIS ROOM.
LOOK AT ALL THE CLOTHES
AH! IT'S PICTURES FROM THE SCHOOL EXCURSION!
flip
flip
!
...!
WHAT'S THIS?

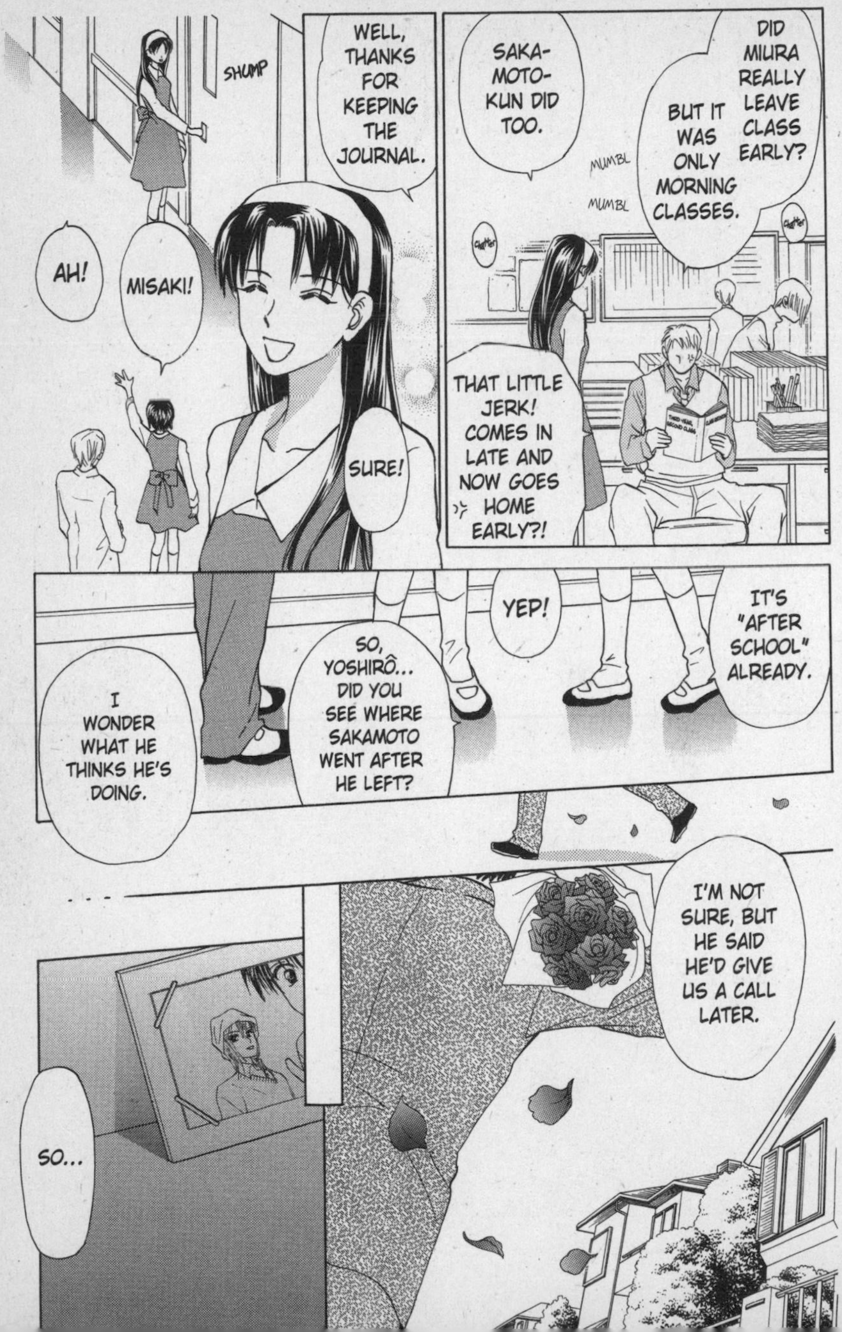
DID MIURA REALLY LEAVE CLASS EARLY?
BUT IT WAS ONLY MORNING CLASSES.
MUMBL
MUMBL
SAKA-MOTO-KUN DID TOO.
THAT LITTLE JERK! COMES IN LATE AND NOW GOES HOME EARLY?!
WELL, THANKS FOR KEEPING THE JOURNAL.
SURE!
SHUMP
MISAKI!
AH!
IT'S "AFTER SCHOOL" ALREADY.
YEP!
SO, YOSHIRÔ... DID YOU SEE WHERE SAKAMOTO WENT AFTER HE LEFT?
I WONDER WHAT HE THINKS HE'S DOING.
I'M NOT SURE, BUT HE SAID HE'D GIVE US A CALL LATER.
...
SO...

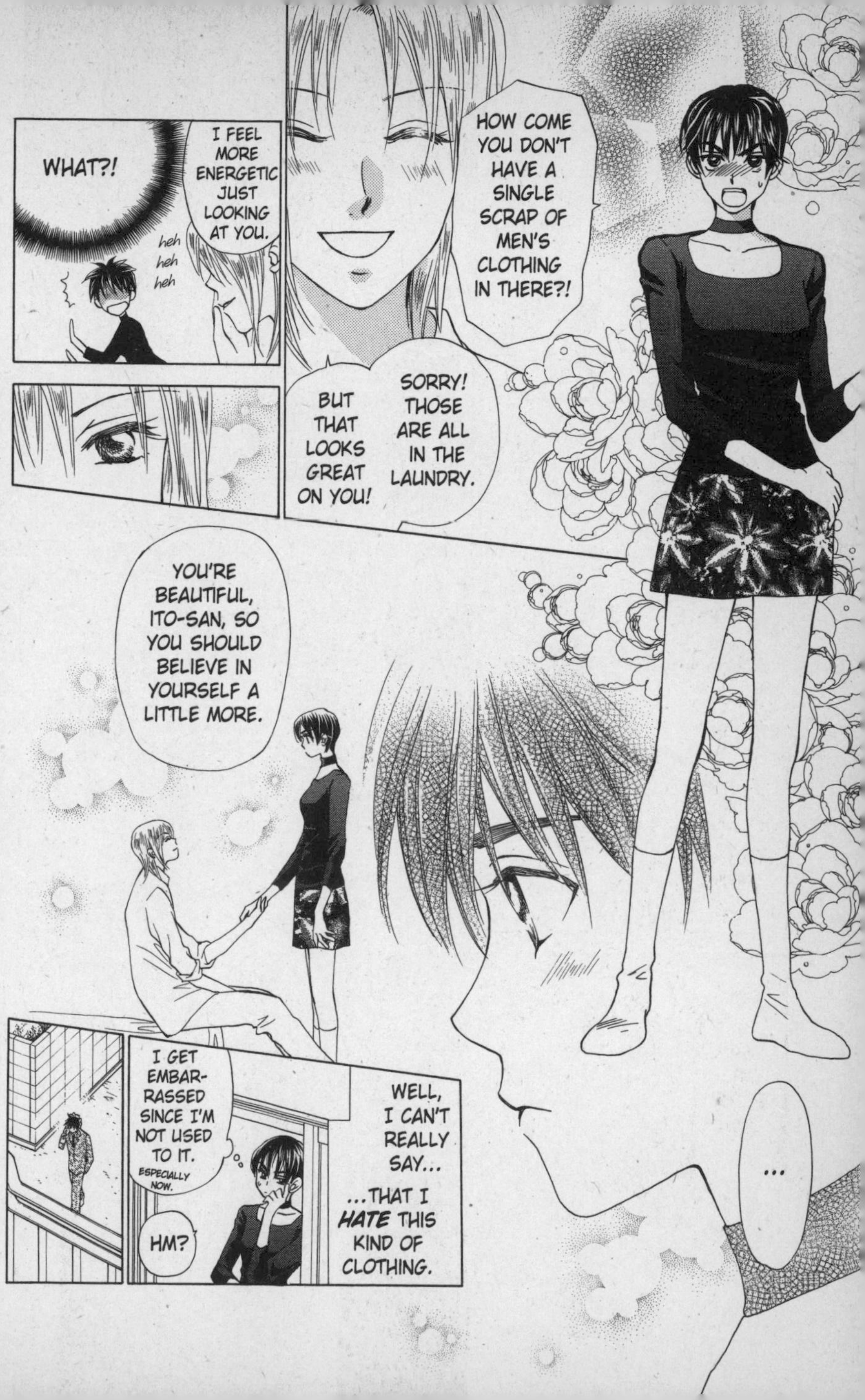
HOW COME YOU DON'T HAVE A SINGLE SCRAP OF MEN'S CLOTHING IN THERE?!
SORRY! THOSE ARE ALL IN THE LAUNDRY.
BUT THAT LOOKS GREAT ON YOU!
I FEEL MORE ENERGETIC JUST LOOKING AT YOU.
heh heh heh
WHAT?!
YOU'RE BEAUTIFUL, ITO-SAN, SO YOU SHOULD BELIEVE IN YOURSELF A LITTLE MORE.
...
WELL, I CAN'T REALLY SAY...
...THAT I *HATE* THIS KIND OF CLOTHING.
I GET EMBARRASSED SINCE I'M NOT USED TO IT.
ESPECIALLY NOW.
HM?

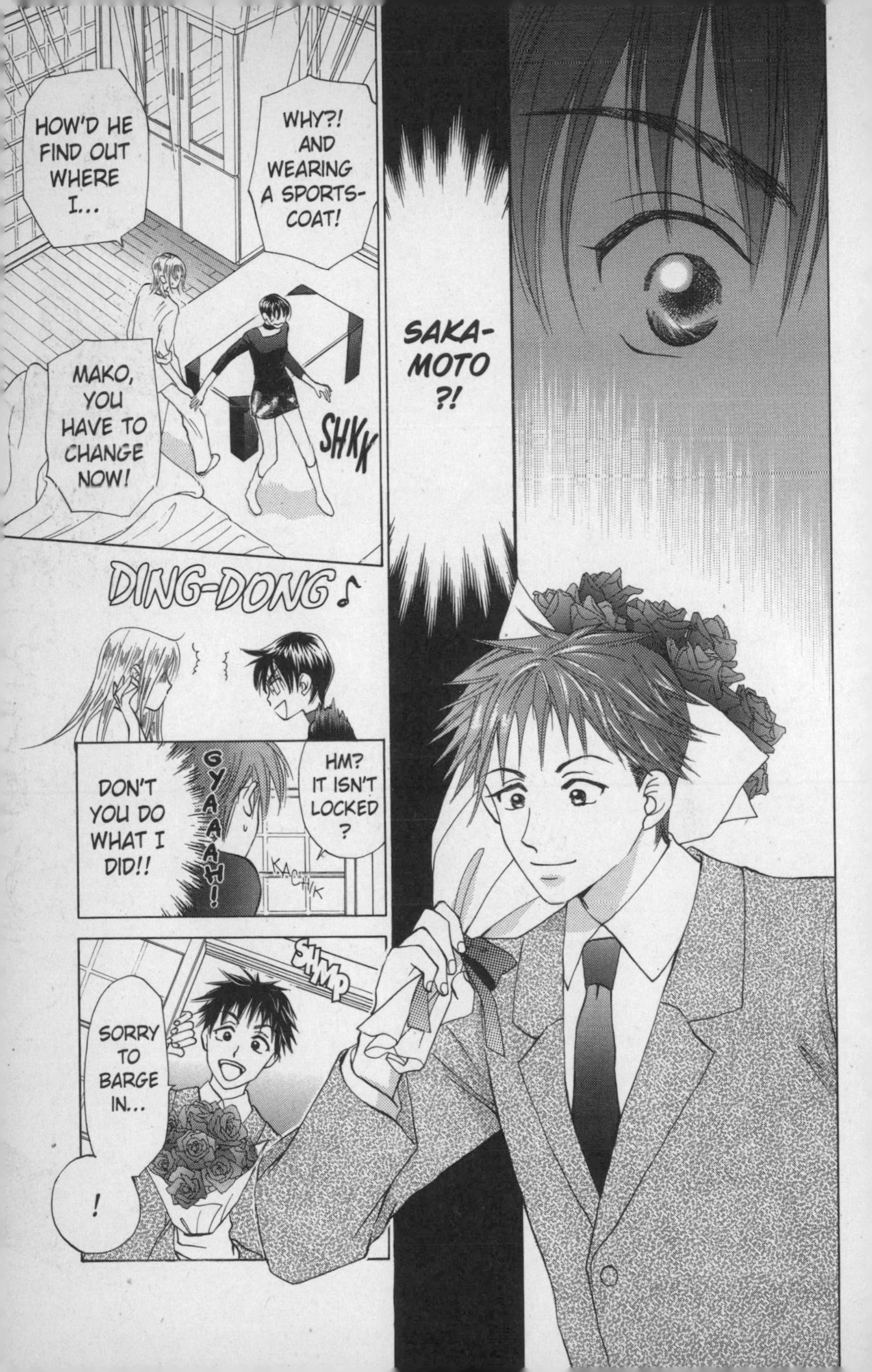
SAKA-MOTO?!
WHY?! AND WEARING A SPORTS-COAT!
HOW'D HE FIND OUT WHERE I...
MAKO, YOU HAVE TO CHANGE NOW!
SHKK
DING-DONG♪
HM? IT ISN'T LOCKED?
GYAAAAH!
DON'T YOU DO WHAT I DID!!
KACHIK
SHMP
SORRY TO BARGE IN...
!

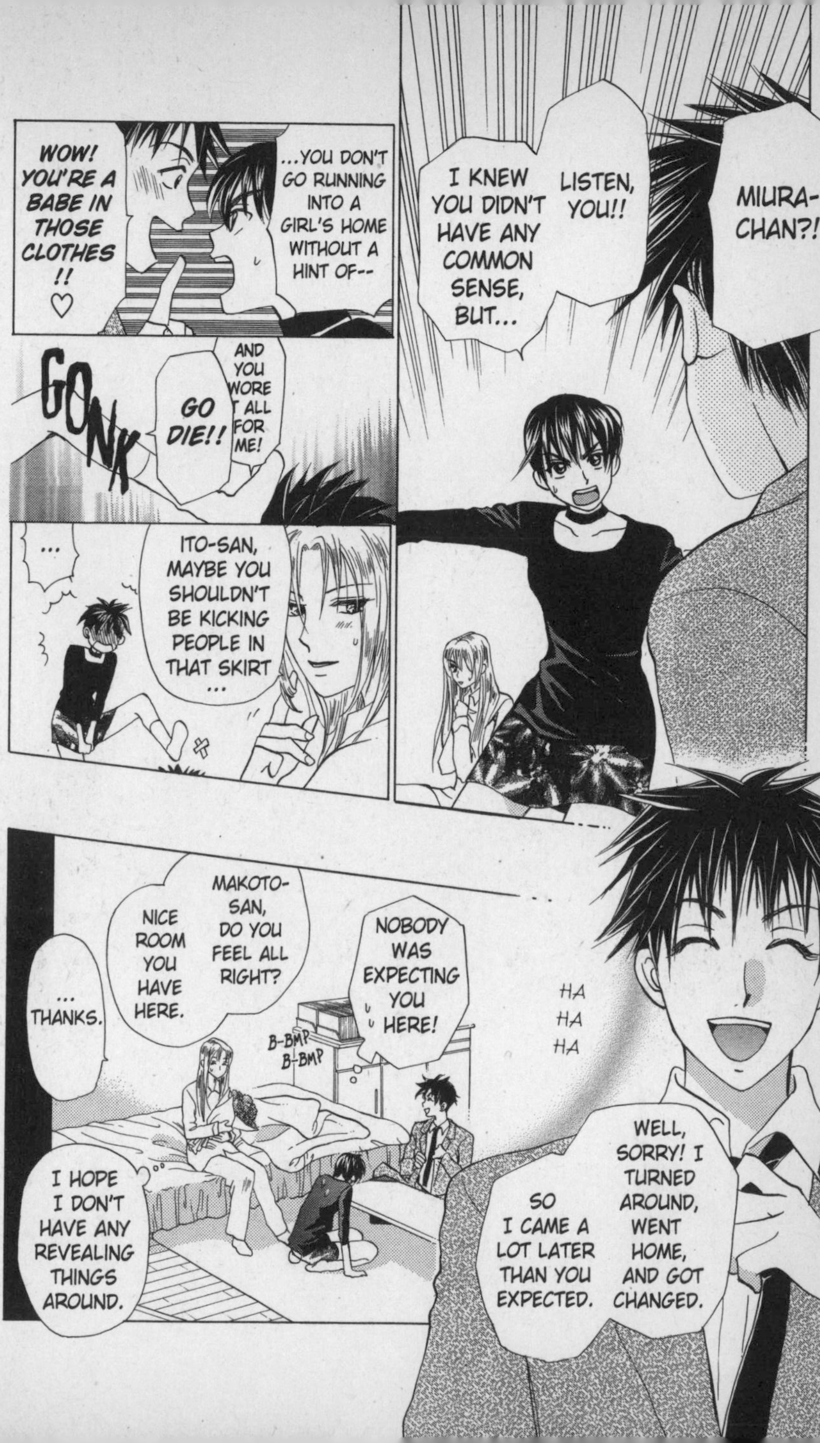
MIURA-CHAN?!
LISTEN, YOU!!
I KNEW YOU DIDN'T HAVE ANY COMMON SENSE, BUT...
...YOU DON'T GO RUNNING INTO A GIRL'S HOME WITHOUT A HINT OF--
WOW! YOU'RE A BABE IN THOSE CLOTHES!! ♡
AND YOU WORE T ALL FOR ME!
GO DIE!!
GONK
ITO-SAN, MAYBE YOU SHOULDN'T BE KICKING PEOPLE IN THAT SKIRT...
...
HA HA HA
WELL, SORRY! I TURNED AROUND, WENT HOME, AND GOT CHANGED.
SO I CAME A LOT LATER THAN YOU EXPECTED.
NOBODY WAS EXPECTING YOU HERE!
MAKOTO-SAN, DO YOU FEEL ALL RIGHT?
NICE ROOM YOU HAVE HERE.
...THANKS.
B-BMP B-BMP
I HOPE I DON'T HAVE ANY REVEALING THINGS AROUND.

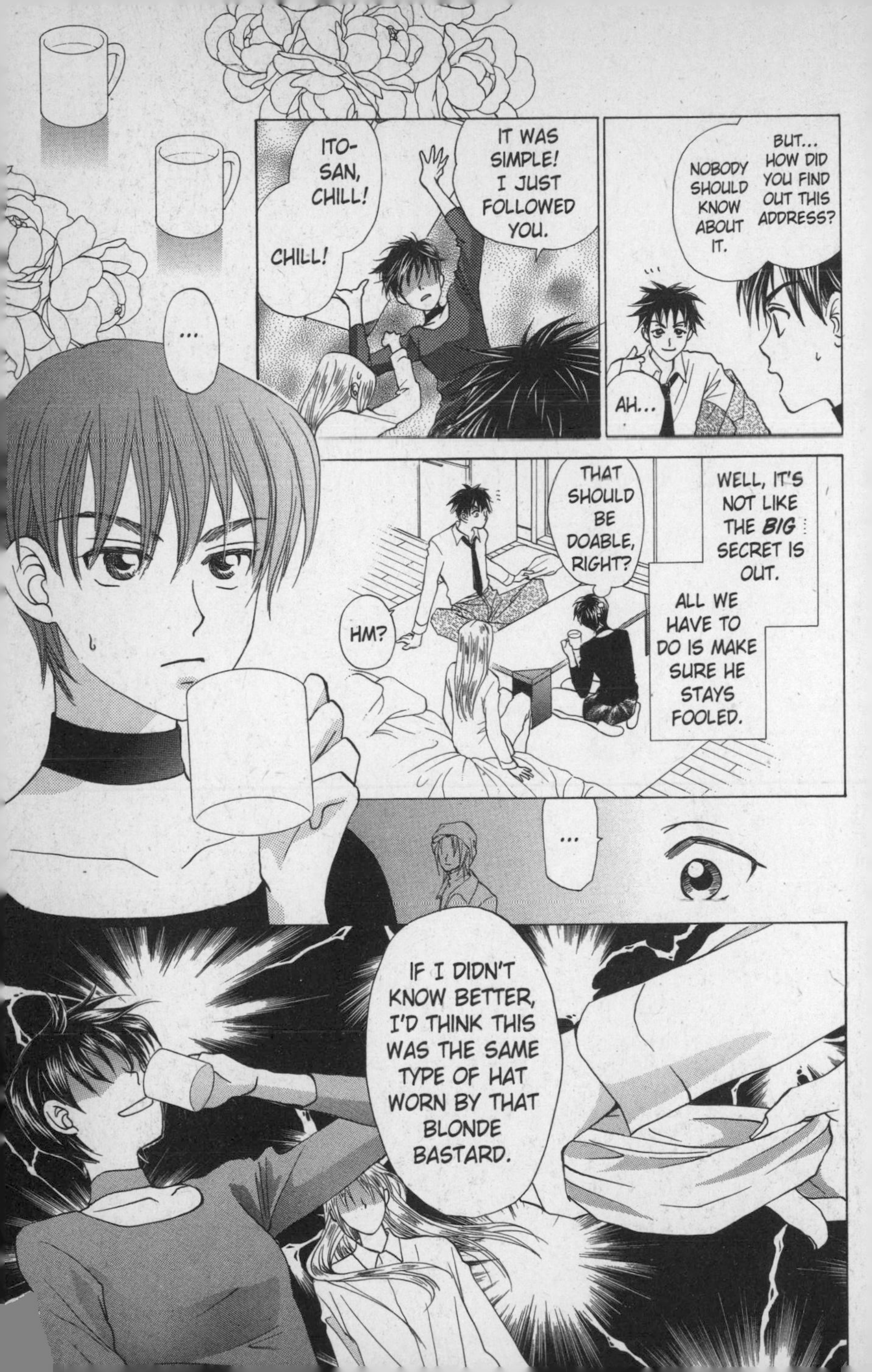
BUT... HOW DID YOU FIND OUT THIS ADDRESS?
NOBODY SHOULD KNOW ABOUT IT.
AH...
IT WAS SIMPLE! I JUST FOLLOWED YOU.
ITO-SAN, CHILL!
CHILL!
...
WELL, IT'S NOT LIKE THE BIG SECRET IS OUT.
ALL WE HAVE TO DO IS MAKE SURE HE STAYS FOOLED.
THAT SHOULD BE DOABLE, RIGHT?
HM?
...
IF I DIDN'T KNOW BETTER, I'D THINK THIS WAS THE SAME TYPE OF HAT WORN BY THAT BLONDE BASTARD.

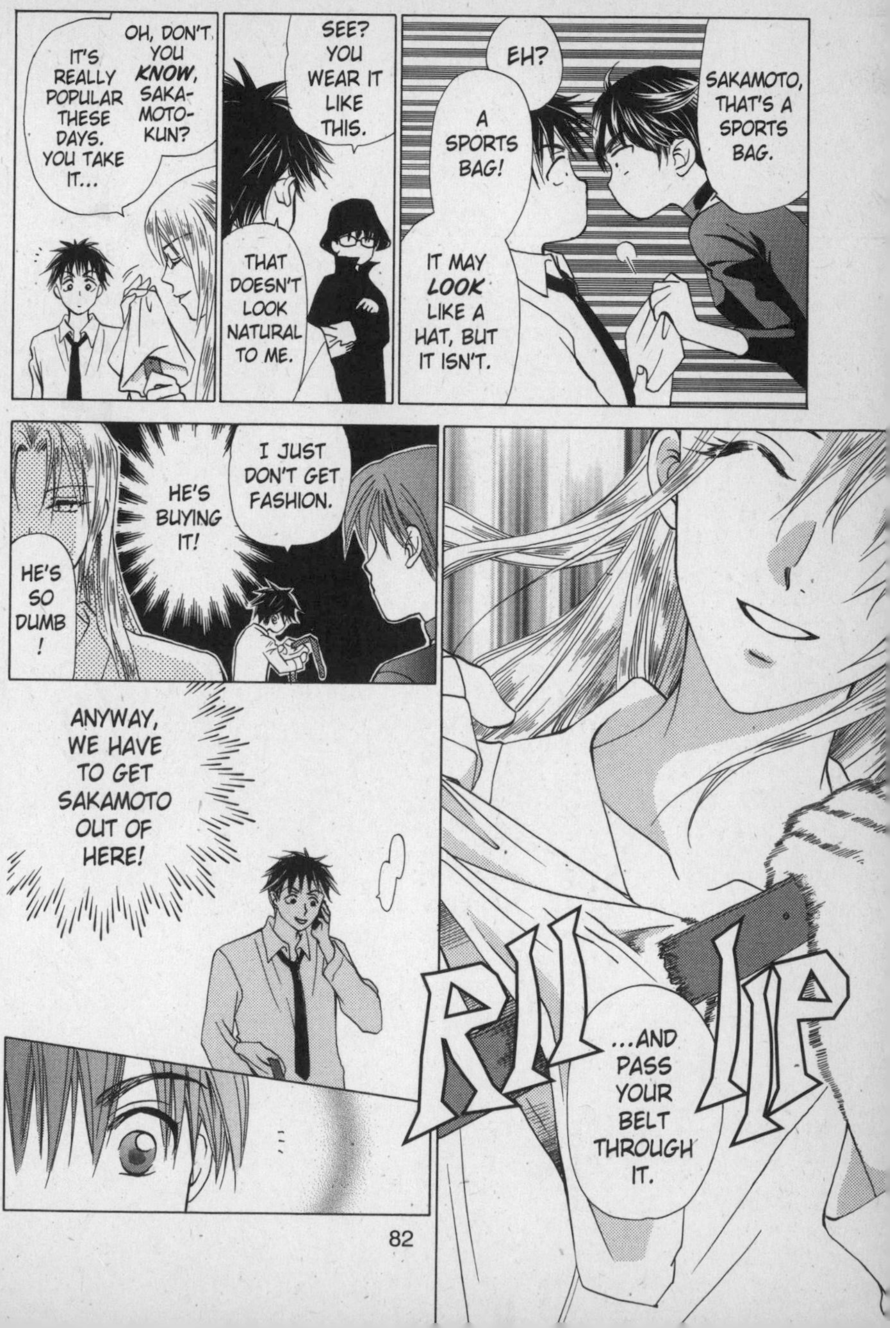
SAKAMOTO, THAT'S A SPORTS BAG.
EH?
A SPORTS BAG!
IT MAY LOOK LIKE A HAT, BUT IT ISN'T.
SEE? YOU WEAR IT LIKE THIS.
THAT DOESN'T LOOK NATURAL TO ME.
OH, DON'T YOU KNOW, SAKA-MOTO-KUN?
IT'S REALLY POPULAR THESE DAYS. YOU TAKE IT...
...AND PASS YOUR BELT THROUGH IT.
RIIIP
I JUST DON'T GET FASHION.
HE'S BUYING IT!
HE'S SO DUMB!
ANYWAY, WE HAVE TO GET SAKAMOTO OUT OF HERE!

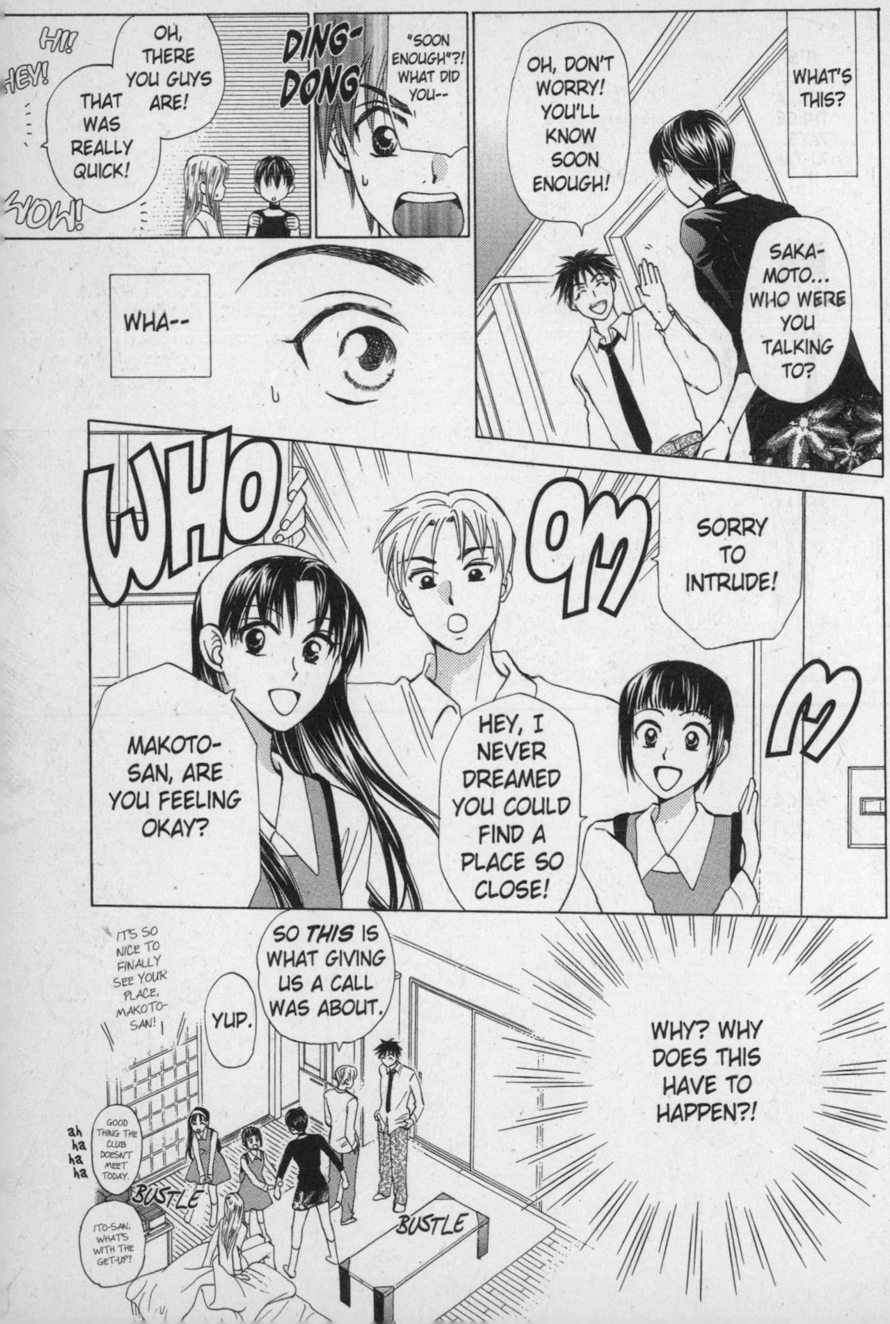
WHAT'S THIS?
SAKA-MOTO... WHO WERE YOU TALKING TO?
OH, DON'T WORRY! YOU'LL KNOW SOON ENOUGH!
DING-DONG
"SOON ENOUGH"?! WHAT DID YOU--
OH, THERE YOU GUYS ARE!
THAT WAS REALLY QUICK!
HI!
HEY!
WOW!
WHA--
SORRY TO INTRUDE!
WHO
OM
M
HEY, I NEVER DREAMED YOU COULD FIND A PLACE SO CLOSE!
MAKOTO-SAN, ARE YOU FEELING OKAY?
WHY? WHY DOES THIS HAVE TO HAPPEN?!
SO *THIS* IS WHAT GIVING US A CALL WAS ABOUT.
YUP.
IT'S SO NICE TO FINALLY SEE YOUR PLACE, MAKOTO-SAN!
GOOD THING THE CLUB DOESN'T MEET TODAY.
ah ha ha ha
BUSTLE
ITO-SAN, WHATS WITH THE GET-UP?
BUSTLE

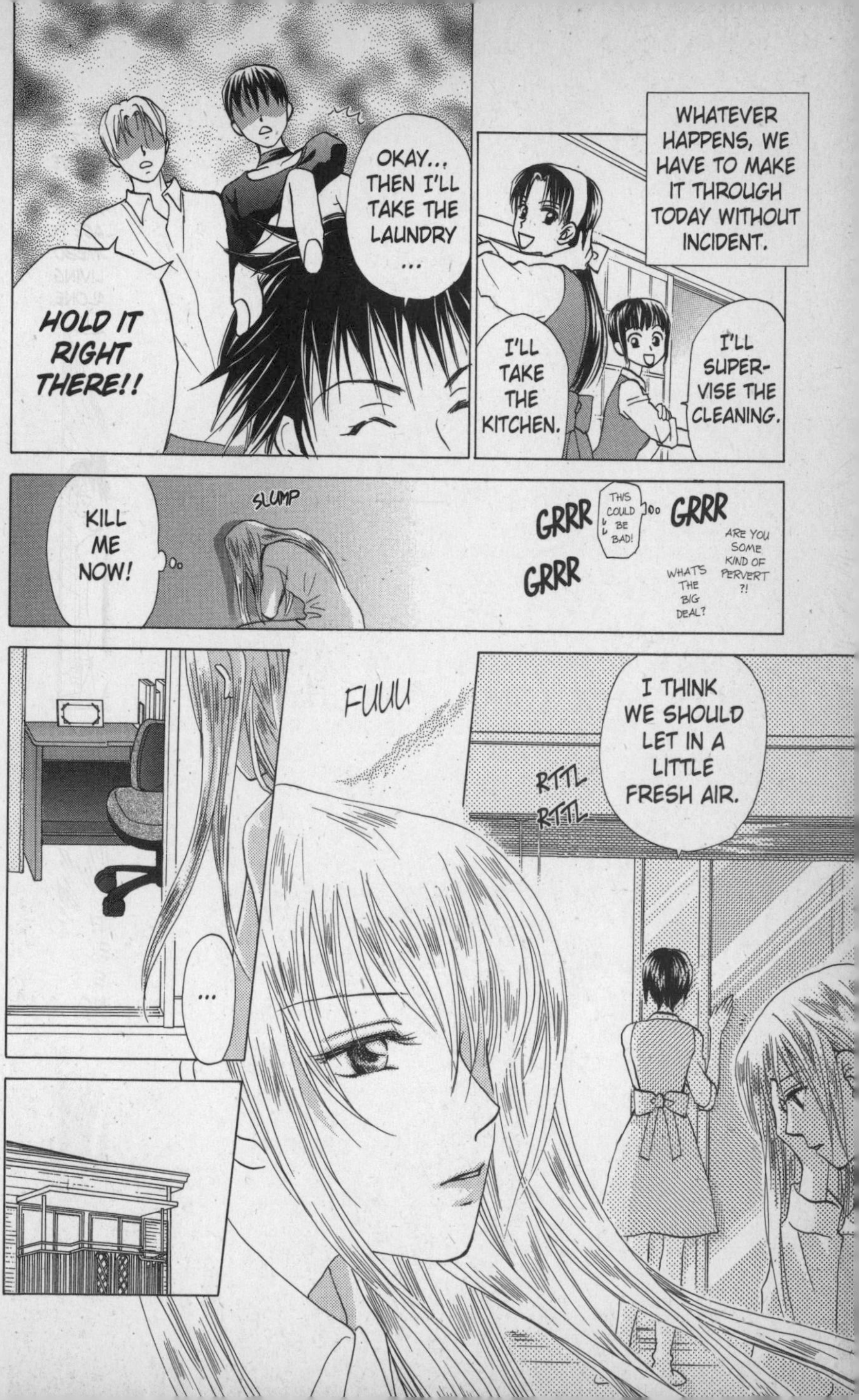
WHATEVER HAPPENS, WE HAVE TO MAKE IT THROUGH TODAY WITHOUT INCIDENT.
I'LL SUPER-VISE THE CLEANING.
I'LL TAKE THE KITCHEN.
OKAY..., THEN I'LL TAKE THE LAUNDRY ...
HOLD IT RIGHT THERE!!
ARE YOU SOME KIND OF PERVERT ?!
WHAT'S THE BIG DEAL?
GRRR
THIS COULD BE BAD!
GRRR
GRRR
SLUMP
KILL ME NOW!
I THINK WE SHOULD LET IN A LITTLE FRESH AIR.
RTTL RTTL
FUUU
...

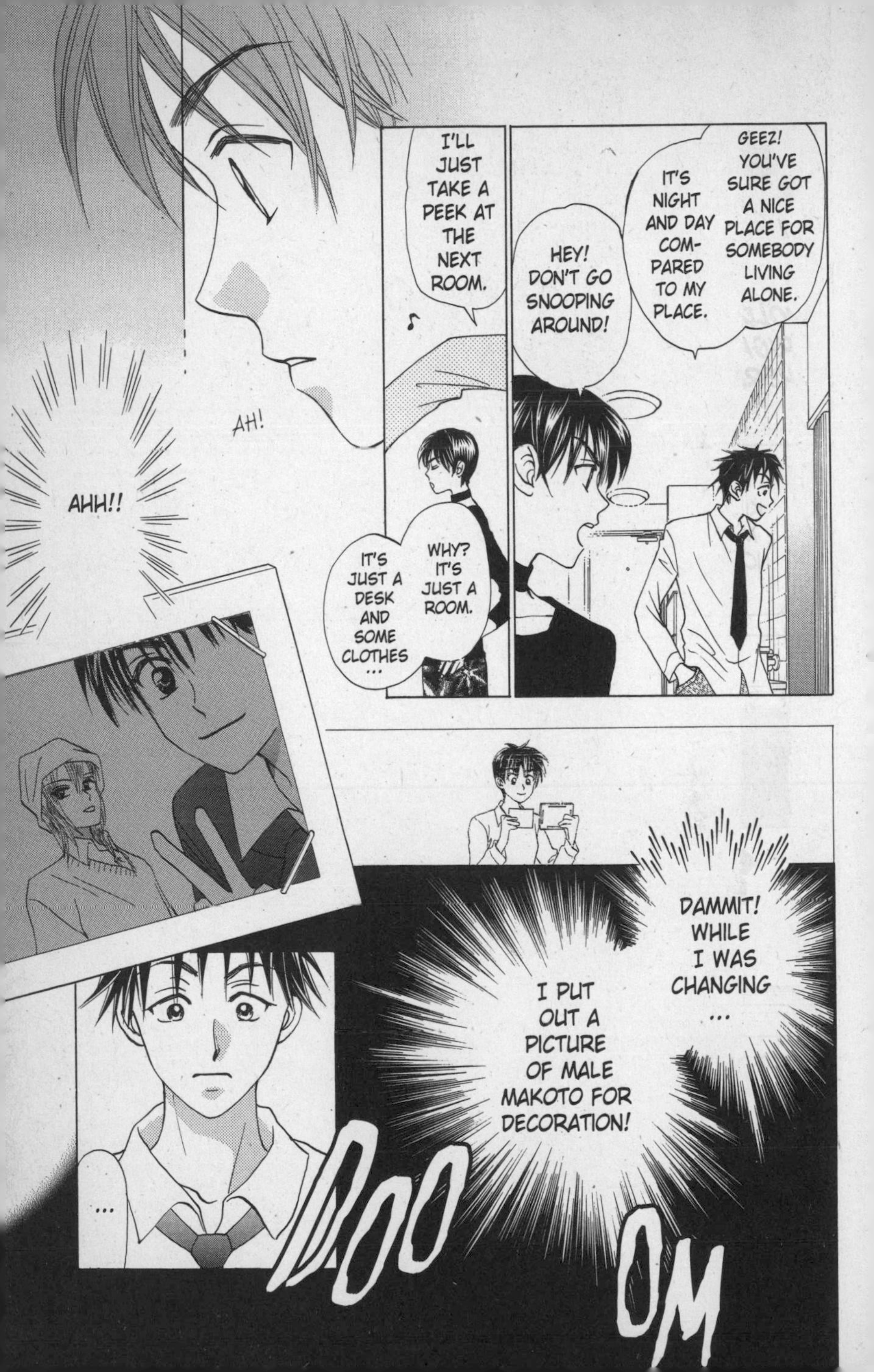
GEEZ! YOU'VE SURE GOT A NICE PLACE FOR SOMEBODY LIVING ALONE.
IT'S NIGHT AND DAY COMPARED TO MY PLACE.
HEY! DON'T GO SNOOPING AROUND!
I'LL JUST TAKE A PEEK AT THE NEXT ROOM.
WHY? IT'S JUST A ROOM.
IT'S JUST A DESK AND SOME CLOTHES ...
AH!
AHH!!
DAMMIT! WHILE I WAS CHANGING ...
I PUT OUT A PICTURE OF MALE MAKOTO FOR DECORATION!
...
DOOOM

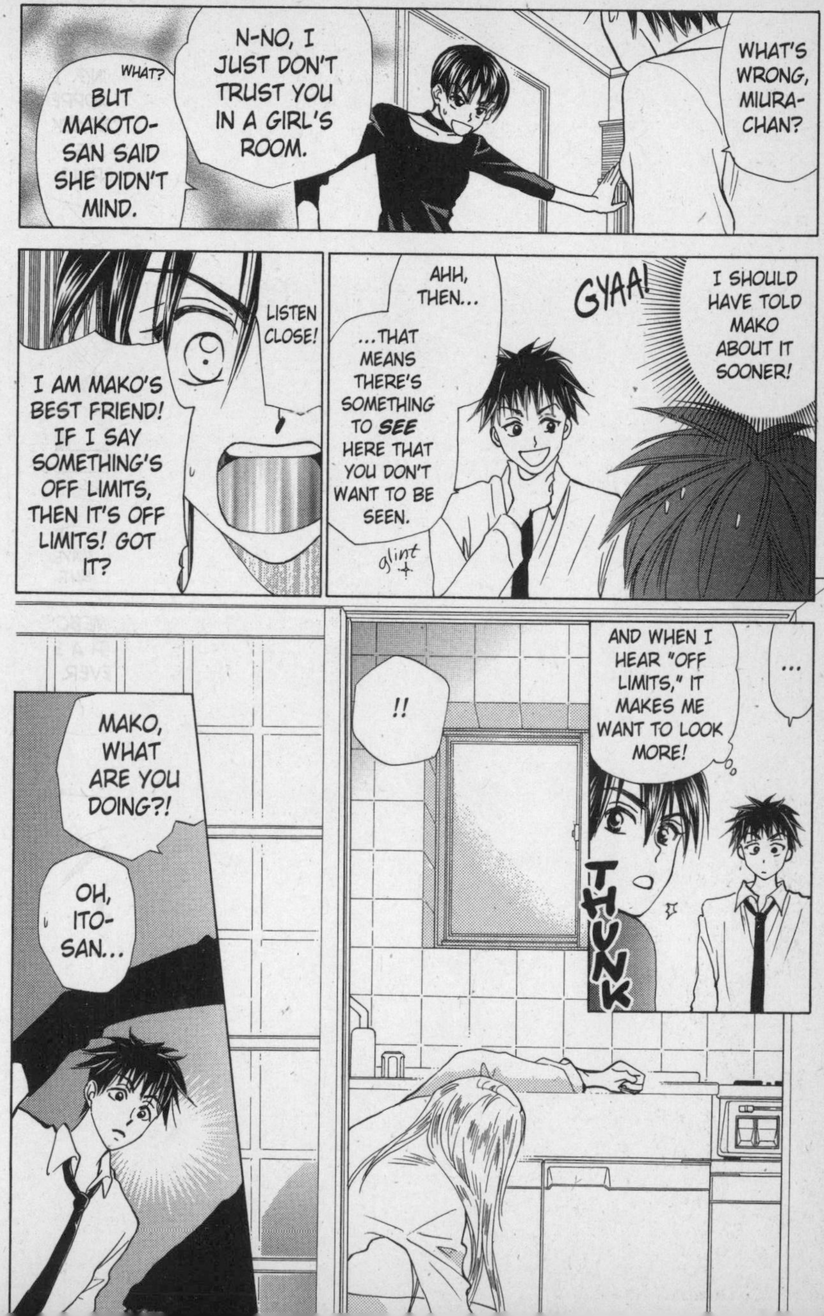
WHAT'S WRONG, MIURA-CHAN?
N-NO, I JUST DON'T TRUST YOU IN A GIRL'S ROOM.
WHAT? BUT MAKOTO-SAN SAID SHE DIDN'T MIND.
I SHOULD HAVE TOLD MAKO ABOUT IT SOONER!
GYAA!
AHH, THEN...
...THAT MEANS THERE'S SOMETHING TO *SEE* HERE THAT YOU DON'T WANT TO BE SEEN.
glint
LISTEN CLOSE!
I AM MAKO'S BEST FRIEND! IF I SAY SOMETHING'S OFF LIMITS, THEN IT'S OFF LIMITS! GOT IT?
...
AND WHEN I HEAR "OFF LIMITS," IT MAKES ME WANT TO LOOK MORE!
THUNK
!!
MAKO, WHAT ARE YOU DOING?!
OH, ITO-SAN...

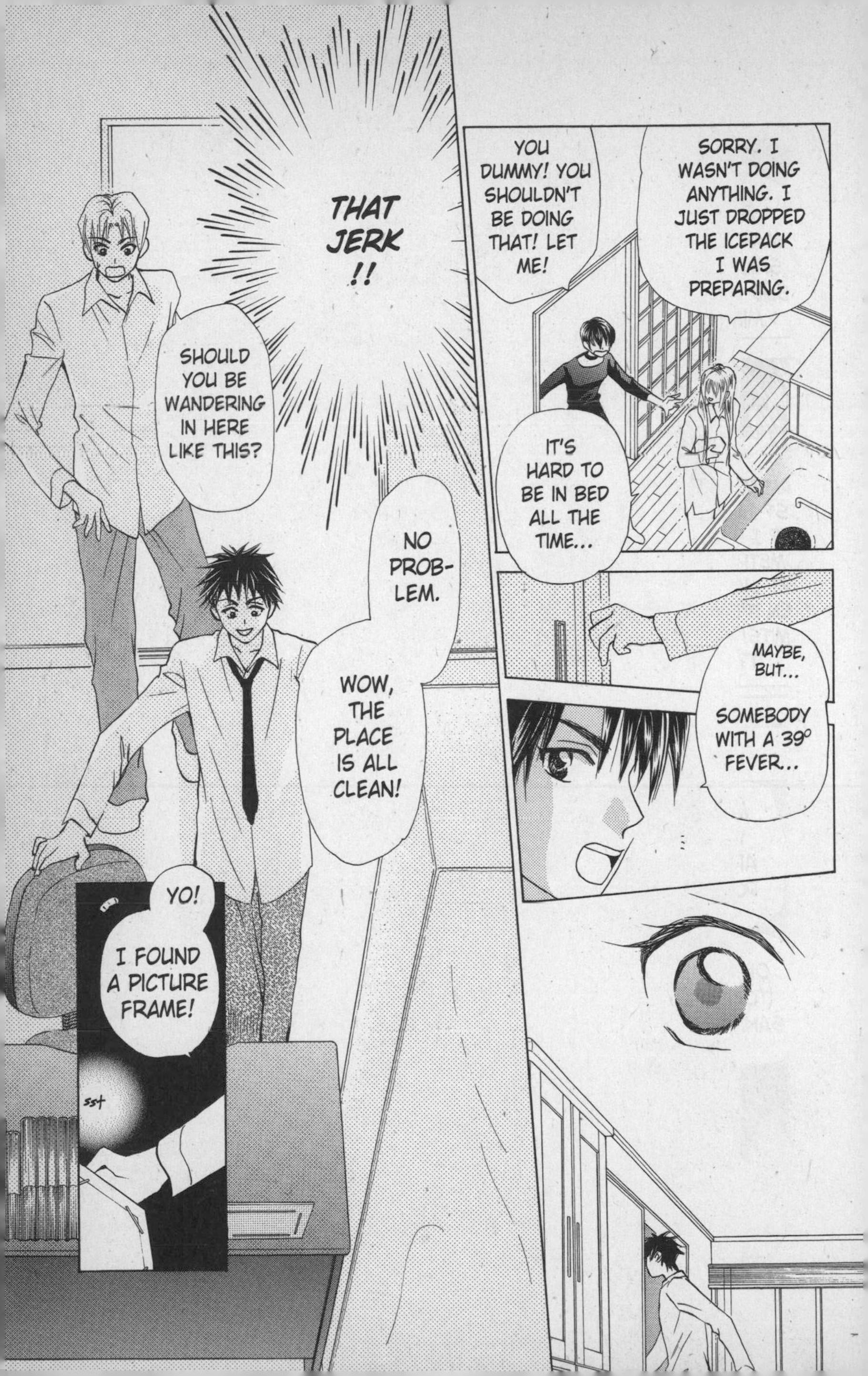
SORRY. I WASN'T DOING ANYTHING. I JUST DROPPED THE ICEPACK I WAS PREPARING.
YOU DUMMY! YOU SHOULDN'T BE DOING THAT! LET ME!
IT'S HARD TO BE IN BED ALL THE TIME...
MAYBE, BUT...
SOMEBODY WITH A 39° FEVER...
THAT JERK!!
SHOULD YOU BE WANDERING IN HERE LIKE THIS?
NO PROB-LEM.
WOW, THE PLACE IS ALL CLEAN!
YO!
I FOUND A PICTURE FRAME!
sst

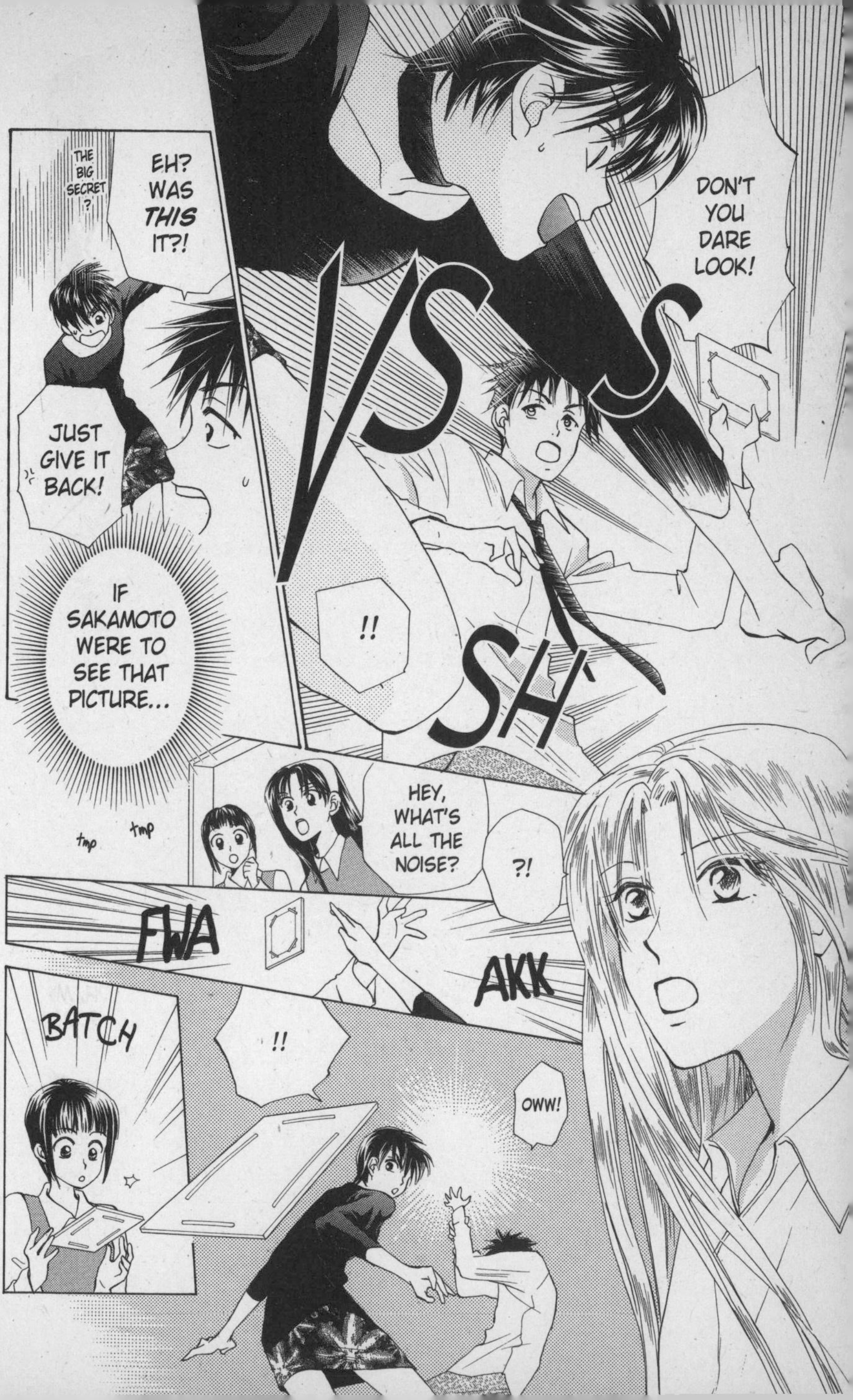
DON'T YOU DARE LOOK!
VS
S
SH
!!
THE BIG SECRET?
EH? WAS *THIS* IT?!
JUST GIVE IT BACK!
IF SAKAMOTO WERE TO SEE THAT PICTURE...
HEY, WHAT'S ALL THE NOISE?
tmp
tmp
?!
FWA
AKK
!!
BATCH
OWW!

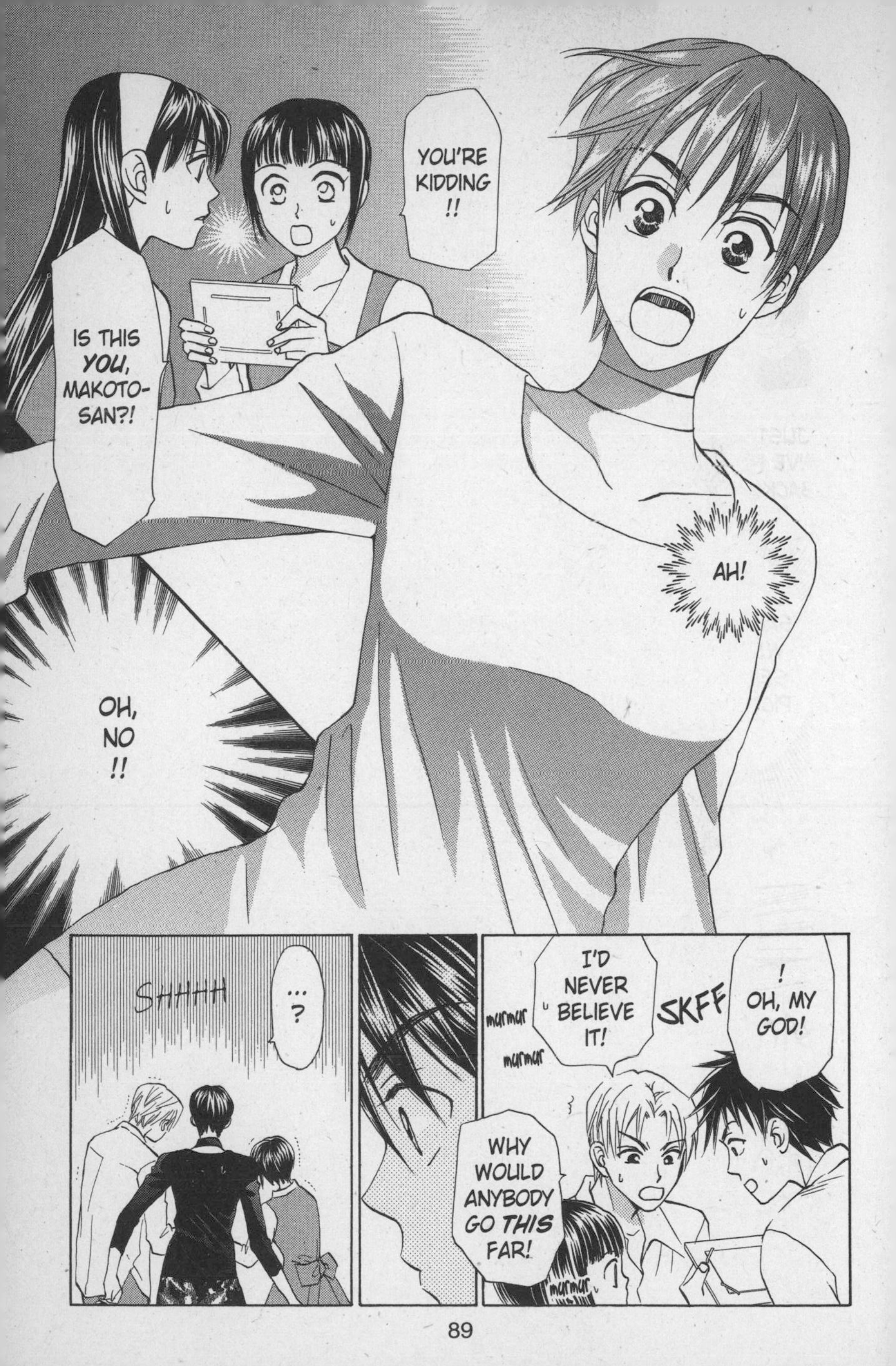
YOU'RE KIDDING !!
AH!
IS THIS *YOU*, MAKOTO-SAN?!
OH, NO !!
! OH, MY GOD!
SKFF
I'D NEVER BELIEVE IT!
murmur
murmur
WHY WOULD ANYBODY GO *THIS* FAR!
murmur
...?
SHHHH

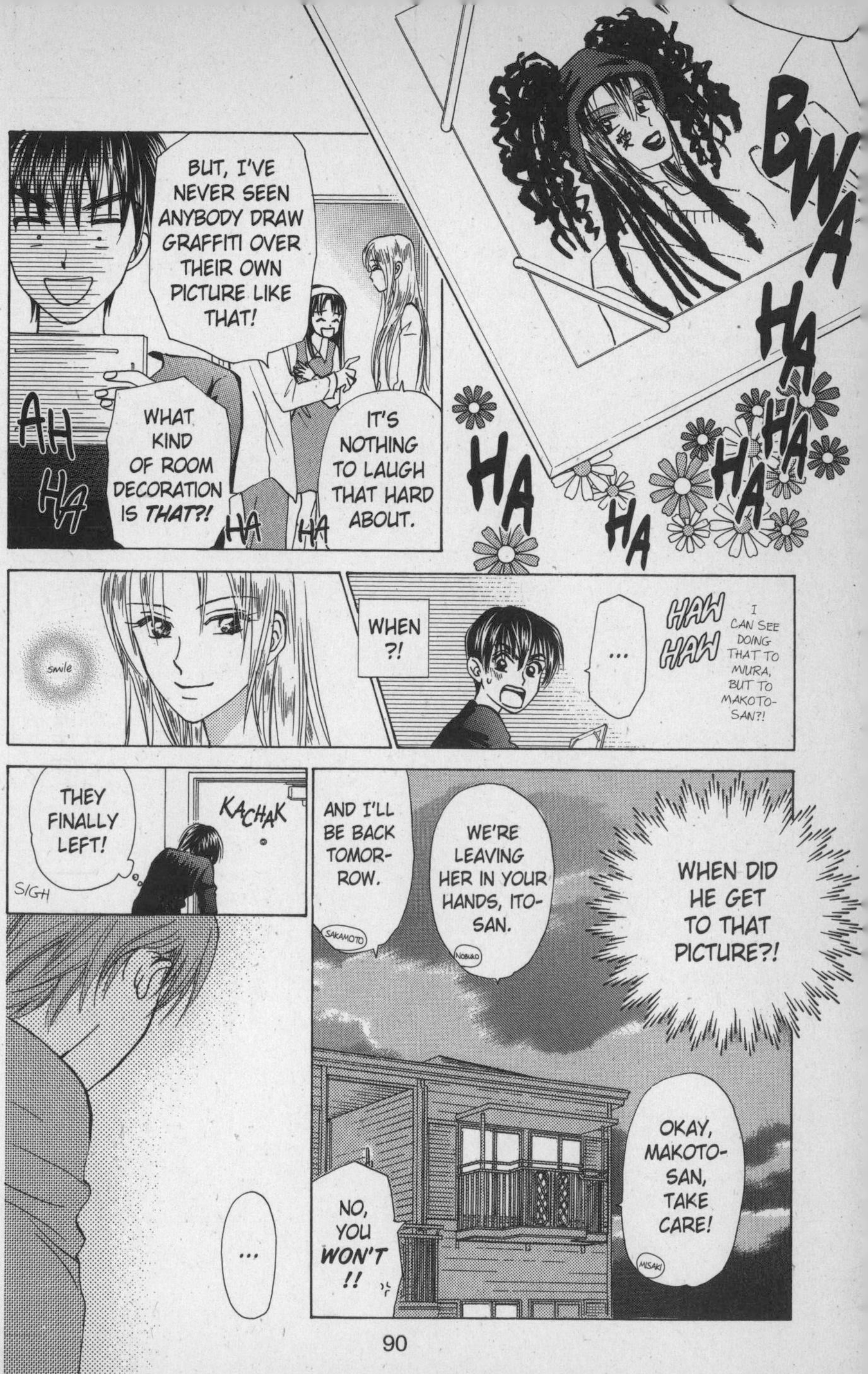
BWAHAHAHAHA
HA HA HA
BUT, I'VE NEVER SEEN ANYBODY DRAW GRAFFITI OVER THEIR OWN PICTURE LIKE THAT!
IT'S NOTHING TO LAUGH THAT HARD ABOUT.
WHAT KIND OF ROOM DECORATION IS *THAT?!*
AH HA HA HA
HAW HAW
I CAN SEE DOING THAT TO MIURA, BUT TO MAKOTO-SAN?!
...
WHEN ?!
smile
WHEN DID HE GET TO THAT PICTURE?!
WE'RE LEAVING HER IN YOUR HANDS, ITO-SAN.
NOBUKO
AND I'LL BE BACK TOMOR-ROW.
SAKAMOTO
OKAY, MAKOTO-SAN, TAKE CARE!
MISAKI
NO, YOU ***WON'T*** !!
THEY FINALLY LEFT!
KACHAK
SIGH
...

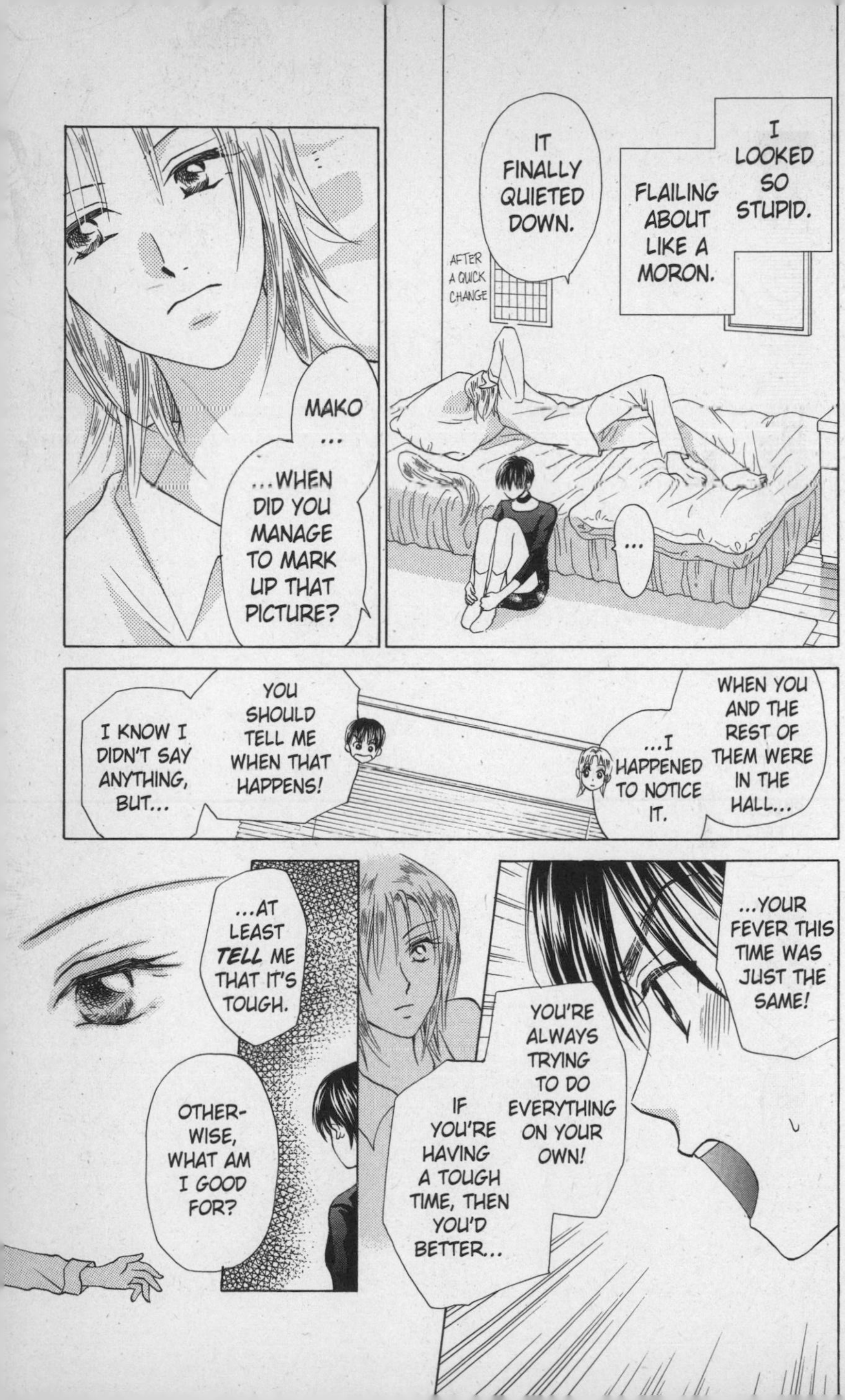
I LOOKED SO STUPID.
FLAILING ABOUT LIKE A MORON.
IT FINALLY QUIETED DOWN.
AFTER A QUICK CHANGE
...
MAKO ...
...WHEN DID YOU MANAGE TO MARK UP THAT PICTURE?
WHEN YOU AND THE REST OF THEM WERE IN THE HALL...
...I HAPPENED TO NOTICE IT.
YOU SHOULD TELL ME WHEN THAT HAPPENS!
I KNOW I DIDN'T SAY ANYTHING, BUT...
...YOUR FEVER THIS TIME WAS JUST THE SAME!
YOU'RE ALWAYS TRYING TO DO EVERYTHING ON YOUR OWN!
IF YOU'RE HAVING A TOUGH TIME, THEN YOU'D BETTER...
...AT LEAST *TELL* ME THAT IT'S TOUGH.
OTHER-WISE, WHAT AM I GOOD FOR?

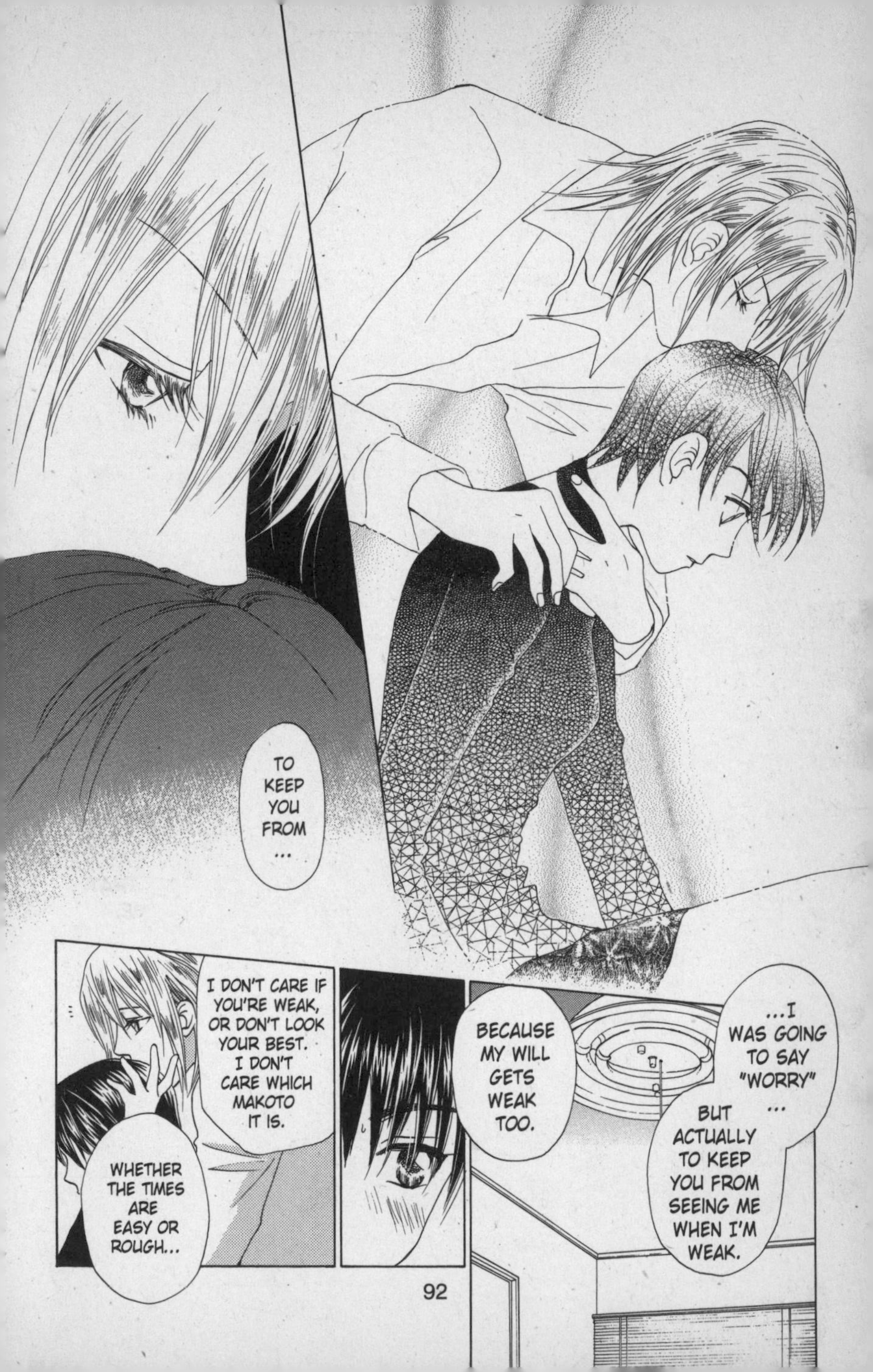
TO KEEP YOU FROM ...
...I WAS GOING TO SAY "WORRY" ...
BUT ACTUALLY TO KEEP YOU FROM SEEING ME WHEN I'M WEAK.
BECAUSE MY WILL GETS WEAK TOO.
I DON'T CARE IF YOU'RE WEAK, OR DON'T LOOK YOUR BEST. I DON'T CARE WHICH MAKOTO IT IS.
WHETHER THE TIMES ARE EASY OR ROUGH...

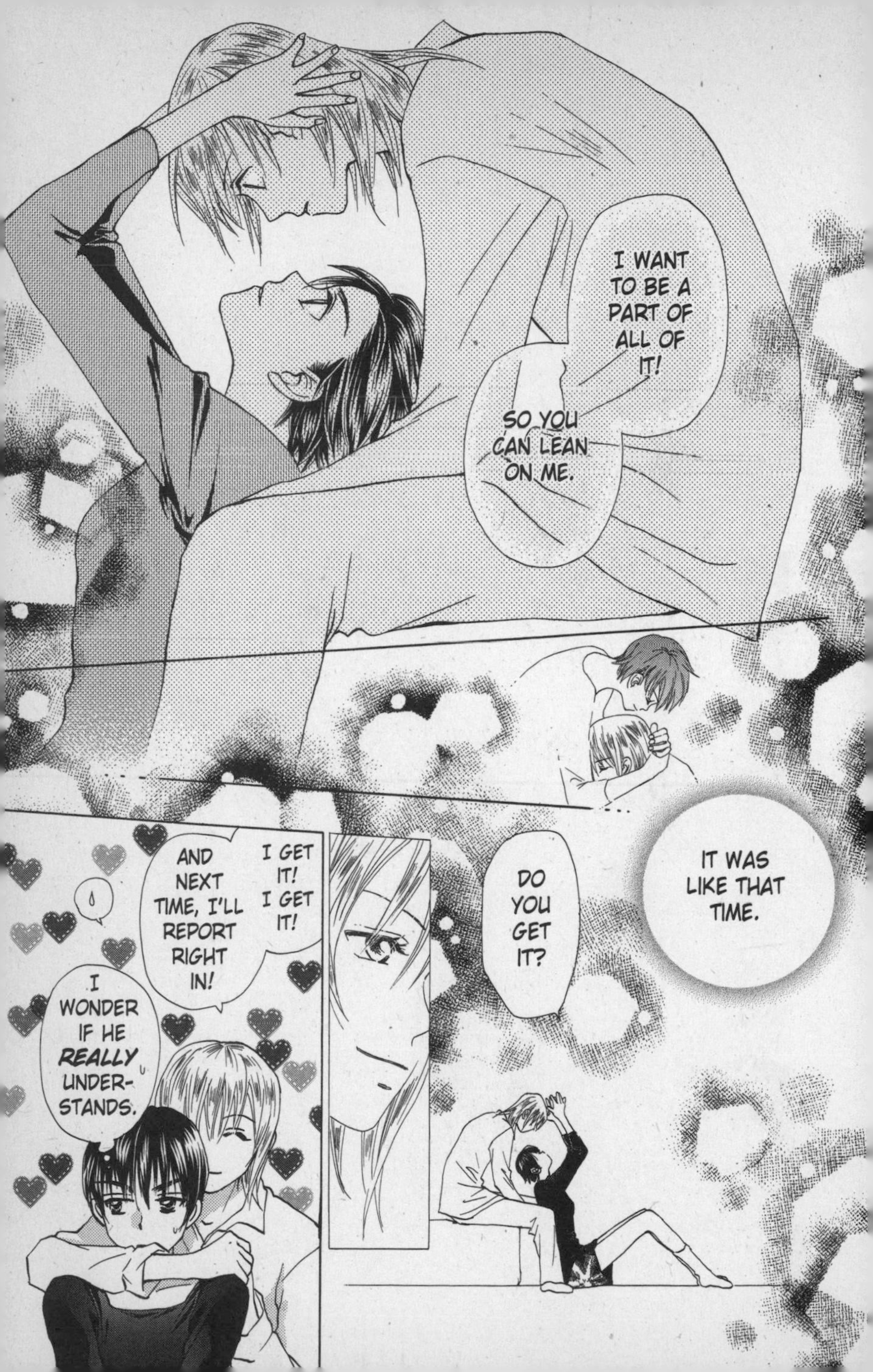
I WANT TO BE A PART OF ALL OF IT!
SO YOU CAN LEAN ON ME.
IT WAS LIKE THAT TIME.
DO YOU GET IT?
I GET IT! I GET IT!
AND NEXT TIME, I'LL REPORT RIGHT IN!
I WONDER IF HE *REALLY* UNDERSTANDS.

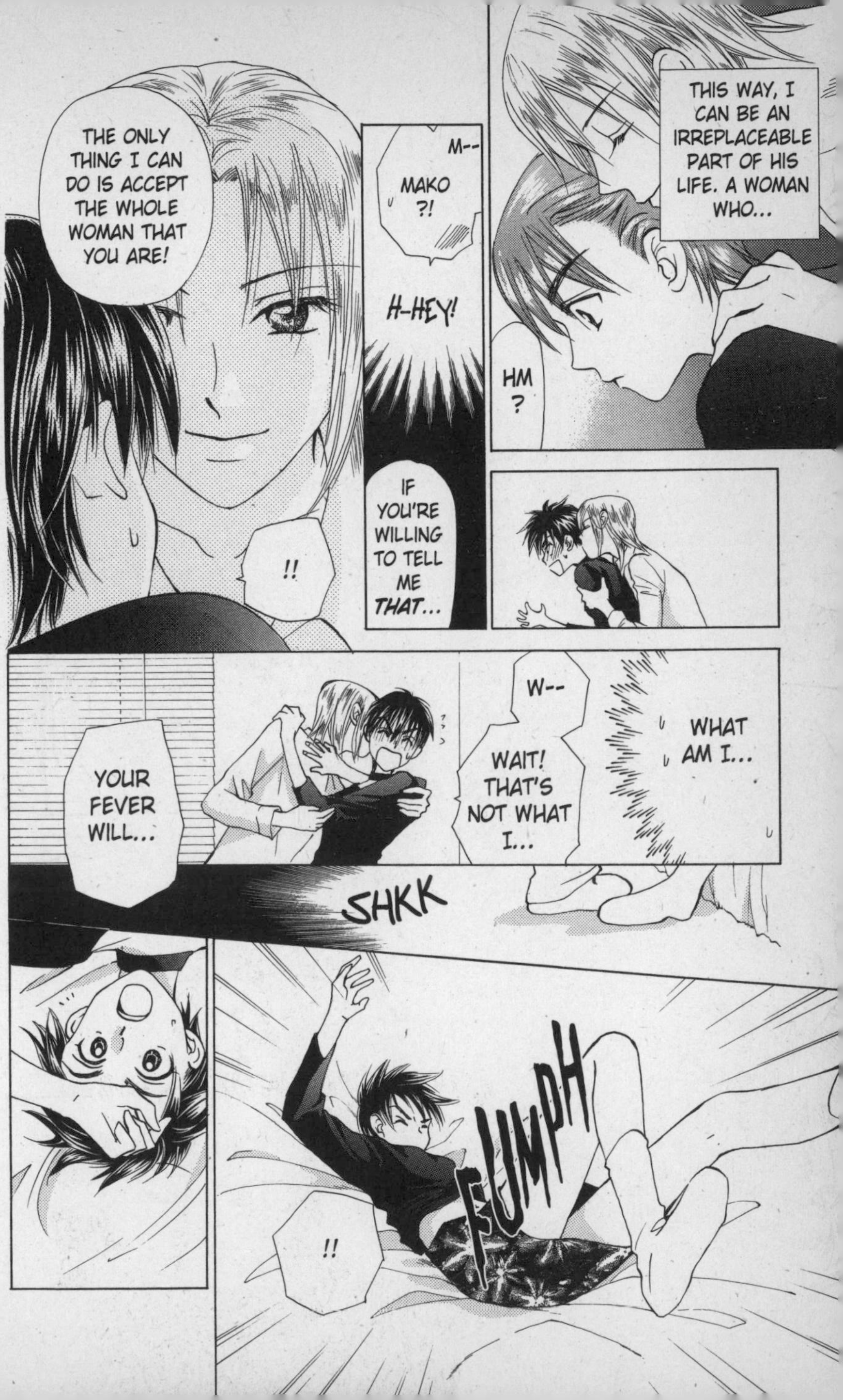
THIS WAY, I CAN BE AN IRREPLACEABLE PART OF HIS LIFE. A WOMAN WHO...
HM ?
M--
MAKO ?!
H-HEY!
IF YOU'RE WILLING TO TELL ME THAT...
THE ONLY THING I CAN DO IS ACCEPT THE WHOLE WOMAN THAT YOU ARE!
!!
WHAT AM I...
W--
WAIT! THAT'S NOT WHAT I...
YOUR FEVER WILL...
SHKK
FUMPH
!!

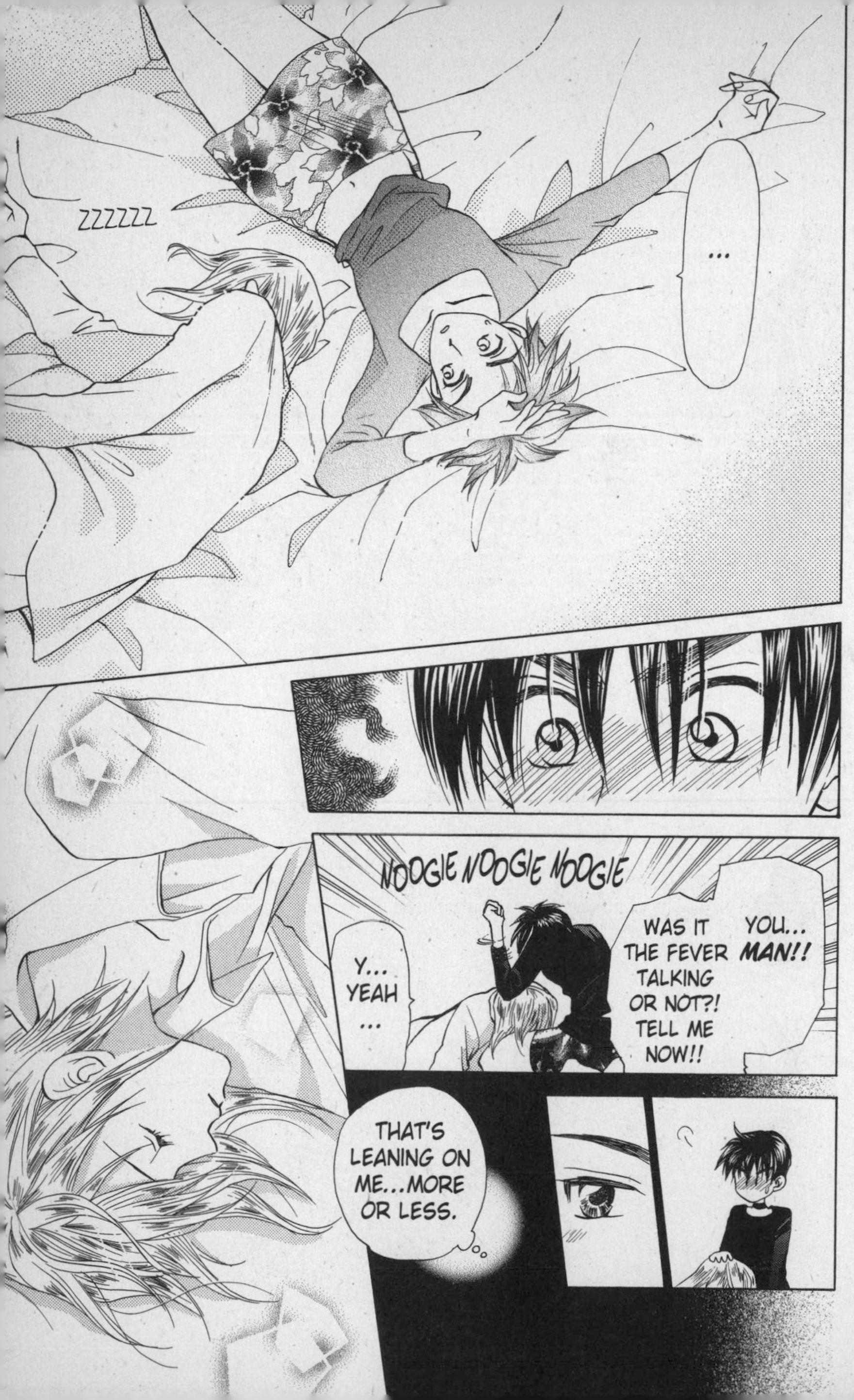
...
ZZZZZZ
YOU... MAN!!
WAS IT THE FEVER TALKING OR NOT?! TELL ME NOW!!
NOOGIE NOOGIE NOOGIE
Y... YEAH ...
THAT'S LEANING ON ME...MORE OR LESS.

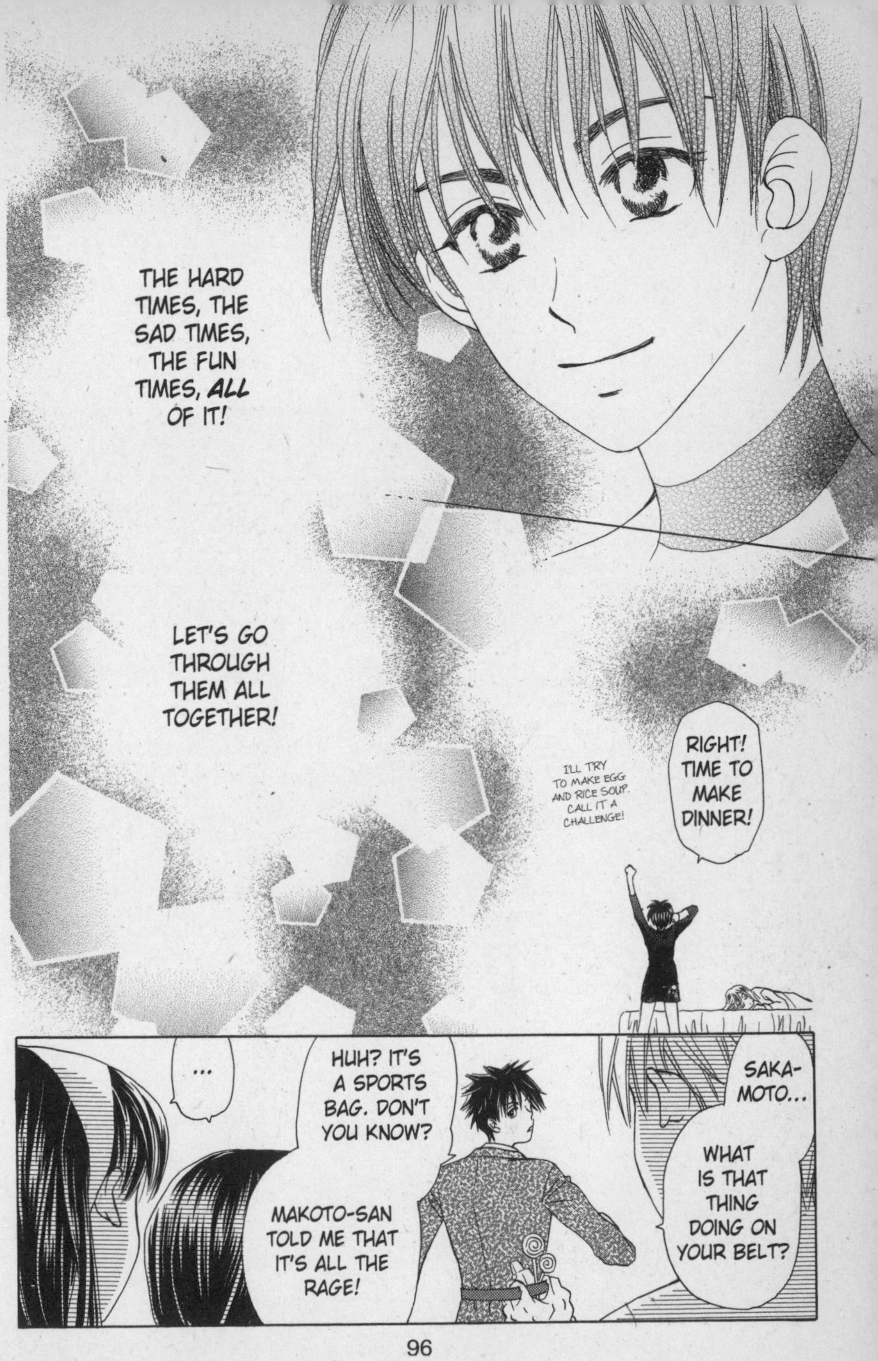
THE HARD TIMES, THE SAD TIMES, THE FUN TIMES, ALL OF IT!
LET'S GO THROUGH THEM ALL TOGETHER!
RIGHT! TIME TO MAKE DINNER!
I'LL TRY TO MAKE EGG AND RICE SOUP. CALL IT A CHALLENGE!
SAKA-MOTO...
WHAT IS THAT THING DOING ON YOUR BELT?
HUH? IT'S A SPORTS BAG. DON'T YOU KNOW?
MAKOTO-SAN TOLD ME THAT IT'S ALL THE RAGE!
...

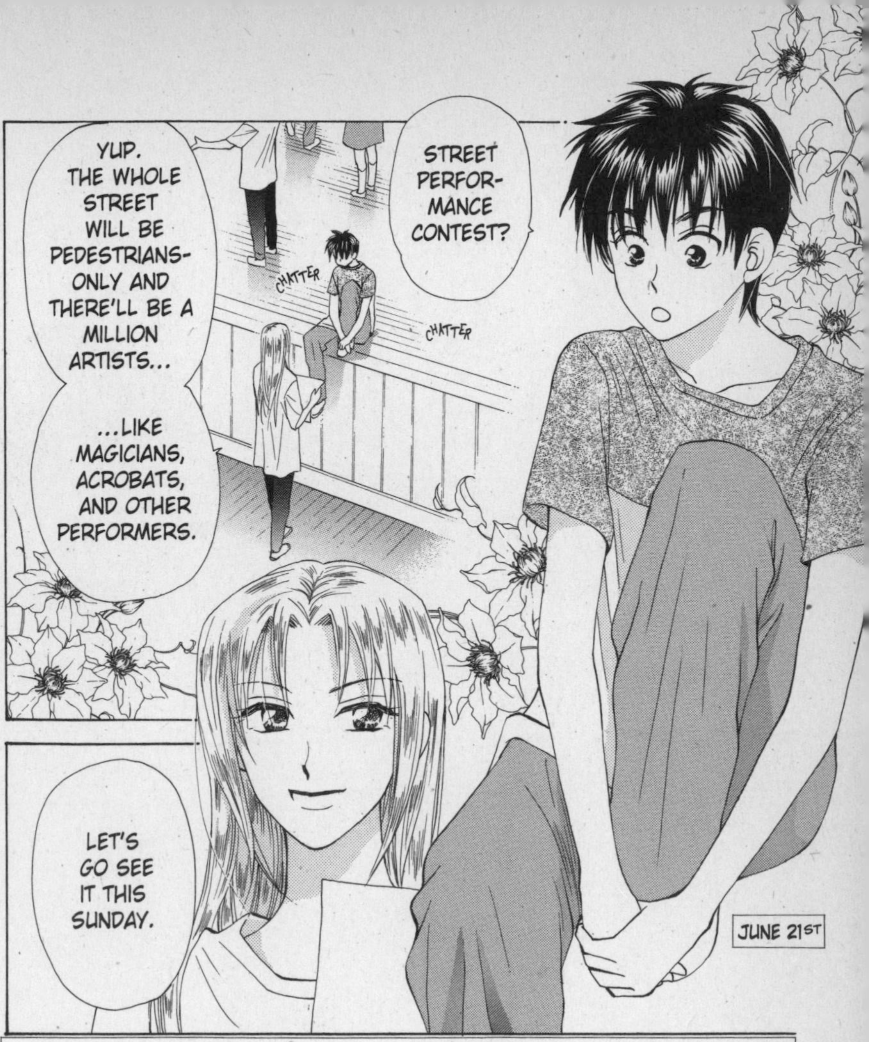
STREET PERFORMANCE CONTEST?
YUP. THE WHOLE STREET WILL BE PEDESTRIANS-ONLY AND THERE'LL BE A MILLION ARTISTS...
...LIKE MAGICIANS, ACROBATS, AND OTHER PERFORMERS.
CHATTER
CHATTER
JUNE 21ST
LET'S GO SEE IT THIS SUNDAY.

-Behind the Scenes Story- ④

This was the first time I drew a story where Ito and Makoto got separated. It was really hard to put together. I wasted a lot of time because it just wouldn't flow without them together... And I still feel it's a half-baked story. But I had fun drawing the scene about Makoto versus his father. I wish I could work more on it, but it was all I could do within the alloted space. I hope I'll have an opportunity to work on this challenging theme again.

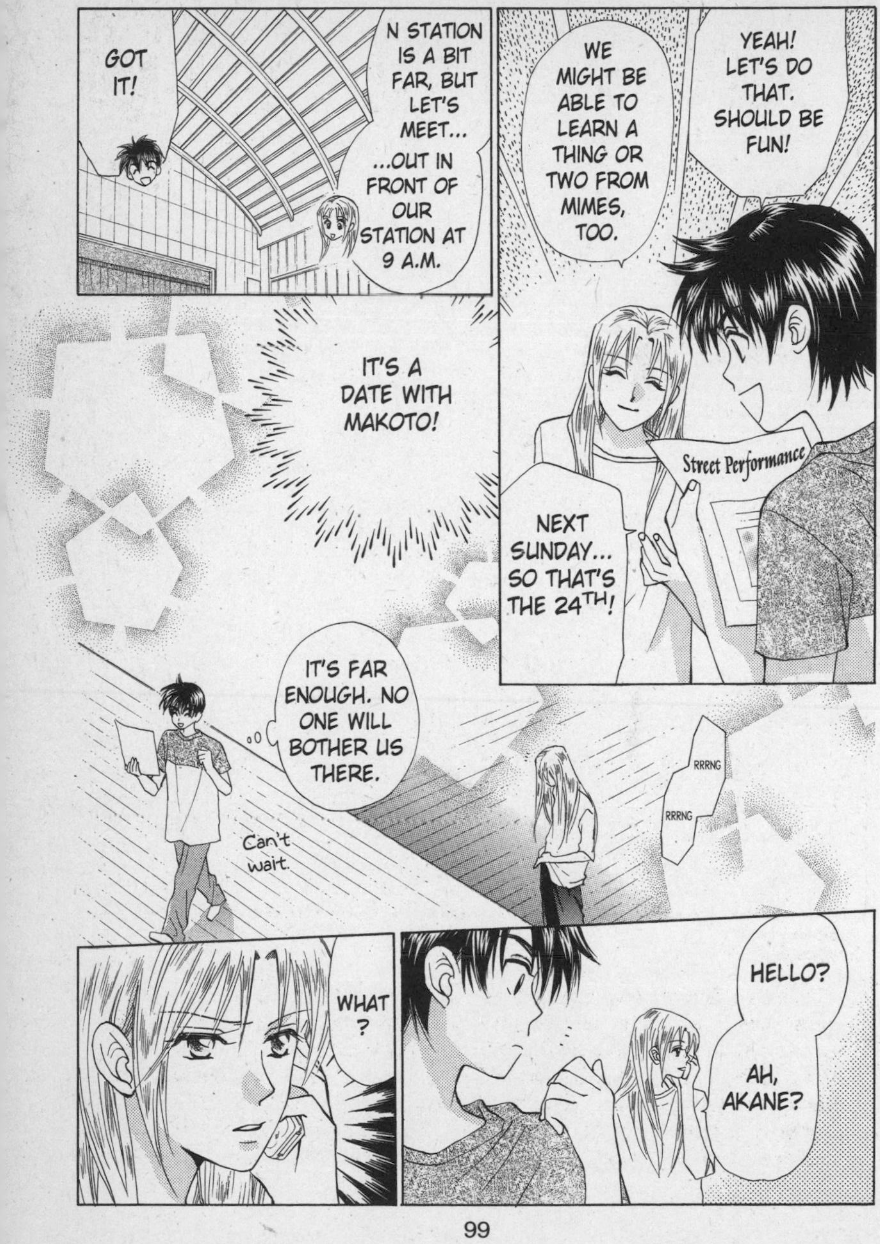
YEAH! LET'S DO THAT. SHOULD BE FUN!
WE MIGHT BE ABLE TO LEARN A THING OR TWO FROM MIMES, TOO.
Street Performance
NEXT SUNDAY... SO THAT'S THE 24TH!
N STATION IS A BIT FAR, BUT LET'S MEET...
...OUT IN FRONT OF OUR STATION AT 9 A.M.
GOT IT!
IT'S A DATE WITH MAKOTO!
IT'S FAR ENOUGH. NO ONE WILL BOTHER US THERE.
Can't wait.
RRRNG
RRRNG
HELLO?
AH, AKANE?
WHAT ?

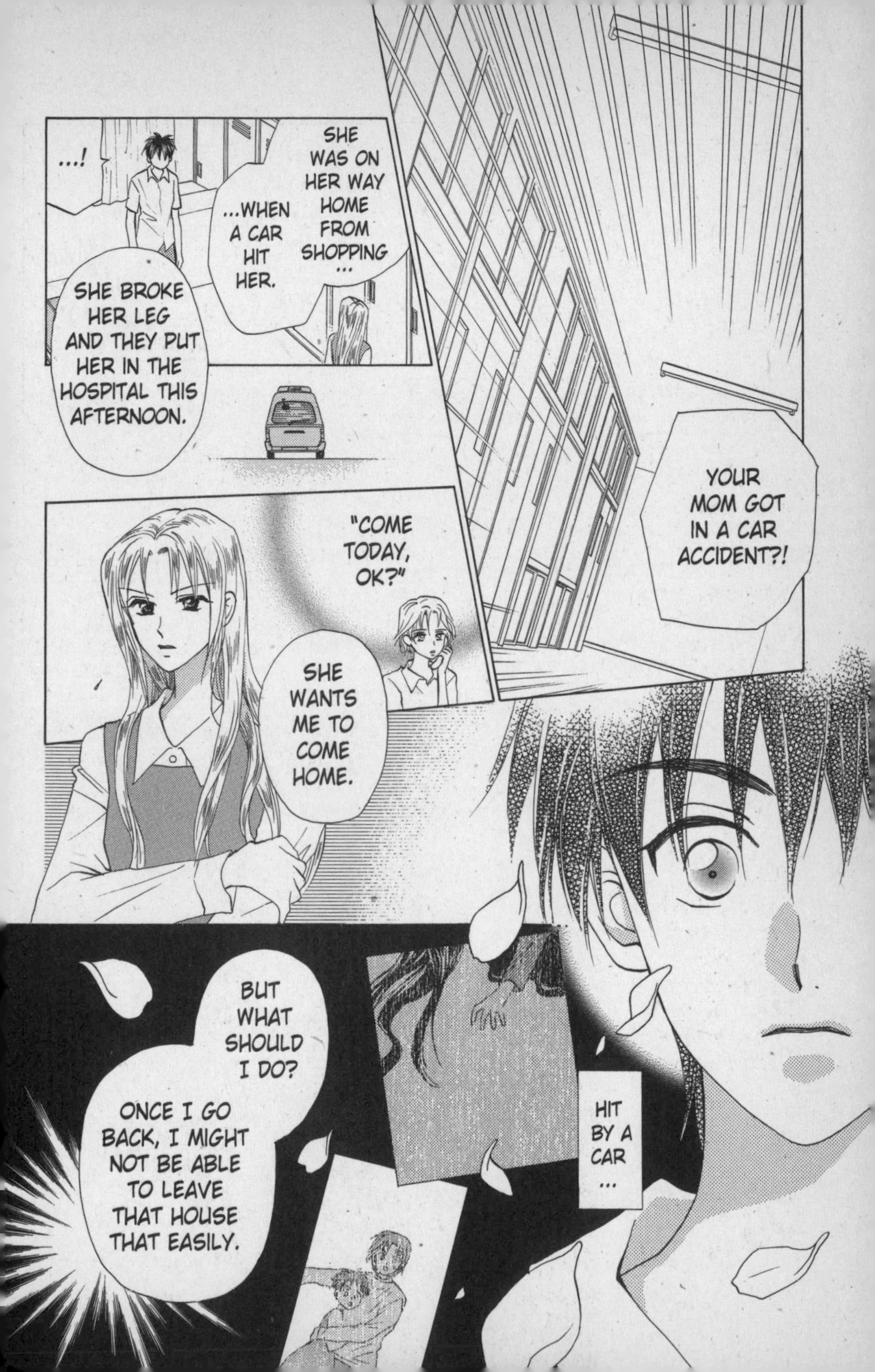
YOUR MOM GOT IN A CAR ACCIDENT?!
SHE WAS ON HER WAY HOME FROM SHOPPING...
...WHEN A CAR HIT HER.
...!
SHE BROKE HER LEG AND THEY PUT HER IN THE HOSPITAL THIS AFTERNOON.
"COME TODAY, OK?"
SHE WANTS ME TO COME HOME.
HIT BY A CAR...
BUT WHAT SHOULD I DO?
ONCE I GO BACK, I MIGHT NOT BE ABLE TO LEAVE THAT HOUSE THAT EASILY.

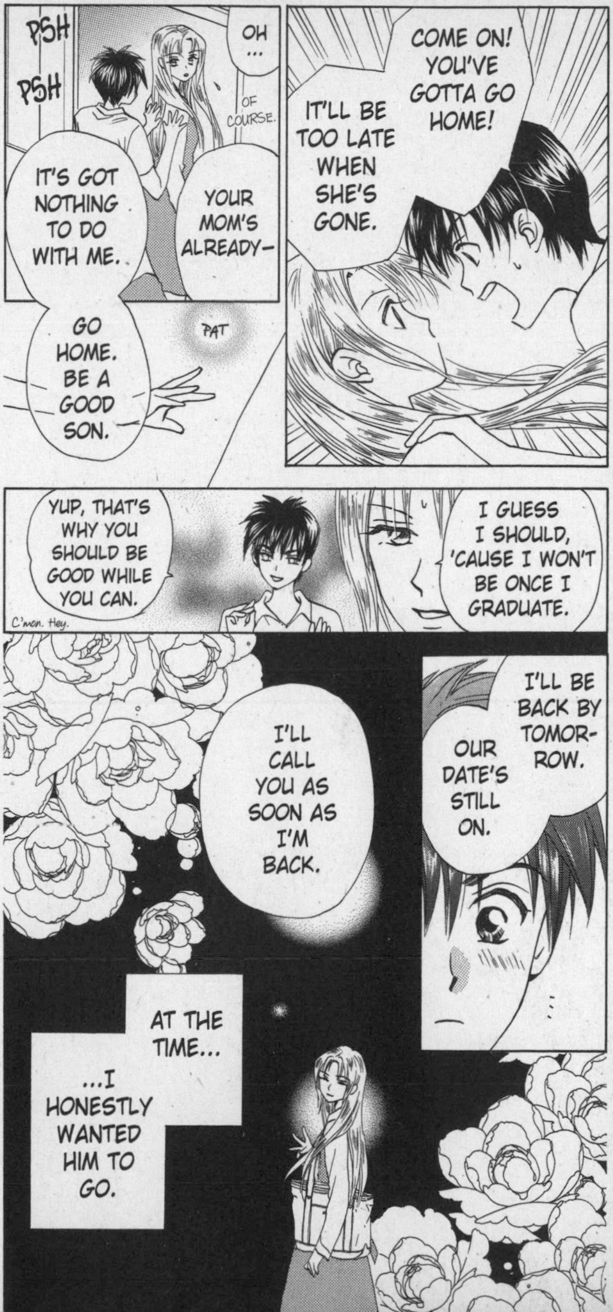
COME ON! YOU'VE GOTTA GO HOME!
IT'LL BE TOO LATE WHEN SHE'S GONE.
OH ...
OF COURSE.
PSH
PSH
YOUR MOM'S ALREADY—
IT'S GOT NOTHING TO DO WITH ME.
GO HOME. BE A GOOD SON.
PAT
I GUESS I SHOULD, 'CAUSE I WON'T BE ONCE I GRADUATE.
YUP, THAT'S WHY YOU SHOULD BE GOOD WHILE YOU CAN.
C'mon. Hey.
I'LL BE BACK BY TOMORROW.
OUR DATE'S STILL ON.
I'LL CALL YOU AS SOON AS I'M BACK.
AT THE TIME...
...I HONESTLY WANTED HIM TO GO.

Continued (from page 75)

- Tsugumi Nomura (Yuko Mizutani)
- Misaki Ichikawa (Satsuki Yukino)
- Nobuko Kataoka (Machiko Toyoshima)
- Yoshiro Ozaki (Atsushi Kisaichi)

A lot of great voice actors and actresses! The CD turned out awesome, I tell you ♥ I'm grateful to everyone who worked on it...and to all the readers who requested a copy! Thank you so much for your submissions. ♥♥ I'll do my best to keep up the good work.

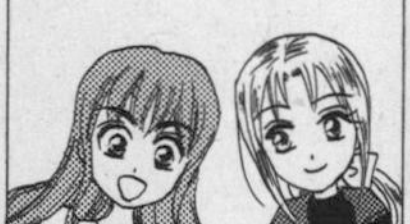

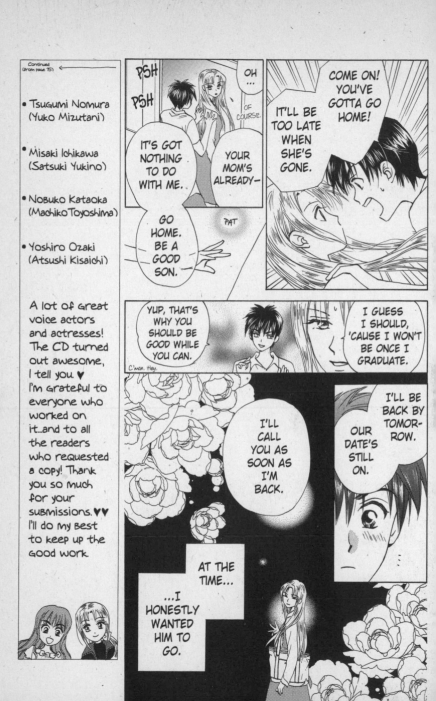

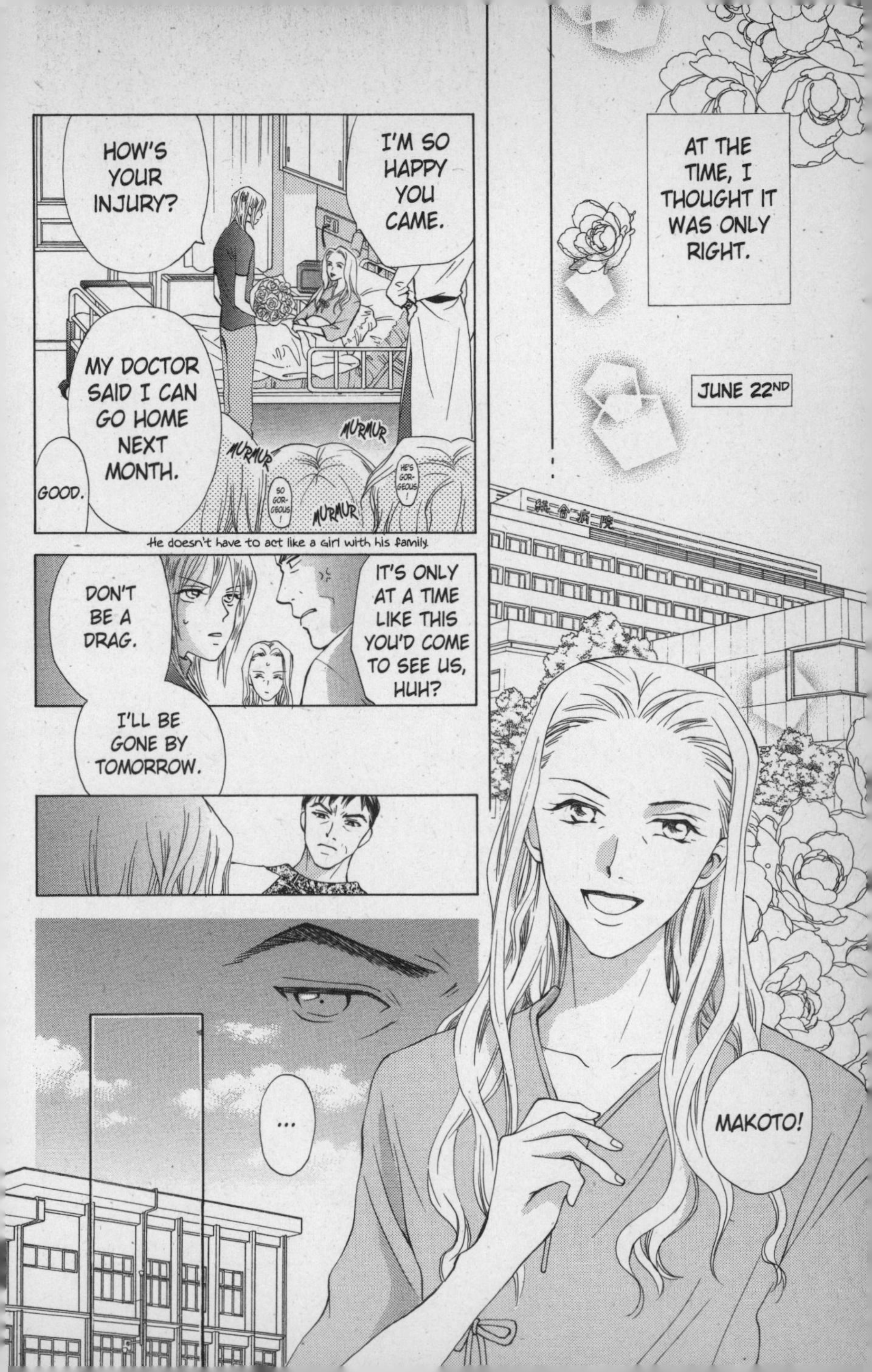
AT THE TIME, I THOUGHT IT WAS ONLY RIGHT.
JUNE 22ND
MAKOTO!
I'M SO HAPPY YOU CAME.
HOW'S YOUR INJURY?
MY DOCTOR SAID I CAN GO HOME NEXT MONTH.
GOOD.
MURMUR
HE'S GORGEOUS!
MURMUR
SO GORGEOUS!
MURMUR
He doesn't have to act like a girl with his family.
IT'S ONLY AT A TIME LIKE THIS YOU'D COME TO SEE US, HUH?
DON'T BE A DRAG.
I'LL BE GONE BY TOMORROW.
...

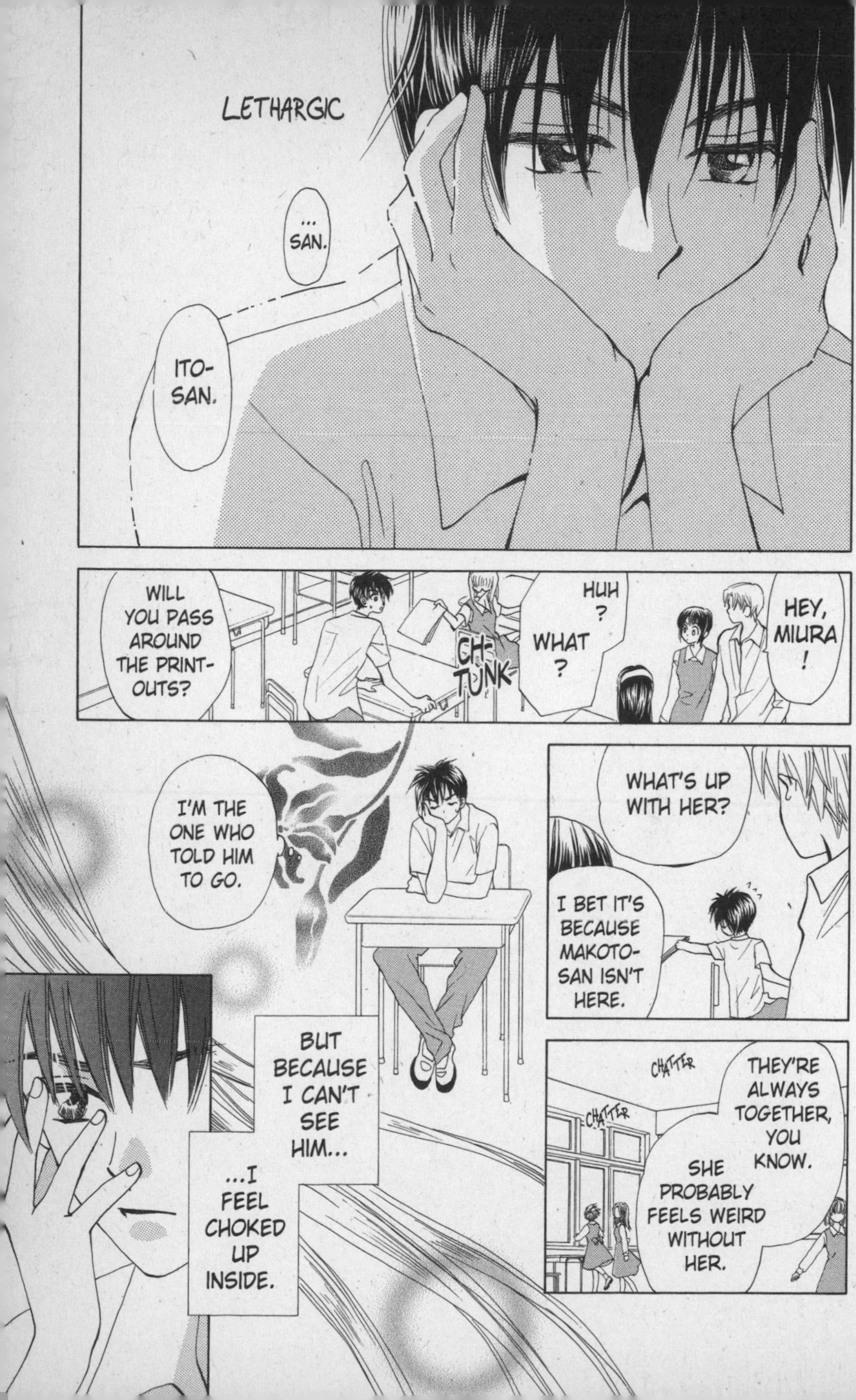
LETHARGIC
... SAN.
ITO-SAN.
HEY, MIURA!
HUH? WHAT?
CH-TUNK
WILL YOU PASS AROUND THE PRINT-OUTS?
WHAT'S UP WITH HER?
I BET IT'S BECAUSE MAKOTO-SAN ISN'T HERE.
CHATTER
CHATTER
THEY'RE ALWAYS TOGETHER, YOU KNOW.
SHE PROBABLY FEELS WEIRD WITHOUT HER.
I'M THE ONE WHO TOLD HIM TO GO.
BUT BECAUSE I CAN'T SEE HIM...
...I FEEL CHOKED UP INSIDE.

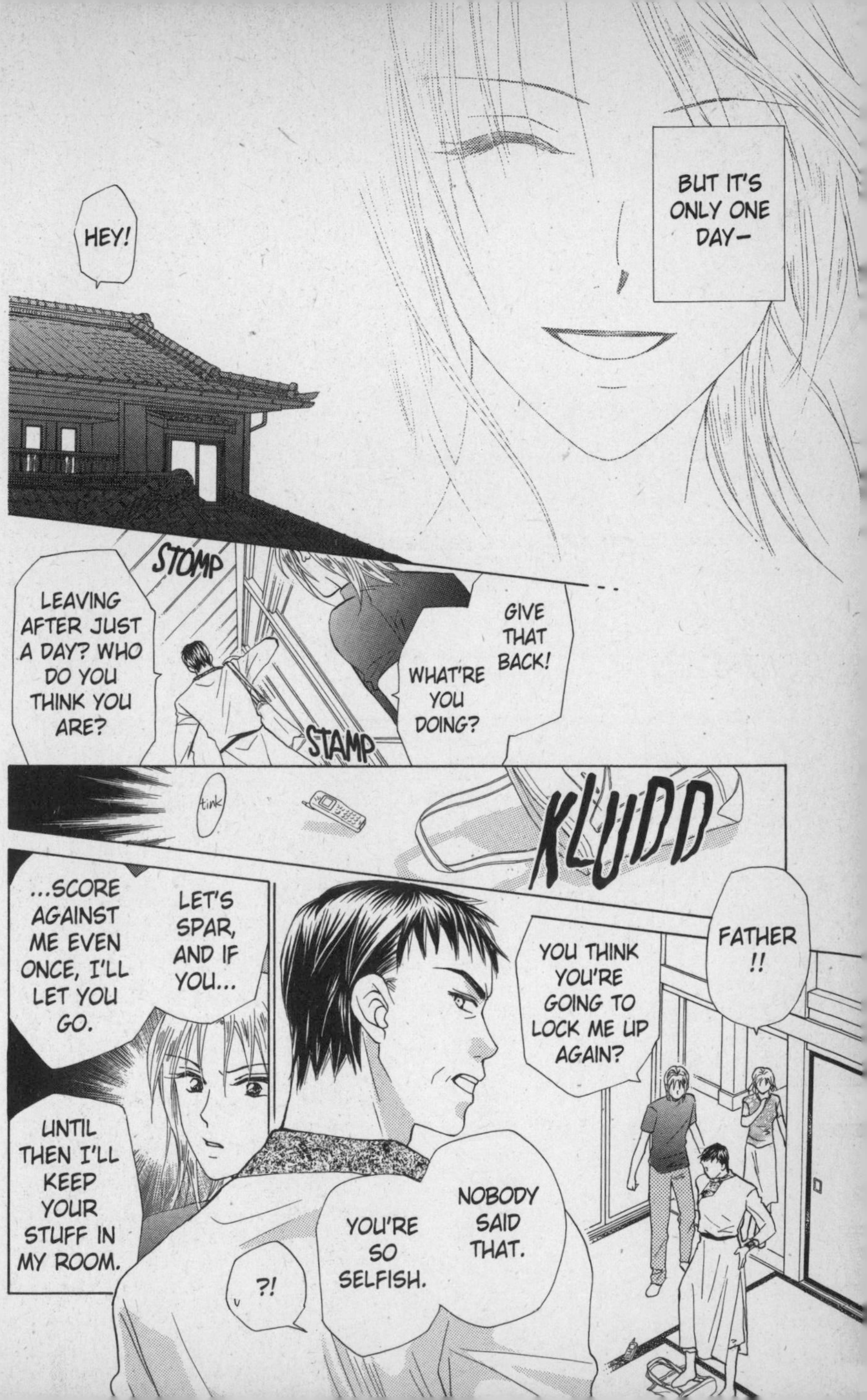
BUT IT'S ONLY ONE DAY—
HEY!
GIVE THAT BACK!
WHAT'RE YOU DOING?
STOMP
LEAVING AFTER JUST A DAY? WHO DO YOU THINK YOU ARE?
STAMP
KLUDD
tink
FATHER !!
YOU THINK YOU'RE GOING TO LOCK ME UP AGAIN?
LET'S SPAR, AND IF YOU...
...SCORE AGAINST ME EVEN ONCE, I'LL LET YOU GO.
NOBODY SAID THAT.
YOU'RE SO SELFISH.
UNTIL THEN I'LL KEEP YOUR STUFF IN MY ROOM.
?!

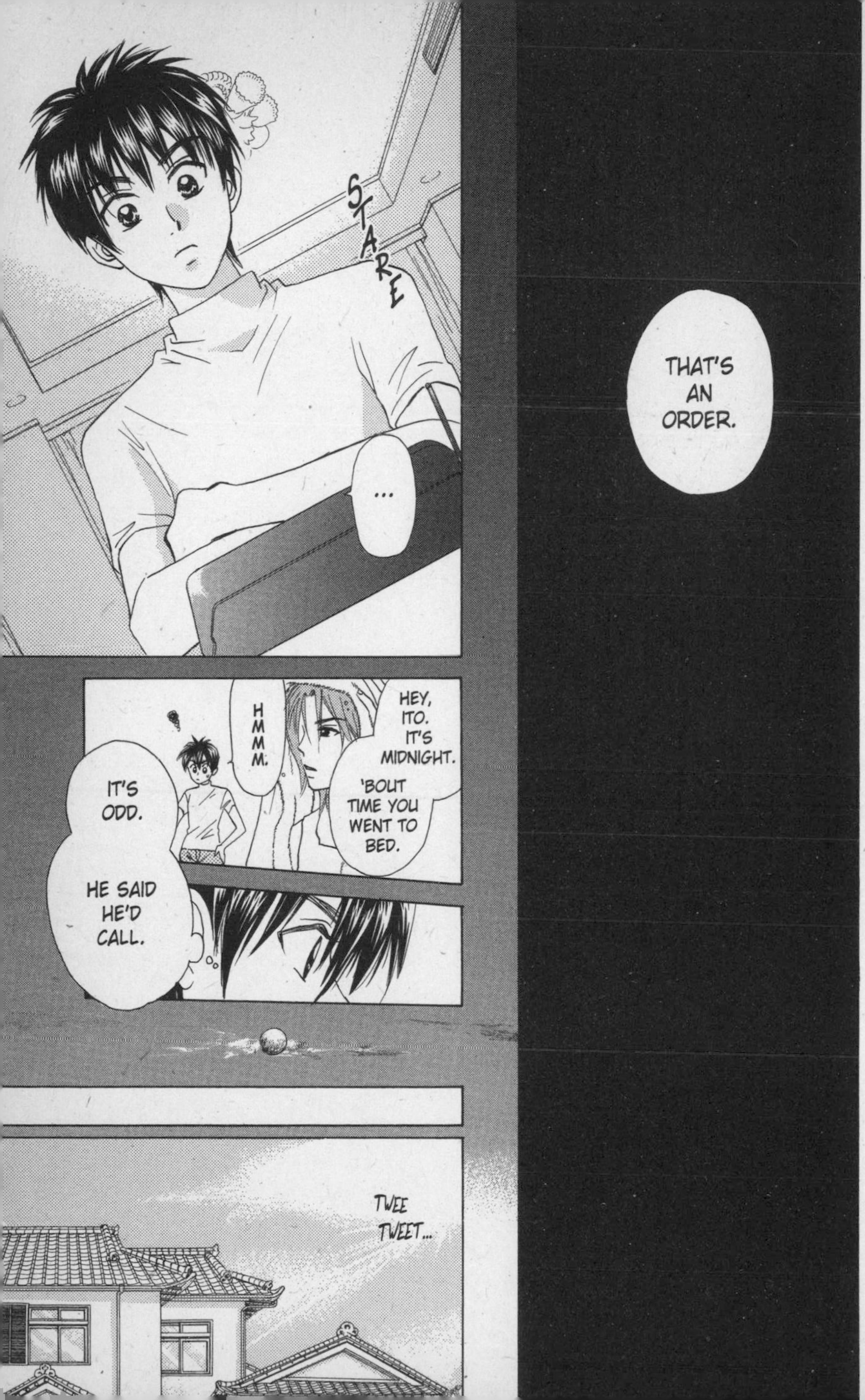
THAT'S AN ORDER.
STARE
...
HEY, ITO. IT'S MIDNIGHT.
'BOUT TIME YOU WENT TO BED.
HMMM.
IT'S ODD.
HE SAID HE'D CALL.
TWEE TWEET...

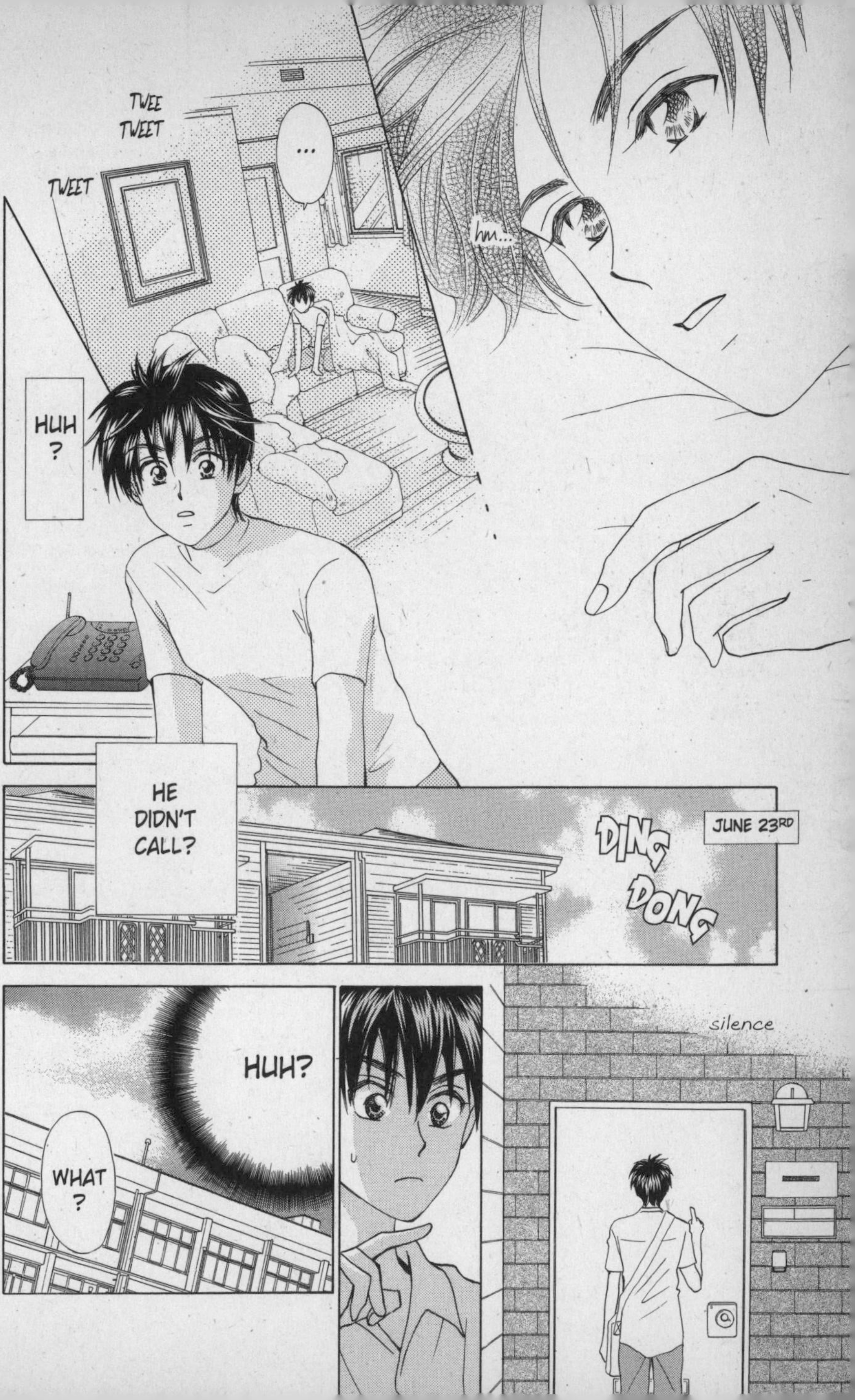
hm...
TWEE TWEET
TWEET
...
HUH ?
HE DIDN'T CALL?
JUNE 23RD
DING DONG
silence
HUH?
WHAT ?

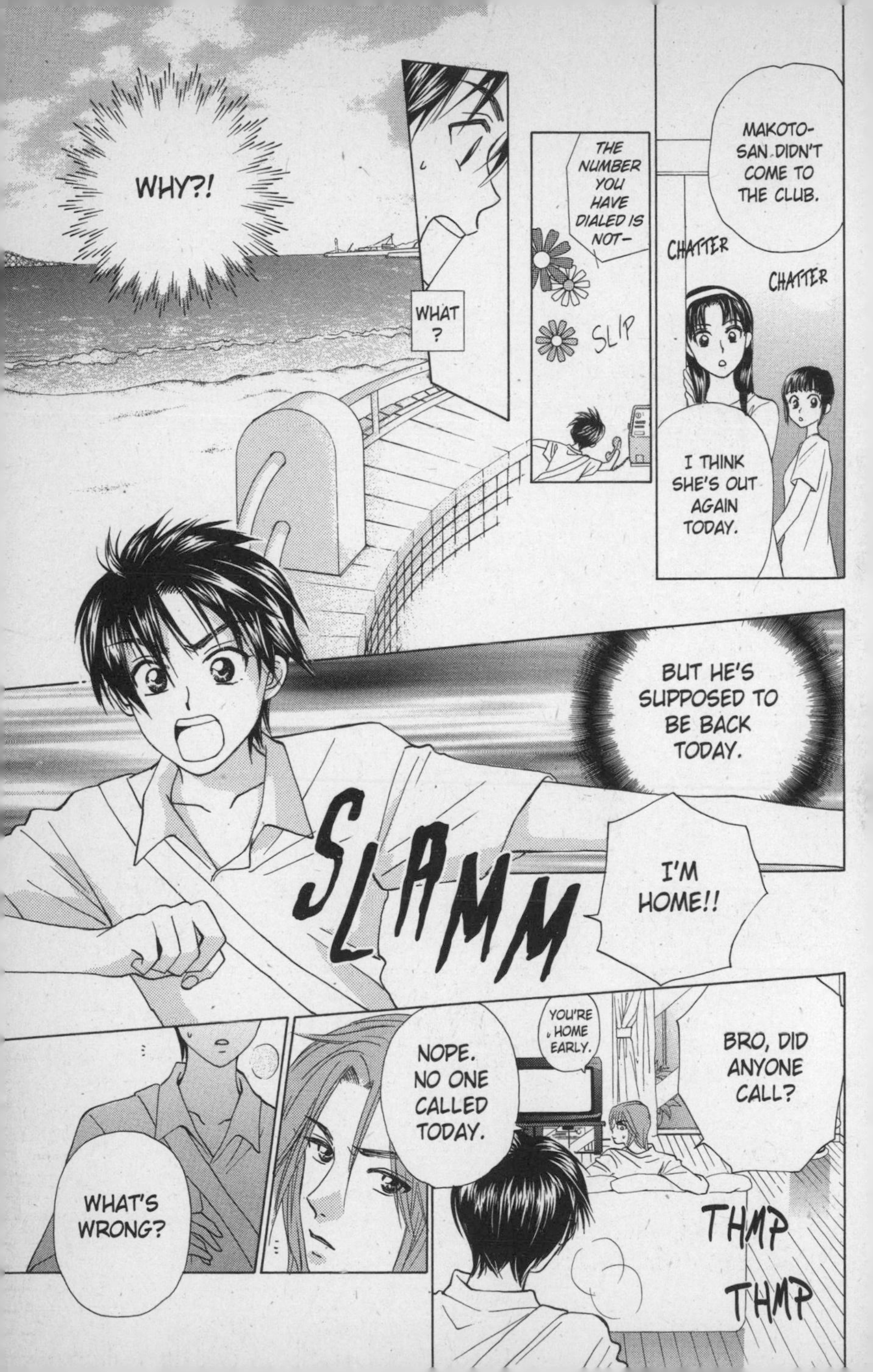
MAKOTO-SAN DIDN'T COME TO THE CLUB.
CHATTER
CHATTER
I THINK SHE'S OUT AGAIN TODAY.
THE NUMBER YOU HAVE DIALED IS NOT—
SLIP
WHAT ?
WHY?!
BUT HE'S SUPPOSED TO BE BACK TODAY.
SLAMM
I'M HOME!!
BRO, DID ANYONE CALL?
YOU'RE HOME EARLY.
THMP
THMP
NOPE. NO ONE CALLED TODAY.
WHAT'S WRONG?

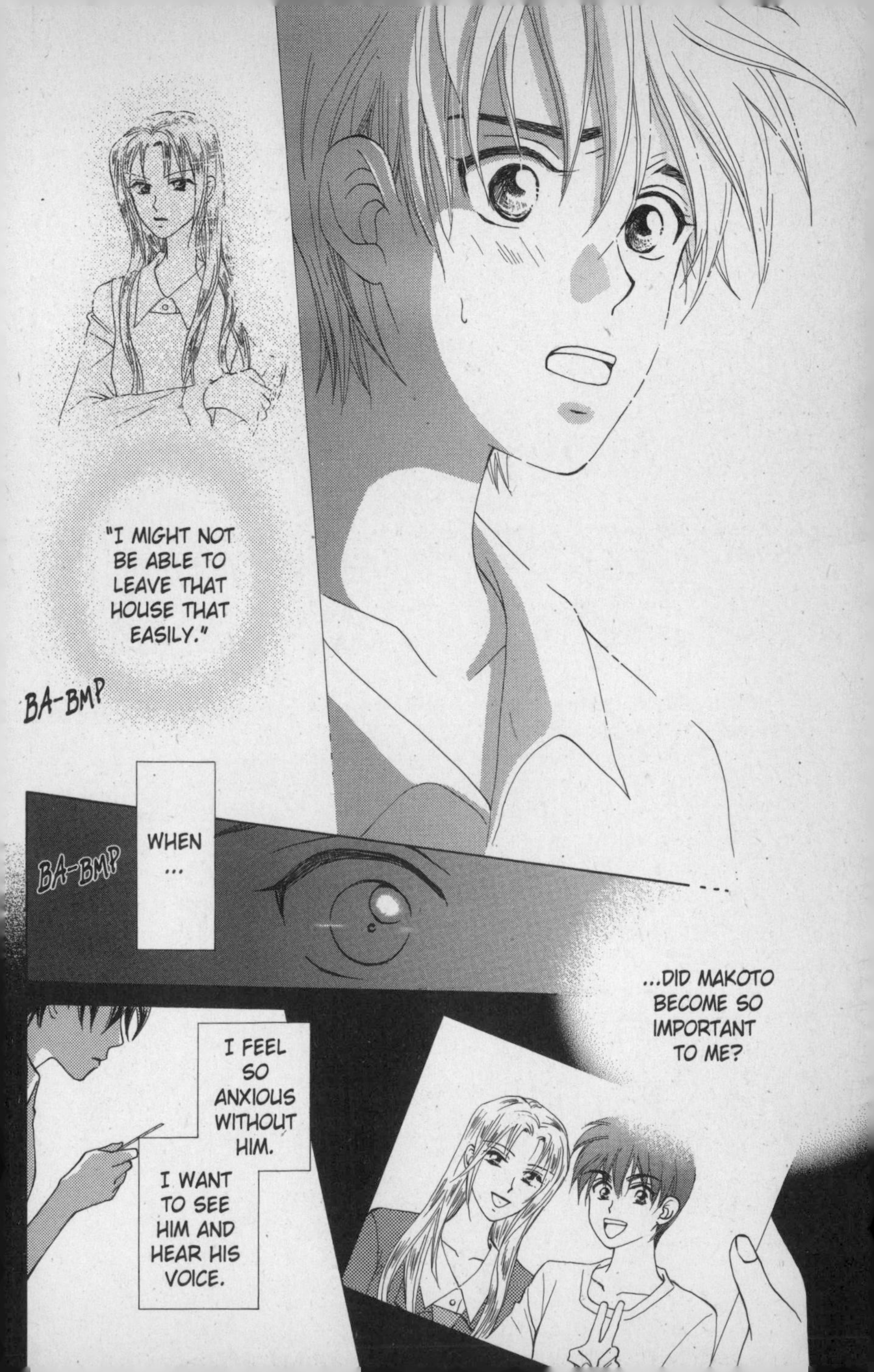
"I MIGHT NOT BE ABLE TO LEAVE THAT HOUSE THAT EASILY."
BA-BMP
WHEN ...
BA-BMP
...DID MAKOTO BECOME SO IMPORTANT TO ME?
I FEEL SO ANXIOUS WITHOUT HIM.
I WANT TO SEE HIM AND HEAR HIS VOICE.

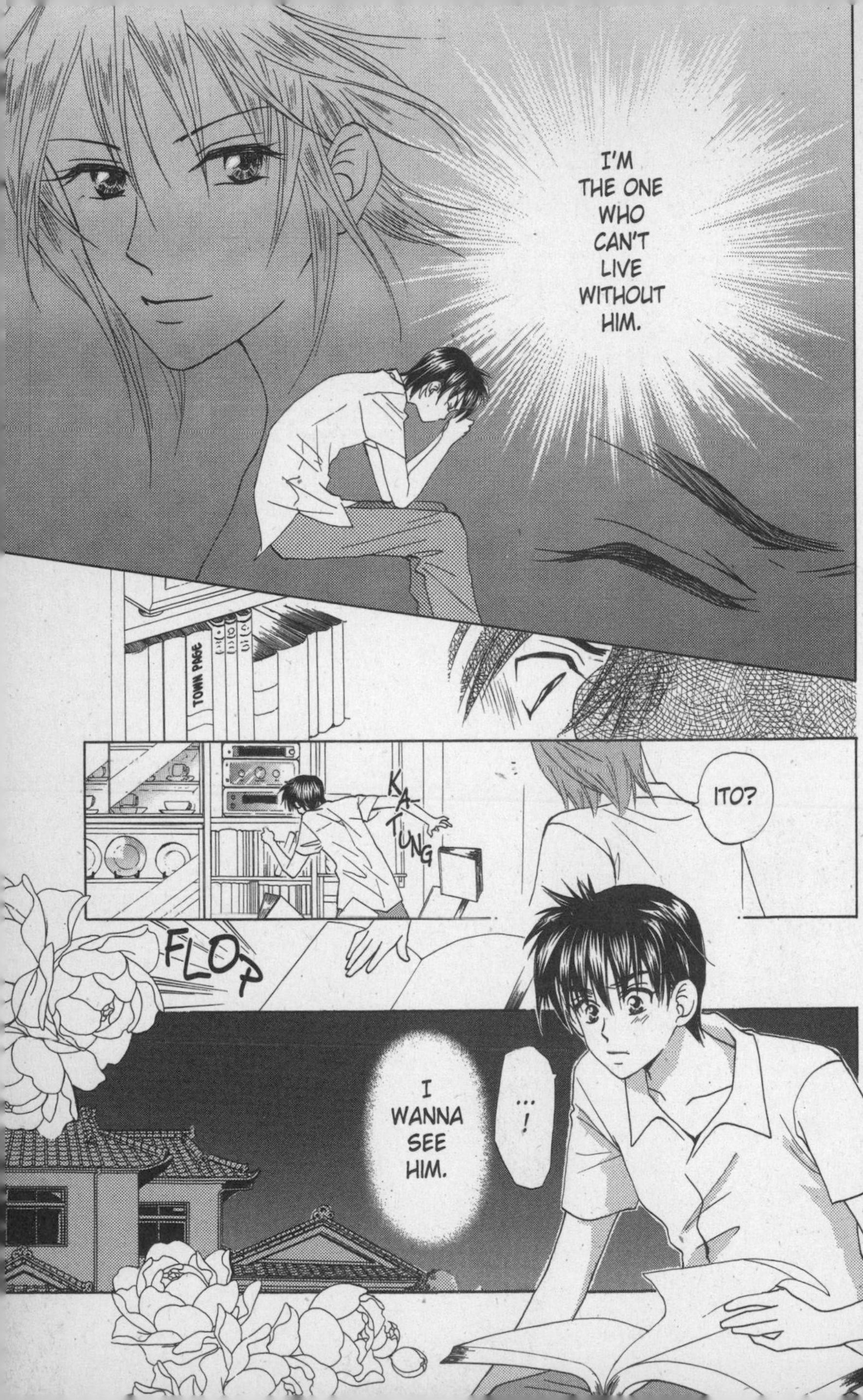
I'M THE ONE WHO CAN'T LIVE WITHOUT HIM.
TOWN PAGE
ITO?
KA-TUNG
FLOP
...!
I WANNA SEE HIM.

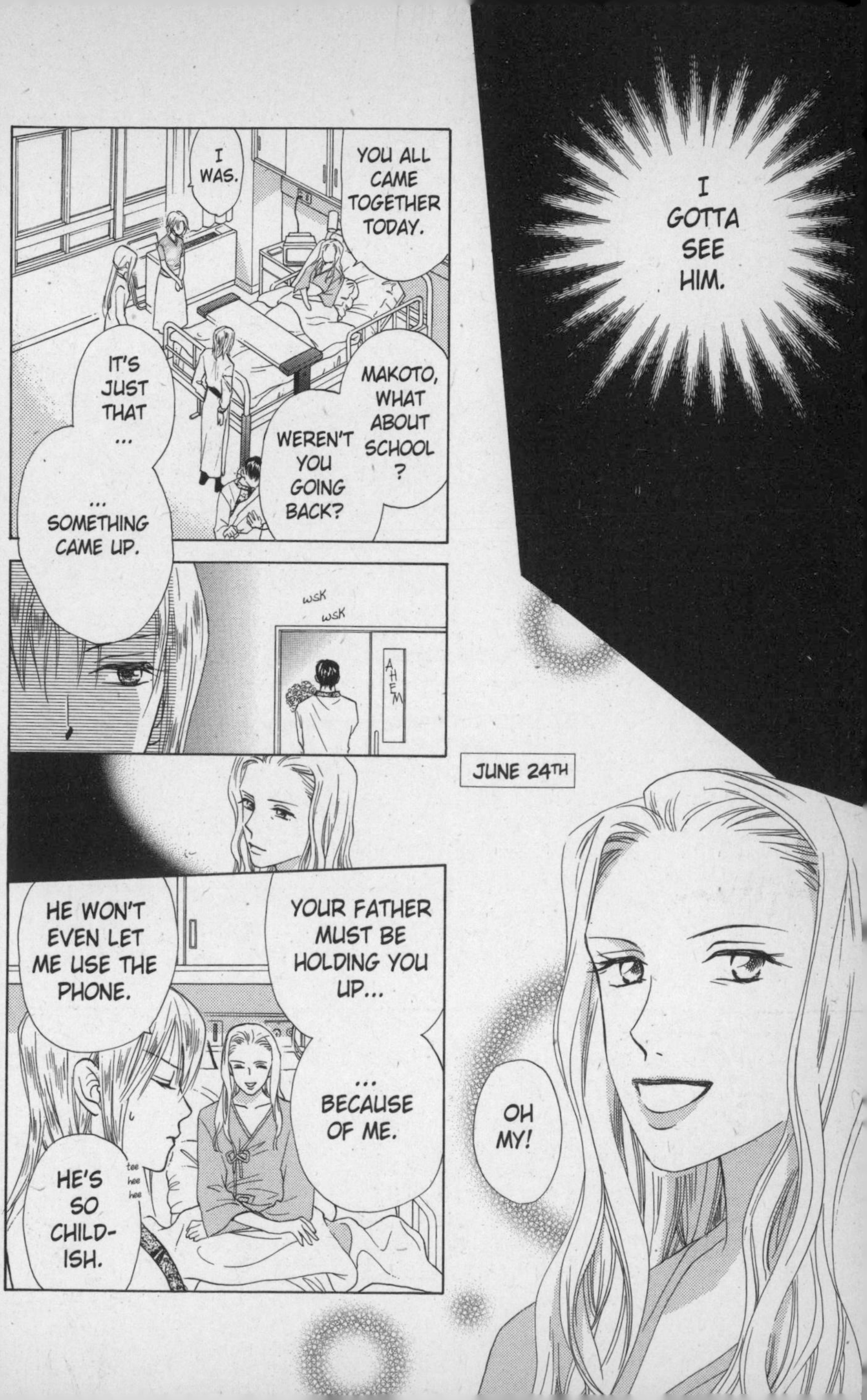
I GOTTA SEE HIM.
JUNE 24TH
OH MY!
YOU ALL CAME TOGETHER TODAY.
I WAS.
MAKOTO, WHAT ABOUT SCHOOL?
WEREN'T YOU GOING BACK?
IT'S JUST THAT ...
... SOMETHING CAME UP.
wsk wsk
AHEM
YOUR FATHER MUST BE HOLDING YOU UP...
... BECAUSE OF ME.
HE WON'T EVEN LET ME USE THE PHONE.
tee hee hee
HE'S SO CHILD-ISH.

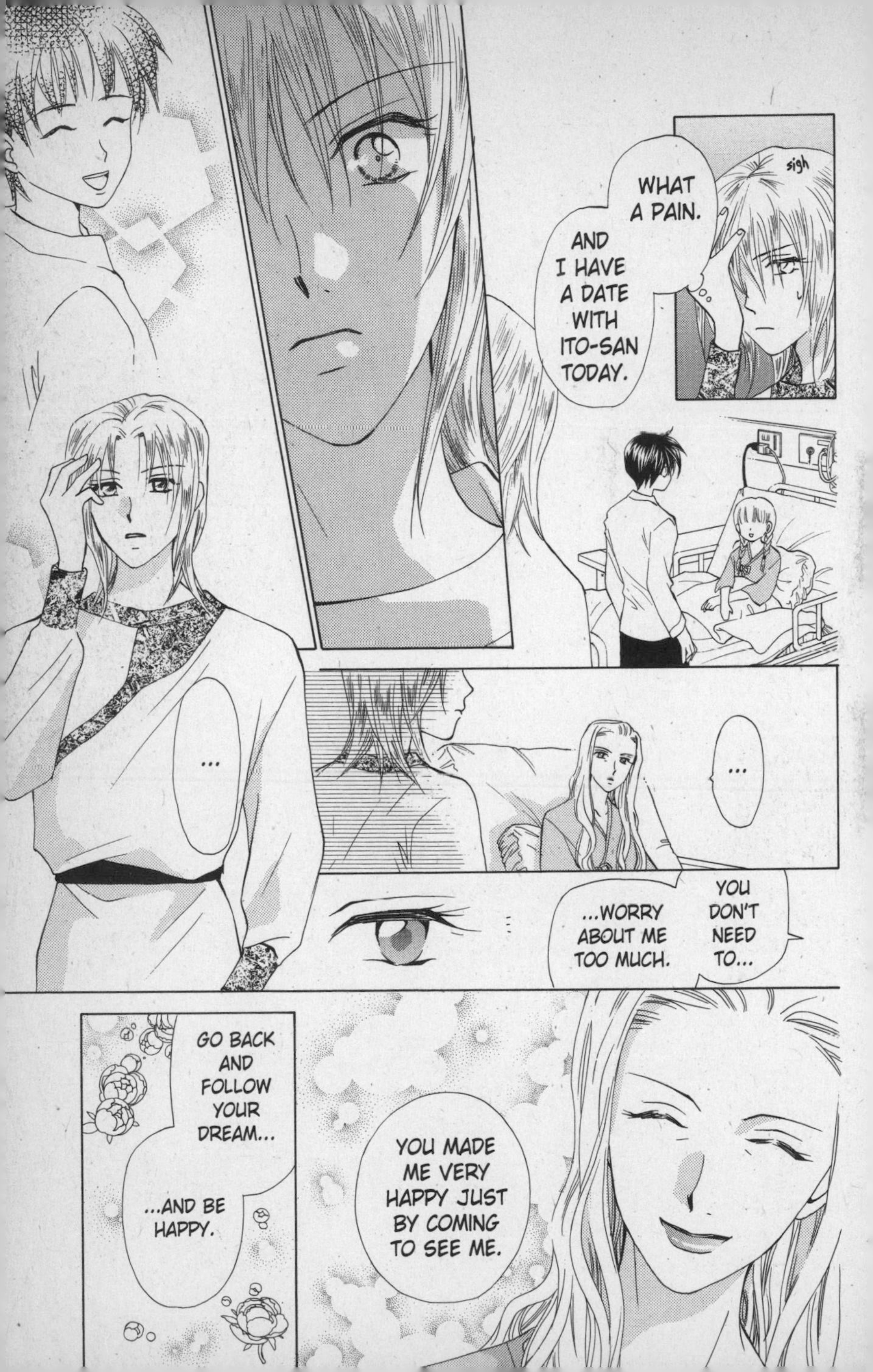
WHAT A PAIN.
AND I HAVE A DATE WITH ITO-SAN TODAY.
sigh
...
YOU DON'T NEED TO...
...WORRY ABOUT ME TOO MUCH.
...
YOU MADE ME VERY HAPPY JUST BY COMING TO SEE ME.
GO BACK AND FOLLOW YOUR DREAM...
...AND BE HAPPY.

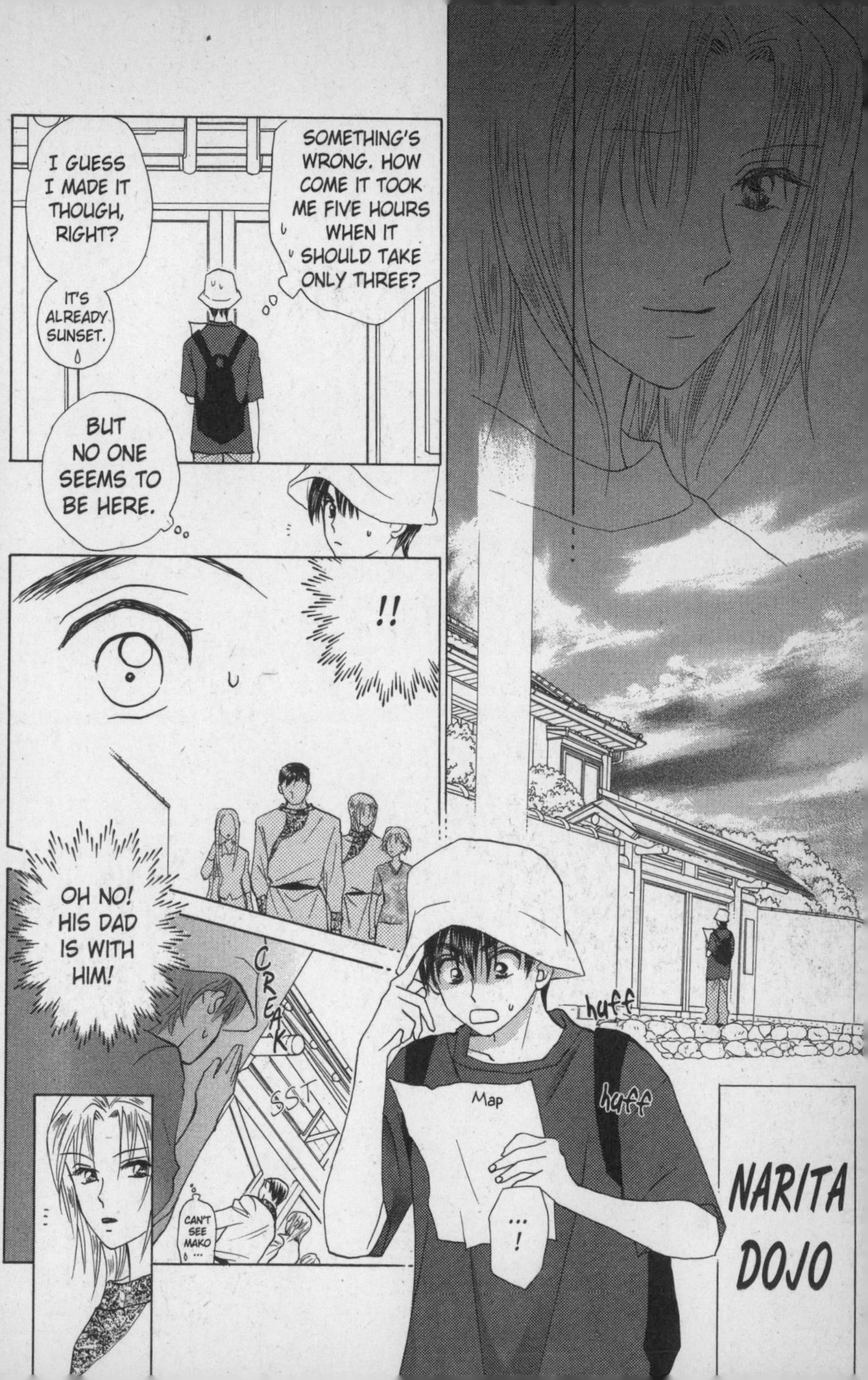
NARITA DOJO
huff
huff
Map
...!
SOMETHING'S WRONG. HOW COME IT TOOK ME FIVE HOURS WHEN IT SHOULD TAKE ONLY THREE?
I GUESS I MADE IT THOUGH, RIGHT?
IT'S ALREADY SUNSET.
BUT NO ONE SEEMS TO BE HERE.
!!
OH NO! HIS DAD IS WITH HIM!
CREAK
SST
...
CAN'T SEE MAKO ...

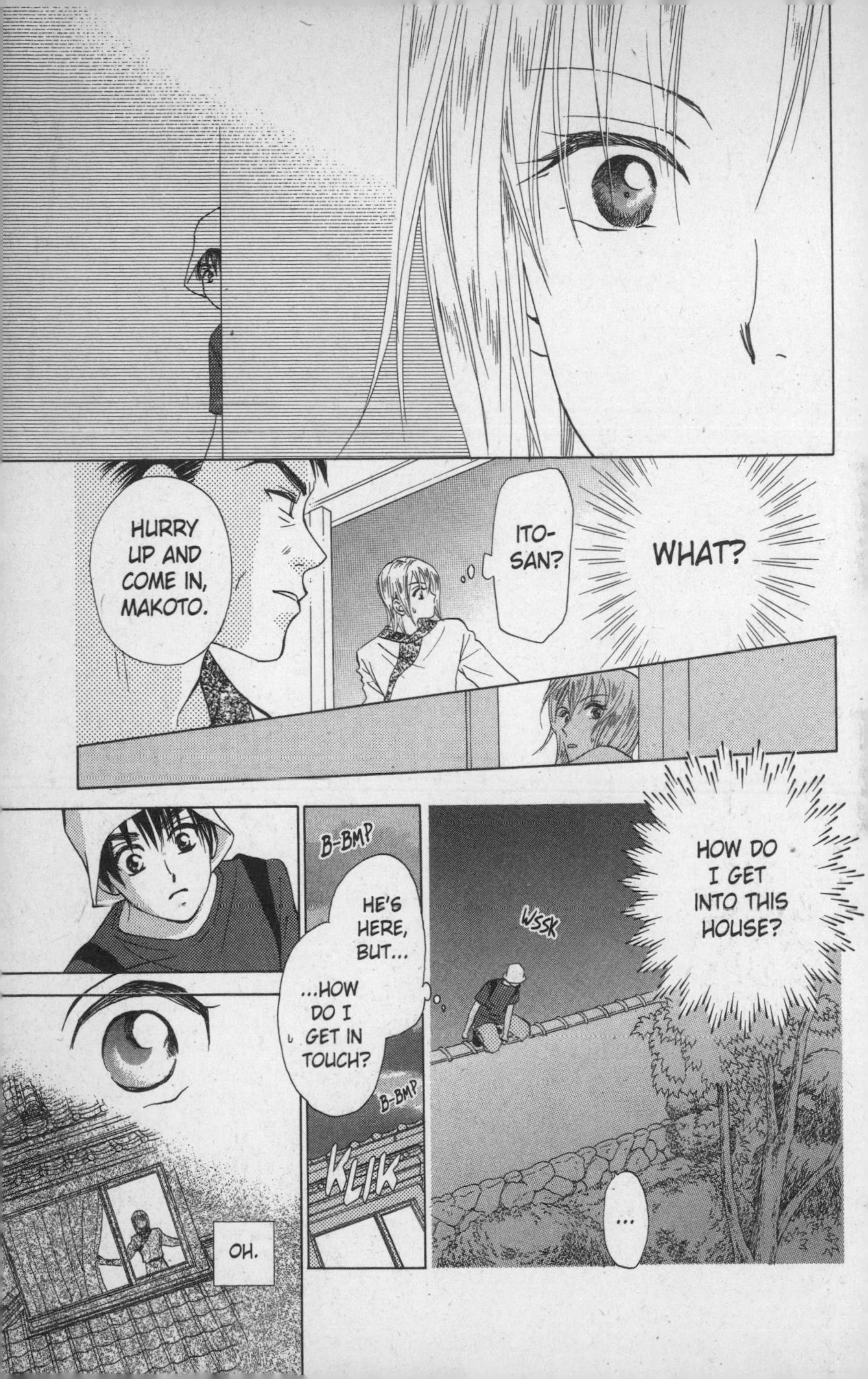
ITO-SAN?
HURRY UP AND COME IN, MAKOTO.
WHAT?
HOW DO I GET INTO THIS HOUSE?
WSSK
...
B-BMP
HE'S HERE, BUT...
...HOW DO I GET IN TOUCH?
B-BMP
KLIK
OH.

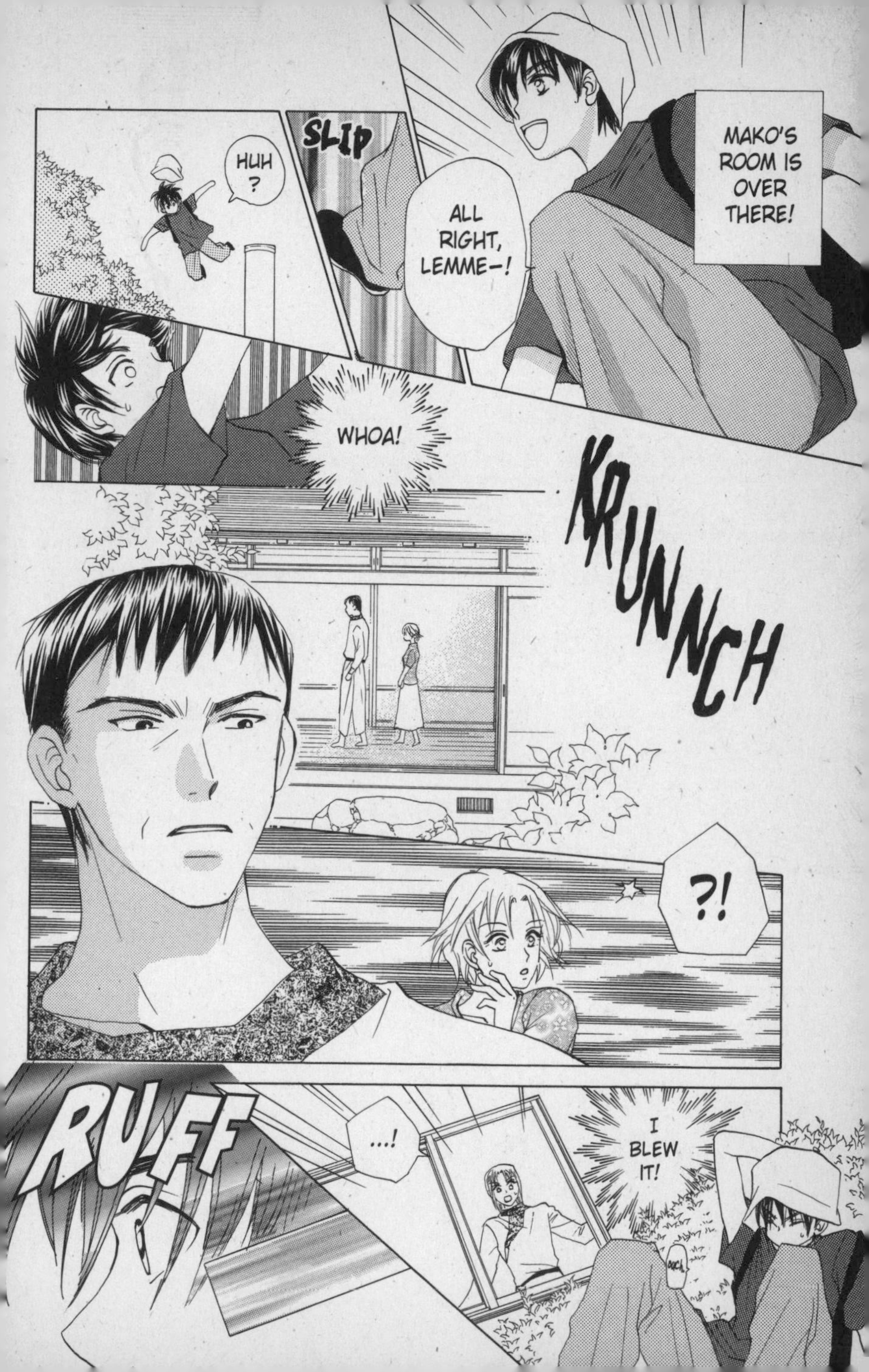
MAKO'S ROOM IS OVER THERE!
ALL RIGHT, LEMME--!
SLIP
HUH?
WHOA!
KRUNNCH
?!
I BLEW IT!
OUCH
...!
RUFF

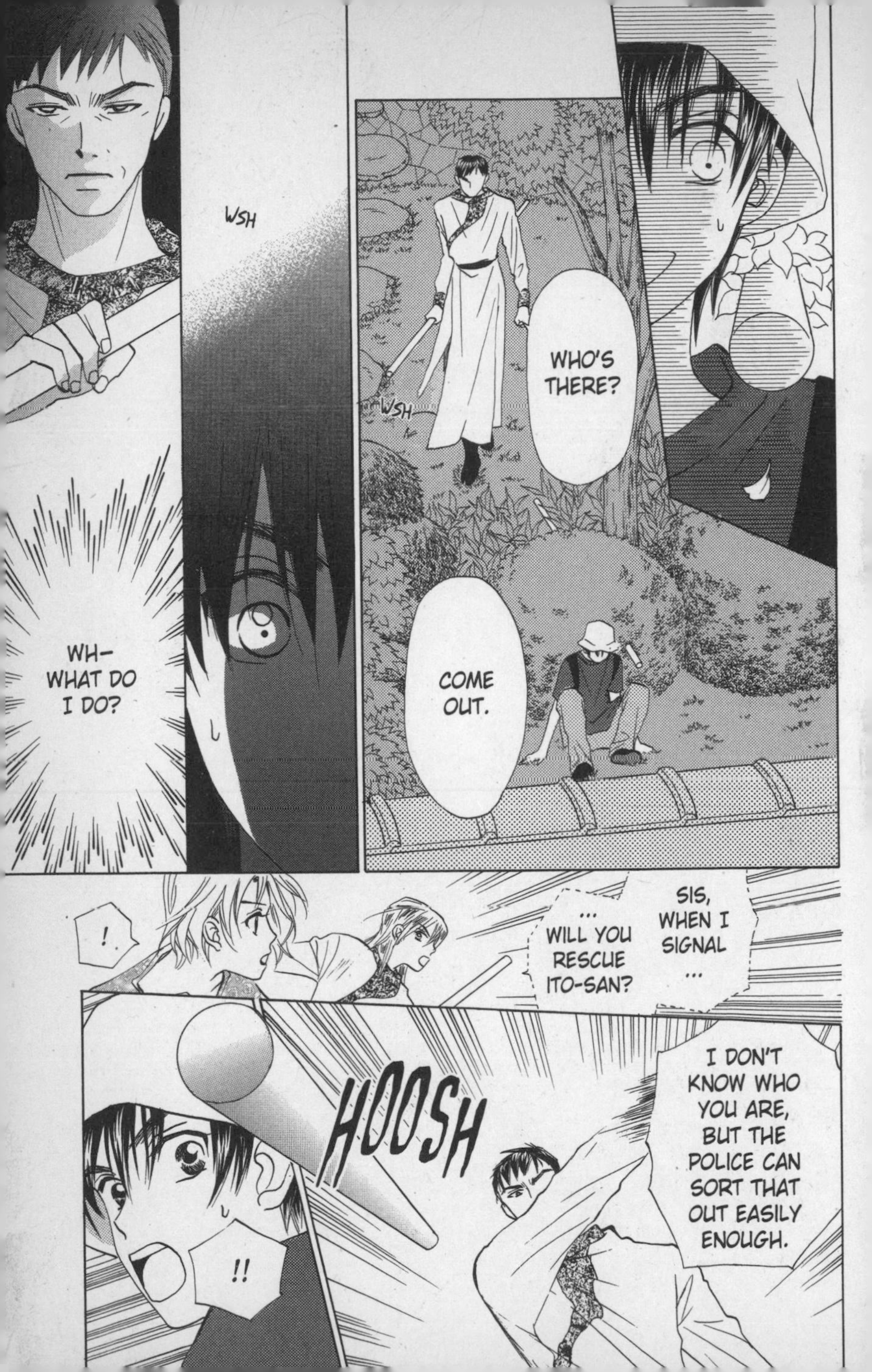
WHO'S THERE?
WSH
COME OUT.
WSH
WH- WHAT DO I DO?
SIS, WHEN I SIGNAL ...
... WILL YOU RESCUE ITO-SAN?
!
I DON'T KNOW WHO YOU ARE, BUT THE POLICE CAN SORT THAT OUT EASILY ENOUGH.
HOOSH
!!

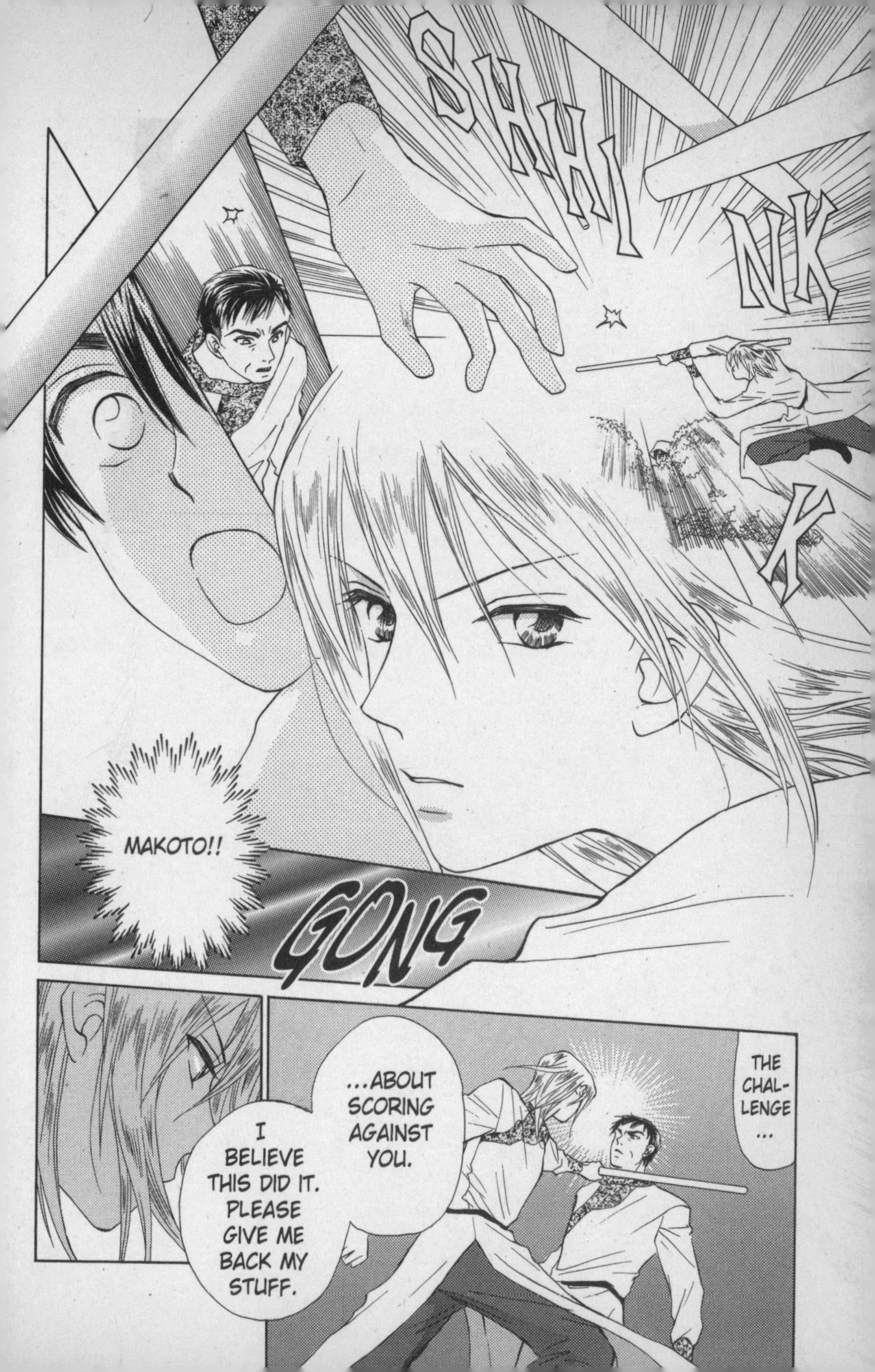
SHHI
NK
K
MAKOTO!!
GONG
THE CHAL-LENGE...
...ABOUT SCORING AGAINST YOU.
I BELIEVE THIS DID IT. PLEASE GIVE ME BACK MY STUFF.

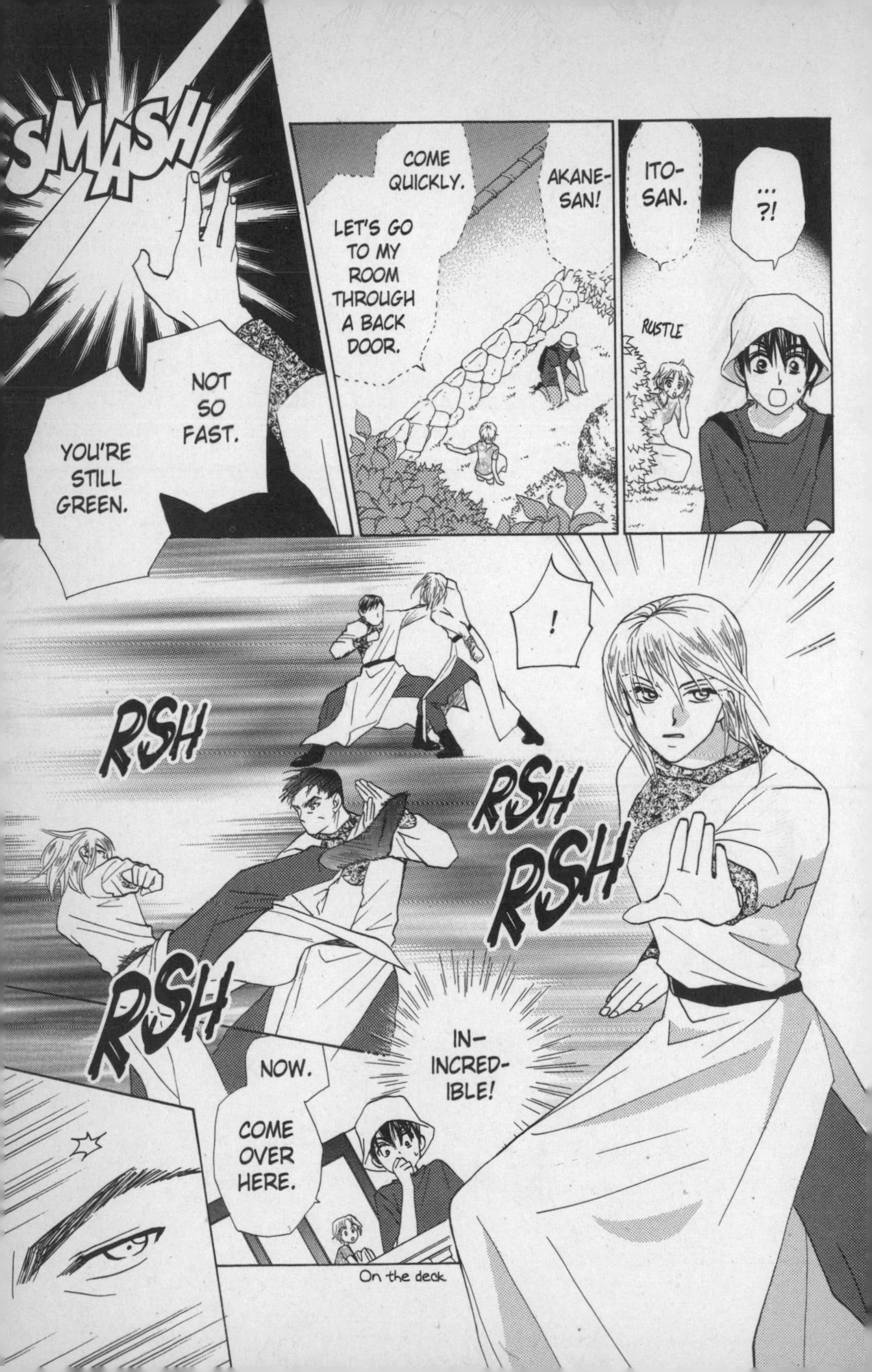
...?!
ITO-SAN.
RUSTLE
AKANE-SAN!
COME QUICKLY.
LET'S GO TO MY ROOM THROUGH A BACK DOOR.
SMASH
NOT SO FAST.
YOU'RE STILL GREEN.
!
RSH
RSH
RSH
RSH
IN-INCREDIBLE!
NOW.
COME OVER HERE.
On the deck

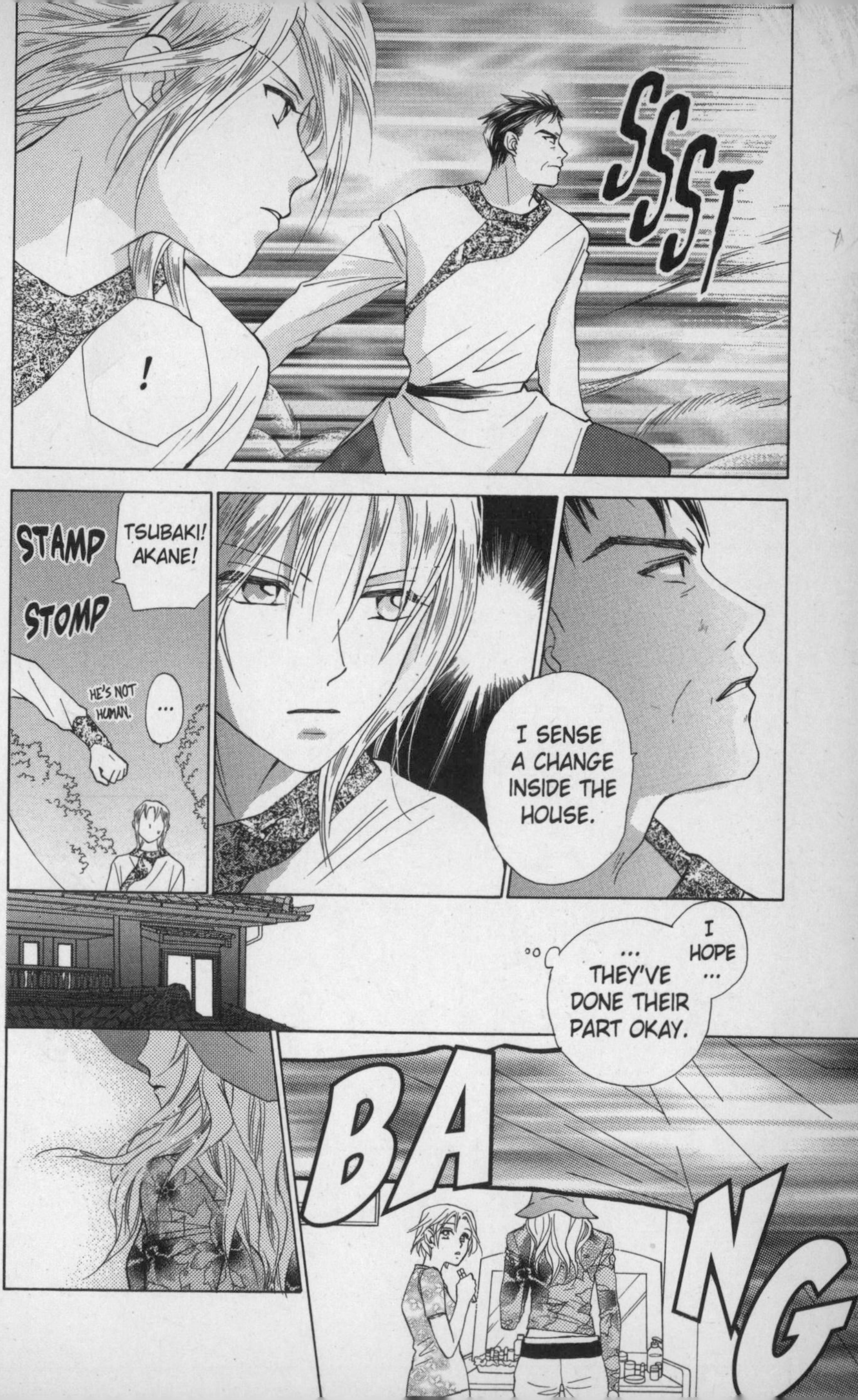
SSST
!
I SENSE A CHANGE INSIDE THE HOUSE.
TSUBAKI! AKANE!
STAMP
STOMP
...
HE'S NOT HUMAN.
I HOPE ... ... THEY'VE DONE THEIR PART OKAY.
BANG

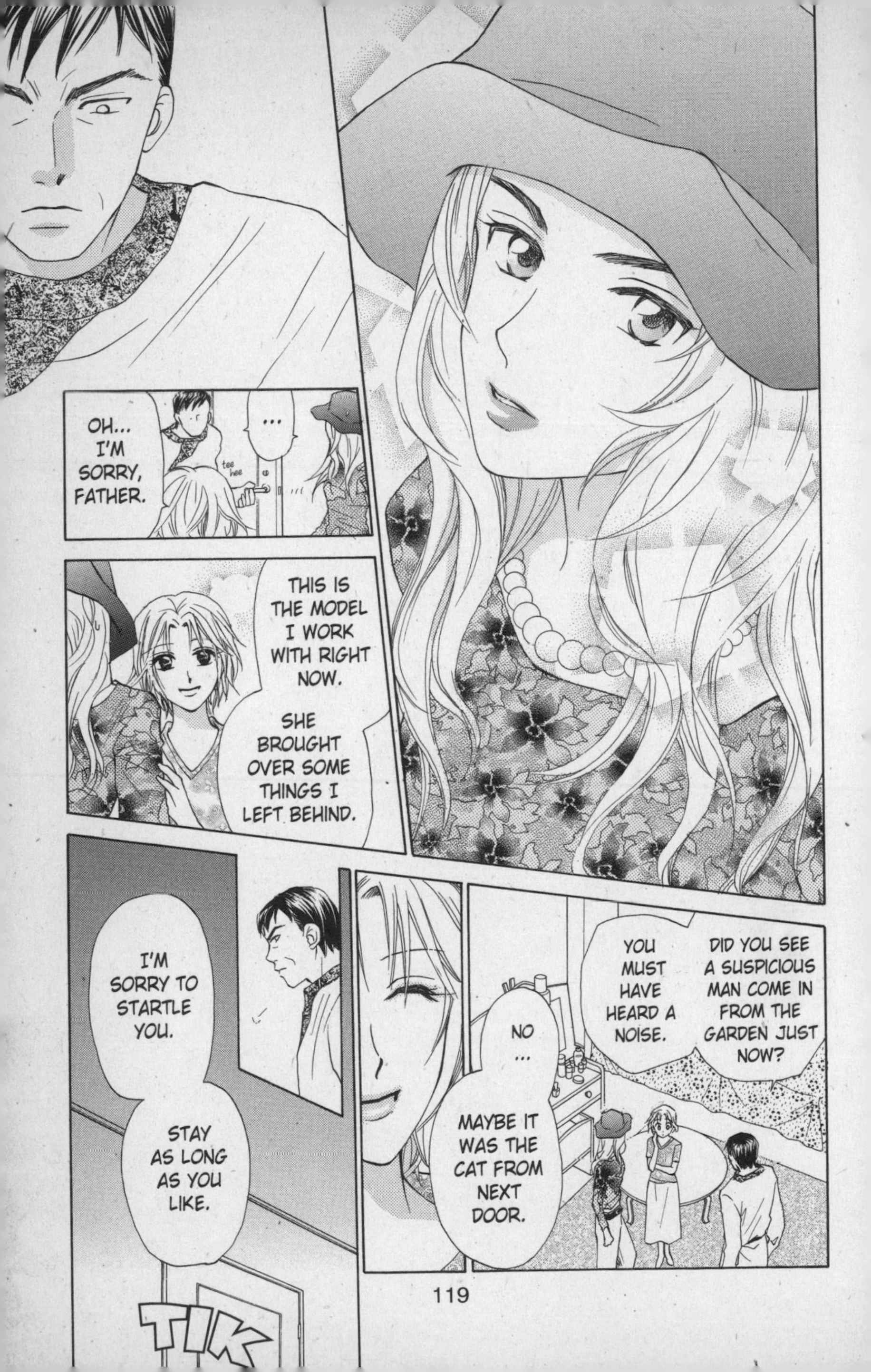
...
tee hee
OH... I'M SORRY, FATHER.
THIS IS THE MODEL I WORK WITH RIGHT NOW.
SHE BROUGHT OVER SOME THINGS I LEFT BEHIND.
DID YOU SEE A SUSPICIOUS MAN COME IN FROM THE GARDEN JUST NOW?
YOU MUST HAVE HEARD A NOISE.
NO ...
MAYBE IT WAS THE CAT FROM NEXT DOOR.
I'M SORRY TO STARTLE YOU.
STAY AS LONG AS YOU LIKE.
TIK

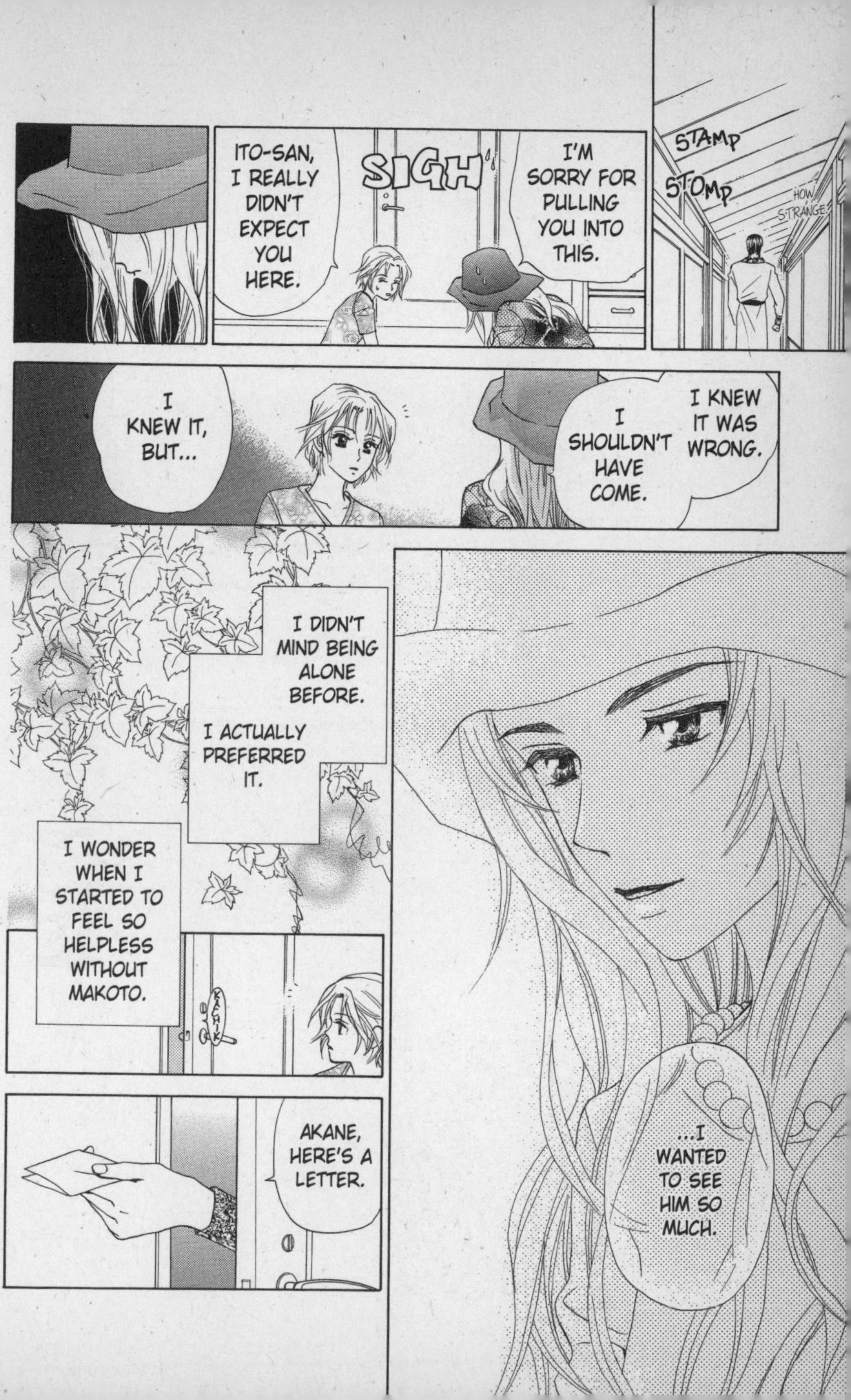
STAMP
STOMP
HOW STRANGE
I'M SORRY FOR PULLING YOU INTO THIS.
SIGH
ITO-SAN, I REALLY DIDN'T EXPECT YOU HERE.
I KNEW IT WAS WRONG.
I SHOULDN'T HAVE COME.
I KNEW IT, BUT...
...I WANTED TO SEE HIM SO MUCH.
I DIDN'T MIND BEING ALONE BEFORE.
I ACTUALLY PREFERRED IT.
I WONDER WHEN I STARTED TO FEEL SO HELPLESS WITHOUT MAKOTO.
KACHIK
AKANE, HERE'S A LETTER.

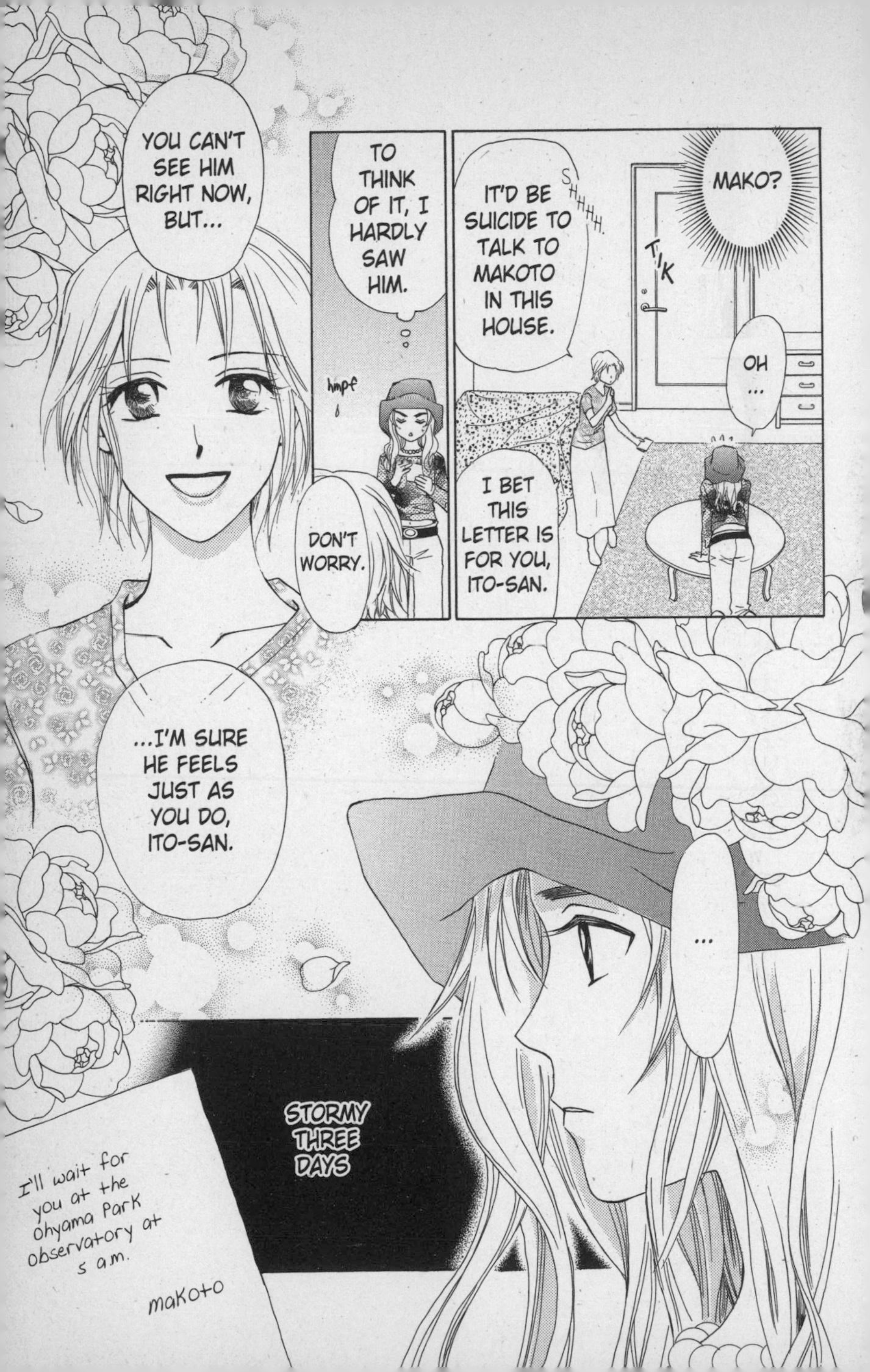
MAKO?
TIK
SHHHHH.
IT'D BE SUICIDE TO TALK TO MAKOTO IN THIS HOUSE.
OH ...
I BET THIS LETTER IS FOR YOU, ITO-SAN.
TO THINK OF IT, I HARDLY SAW HIM.
hmpf
DON'T WORRY.
YOU CAN'T SEE HIM RIGHT NOW, BUT...
...I'M SURE HE FEELS JUST AS YOU DO, ITO-SAN.
...
STORMY THREE DAYS
I'll wait for you at the ohyama Park observatory at 5 a.m.
makoto

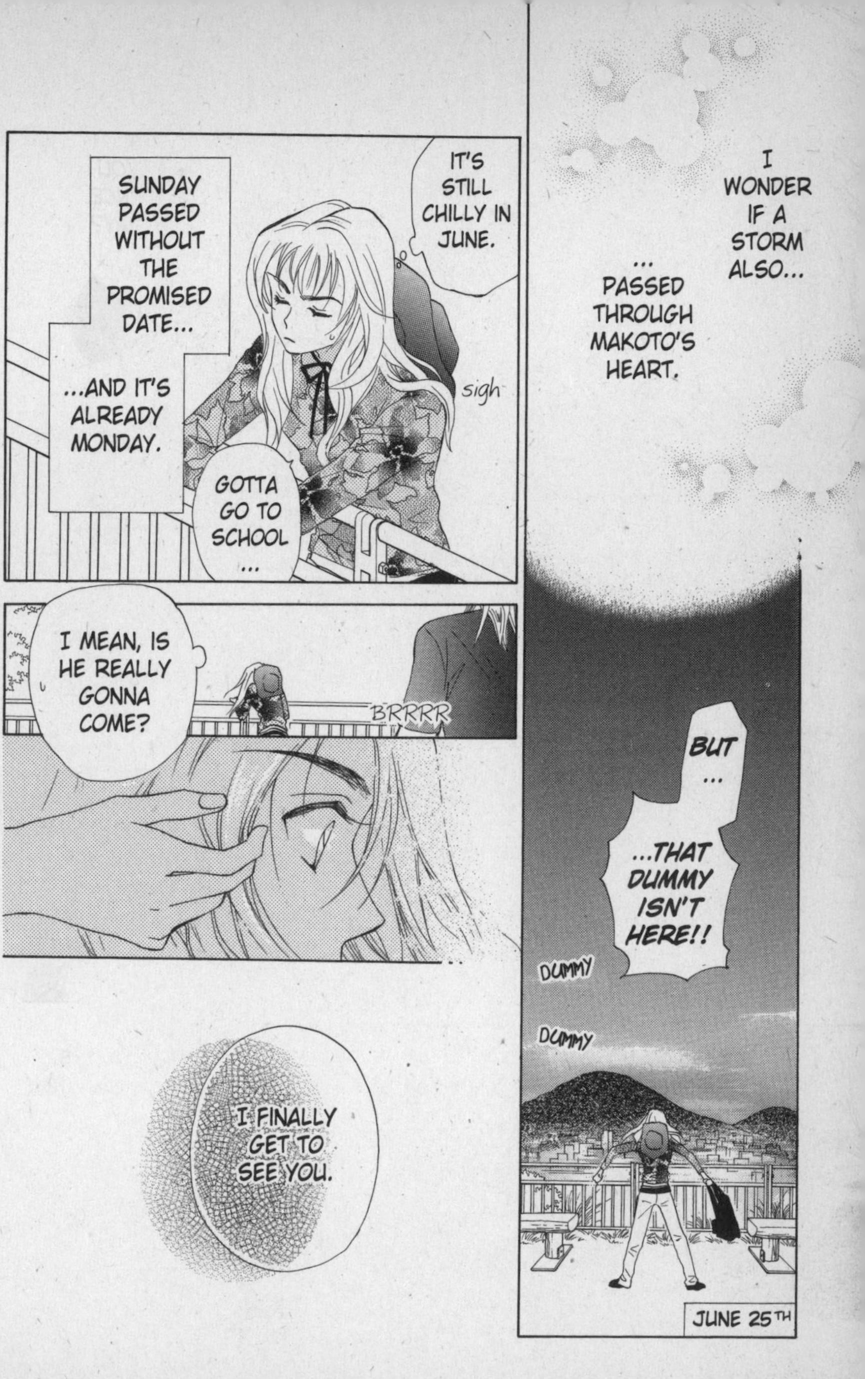
I WONDER IF A STORM ALSO...
... PASSED THROUGH MAKOTO'S HEART.
BUT ...
...THAT DUMMY ISN'T HERE!!
DUMMY
DUMMY
JUNE 25TH
IT'S STILL CHILLY IN JUNE.
SUNDAY PASSED WITHOUT THE PROMISED DATE...
...AND IT'S ALREADY MONDAY.
sigh
GOTTA GO TO SCHOOL ...
BRRRR
I MEAN, IS HE REALLY GONNA COME?
I FINALLY GET TO SEE YOU.

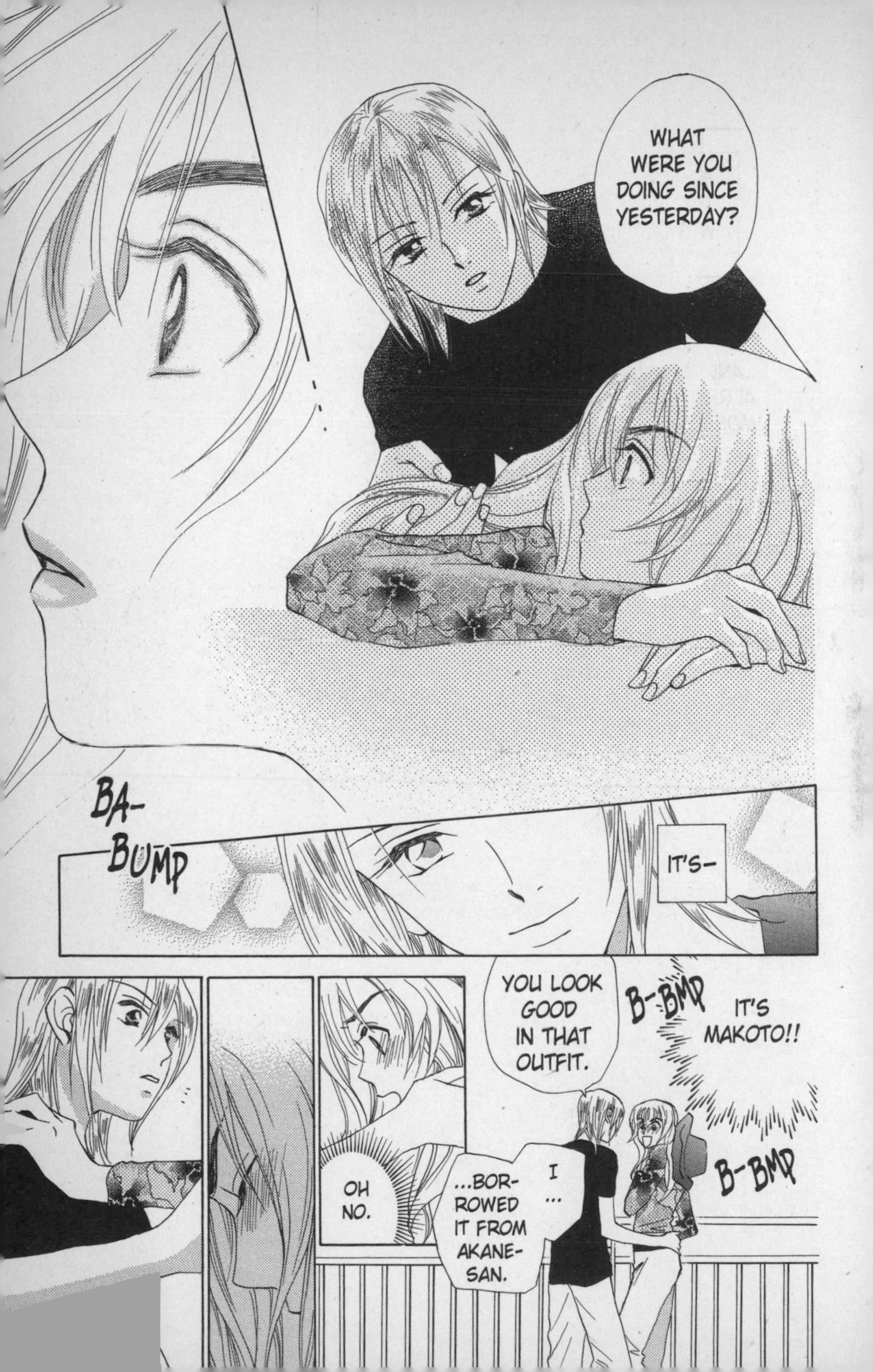
WHAT WERE YOU DOING SINCE YESTERDAY?
BA-BUMP
IT'S—
IT'S MAKOTO!!
B-BMP
YOU LOOK GOOD IN THAT OUTFIT.
B-BMP
I ...
...BOR-ROWED IT FROM AKANE-SAN.
OH NO.

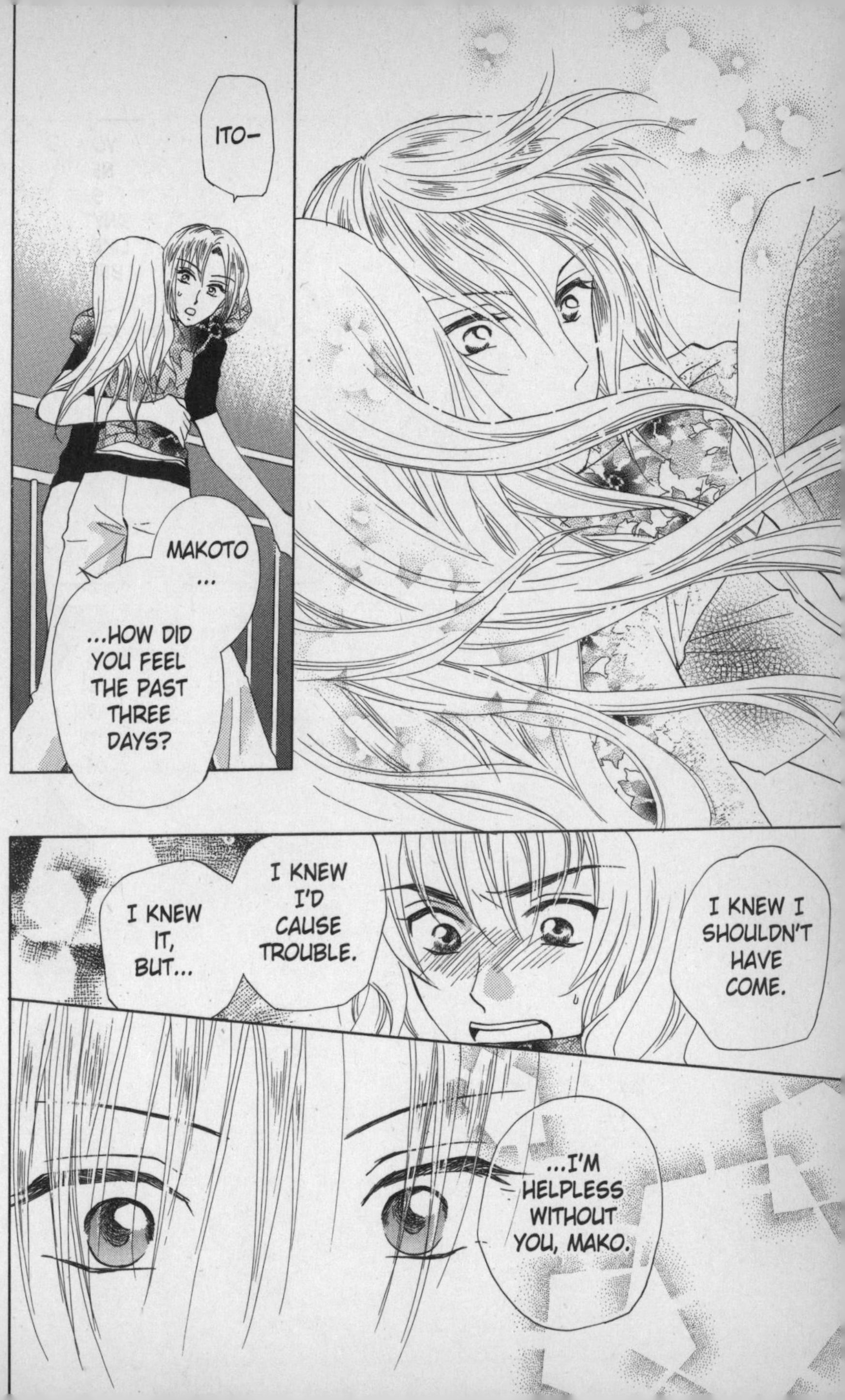
ITO–
MAKOTO ...
...HOW DID YOU FEEL THE PAST THREE DAYS?
I KNEW I SHOULDN'T HAVE COME.
I KNEW I'D CAUSE TROUBLE.
I KNEW IT, BUT...
...I'M HELPLESS WITHOUT YOU, MAKO.

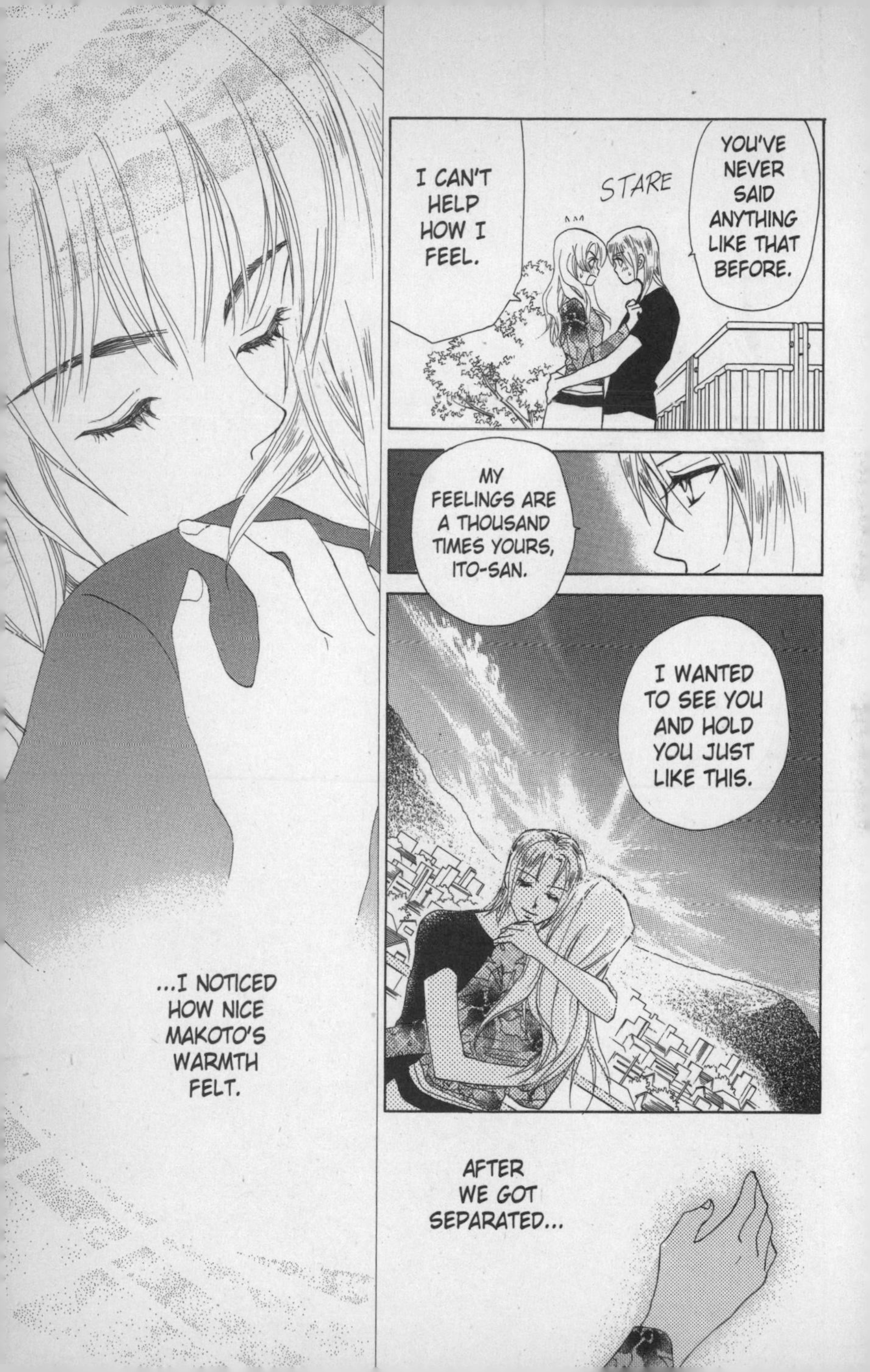
YOU'VE NEVER SAID ANYTHING LIKE THAT BEFORE.
STARE
I CAN'T HELP HOW I FEEL.
MY FEELINGS ARE A THOUSAND TIMES YOURS, ITO-SAN.
I WANTED TO SEE YOU AND HOLD YOU JUST LIKE THIS.
AFTER WE GOT SEPARATED...
...I NOTICED HOW NICE MAKOTO'S WARMTH FELT.

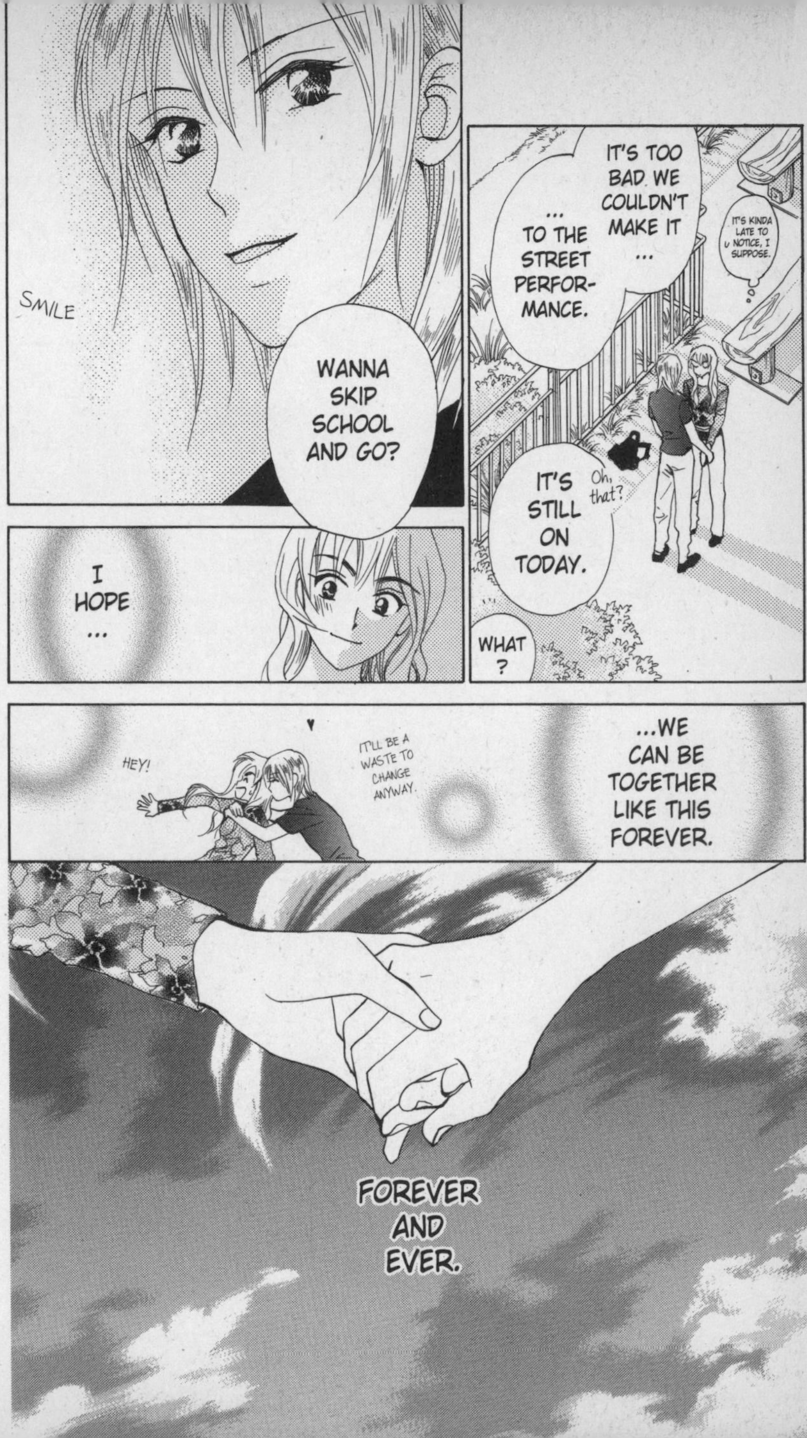
IT'S TOO BAD WE COULDN'T MAKE IT ...
IT'S KINDA LATE TO NOTICE, I SUPPOSE.
... TO THE STREET PERFORMANCE.
Oh, that?
IT'S STILL ON TODAY.
WHAT?
SMILE
WANNA SKIP SCHOOL AND GO?
I HOPE ...
...WE CAN BE TOGETHER LIKE THIS FOREVER.
IT'LL BE A WASTE TO CHANGE ANYWAY.
HEY!
FOREVER AND EVER.

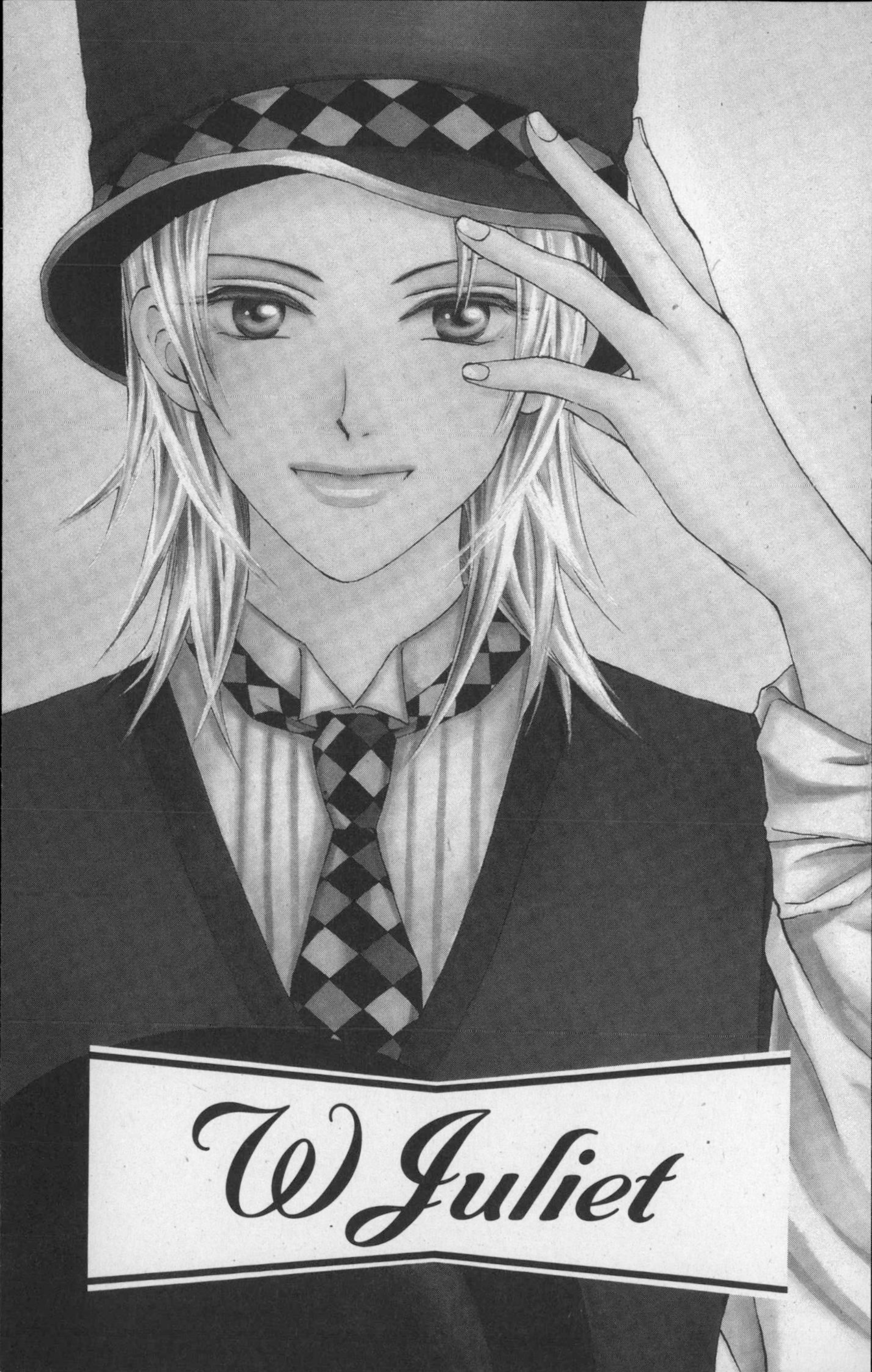
W Juliet

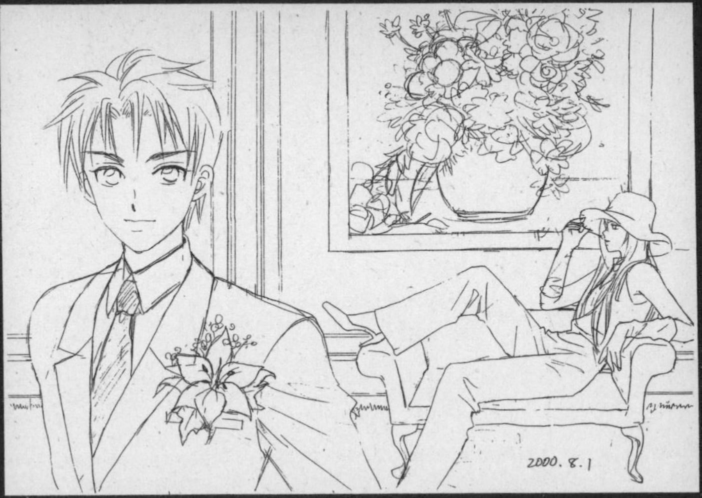
2000. 8. 1

↑ Draft (B5 size)

↓ Draft for Bonus Calendar (B4 size)

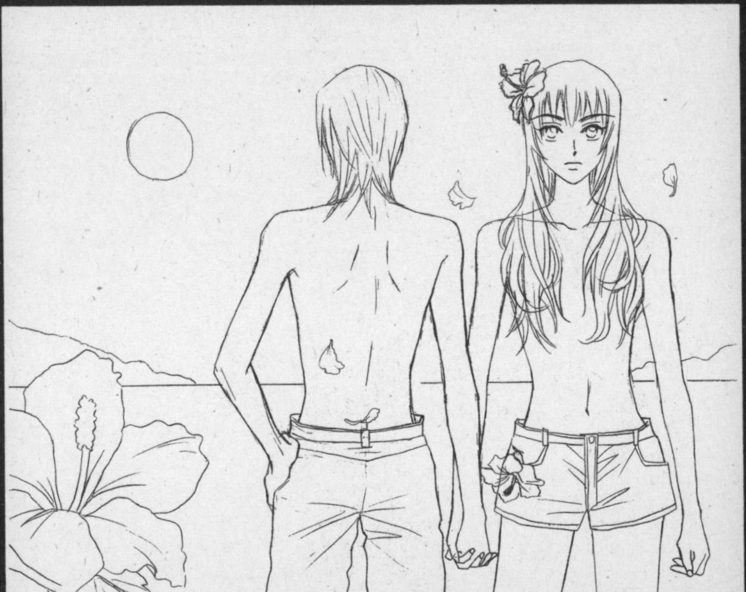
2000. 10.

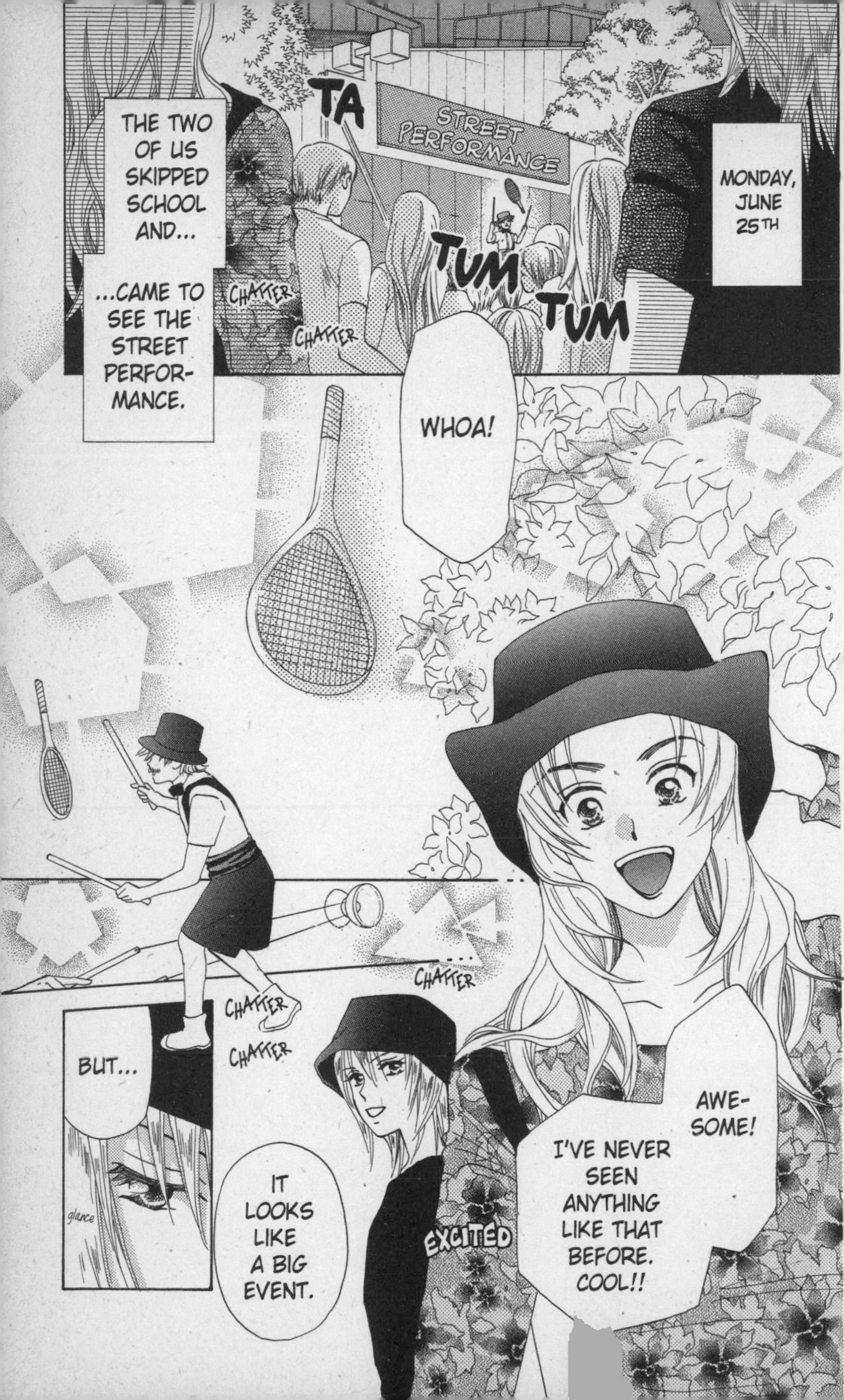
MONDAY, JUNE 25TH
TA
STREET PERFORMANCE
TUM
TUM
CHATTER
CHATTER
THE TWO OF US SKIPPED SCHOOL AND...
...CAME TO SEE THE STREET PERFORMANCE.
WHOA!
CHATTER
CHATTER
CHATTER
AWESOME!
I'VE NEVER SEEN ANYTHING LIKE THAT BEFORE. COOL!!
EXCITED
IT LOOKS LIKE A BIG EVENT.
BUT...
glance

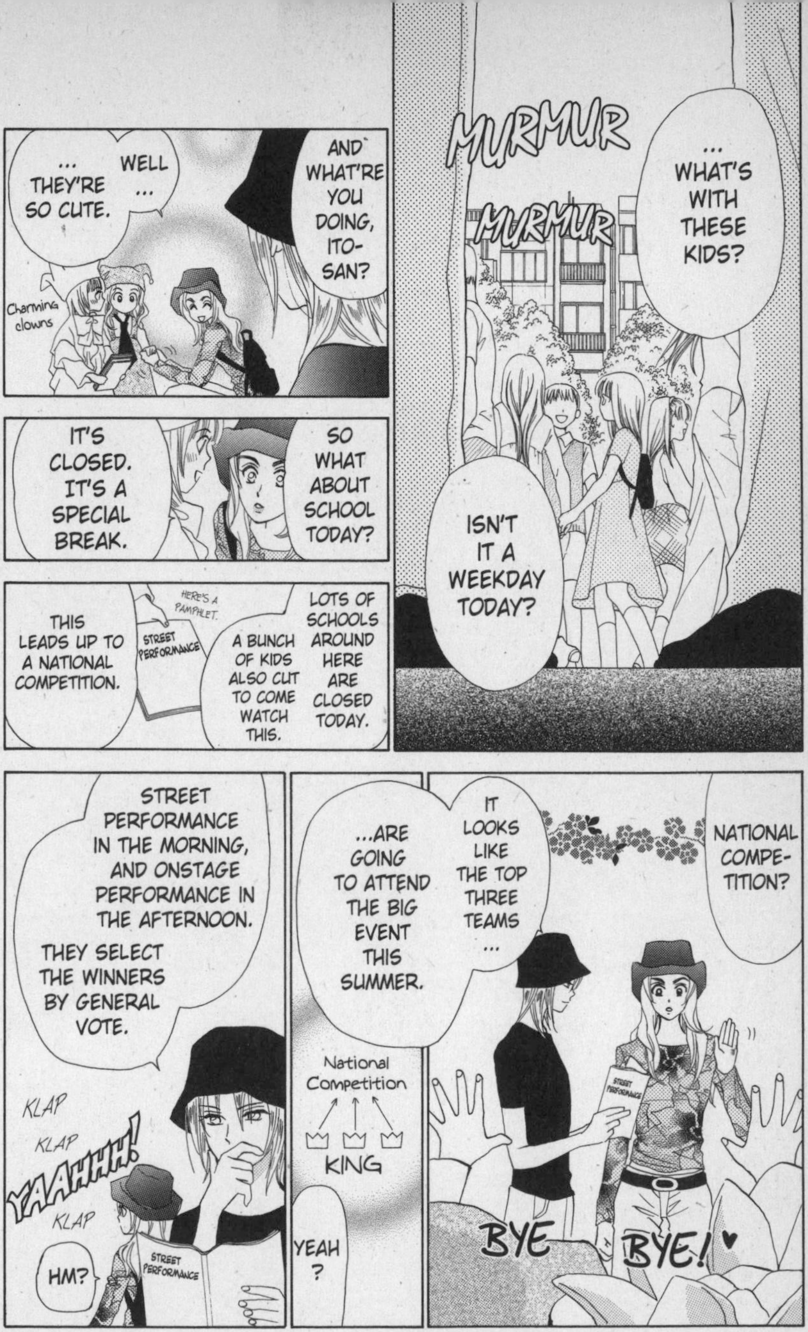
MURMUR
MURMUR
... WHAT'S WITH THESE KIDS?
ISN'T IT A WEEKDAY TODAY?
AND WHAT'RE YOU DOING, ITO-SAN?
WELL ...
... THEY'RE SO CUTE.
Charming clowns
SO WHAT ABOUT SCHOOL TODAY?
IT'S CLOSED. IT'S A SPECIAL BREAK.
LOTS OF SCHOOLS AROUND HERE ARE CLOSED TODAY.
A BUNCH OF KIDS ALSO CUT TO COME WATCH THIS.
HERE'S A PAMPHLET.
STREET PERFORMANCE
THIS LEADS UP TO A NATIONAL COMPETITION.
NATIONAL COMPE-TITION?
STREET PERFORMANCE
BYE
BYE!
IT LOOKS LIKE THE TOP THREE TEAMS ...
...ARE GOING TO ATTEND THE BIG EVENT THIS SUMMER.
National Competition
KING
YEAH ?
STREET PERFORMANCE IN THE MORNING, AND ONSTAGE PERFORMANCE IN THE AFTERNOON.
THEY SELECT THE WINNERS BY GENERAL VOTE.
KLAP
KLAP
YAAHHH!
KLAP
HM?
STREET PERFORMANCE

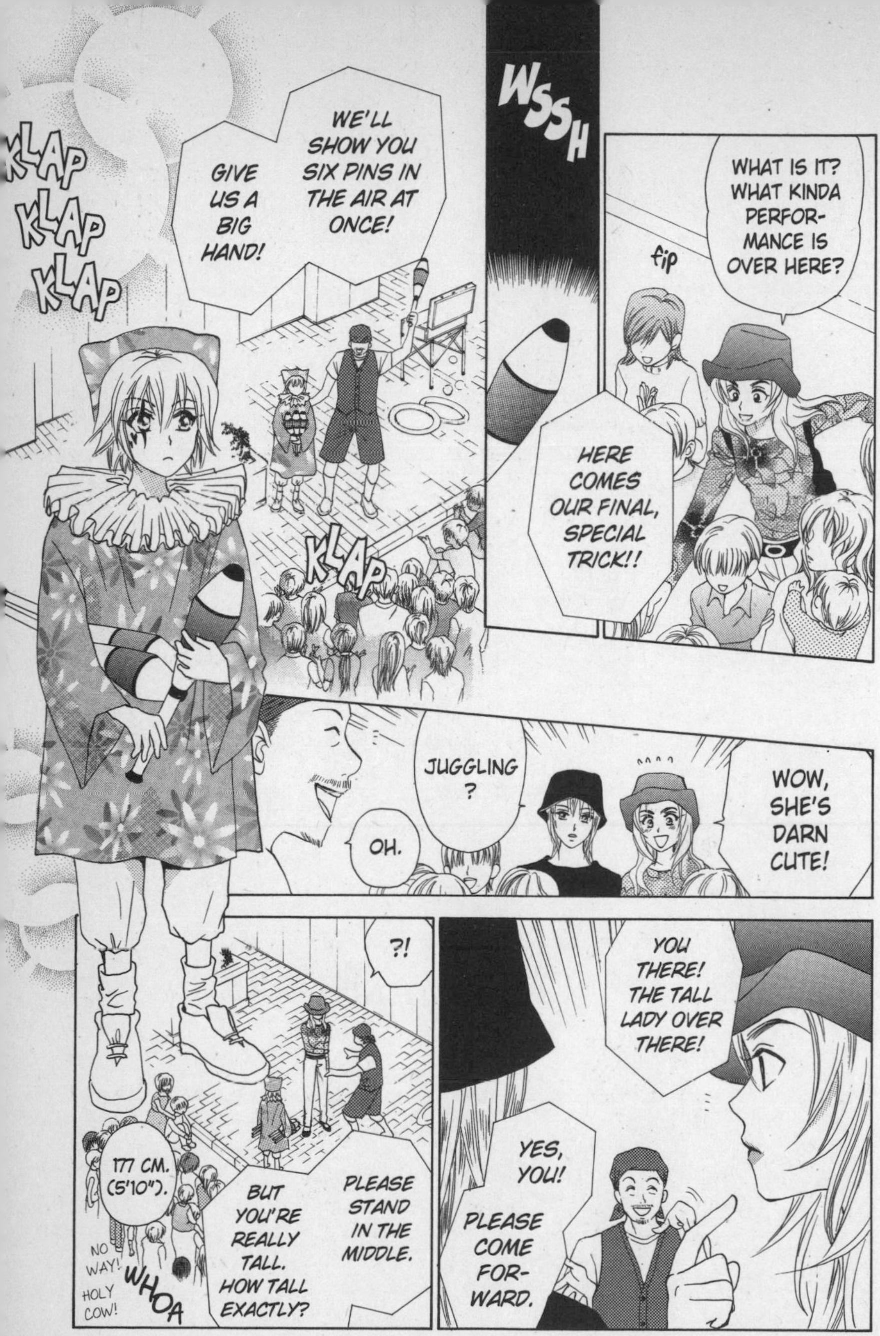
WHAT IS IT? WHAT KINDA PERFORMANCE IS OVER HERE?
fip
HERE COMES OUR FINAL, SPECIAL TRICK!!
WSSH
WE'LL SHOW YOU SIX PINS IN THE AIR AT ONCE!
GIVE US A BIG HAND!
KLAP KLAP KLAP
KLAP
WOW, SHE'S DARN CUTE!
JUGGLING?
OH.
YOU THERE! THE TALL LADY OVER THERE!
YES, YOU!
PLEASE COME FORWARD.
?!
PLEASE STAND IN THE MIDDLE.
BUT YOU'RE REALLY TALL. HOW TALL EXACTLY?
177 CM. (5'10").
NO WAY!
WHOA
HOLY COW!

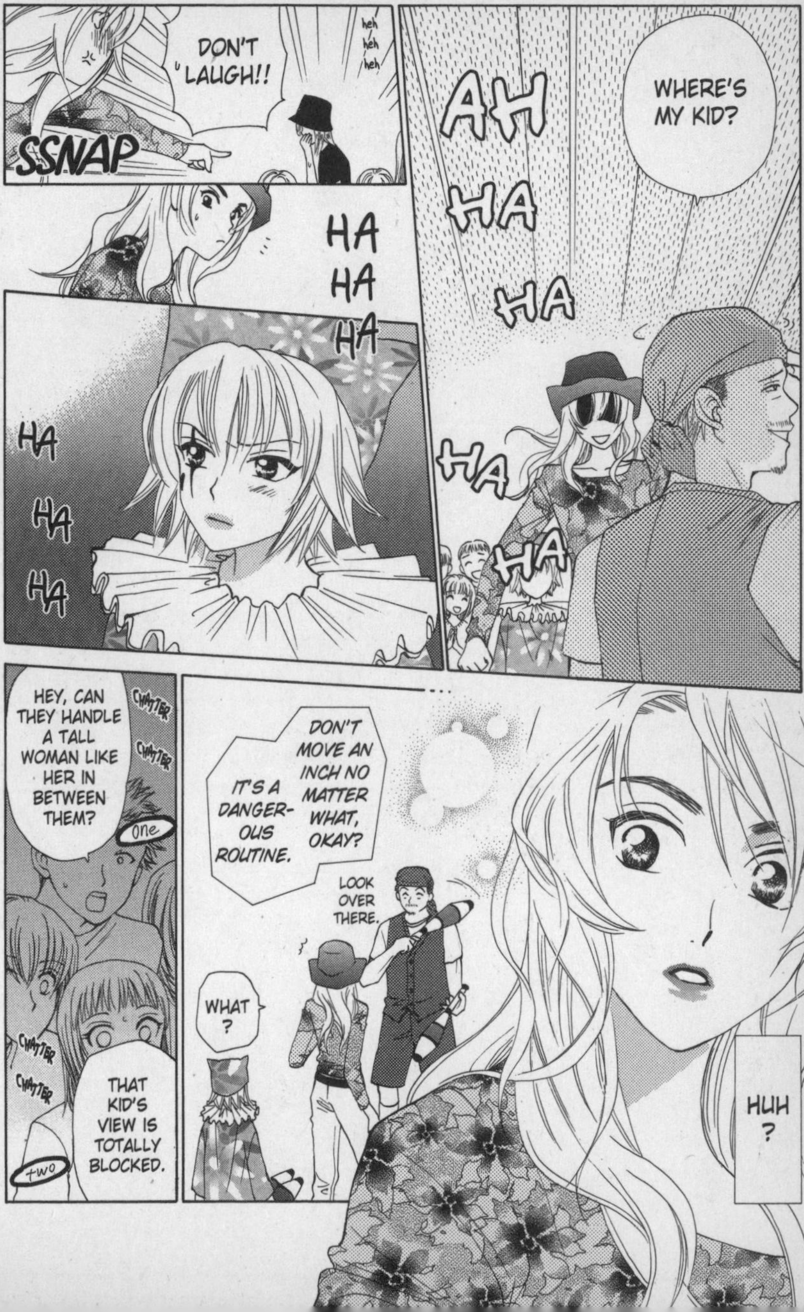
WHERE'S MY KID?
AH HA HA HA HA HA
heh heh heh
DON'T LAUGH!!
SSNAP
HA HA HA
HA HA HA
...
HUH ?
DON'T MOVE AN INCH NO MATTER WHAT, OKAY?
IT'S A DANGEROUS ROUTINE.
LOOK OVER THERE.
WHAT ?
HEY, CAN THEY HANDLE A TALL WOMAN LIKE HER IN BETWEEN THEM?
CHATTER CHATTER
one
CHATTER CHATTER
THAT KID'S VIEW IS TOTALLY BLOCKED.
two

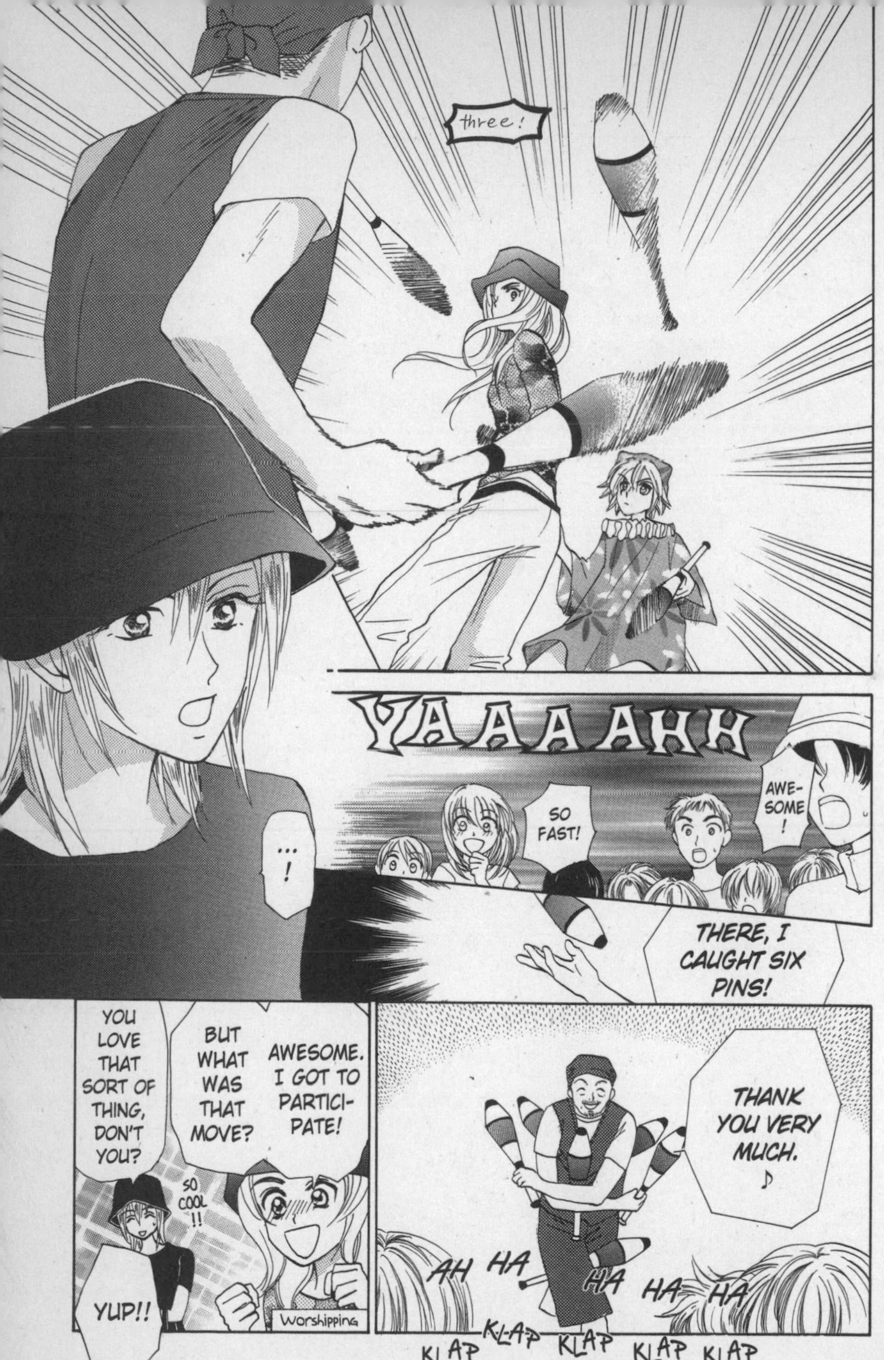
three!
YAAAAHH
AWESOME!
SO FAST!
...!
THERE, I CAUGHT SIX PINS!
THANK YOU VERY MUCH. ♪
AH HA HA HA HA
KLAP K-LAP KLAP KLAP KLAP
AWESOME. I GOT TO PARTICIPATE!
BUT WHAT WAS THAT MOVE?
SO COOL!!
YOU LOVE THAT SORT OF THING, DON'T YOU?
YUP!!
Worshipping

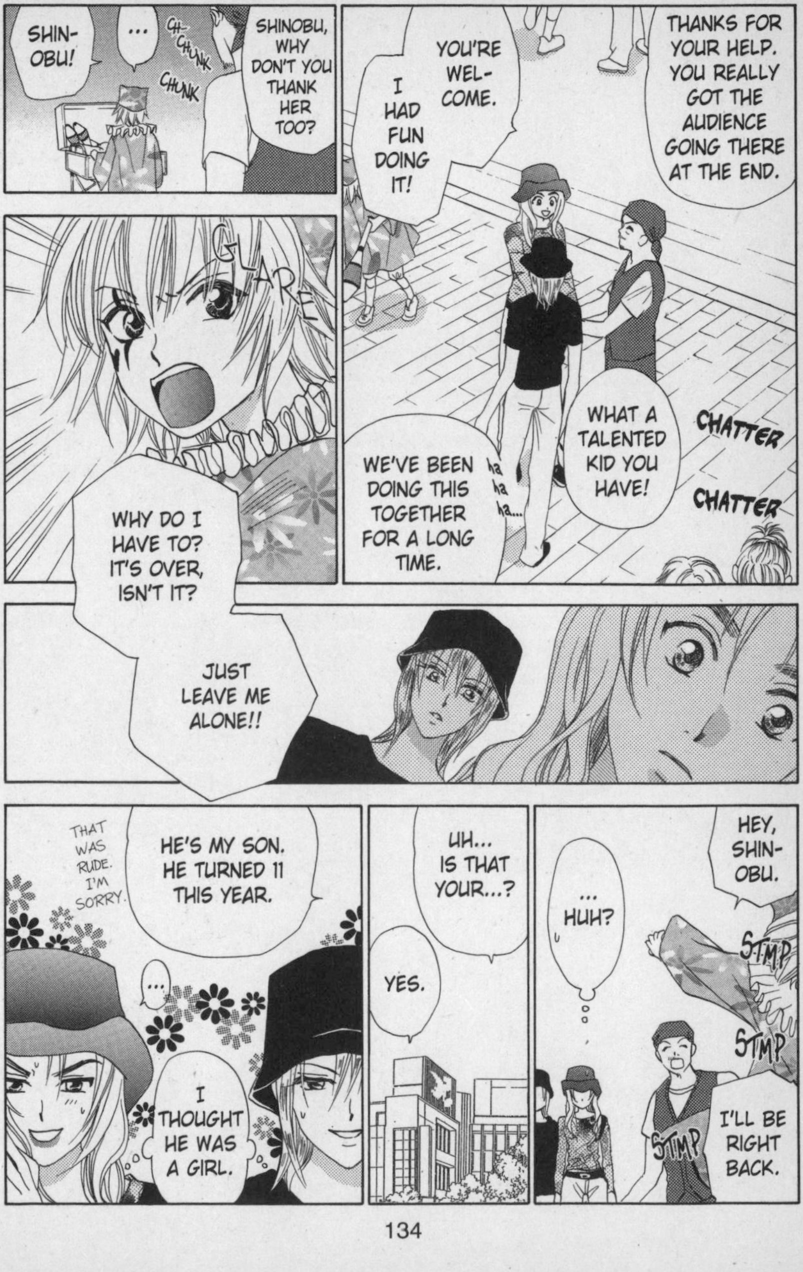
THANKS FOR YOUR HELP. YOU REALLY GOT THE AUDIENCE GOING THERE AT THE END.
YOU'RE WELCOME.
I HAD FUN DOING IT!
WHAT A TALENTED KID YOU HAVE!
CHATTER
CHATTER
WE'VE BEEN DOING THIS TOGETHER FOR A LONG TIME.
ha ha ha...
SHINOBU, WHY DON'T YOU THANK HER TOO?
CH-CHUNK
CHUNK
...
SHIN-OBU!
GLARE
WHY DO I HAVE TO? IT'S OVER, ISN'T IT?
JUST LEAVE ME ALONE!!
HEY, SHIN-OBU.
STMP
STMP
I'LL BE RIGHT BACK.
STMP
... HUH?
UH... IS THAT YOUR...?
YES.
HE'S MY SON. HE TURNED 11 THIS YEAR.
THAT WAS RUDE. I'M SORRY.
...
I THOUGHT HE WAS A GIRL.

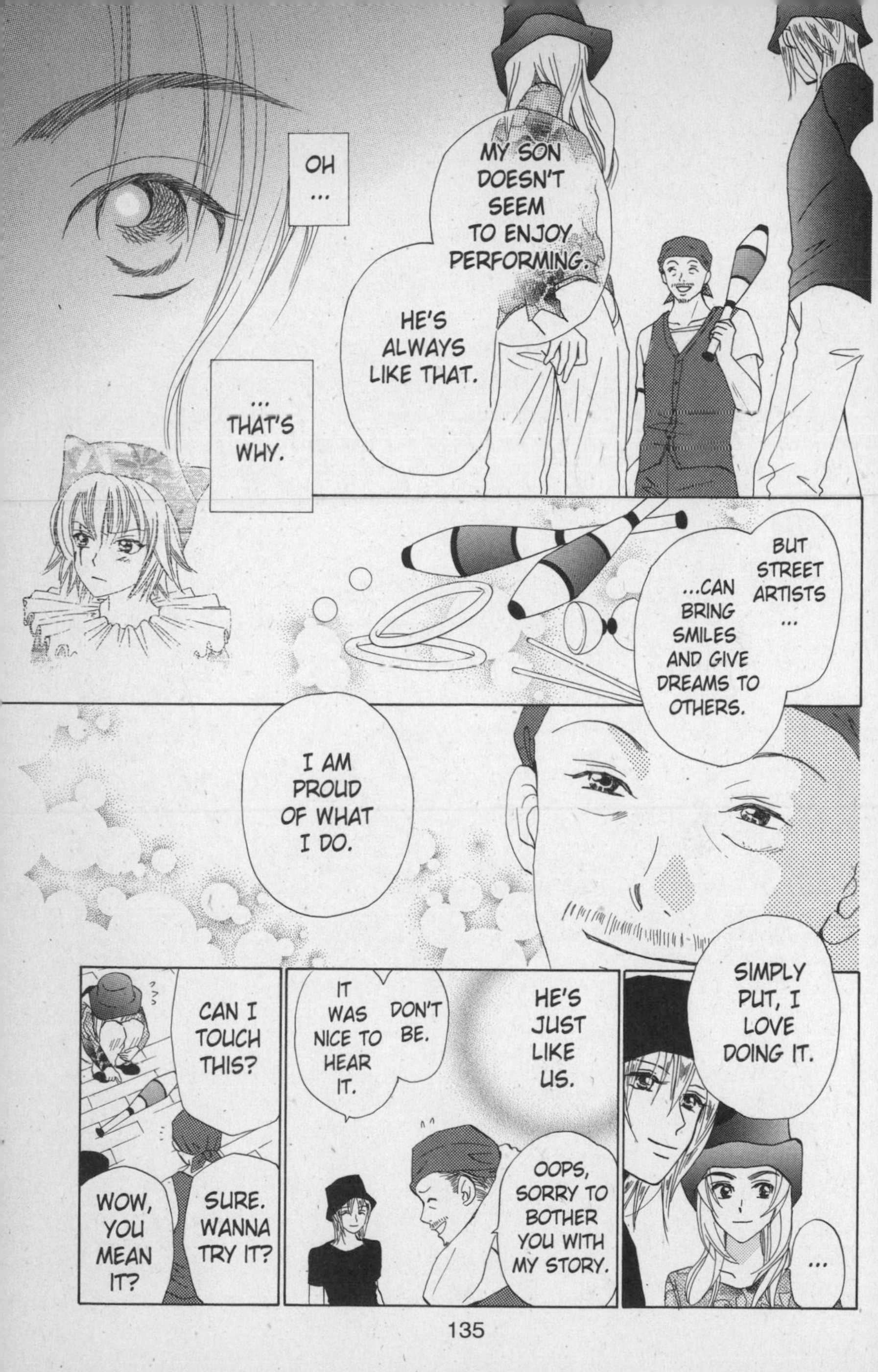
MY SON DOESN'T SEEM TO ENJOY PERFORMING.
HE'S ALWAYS LIKE THAT.
OH ...
... THAT'S WHY.
BUT STREET ARTISTS ...
...CAN BRING SMILES AND GIVE DREAMS TO OTHERS.
I AM PROUD OF WHAT I DO.
SIMPLY PUT, I LOVE DOING IT.
HE'S JUST LIKE US.
...
OOPS, SORRY TO BOTHER YOU WITH MY STORY.
DON'T BE.
IT WAS NICE TO HEAR IT.
CAN I TOUCH THIS?
SURE. WANNA TRY IT?
WOW, YOU MEAN IT?

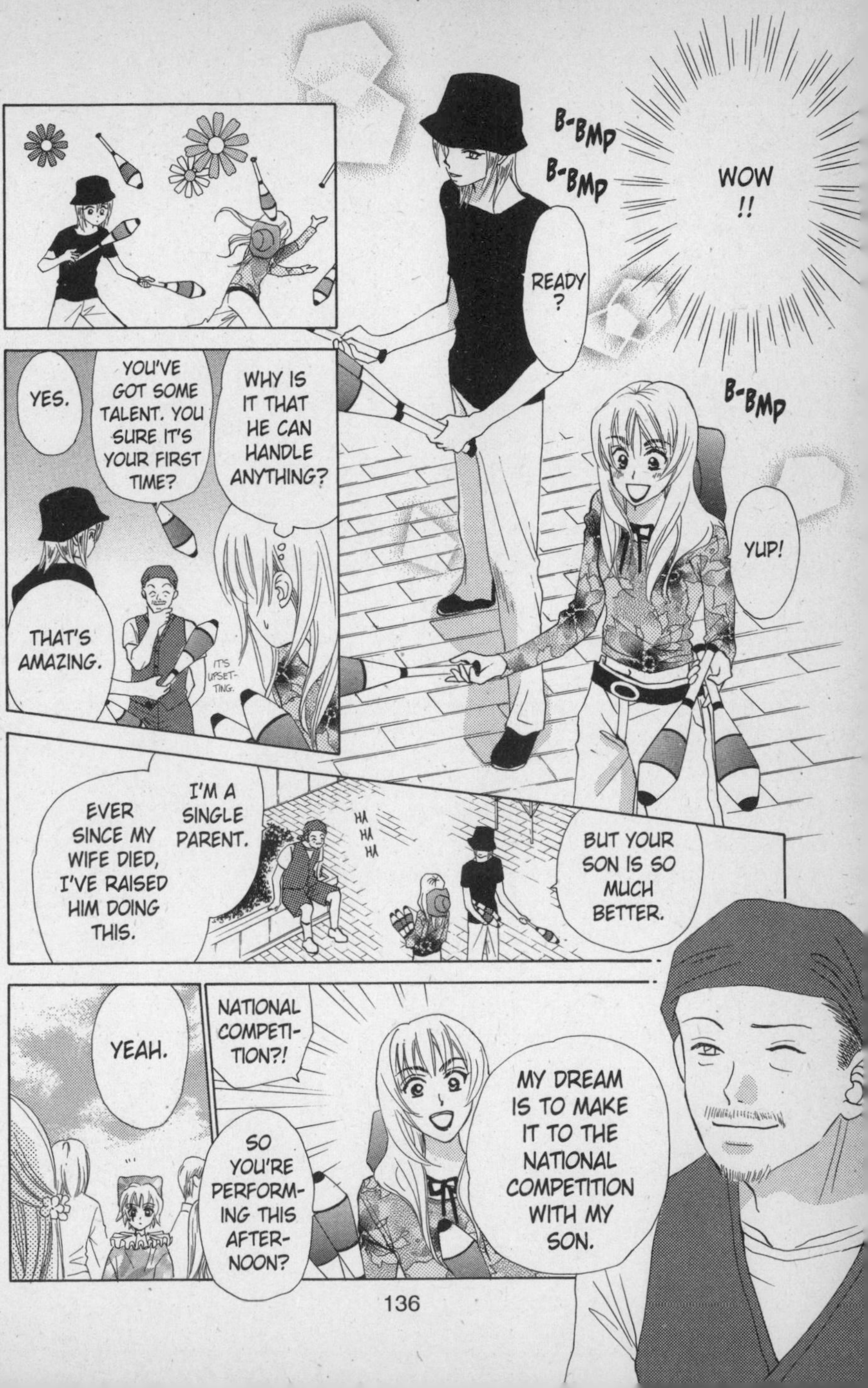
WOW !!
B-BMP
B-BMP
READY ?
B-BMP
YUP!
WHY IS IT THAT HE CAN HANDLE ANYTHING?
YOU'VE GOT SOME TALENT. YOU SURE IT'S YOUR FIRST TIME?
YES.
IT'S UPSETTING.
THAT'S AMAZING.
BUT YOUR SON IS SO MUCH BETTER.
HA HA HA
I'M A SINGLE PARENT.
EVER SINCE MY WIFE DIED, I'VE RAISED HIM DOING THIS.
MY DREAM IS TO MAKE IT TO THE NATIONAL COMPETITION WITH MY SON.
NATIONAL COMPETITION?!
SO YOU'RE PERFORMING THIS AFTERNOON?
YEAH.

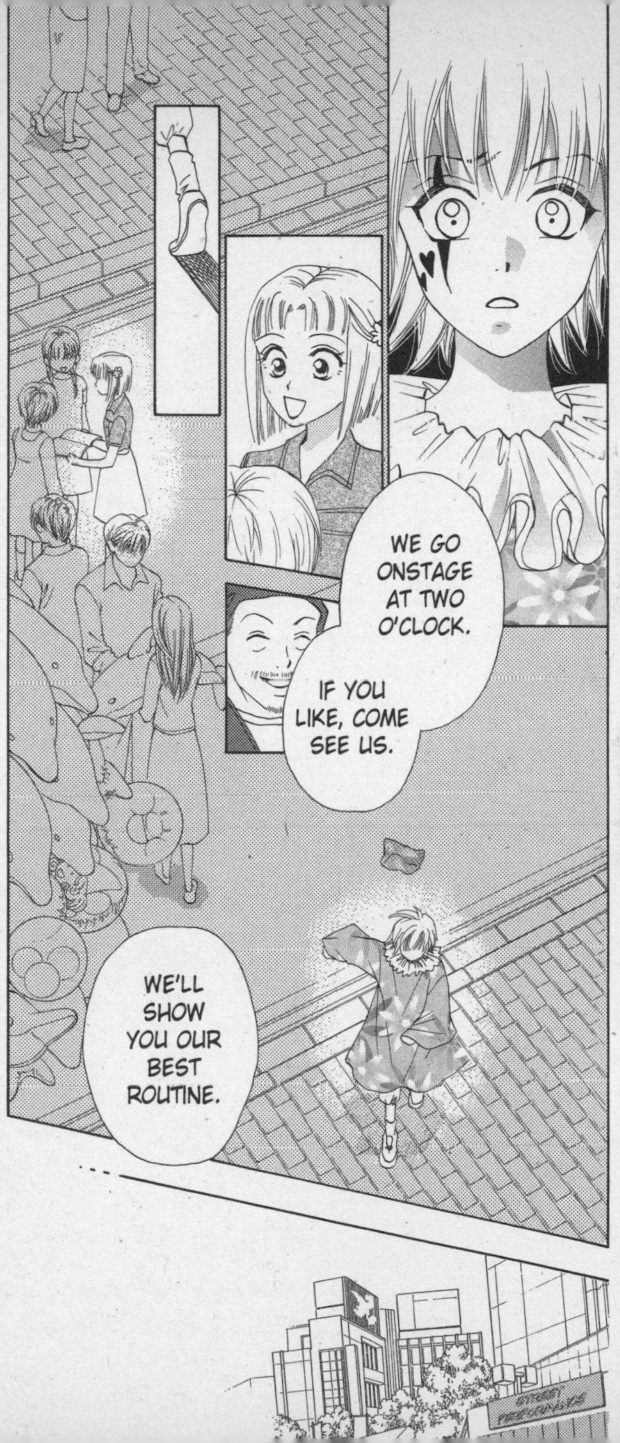
WE GO ONSTAGE AT TWO O'CLOCK.
IF YOU LIKE, COME SEE US.
WE'LL SHOW YOU OUR BEST ROUTINE.
STREET PERFORMANCE

-Behind the Scenes Story- ⑤

There aren't as many horizontal-spaces in this volume. So I decided to use the vertical for this. I enjoy watching street artists. I go and watch them often ♥ (I mean, only when I can spare the time.) In fact, Ito is wearing my hat. It's black and pink, and so cute.✳ But the color faded only on one side after it sat in my room too long. How sad. Good grief! But I'm very happy I finally got to draw a cute boy again.♥ But it was a girl's face... I wanna go see a street performance again.

Well, the space is getting quite tight. I must say good-bye for now. Lots of action with Yûto next.♥ Look forward to it

Ⓔ

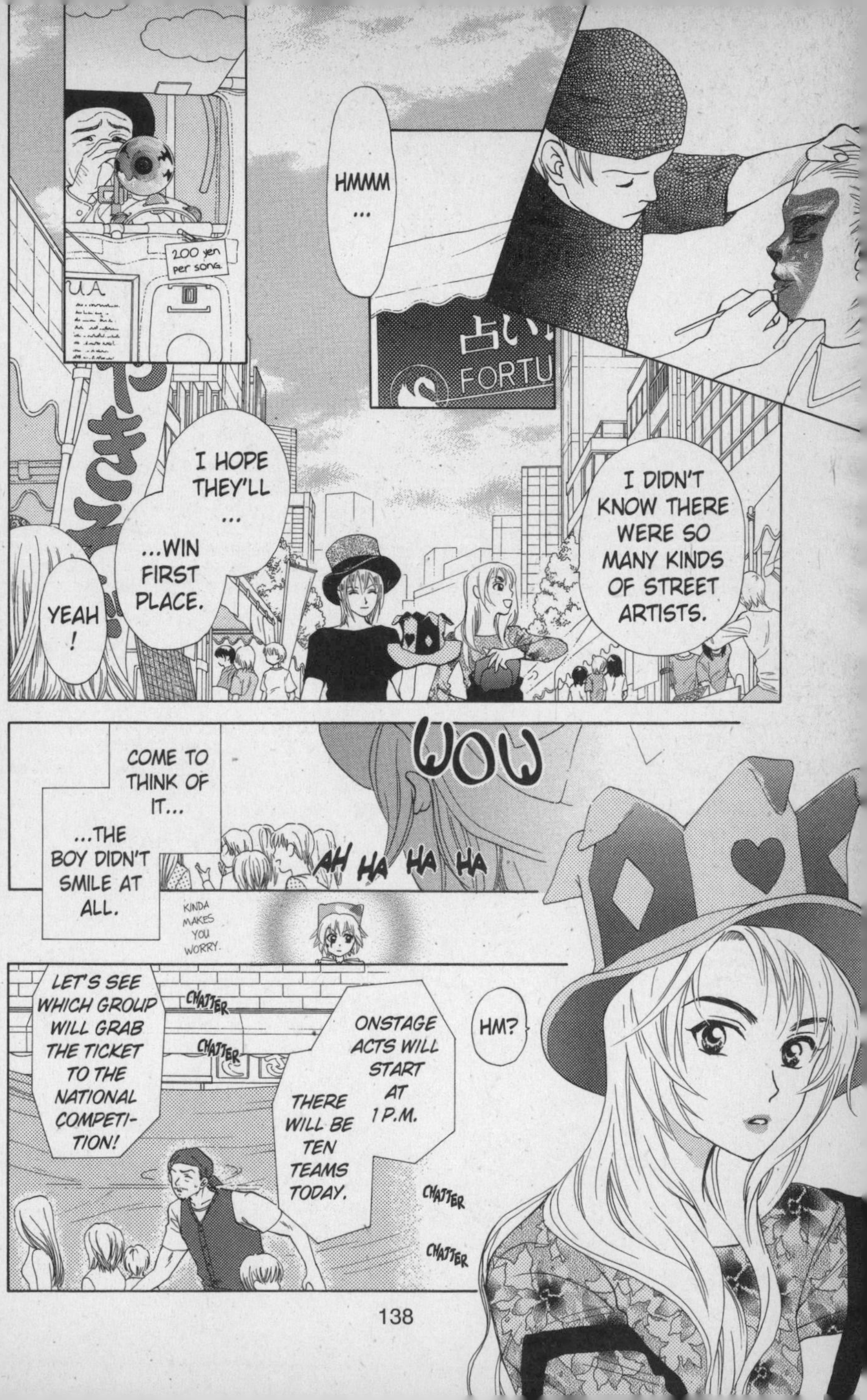

FORTU
HMMM
...
200 yen per song
I DIDN'T KNOW THERE WERE SO MANY KINDS OF STREET ARTISTS.
I HOPE THEY'LL ...
...WIN FIRST PLACE.
YEAH!
WOW
AH HA HA HA
COME TO THINK OF IT...
...THE BOY DIDN'T SMILE AT ALL.
KINDA MAKES YOU WORRY.
HM?
ONSTAGE ACTS WILL START AT 1 P.M.
THERE WILL BE TEN TEAMS TODAY.
CHATTER
CHATTER
LET'S SEE WHICH GROUP WILL GRAB THE TICKET TO THE NATIONAL COMPETITION!
CHATTER
CHATTER

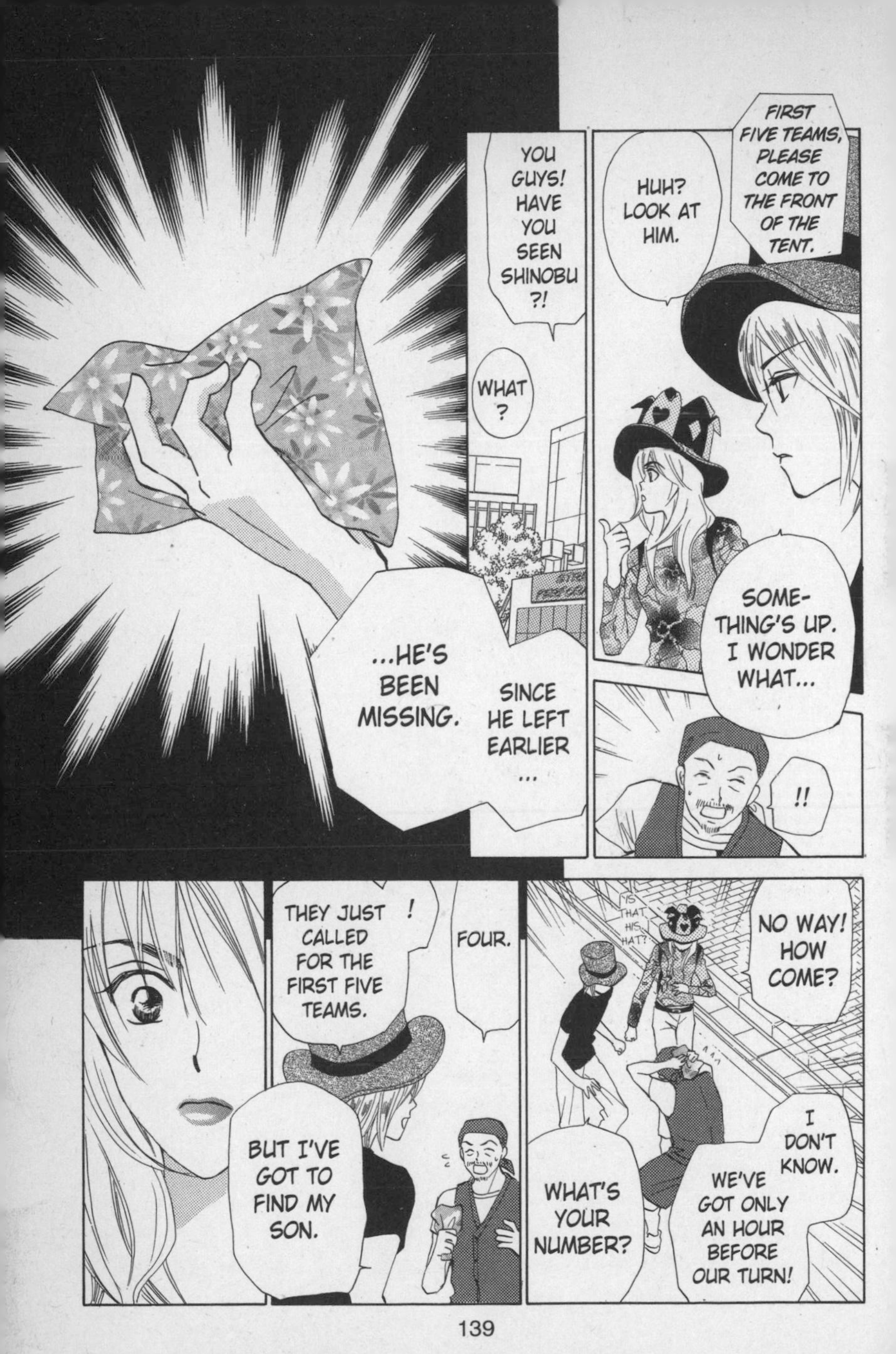
FIRST FIVE TEAMS, PLEASE COME TO THE FRONT OF THE TENT.
HUH? LOOK AT HIM.
SOME-THING'S UP. I WONDER WHAT...
YOU GUYS! HAVE YOU SEEN SHINOBU ?!
WHAT ?
!!
SINCE HE LEFT EARLIER ...
...HE'S BEEN MISSING.
IS THAT HIS HAT?
NO WAY! HOW COME?
I DON'T KNOW.
WE'VE GOT ONLY AN HOUR BEFORE OUR TURN!
WHAT'S YOUR NUMBER?
FOUR.
THEY JUST CALLED FOR THE FIRST FIVE TEAMS.
!
BUT I'VE GOT TO FIND MY SON.

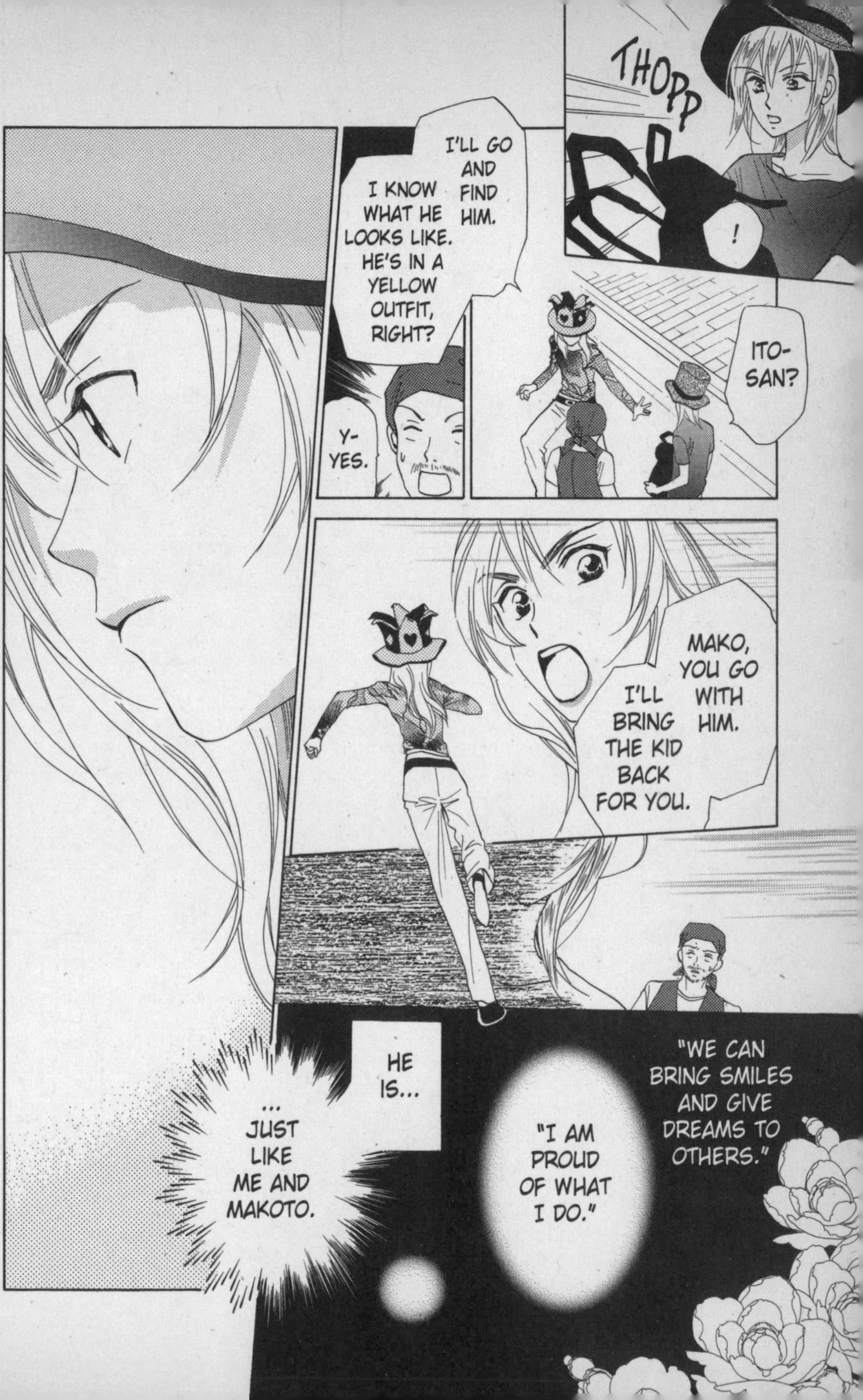
THOPP
!
ITO-SAN?
I'LL GO AND FIND HIM.
I KNOW WHAT HE LOOKS LIKE. HE'S IN A YELLOW OUTFIT, RIGHT?
Y-YES.
MAKO, YOU GO WITH HIM.
I'LL BRING THE KID BACK FOR YOU.
"WE CAN BRING SMILES AND GIVE DREAMS TO OTHERS."
"I AM PROUD OF WHAT I DO."
HE IS...
...JUST LIKE ME AND MAKOTO.

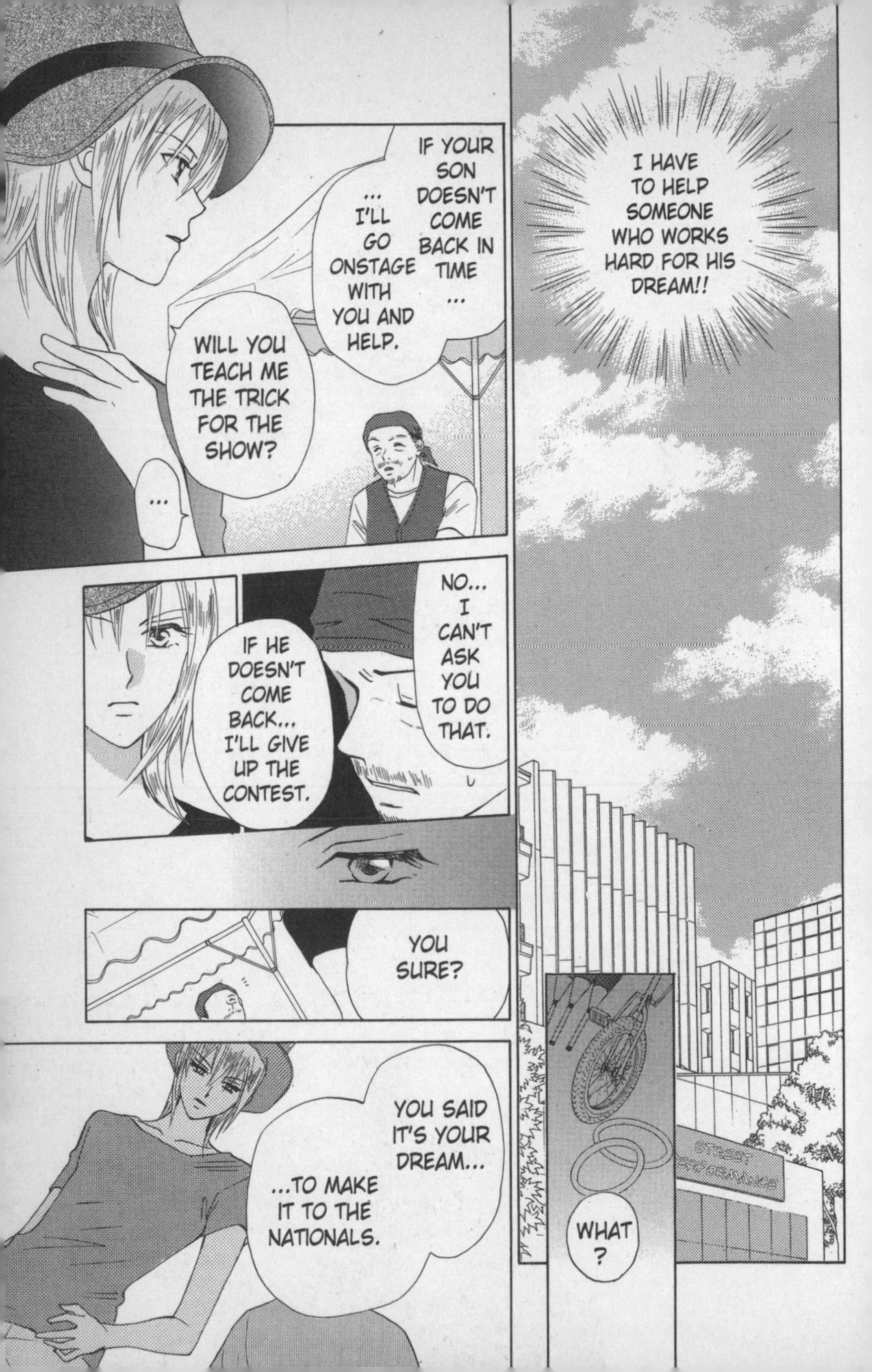
I HAVE TO HELP SOMEONE WHO WORKS HARD FOR HIS DREAM!!
STREET PERFORMANCE
WHAT?
IF YOUR SON DOESN'T COME BACK IN TIME...
...I'LL GO ONSTAGE WITH YOU AND HELP.
WILL YOU TEACH ME THE TRICK FOR THE SHOW?
...
NO... I CAN'T ASK YOU TO DO THAT.
IF HE DOESN'T COME BACK... I'LL GIVE UP THE CONTEST.
YOU SURE?
YOU SAID IT'S YOUR DREAM...
...TO MAKE IT TO THE NATIONALS.

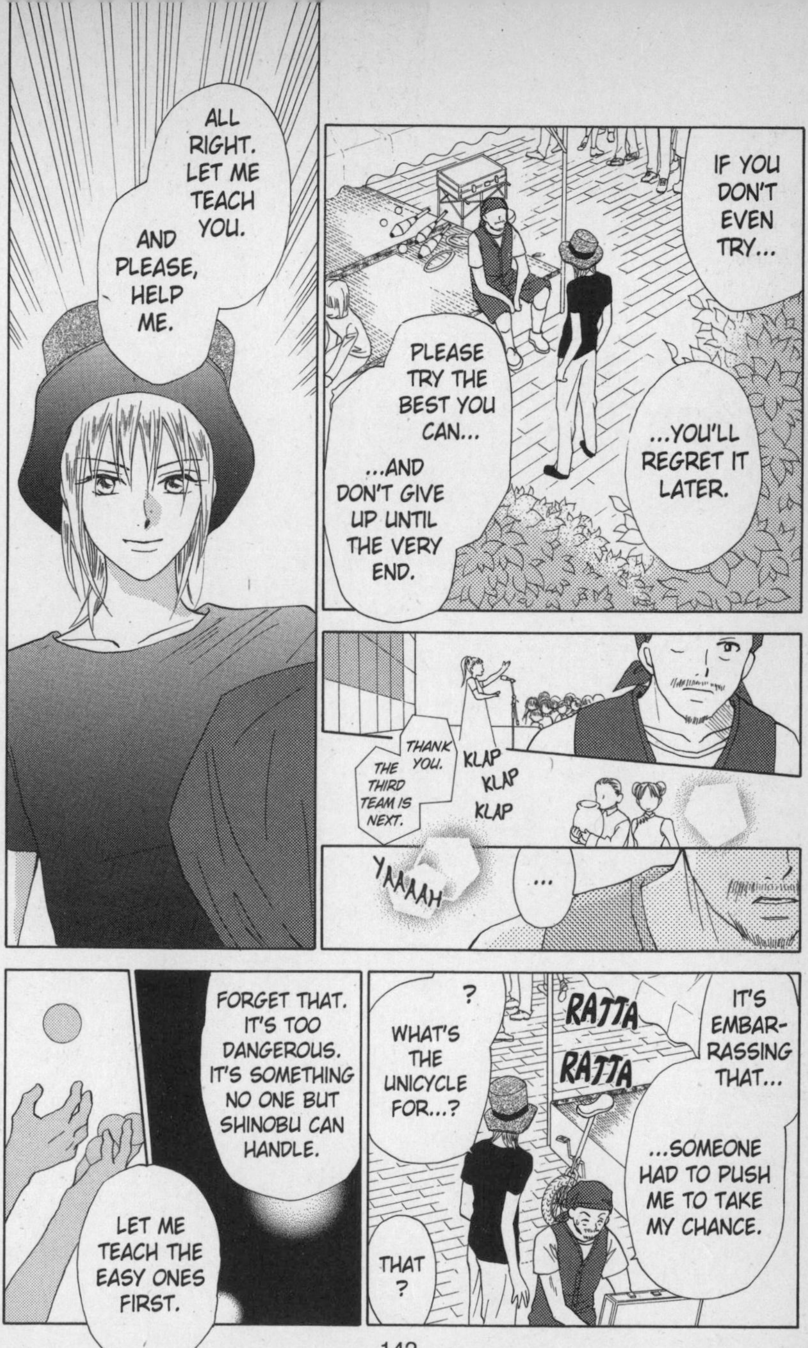
IF YOU DON'T EVEN TRY...
...YOU'LL REGRET IT LATER.
PLEASE TRY THE BEST YOU CAN...
...AND DON'T GIVE UP UNTIL THE VERY END.
THANK YOU.
THE THIRD TEAM IS NEXT.
KLAP
KLAP
KLAP
...
YAAAAH
ALL RIGHT. LET ME TEACH YOU.
AND PLEASE, HELP ME.
IT'S EMBARRASSING THAT...
...SOMEONE HAD TO PUSH ME TO TAKE MY CHANCE.
RATTA
RATTA
?
WHAT'S THE UNICYCLE FOR...?
THAT ?
FORGET THAT. IT'S TOO DANGEROUS. IT'S SOMETHING NO ONE BUT SHINOBU CAN HANDLE.
LET ME TEACH THE EASY ONES FIRST.

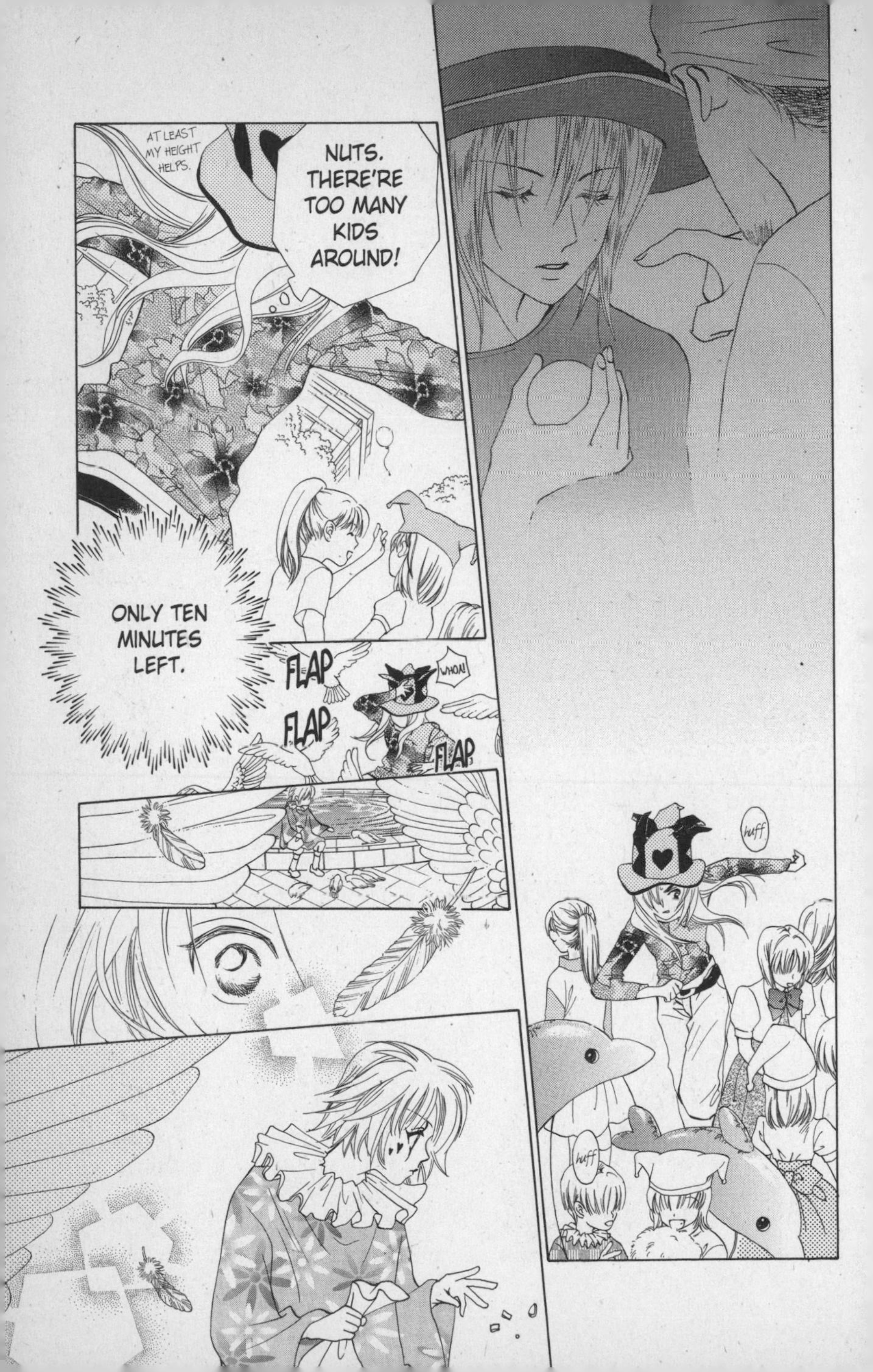
huff
huff
AT LEAST MY HEIGHT HELPS.
NUTS. THERE'RE TOO MANY KIDS AROUND!
ONLY TEN MINUTES LEFT.
WHOA!
FLAP
FLAP
FLAP

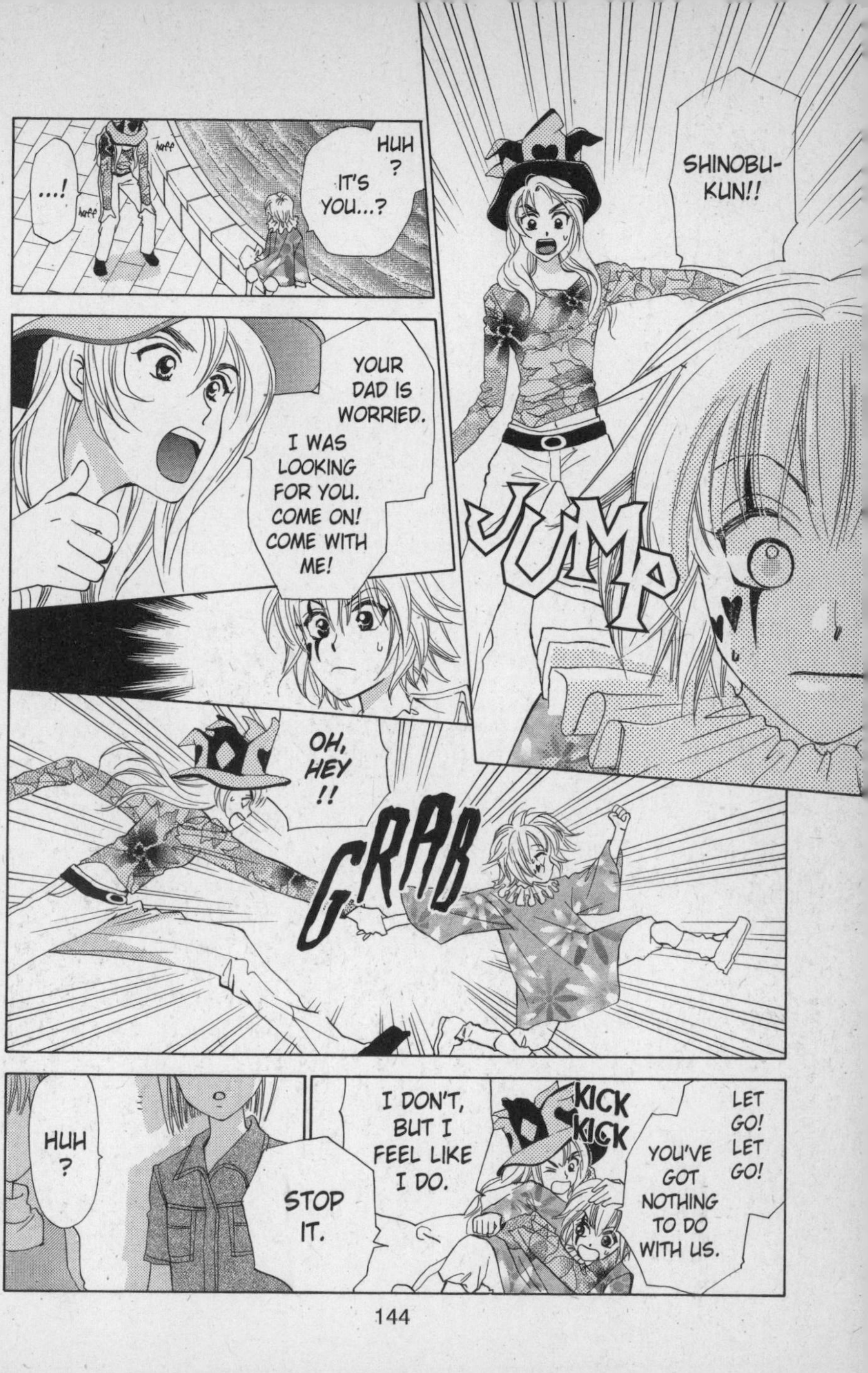
SHINOBU-KUN!!
JUMP
HUH? IT'S YOU...?
haff
haff
...!
YOUR DAD IS WORRIED.
I WAS LOOKING FOR YOU. COME ON! COME WITH ME!
OH, HEY!!
GRAB
LET GO! LET GO!
KICK KICK
YOU'VE GOT NOTHING TO DO WITH US.
I DON'T, BUT I FEEL LIKE I DO.
STOP IT.
HUH?

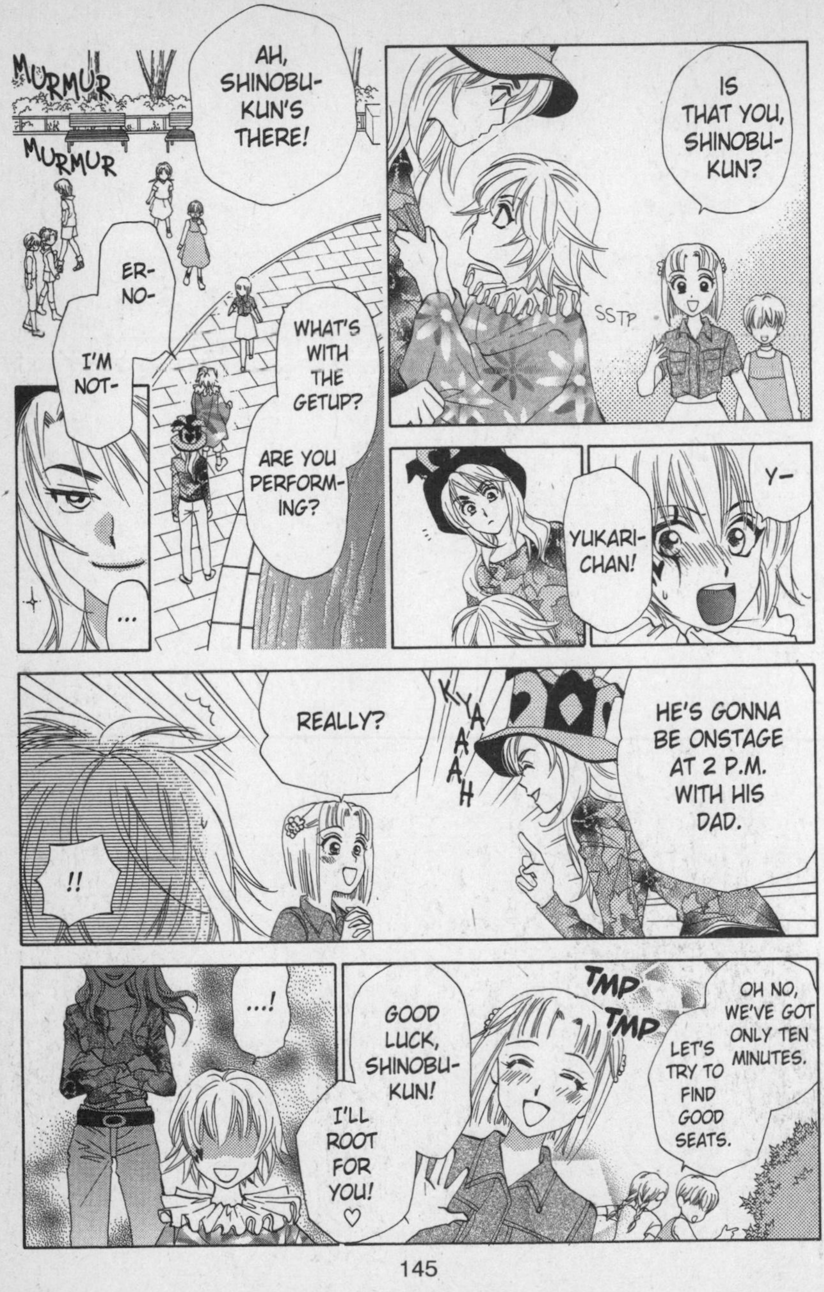
IS THAT YOU, SHINOBU-KUN?
SSTP
AH, SHINOBU-KUN'S THERE!
MURMUR
MURMUR
WHAT'S WITH THE GETUP?
ARE YOU PERFORMING?
ER- NO-
I'M NOT-
...
Y-
YUKARI-CHAN!
HE'S GONNA BE ONSTAGE AT 2 P.M. WITH HIS DAD.
KYAAAAH
REALLY?
!!
OH NO, WE'VE GOT ONLY TEN MINUTES.
LET'S TRY TO FIND GOOD SEATS.
TMP
TMP
GOOD LUCK, SHINOBU-KUN!
I'LL ROOT FOR YOU! ♡
...!

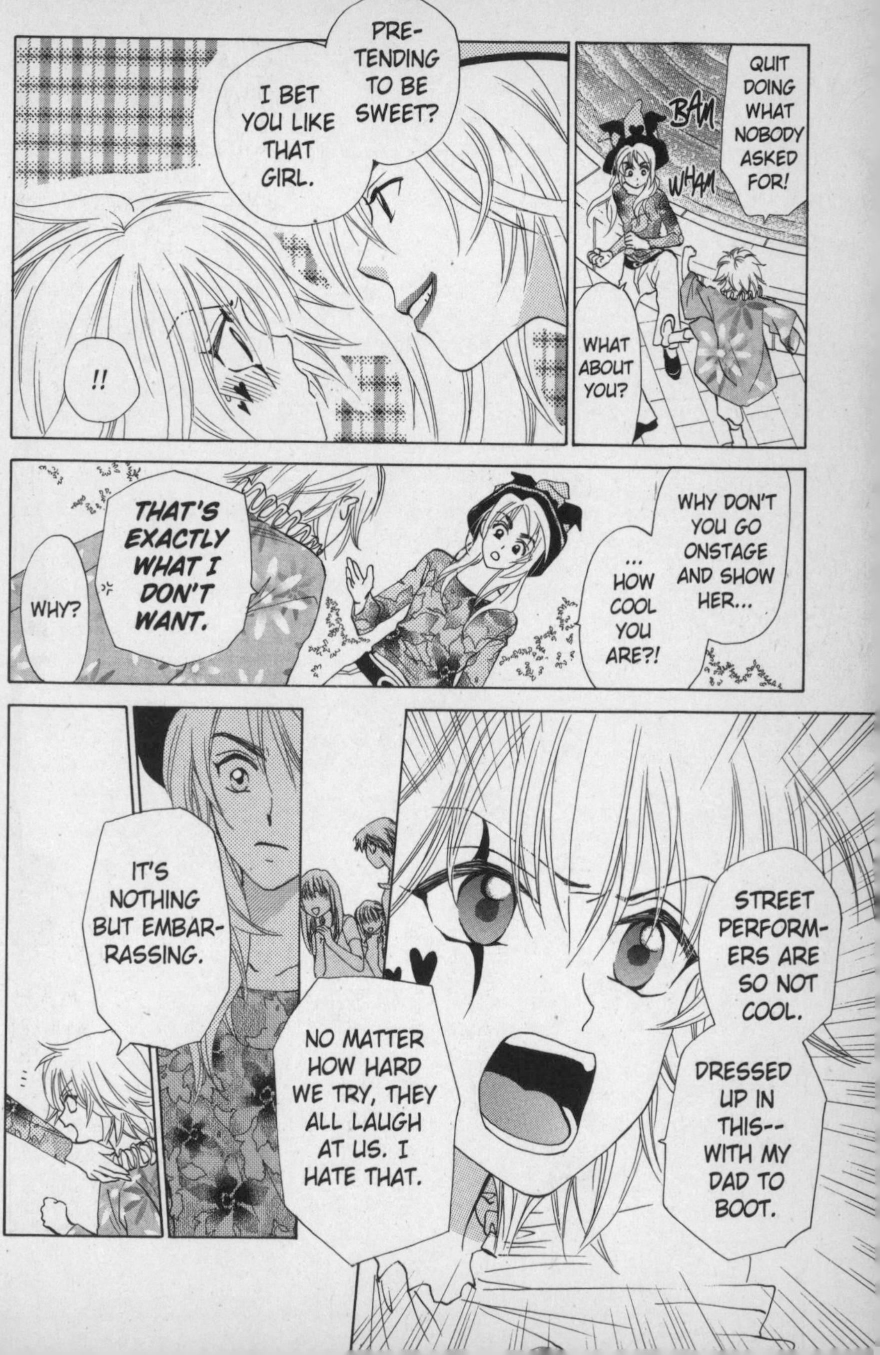
QUIT DOING WHAT NOBODY ASKED FOR!
BAM
WHAM
WHAT ABOUT YOU?
PRE-TENDING TO BE SWEET? I BET YOU LIKE THAT GIRL.
!!
WHY DON'T YOU GO ONSTAGE AND SHOW HER...
...HOW COOL YOU ARE?!
THAT'S EXACTLY WHAT I DON'T WANT.
WHY?
STREET PERFORM-ERS ARE SO NOT COOL.
DRESSED UP IN THIS--WITH MY DAD TO BOOT.
NO MATTER HOW HARD WE TRY, THEY ALL LAUGH AT US. I HATE THAT.
IT'S NOTHING BUT EMBAR-RASSING.

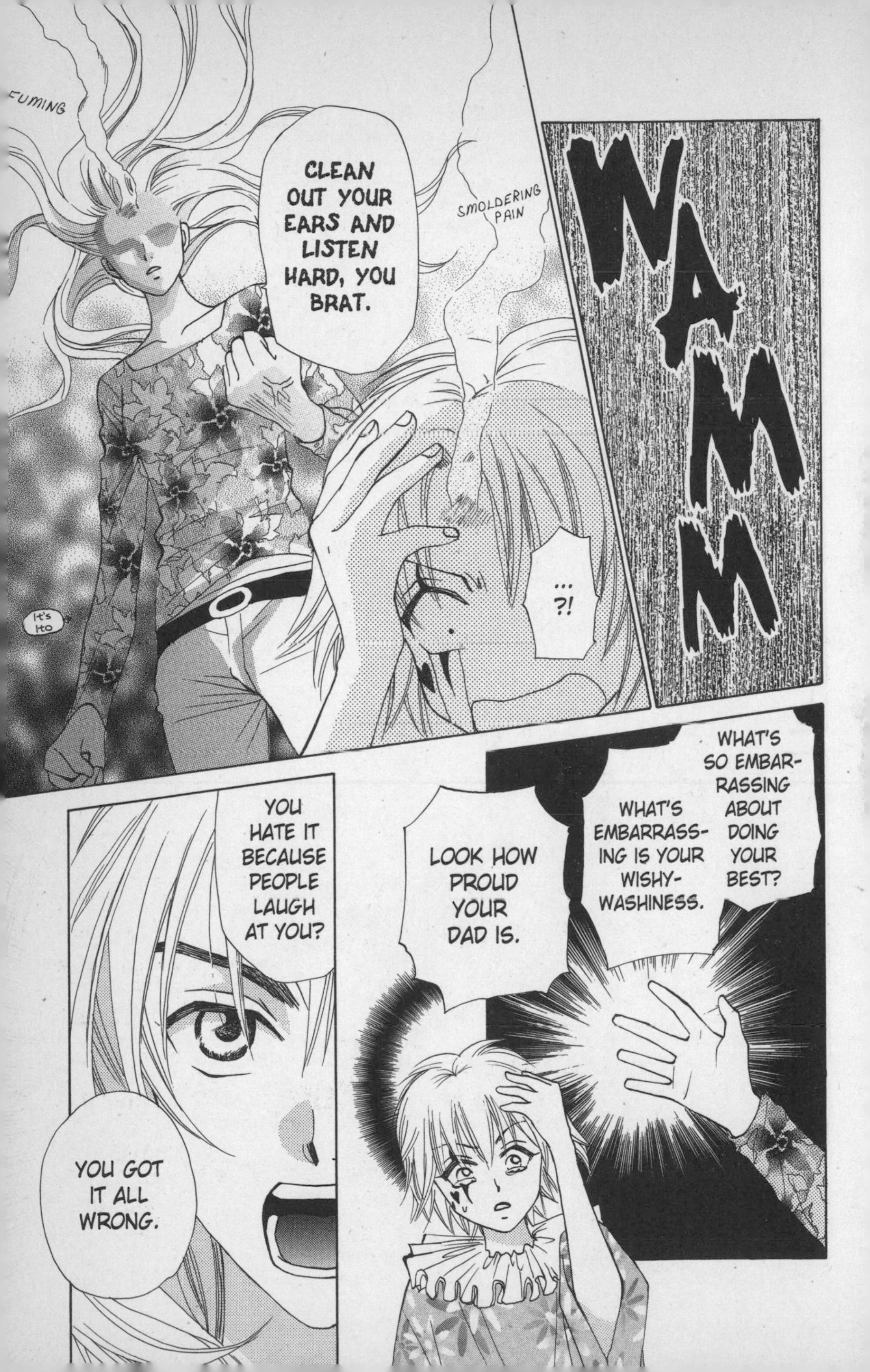
WAMM
CLEAN OUT YOUR EARS AND LISTEN HARD, YOU BRAT.
SMOLDERING PAIN
FUMING
...?!
It's Ito
WHAT'S SO EMBARRASSING ABOUT DOING YOUR BEST?
WHAT'S EMBARRASSING IS YOUR WISHY-WASHINESS.
LOOK HOW PROUD YOUR DAD IS.
YOU HATE IT BECAUSE PEOPLE LAUGH AT YOU?
YOU GOT IT ALL WRONG.

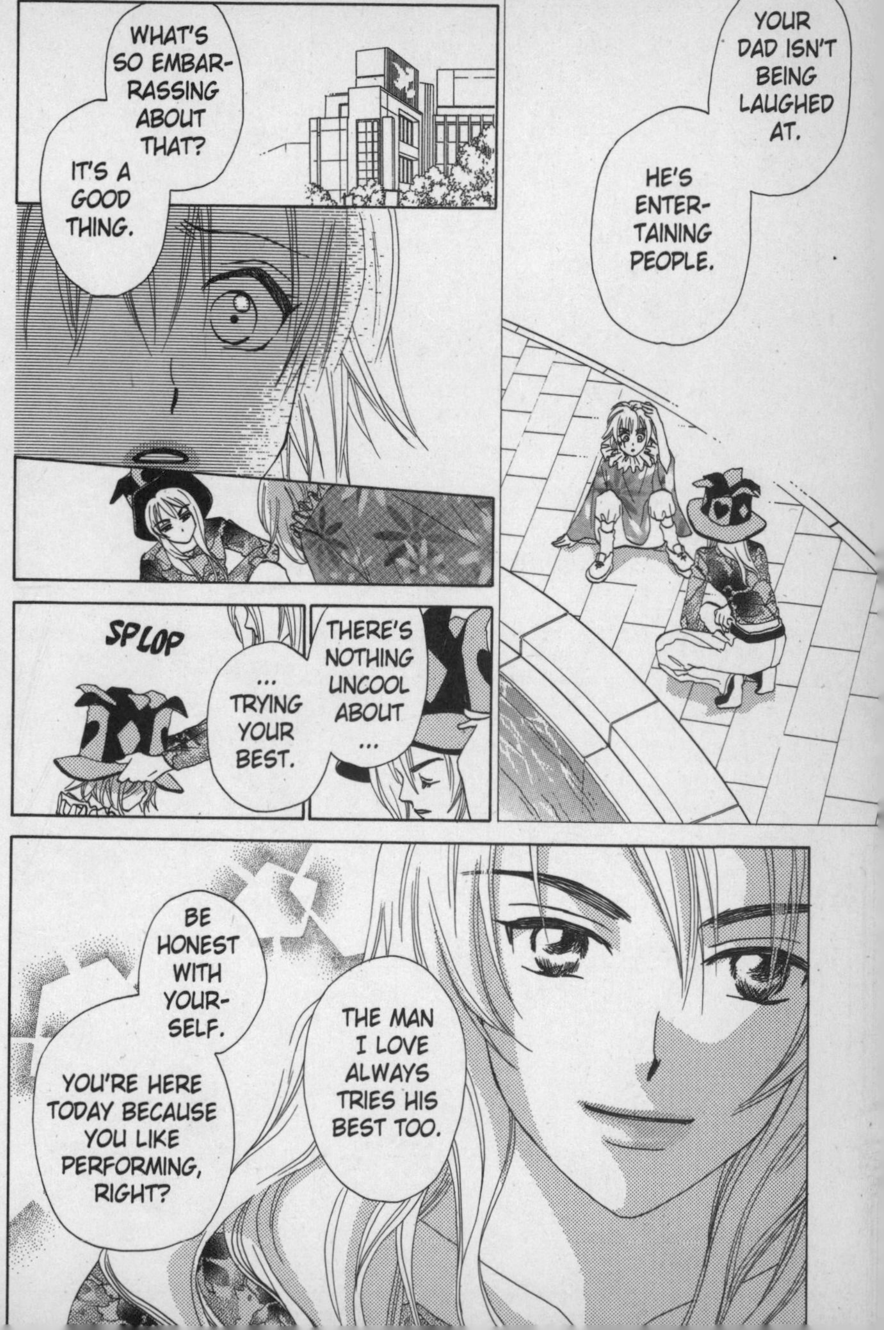
YOUR DAD ISN'T BEING LAUGHED AT.
HE'S ENTERTAINING PEOPLE.
WHAT'S SO EMBARRASSING ABOUT THAT?
IT'S A GOOD THING.
THERE'S NOTHING UNCOOL ABOUT ...
... TRYING YOUR BEST.
SPLOP
THE MAN I LOVE ALWAYS TRIES HIS BEST TOO.
BE HONEST WITH YOURSELF.
YOU'RE HERE TODAY BECAUSE YOU LIKE PERFORMING, RIGHT?

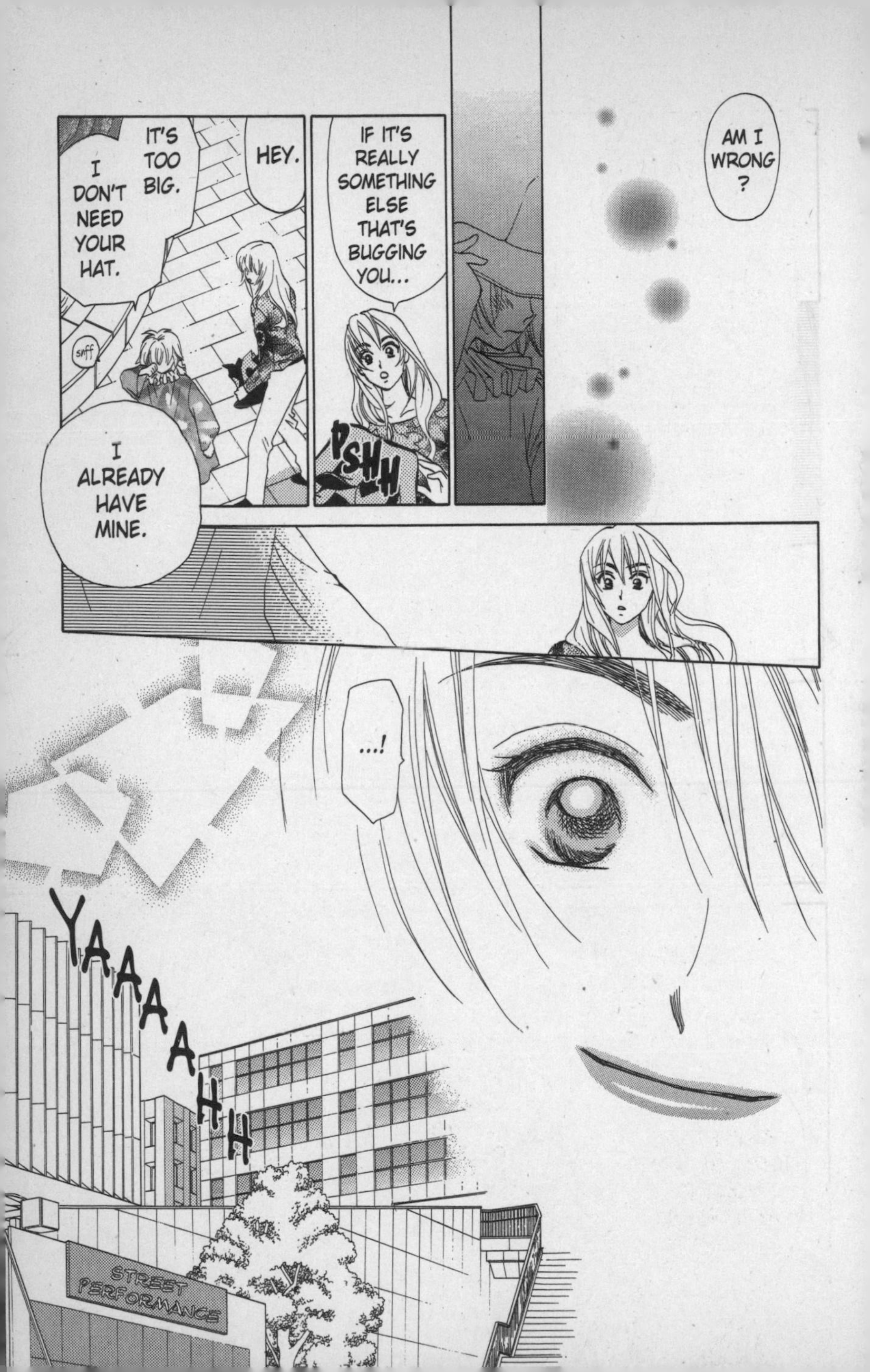
AM I WRONG ?
IF IT'S REALLY SOMETHING ELSE THAT'S BUGGING YOU...
PSHH
HEY.
IT'S TOO BIG.
I DON'T NEED YOUR HAT.
snff
I ALREADY HAVE MINE.
...!
YAAAAHH
STREET PERFORMANCE

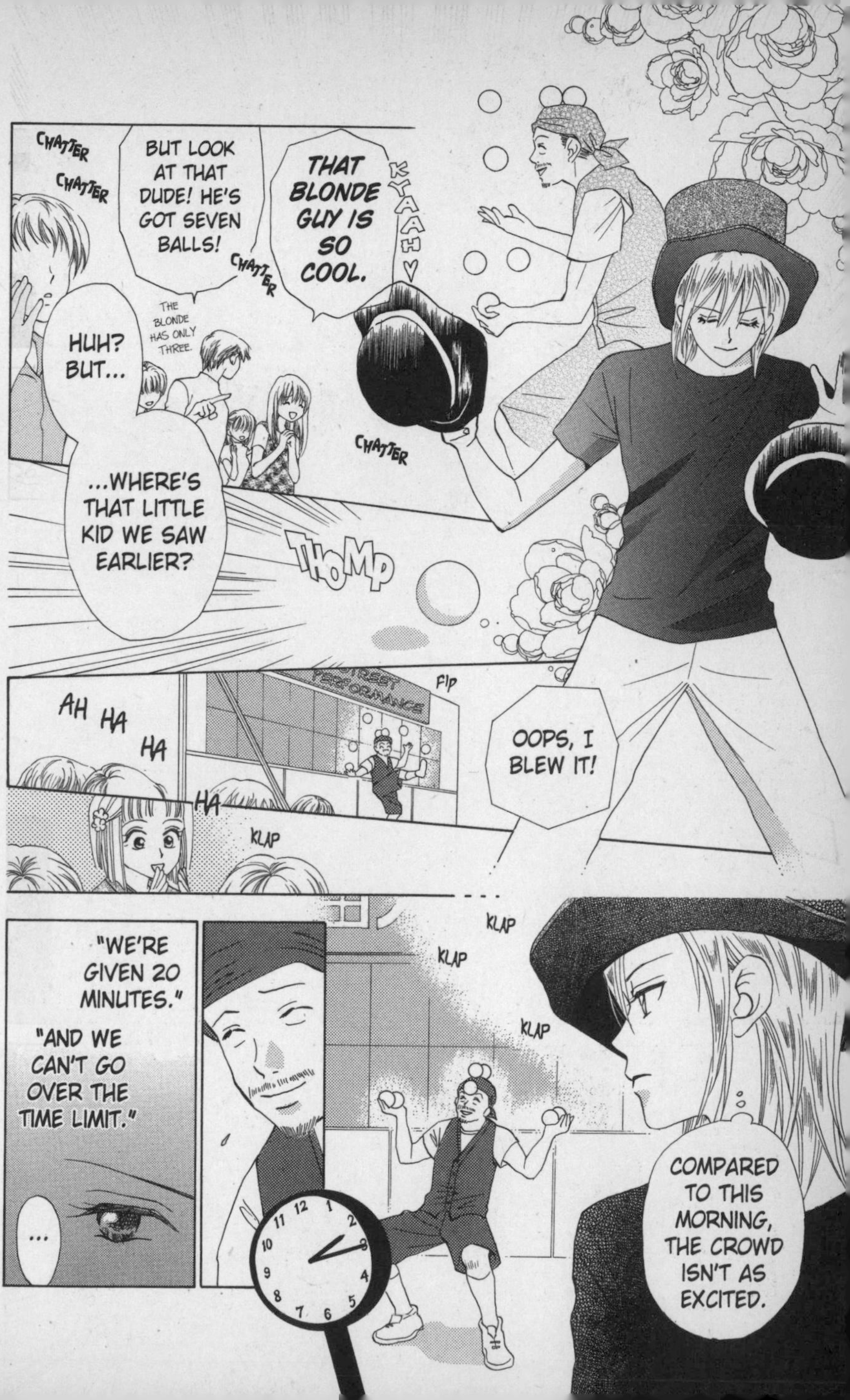
KYAAH♥
THAT BLONDE GUY IS SO COOL.
BUT LOOK AT THAT DUDE! HE'S GOT SEVEN BALLS!
CHATTER
CHATTER
CHATTER
THE BLONDE HAS ONLY THREE.
HUH? BUT...
...WHERE'S THAT LITTLE KID WE SAW EARLIER?
CHATTER
THOMP
OOPS, I BLEW IT!
FLIP
STREET PERFORMANCE
AH HA HA
HA
KLAP
COMPARED TO THIS MORNING, THE CROWD ISN'T AS EXCITED.
KLAP
KLAP
KLAP
"WE'RE GIVEN 20 MINUTES."
"AND WE CAN'T GO OVER THE TIME LIMIT."
...

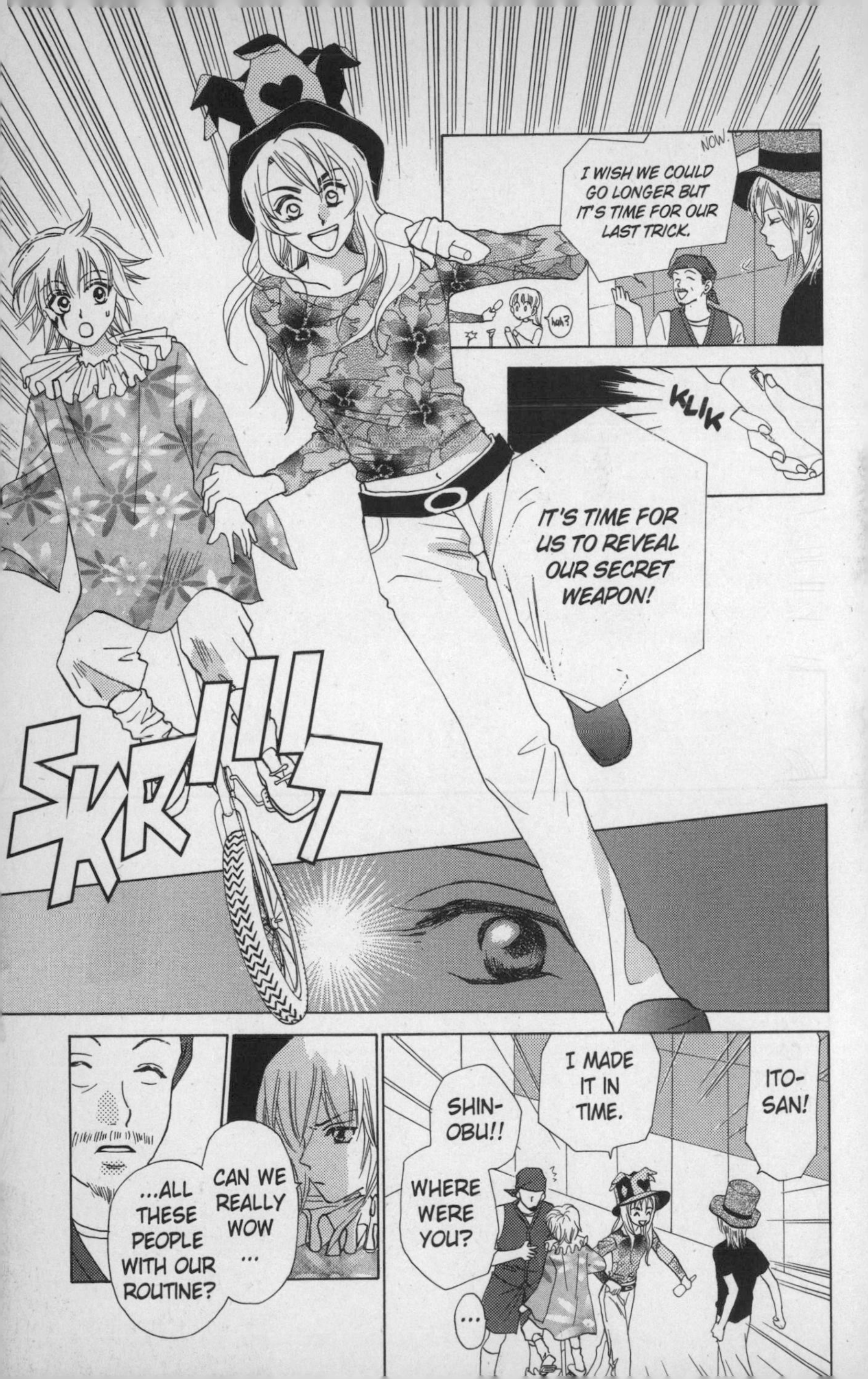
NOW.
I WISH WE COULD GO LONGER BUT IT'S TIME FOR OUR LAST TRICK.
KLIK
IT'S TIME FOR US TO REVEAL OUR SECRET WEAPON!
SKRILLT
ITO-SAN!
I MADE IT IN TIME.
SHIN-OBU!!
WHERE WERE YOU?
...
CAN WE REALLY WOW ...
...ALL THESE PEOPLE WITH OUR ROUTINE?

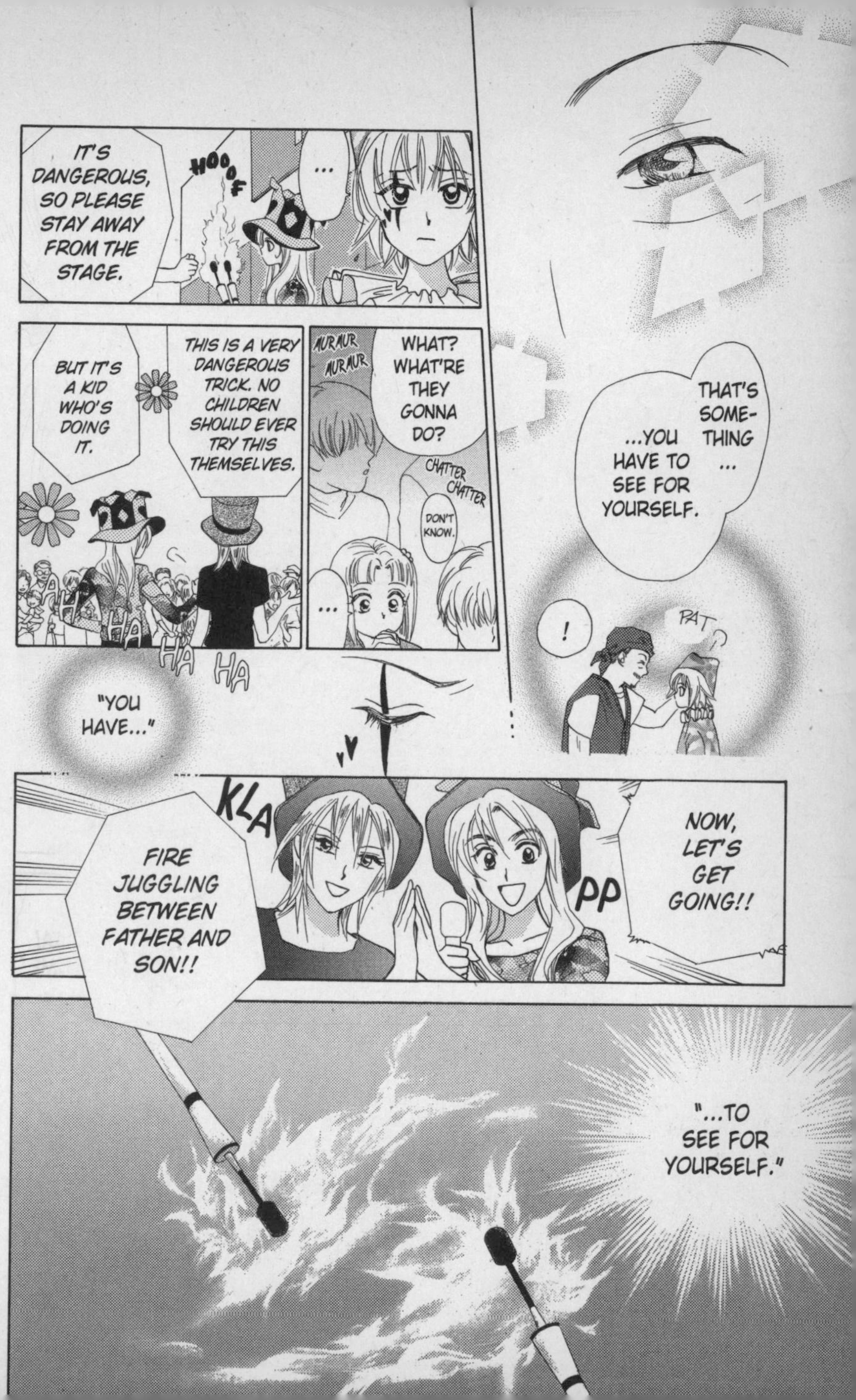
THAT'S SOMETHING...
...YOU HAVE TO SEE FOR YOURSELF.
!
PAT
...
HOOOF
IT'S DANGEROUS, SO PLEASE STAY AWAY FROM THE STAGE.
WHAT? WHAT'RE THEY GONNA DO?
MURMUR MURMUR
CHATTER CHATTER
DON'T KNOW.
...
THIS IS A VERY DANGEROUS TRICK. NO CHILDREN SHOULD EVER TRY THIS THEMSELVES.
BUT IT'S A KID WHO'S DOING IT.
AH HA HA HA HA
"YOU HAVE..."
NOW, LET'S GET GOING!!
KLAPP
FIRE JUGGLING BETWEEN FATHER AND SON!!
"...TO SEE FOR YOURSELF."

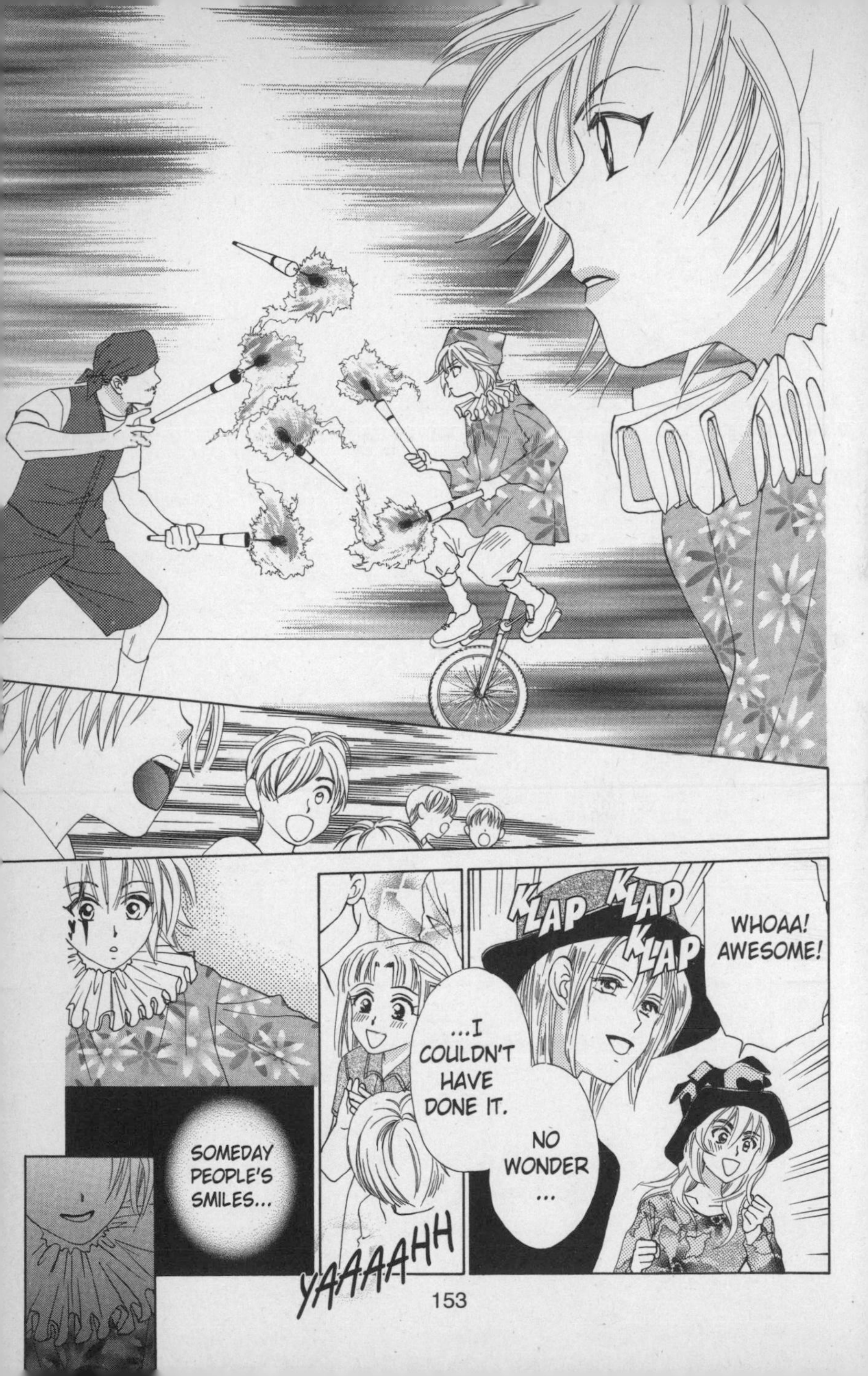
KLAP KLAP KLAP
WHOAA! AWESOME!
...I COULDN'T HAVE DONE IT.
NO WONDER ...
YAAAAHH
SOMEDAY PEOPLE'S SMILES...

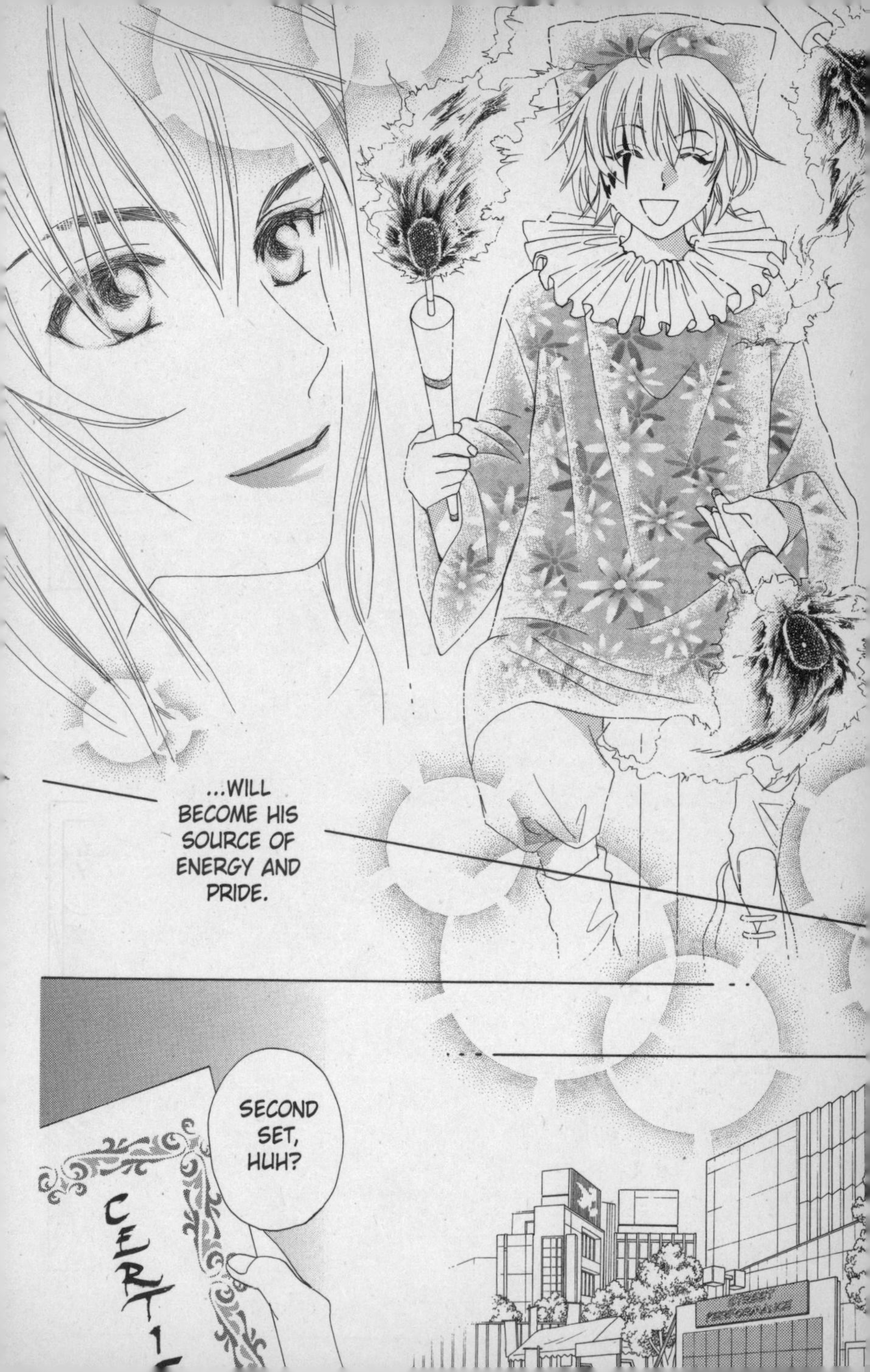
...WILL BECOME HIS SOURCE OF ENERGY AND PRIDE.
SECOND SET, HUH?

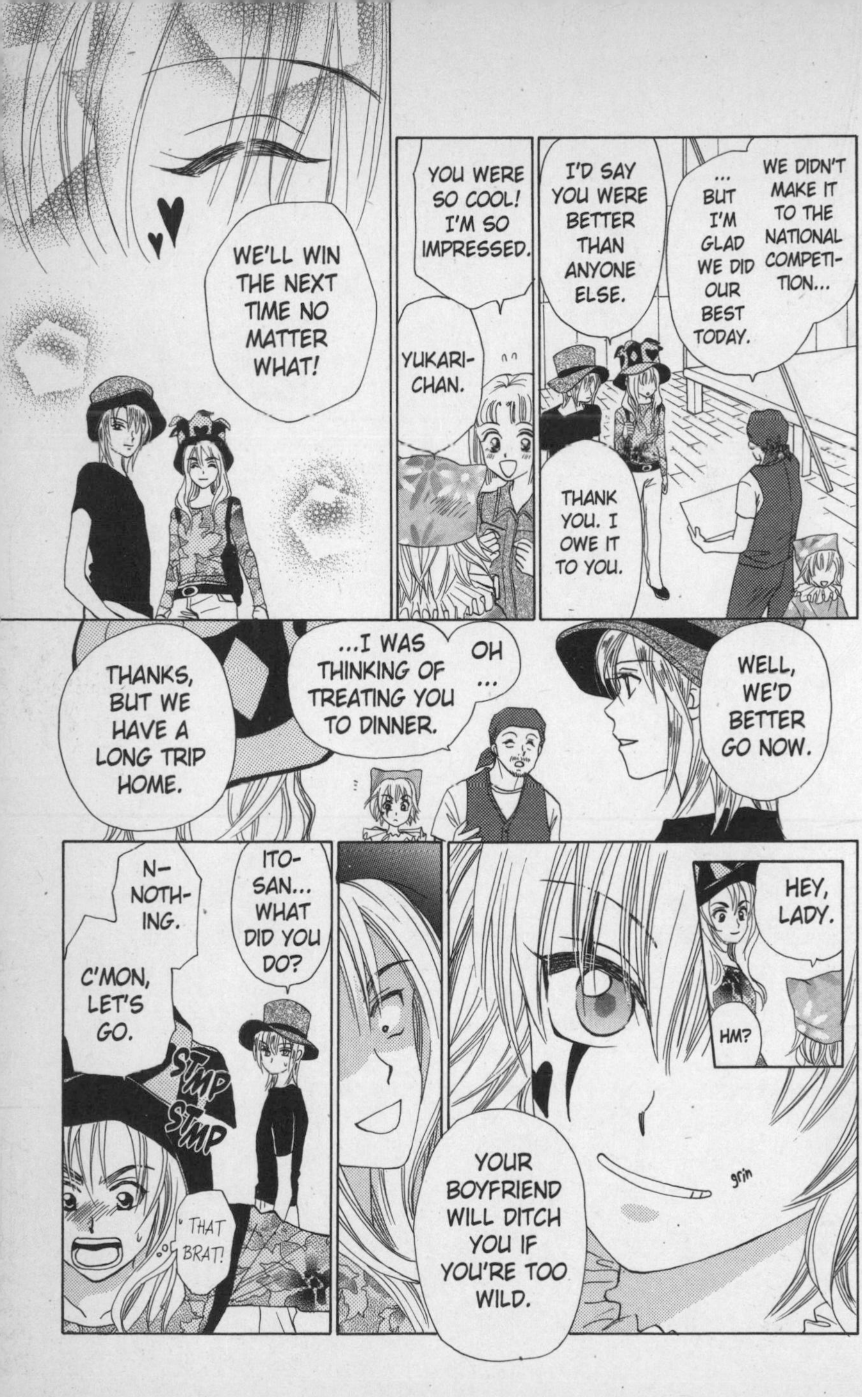
WE DIDN'T MAKE IT TO THE NATIONAL COMPETITION...
... BUT I'M GLAD WE DID OUR BEST TODAY.
I'D SAY YOU WERE BETTER THAN ANYONE ELSE.
THANK YOU. I OWE IT TO YOU.
YOU WERE SO COOL! I'M SO IMPRESSED.
YUKARI-CHAN.
WE'LL WIN THE NEXT TIME NO MATTER WHAT!
WELL, WE'D BETTER GO NOW.
OH ...
...I WAS THINKING OF TREATING YOU TO DINNER.
THANKS, BUT WE HAVE A LONG TRIP HOME.
HEY, LADY.
HM?
grin
YOUR BOYFRIEND WILL DITCH YOU IF YOU'RE TOO WILD.
ITO-SAN... WHAT DID YOU DO?
N-NOTHING.
C'MON, LET'S GO.
STMP STMP
THAT BRAT!

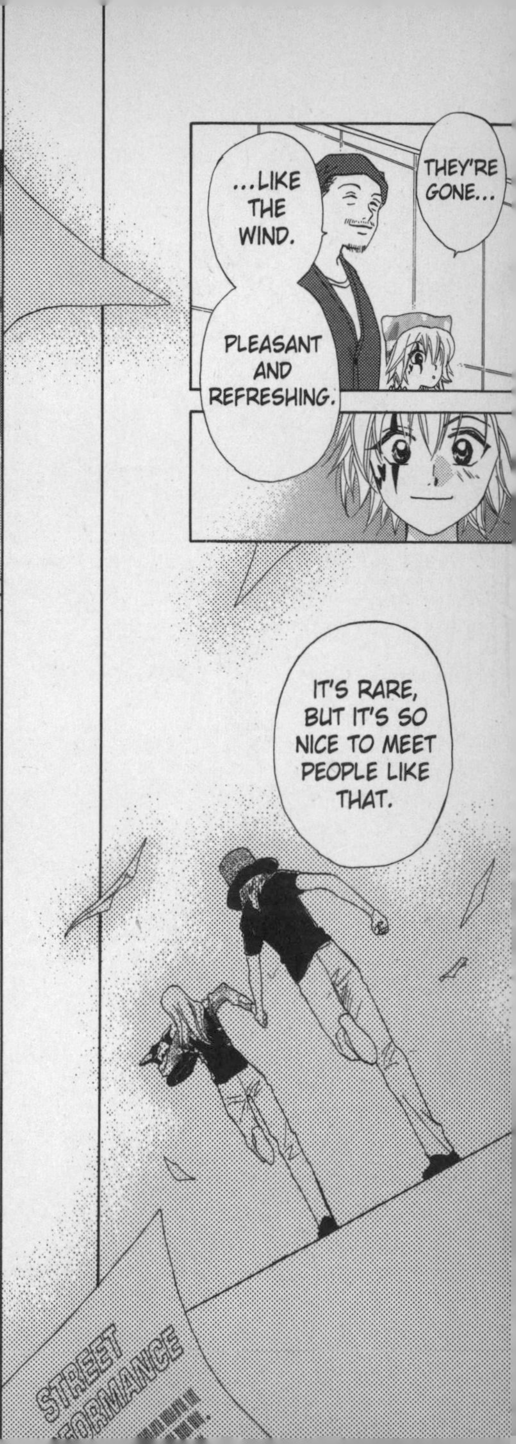
THEY'RE GONE...
...LIKE THE WIND.
PLEASANT AND REFRESHING.
IT'S RARE, BUT IT'S SO NICE TO MEET PEOPLE LIKE THAT.
STREET
FORMANCE

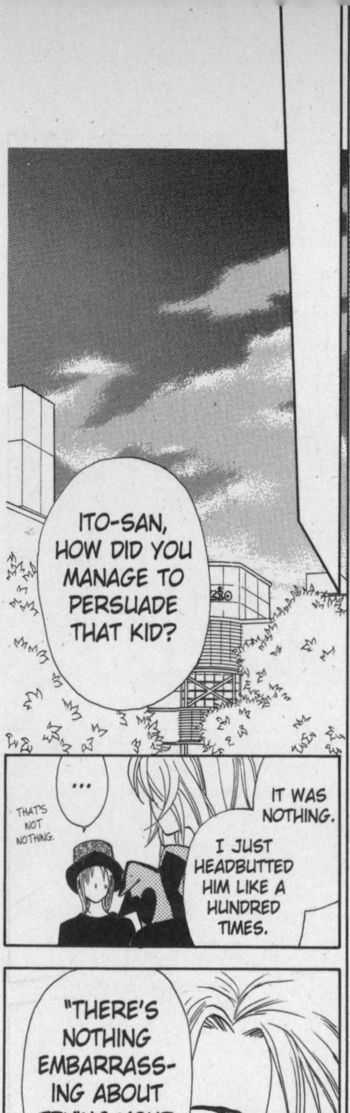
ITO-SAN, HOW DID YOU MANAGE TO PERSUADE THAT KID?
IT WAS NOTHING.
I JUST HEADBUTTED HIM LIKE A HUNDRED TIMES.
...
THAT'S NOT NOTHING.
"THERE'S NOTHING EMBARRASS-ING ABOUT TRYING YOUR BEST."
I SAID SOMETHING LIKE THAT.

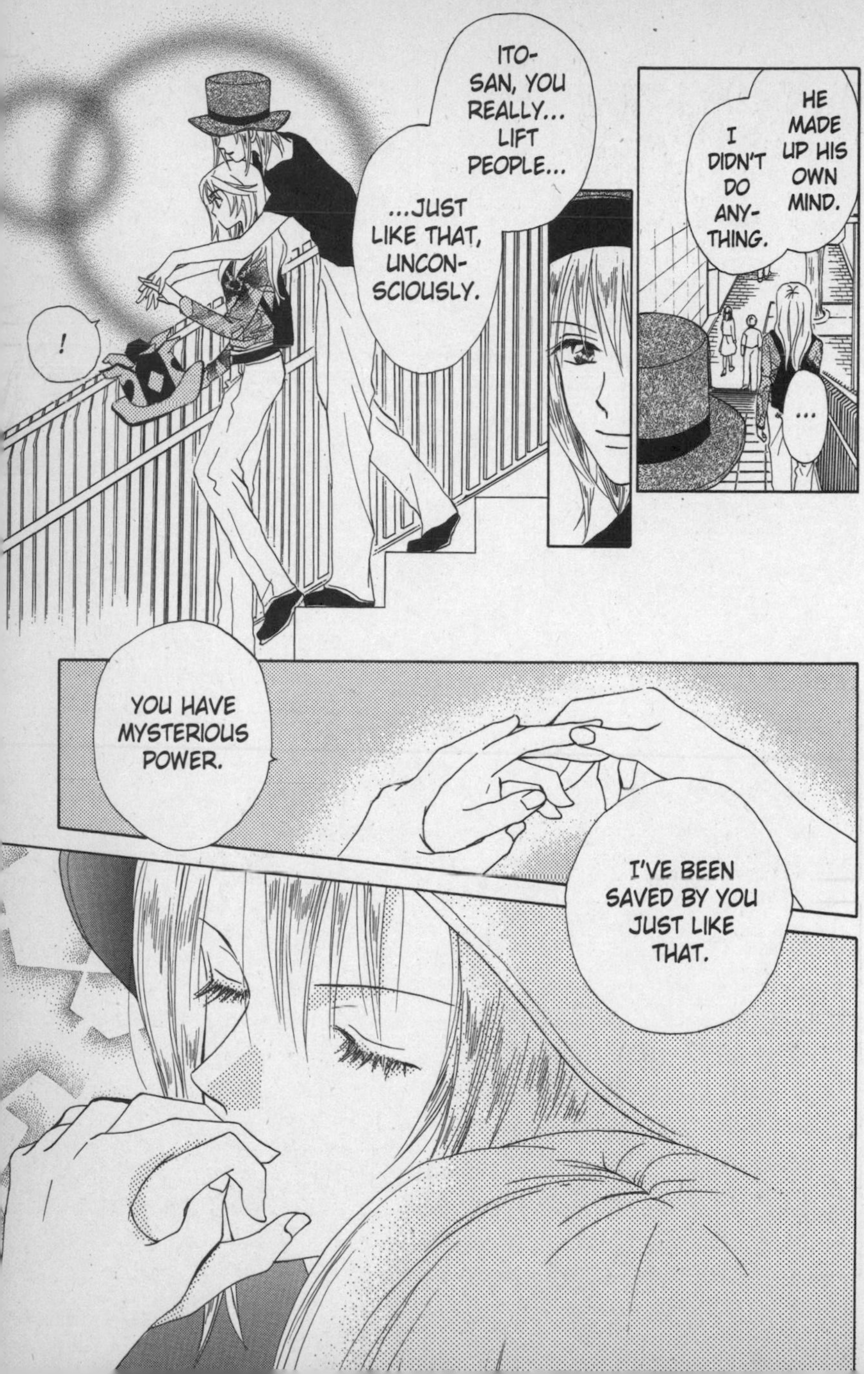
HE MADE UP HIS OWN MIND.
I DIDN'T DO ANYTHING.
...
ITO-SAN, YOU REALLY... LIFT PEOPLE...
...JUST LIKE THAT, UNCONSCIOUSLY.
!
YOU HAVE MYSTERIOUS POWER.
I'VE BEEN SAVED BY YOU JUST LIKE THAT.

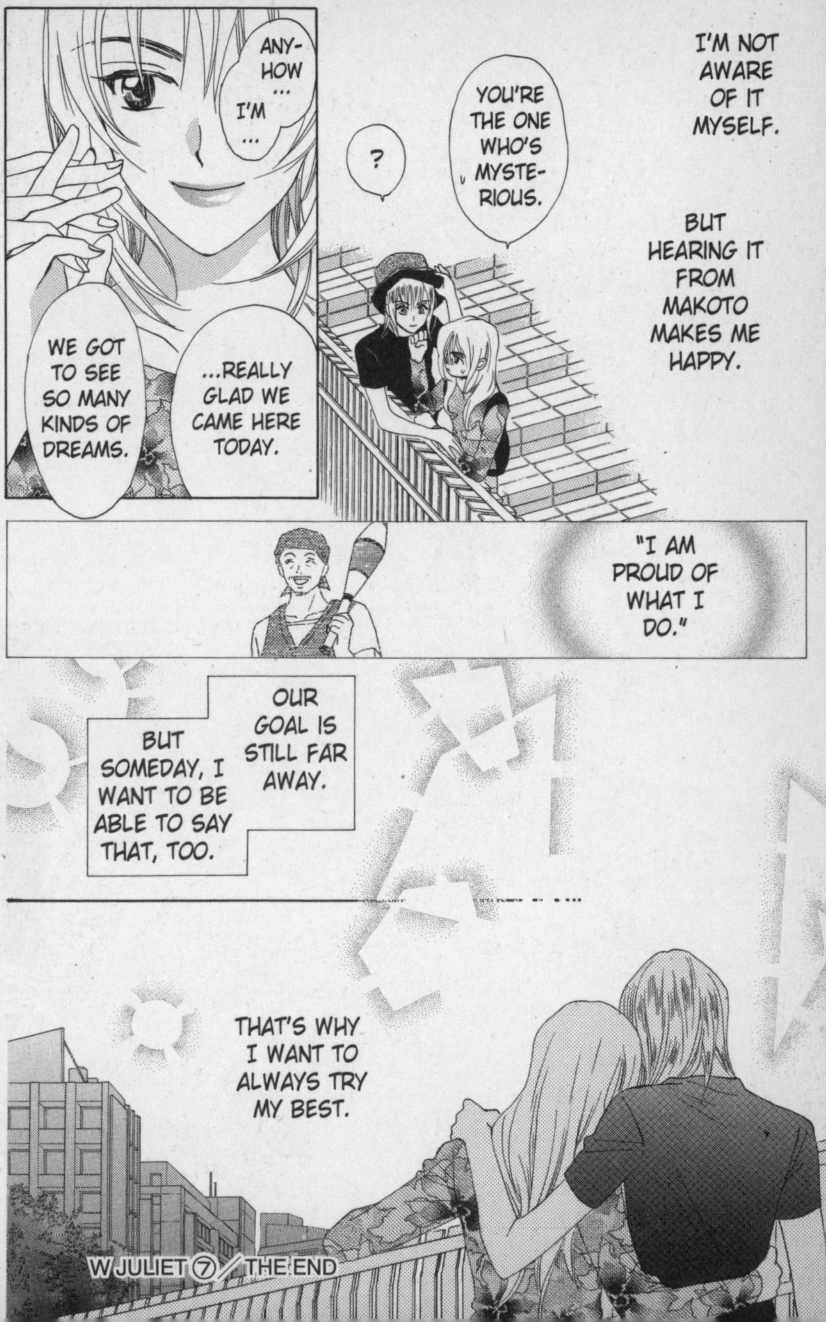
YOU'RE THE ONE WHO'S MYSTE-RIOUS.
?
I'M NOT AWARE OF IT MYSELF.
BUT HEARING IT FROM MAKOTO MAKES ME HAPPY.
ANY-HOW ... I'M ...
...REALLY GLAD WE CAME HERE TODAY.
WE GOT TO SEE SO MANY KINDS OF DREAMS.
"I AM PROUD OF WHAT I DO."
OUR GOAL IS STILL FAR AWAY.
BUT SOMEDAY, I WANT TO BE ABLE TO SAY THAT, TOO.
THAT'S WHY I WANT TO ALWAYS TRY MY BEST.
W JULIET 7 / THE END

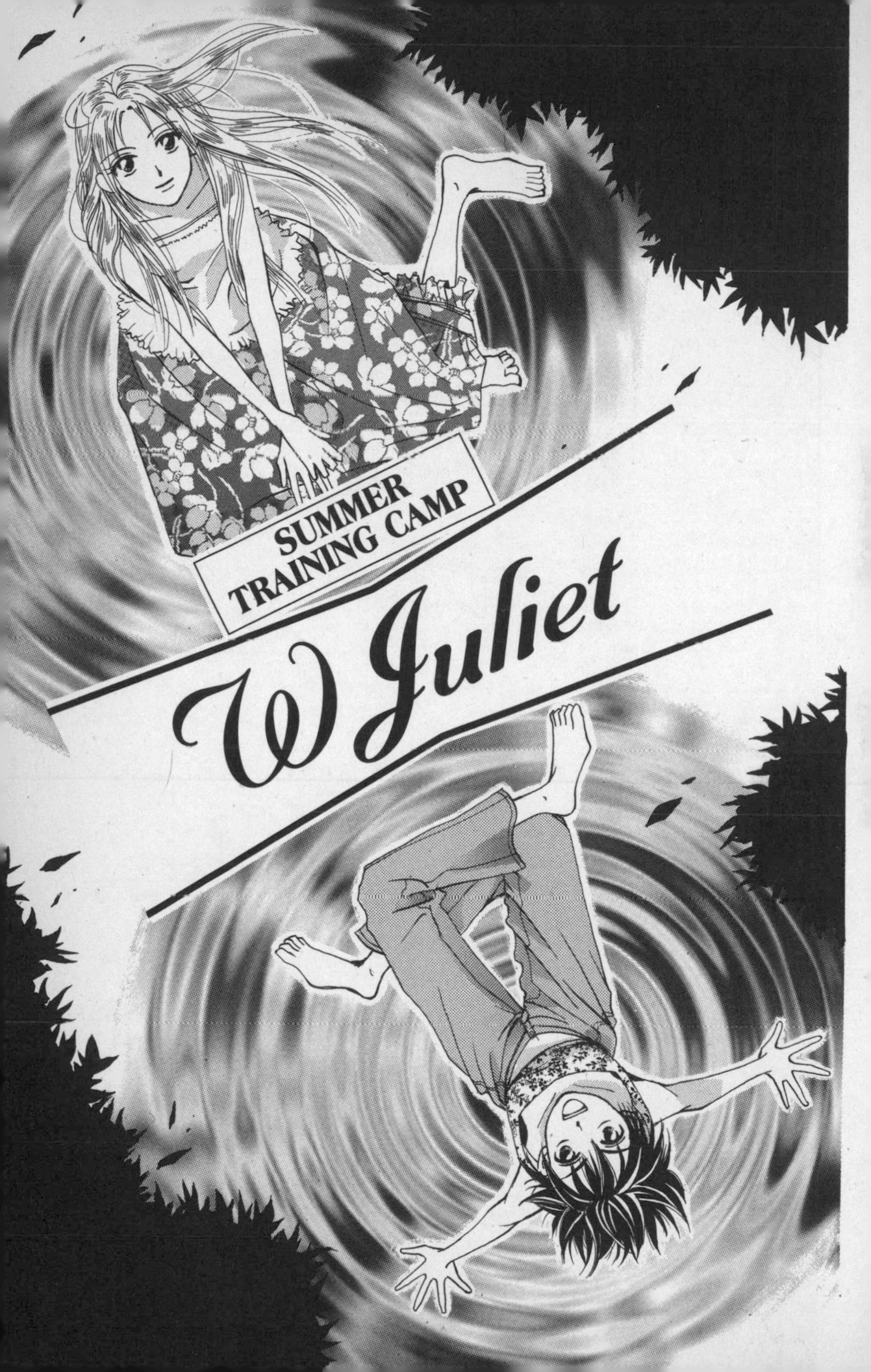
SUMMER TRAINING CAMP
W Juliet

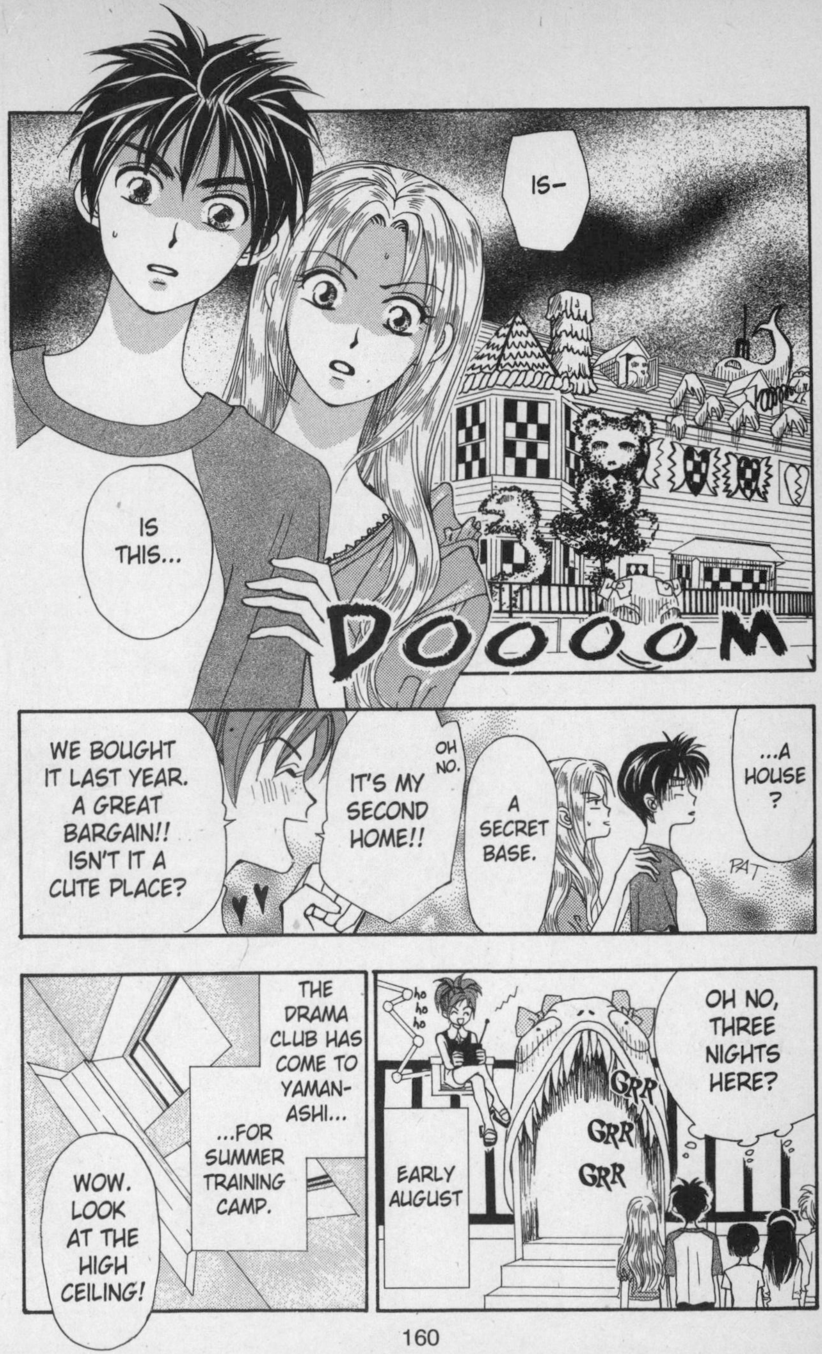
IS-
IS THIS...
DOOOOM
...A HOUSE?
PAT
A SECRET BASE.
OH NO.
IT'S MY SECOND HOME!!
WE BOUGHT IT LAST YEAR. A GREAT BARGAIN!! ISN'T IT A CUTE PLACE?
OH NO, THREE NIGHTS HERE?
ho ho ho
GRR
GRR
GRR
EARLY AUGUST
THE DRAMA CLUB HAS COME TO YAMAN-ASHI...
...FOR SUMMER TRAINING CAMP.
WOW. LOOK AT THE HIGH CEILING!

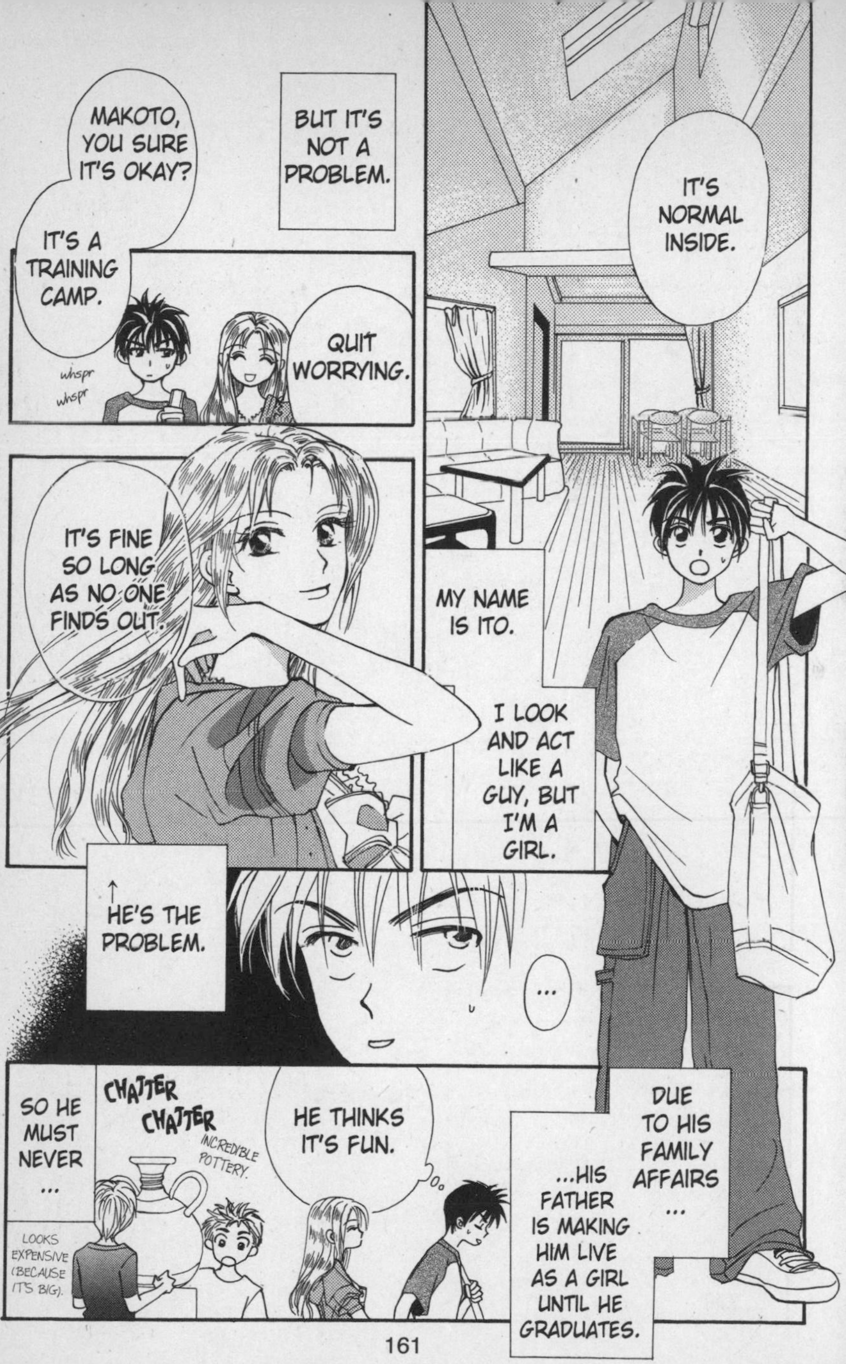
IT'S NORMAL INSIDE.
MY NAME IS ITO.
I LOOK AND ACT LIKE A GUY, BUT I'M A GIRL.
BUT IT'S NOT A PROBLEM.
MAKOTO, YOU SURE IT'S OKAY?
IT'S A TRAINING CAMP.
QUIT WORRYING.
whspr
whspr
IT'S FINE SO LONG AS NO ONE FINDS OUT.
...
↑ HE'S THE PROBLEM.
DUE TO HIS FAMILY AFFAIRS ...
...HIS FATHER IS MAKING HIM LIVE AS A GIRL UNTIL HE GRADUATES.
HE THINKS IT'S FUN.
CHATTER
CHATTER
INCREDIBLE POTTERY.
SO HE MUST NEVER ...
LOOKS EXPENSIVE (BECAUSE IT'S BIG).

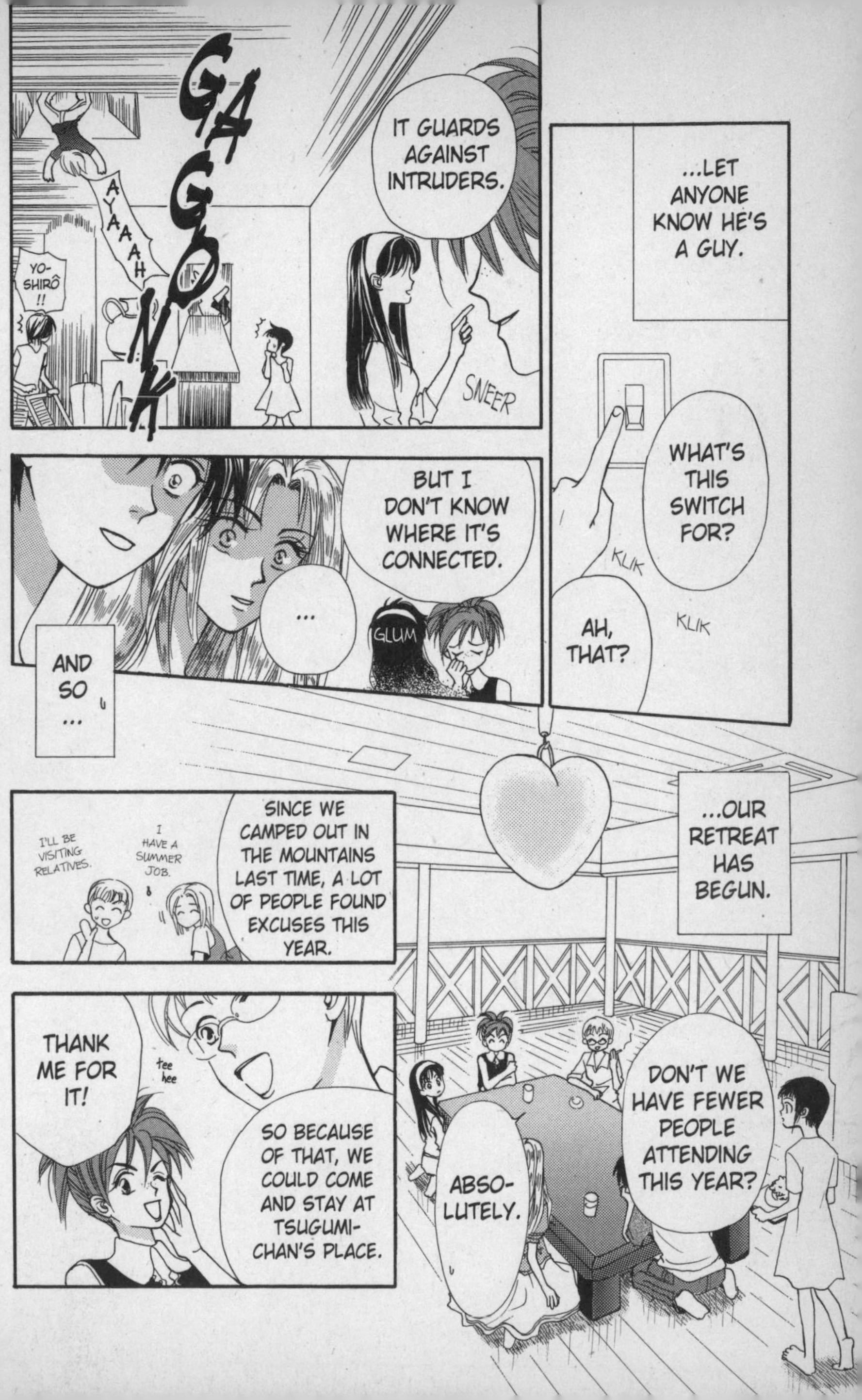
...LET ANYONE KNOW HE'S A GUY.
WHAT'S THIS SWITCH FOR?
KLIK
KLIK
AH, THAT?
IT GUARDS AGAINST INTRUDERS.
GAGONK
AYAAAH
YO-SHIRÔ !!
SNEER
BUT I DON'T KNOW WHERE IT'S CONNECTED.
...
GLUM
AND SO ...
...OUR RETREAT HAS BEGUN.
DON'T WE HAVE FEWER PEOPLE ATTENDING THIS YEAR?
ABSO-LUTELY.
SINCE WE CAMPED OUT IN THE MOUNTAINS LAST TIME, A LOT OF PEOPLE FOUND EXCUSES THIS YEAR.
I HAVE A SUMMER JOB.
I'LL BE VISITING RELATIVES.
SO BECAUSE OF THAT, WE COULD COME AND STAY AT TSUGUMI-CHAN'S PLACE.
THANK ME FOR IT!
tee hee

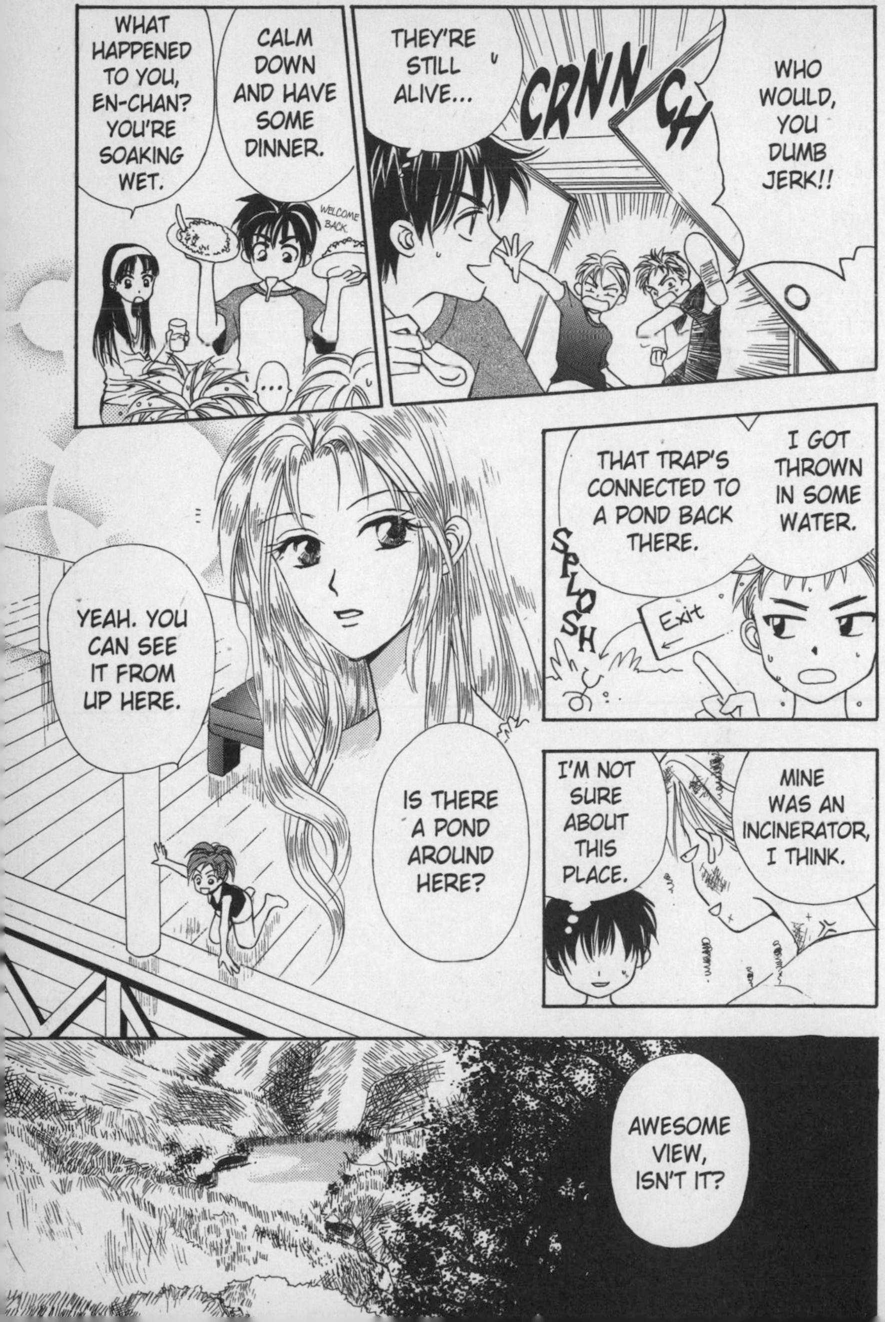
THEY'RE STILL ALIVE...
CRNNCH
WHO WOULD, YOU DUMB JERK!!
CALM DOWN AND HAVE SOME DINNER.
WELCOME BACK.
WHAT HAPPENED TO YOU, EN-CHAN? YOU'RE SOAKING WET.
...
I GOT THROWN IN SOME WATER.
THAT TRAP'S CONNECTED TO A POND BACK THERE.
SPLOSH
Exit
MINE WAS AN INCINERATOR, I THINK.
I'M NOT SURE ABOUT THIS PLACE.
IS THERE A POND AROUND HERE?
YEAH. YOU CAN SEE IT FROM UP HERE.
AWESOME VIEW, ISN'T IT?

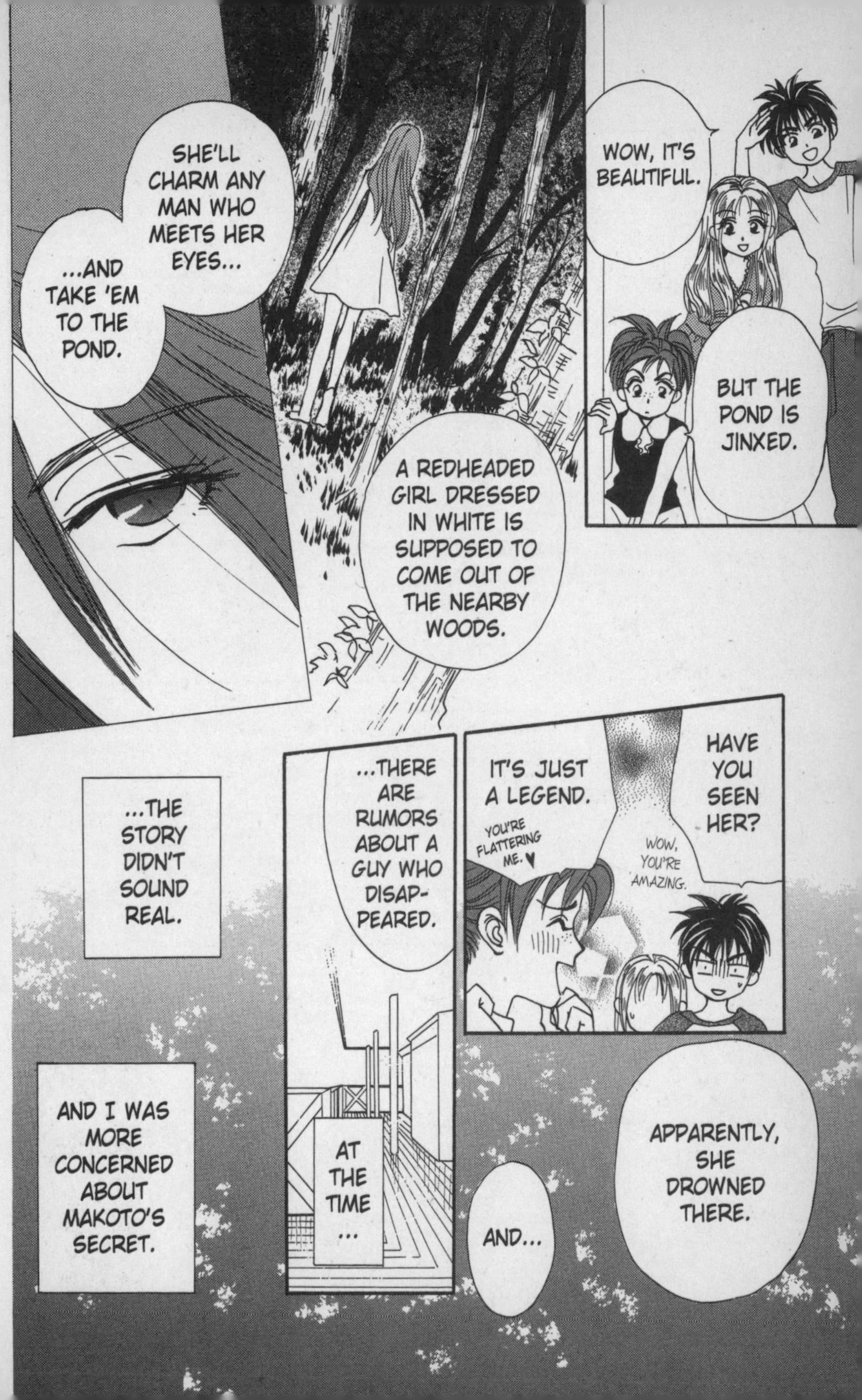
WOW, IT'S BEAUTIFUL.
BUT THE POND IS JINXED.
A REDHEADED GIRL DRESSED IN WHITE IS SUPPOSED TO COME OUT OF THE NEARBY WOODS.
SHE'LL CHARM ANY MAN WHO MEETS HER EYES...
...AND TAKE 'EM TO THE POND.
HAVE YOU SEEN HER?
IT'S JUST A LEGEND.
WOW, YOU'RE AMAZING.
YOU'RE FLATTERING ME. ♥
APPARENTLY, SHE DROWNED THERE.
AND...
...THERE ARE RUMORS ABOUT A GUY WHO DISAP-PEARED.
AT THE TIME...
...THE STORY DIDN'T SOUND REAL.
AND I WAS MORE CONCERNED ABOUT MAKOTO'S SECRET.

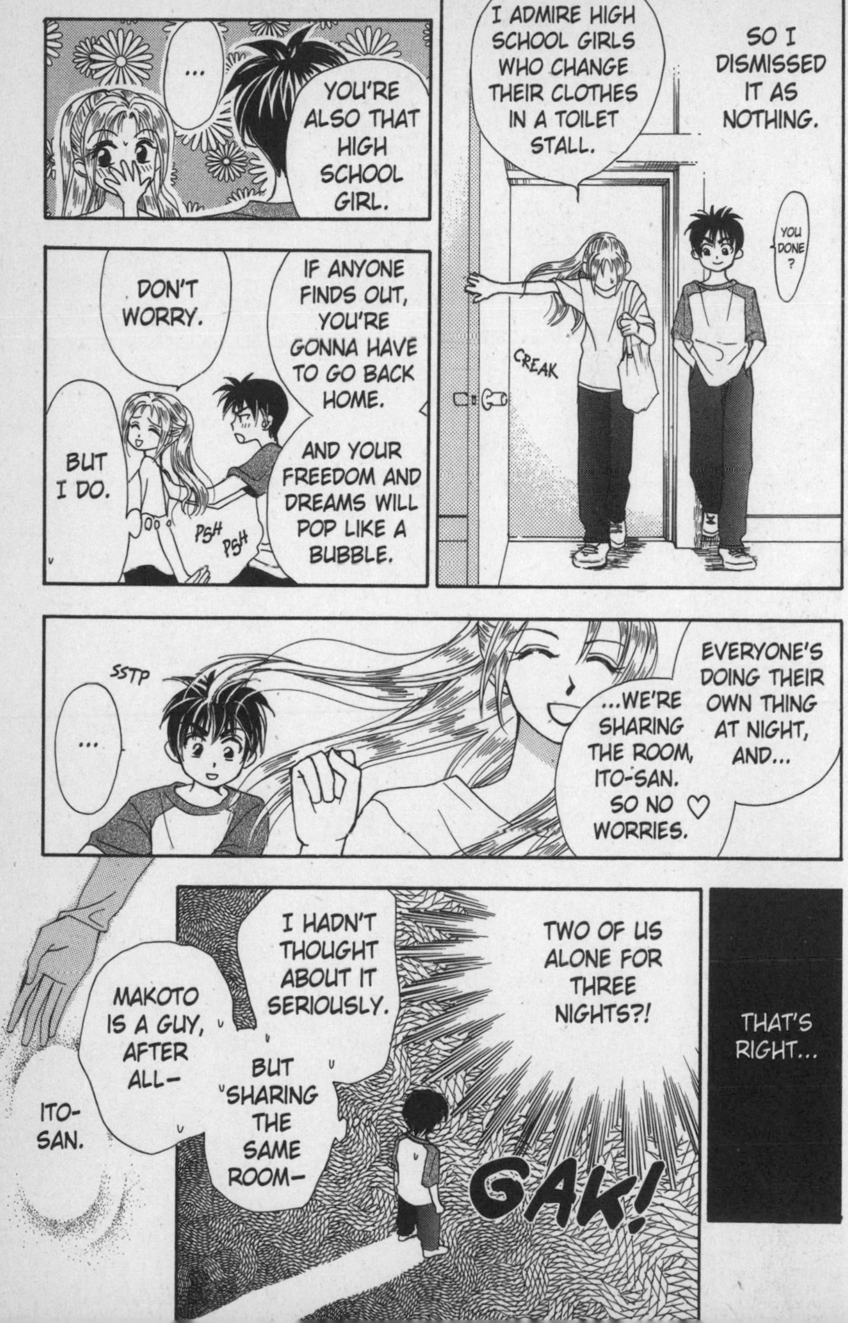
SO I DISMISSED IT AS NOTHING.
I ADMIRE HIGH SCHOOL GIRLS WHO CHANGE THEIR CLOTHES IN A TOILET STALL.
YOU DONE?
CREAK
YOU'RE ALSO THAT HIGH SCHOOL GIRL.
...
IF ANYONE FINDS OUT, YOU'RE GONNA HAVE TO GO BACK HOME.
AND YOUR FREEDOM AND DREAMS WILL POP LIKE A BUBBLE.
DON'T WORRY.
BUT I DO.
PSH PSH
EVERYONE'S DOING THEIR OWN THING AT NIGHT, AND...
...WE'RE SHARING THE ROOM, ITO-SAN. SO NO WORRIES. ♡
SSTP
...
THAT'S RIGHT...
TWO OF US ALONE FOR THREE NIGHTS?!
I HADN'T THOUGHT ABOUT IT SERIOUSLY.
BUT SHARING THE SAME ROOM—
MAKOTO IS A GUY, AFTER ALL—
GAK!
ITO-SAN.

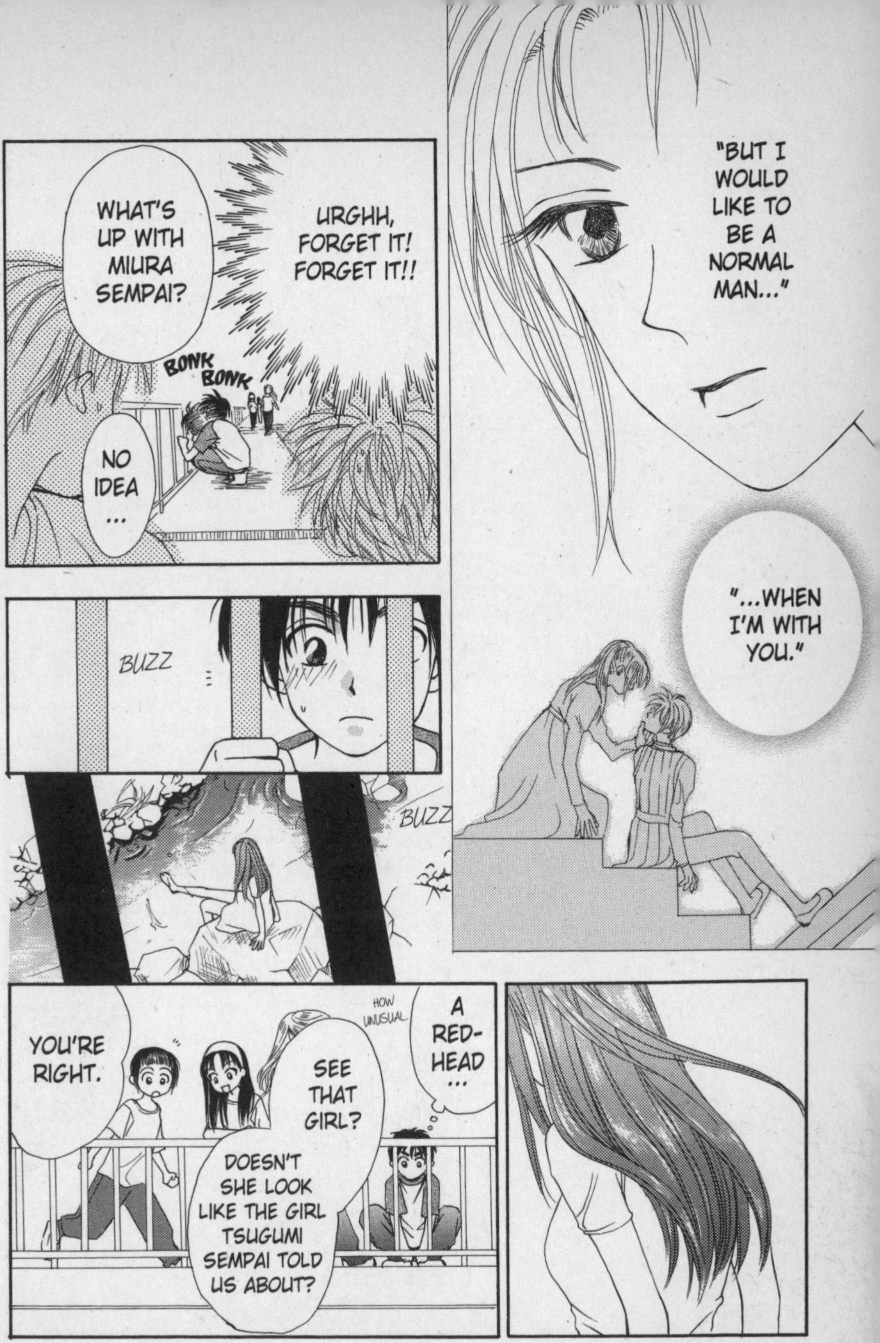
"BUT I WOULD LIKE TO BE A NORMAL MAN..."
"...WHEN I'M WITH YOU."
URGHH, FORGET IT! FORGET IT!!
WHAT'S UP WITH MIURA SEMPAI?
BONK BONK
NO IDEA ...
BUZZ
BUZZ
A RED-HEAD ...
HOW UNUSUAL.
SEE THAT GIRL?
DOESN'T SHE LOOK LIKE THE GIRL TSUGUMI SEMPAI TOLD US ABOUT?
YOU'RE RIGHT.

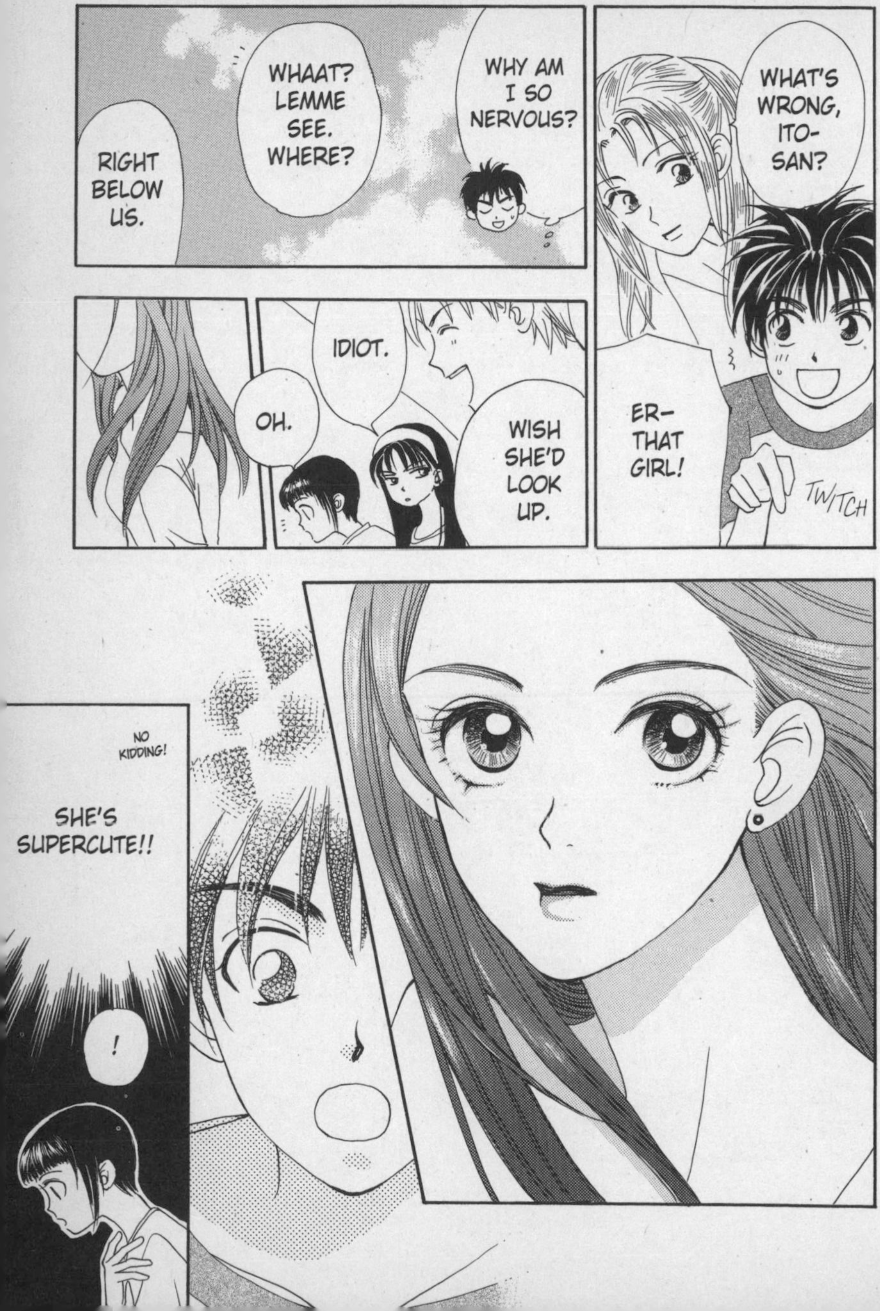
WHAT'S WRONG, ITO-SAN?
ER— THAT GIRL!
TWITCH
WHY AM I SO NERVOUS?
WHAAT? LEMME SEE. WHERE?
RIGHT BELOW US.
IDIOT.
WISH SHE'D LOOK UP.
OH.
NO KIDDING!
SHE'S SUPERCUTE!!
!

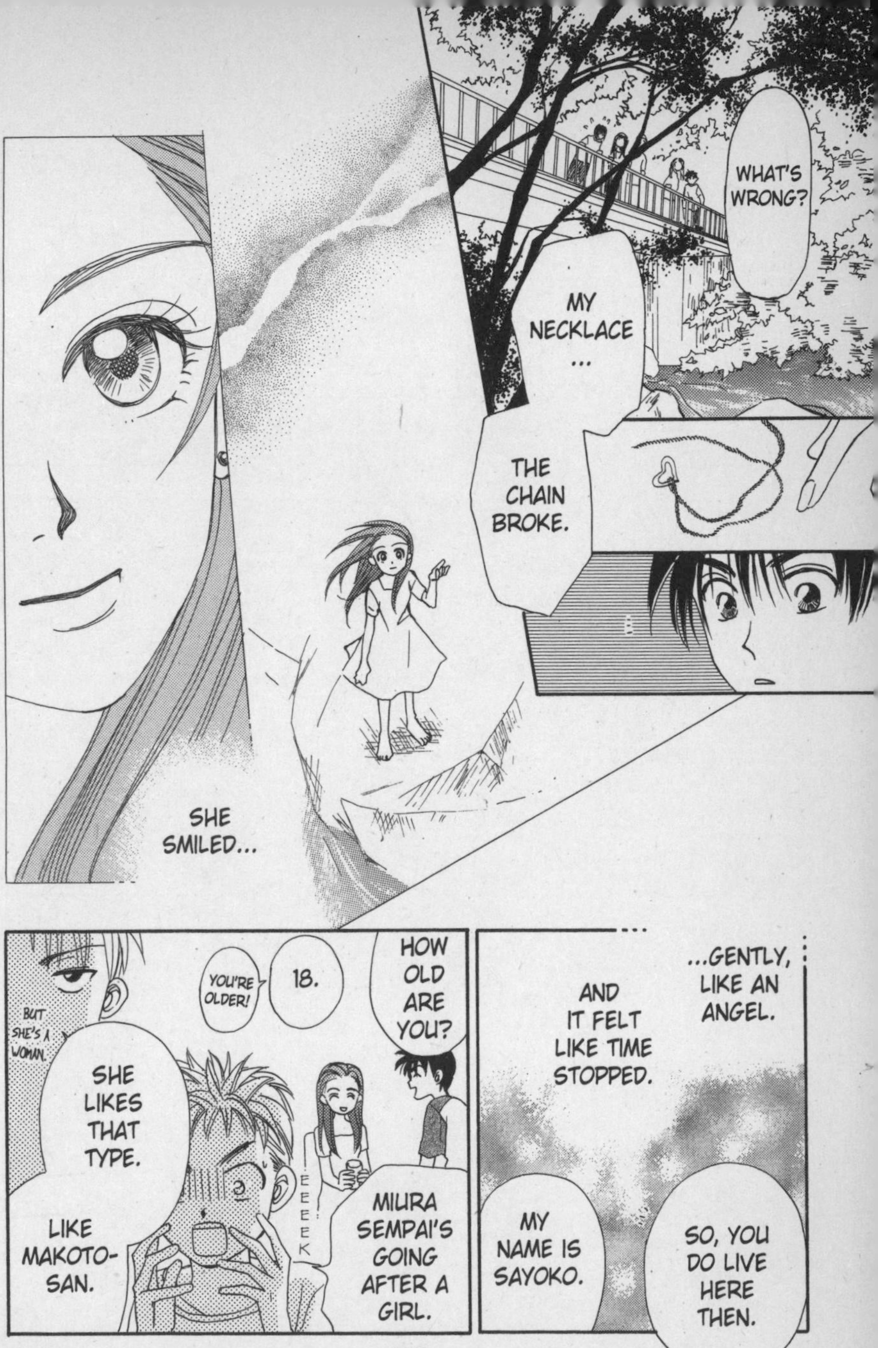
WHAT'S WRONG?
MY NECKLACE ...
THE CHAIN BROKE.
SHE SMILED...
...GENTLY, LIKE AN ANGEL.
AND IT FELT LIKE TIME STOPPED.
SO, YOU DO LIVE HERE THEN.
MY NAME IS SAYOKO.
HOW OLD ARE YOU?
18.
YOU'RE OLDER!
BUT SHE'S A WOMAN.
MIURA SEMPAI'S GOING AFTER A GIRL.
EEEEK
SHE LIKES THAT TYPE.
LIKE MAKOTO-SAN.

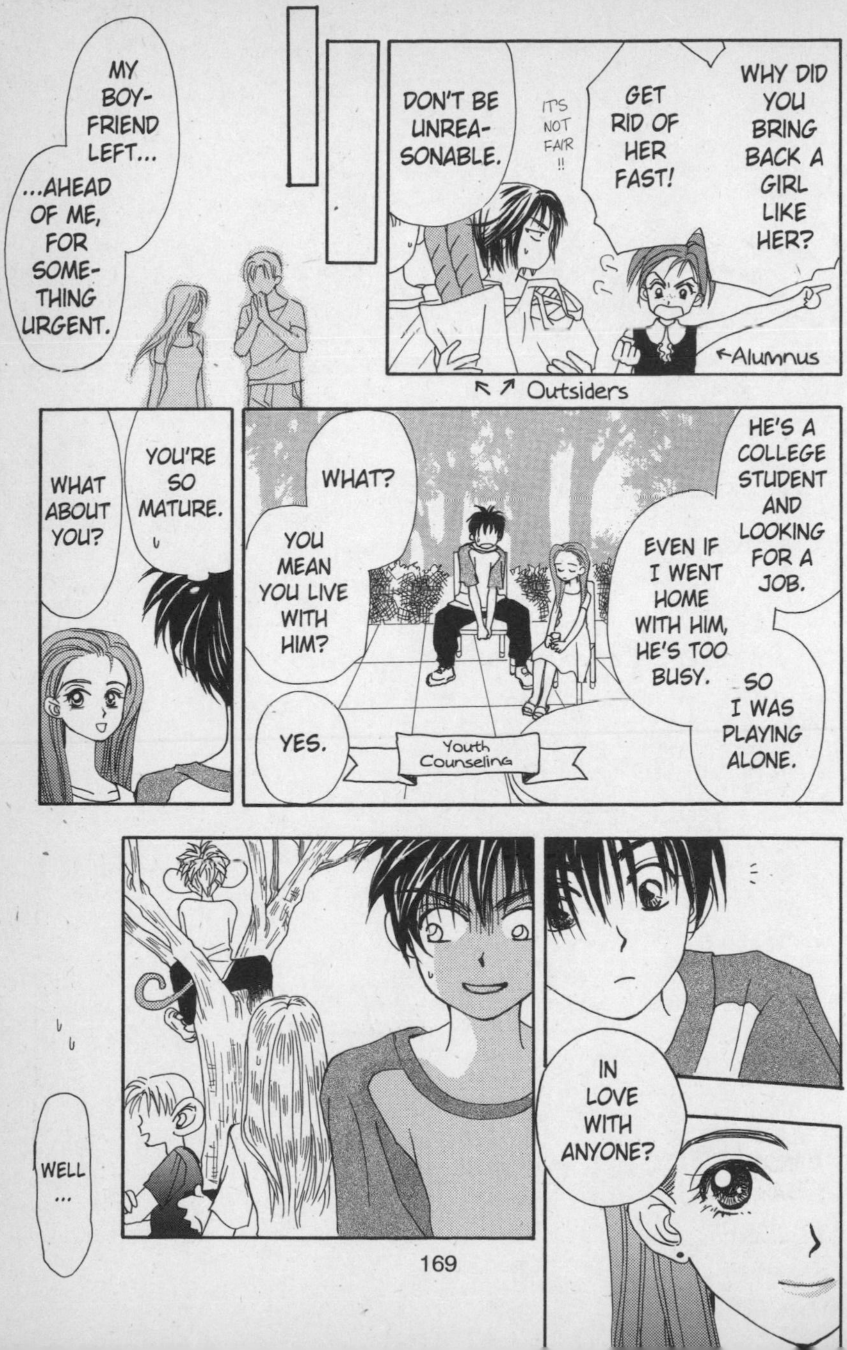
WHY DID YOU BRING BACK A GIRL LIKE HER?
GET RID OF HER FAST!
IT'S NOT FAIR !!
DON'T BE UNREA-SONABLE.
←Alumnus
↖↗ Outsiders
MY BOY-FRIEND LEFT...
...AHEAD OF ME, FOR SOME-THING URGENT.
HE'S A COLLEGE STUDENT AND LOOKING FOR A JOB.
EVEN IF I WENT HOME WITH HIM, HE'S TOO BUSY.
SO I WAS PLAYING ALONE.
WHAT?
YOU MEAN YOU LIVE WITH HIM?
YES.
Youth Counseling
YOU'RE SO MATURE.
WHAT ABOUT YOU?
IN LOVE WITH ANYONE?
WELL ...

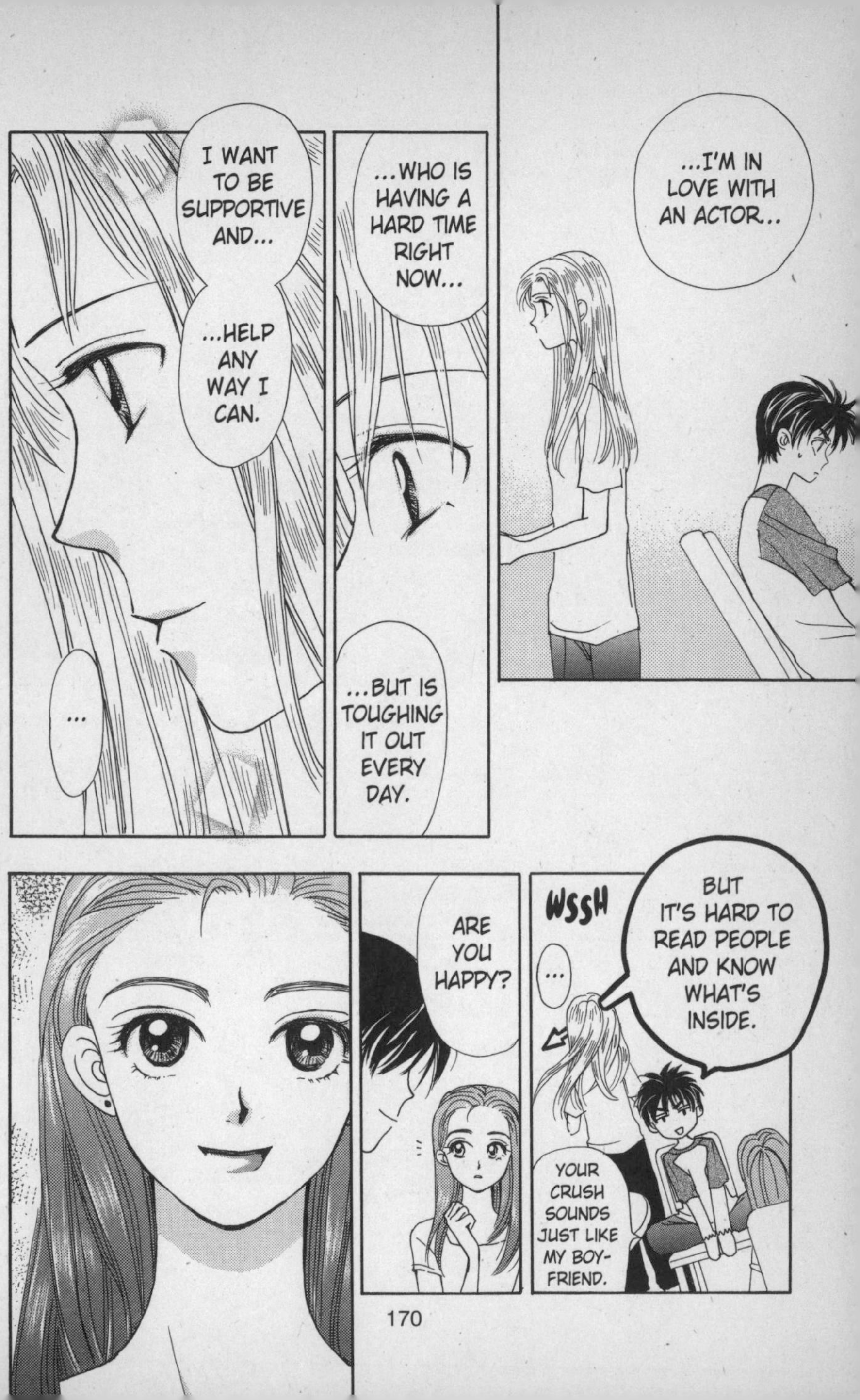
...I'M IN LOVE WITH AN ACTOR...
...WHO IS HAVING A HARD TIME RIGHT NOW...
...BUT IS TOUGHING IT OUT EVERY DAY.
I WANT TO BE SUPPORTIVE AND...
...HELP ANY WAY I CAN.
...
BUT IT'S HARD TO READ PEOPLE AND KNOW WHAT'S INSIDE.
WSSH
...
YOUR CRUSH SOUNDS JUST LIKE MY BOY-FRIEND.
ARE YOU HAPPY?

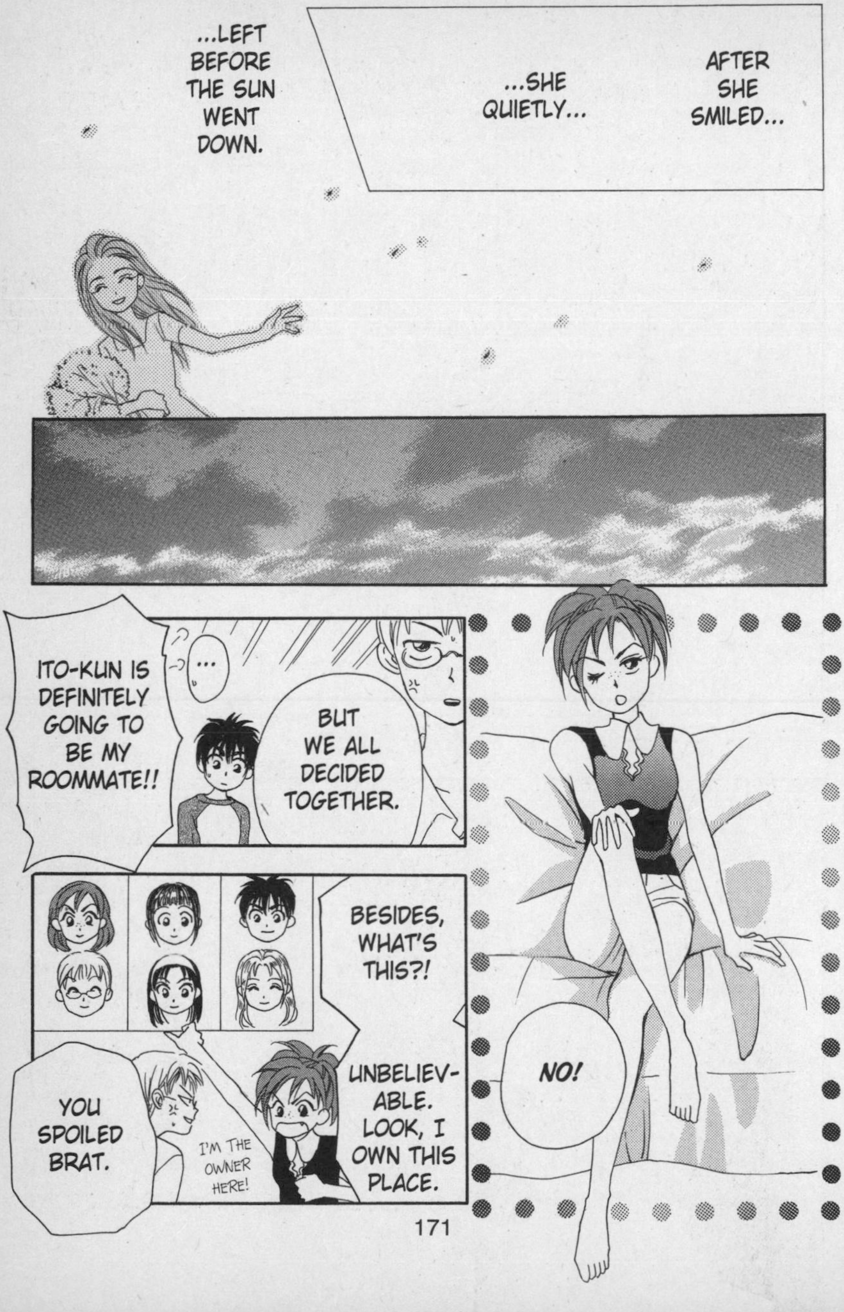
AFTER SHE SMILED...
...SHE QUIETLY...
...LEFT BEFORE THE SUN WENT DOWN.
NO!
BUT WE ALL DECIDED TOGETHER.
...
ITO-KUN IS DEFINITELY GOING TO BE MY ROOMMATE!!
BESIDES, WHAT'S THIS?!
UNBELIEV-ABLE. LOOK, I OWN THIS PLACE.
I'M THE OWNER HERE!
YOU SPOILED BRAT.

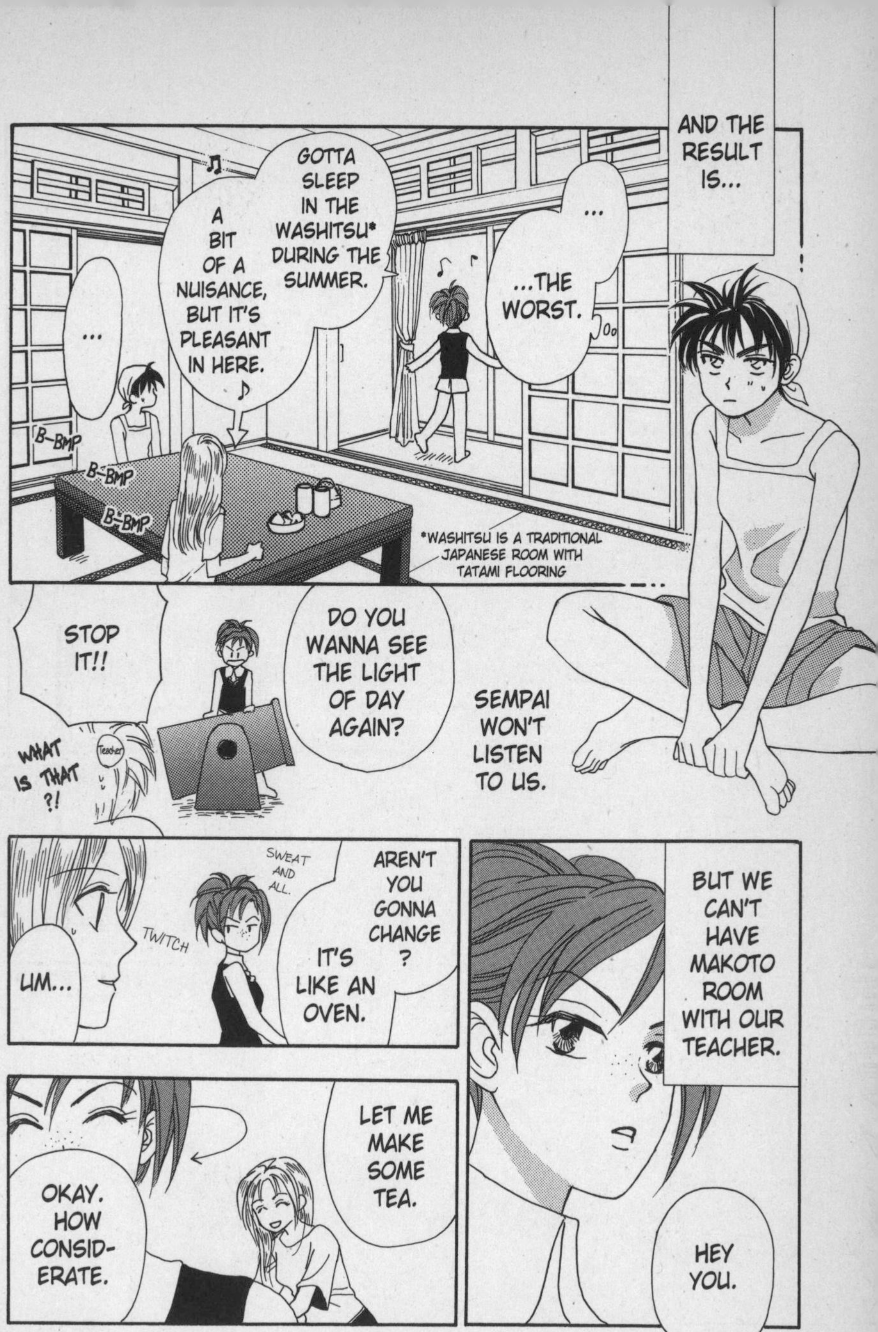
AND THE RESULT IS...
...
...THE WORST.
GOTTA SLEEP IN THE WASHITSU* DURING THE SUMMER.
A BIT OF A NUISANCE, BUT IT'S PLEASANT IN HERE. ♪
...
B-BMP
B-BMP
B-BMP
*WASHITSU IS A TRADITIONAL JAPANESE ROOM WITH TATAMI FLOORING
SEMPAI WON'T LISTEN TO US.
DO YOU WANNA SEE THE LIGHT OF DAY AGAIN?
STOP IT!!
Teacher
WHAT IS THAT ?!
BUT WE CAN'T HAVE MAKOTO ROOM WITH OUR TEACHER.
HEY YOU.
AREN'T YOU GONNA CHANGE ?
SWEAT AND ALL.
IT'S LIKE AN OVEN.
TWITCH
UM...
LET ME MAKE SOME TEA.
OKAY. HOW CONSID-ERATE.

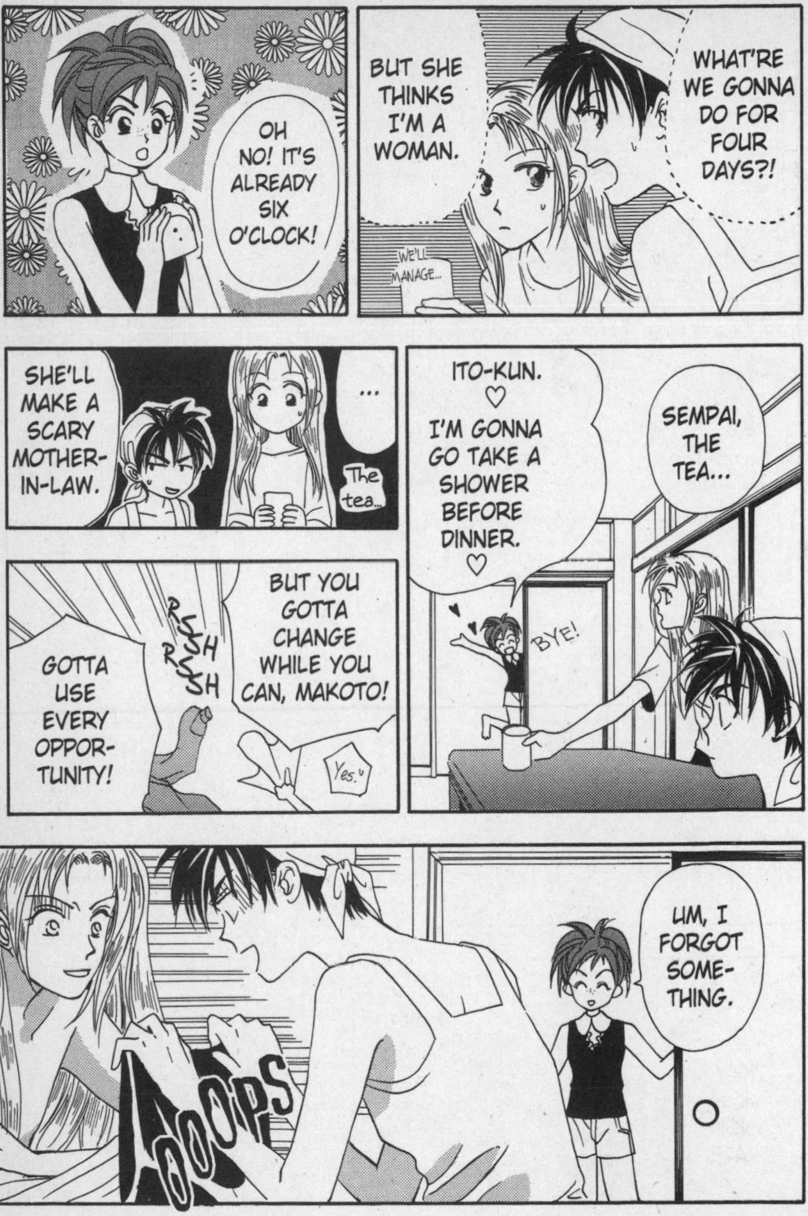
WHAT'RE WE GONNA DO FOR FOUR DAYS?!
BUT SHE THINKS I'M A WOMAN.
WE'LL MANAGE...
OH NO! IT'S ALREADY SIX O'CLOCK!
SEMPAI, THE TEA...
ITO-KUN. ♡ I'M GONNA GO TAKE A SHOWER BEFORE DINNER. ♡
BYE!
...
The tea...
SHE'LL MAKE A SCARY MOTHER-IN-LAW.
BUT YOU GOTTA CHANGE WHILE YOU CAN, MAKOTO!
RSSH RSSH
Yes.
GOTTA USE EVERY OPPORTUNITY!
UM, I FORGOT SOMETHING.
OOOOPS

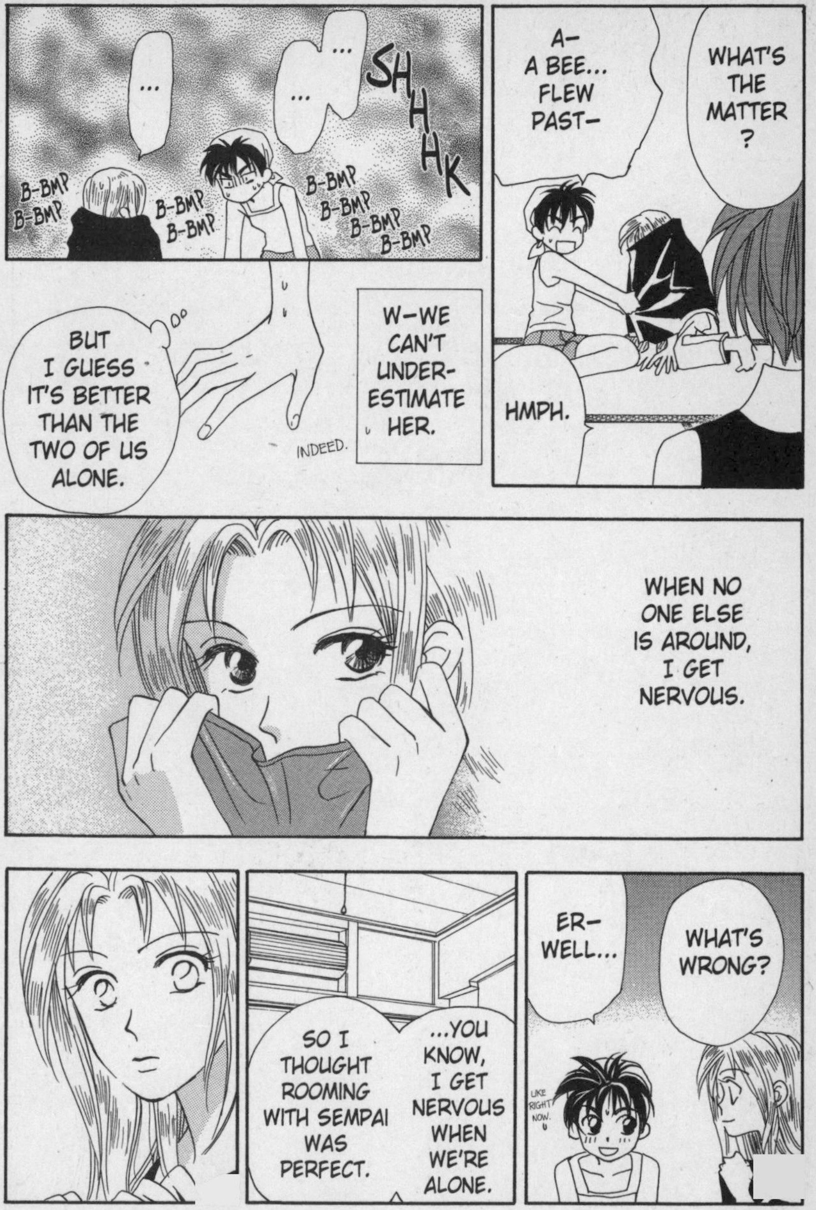
WHAT'S THE MATTER ?
A- A BEE... FLEW PAST-
HMPH.
...
...
...
SHHHK
B-BMP B-BMP B-BMP B-BMP
B-BMP B-BMP
B-BMP B-BMP
W-WE CAN'T UNDER-ESTIMATE HER.
INDEED.
BUT I GUESS IT'S BETTER THAN THE TWO OF US ALONE.
WHEN NO ONE ELSE IS AROUND, I GET NERVOUS.
WHAT'S WRONG?
ER- WELL...
LIKE RIGHT NOW.
...YOU KNOW, I GET NERVOUS WHEN WE'RE ALONE.
SO I THOUGHT ROOMING WITH SEMPAI WAS PERFECT.

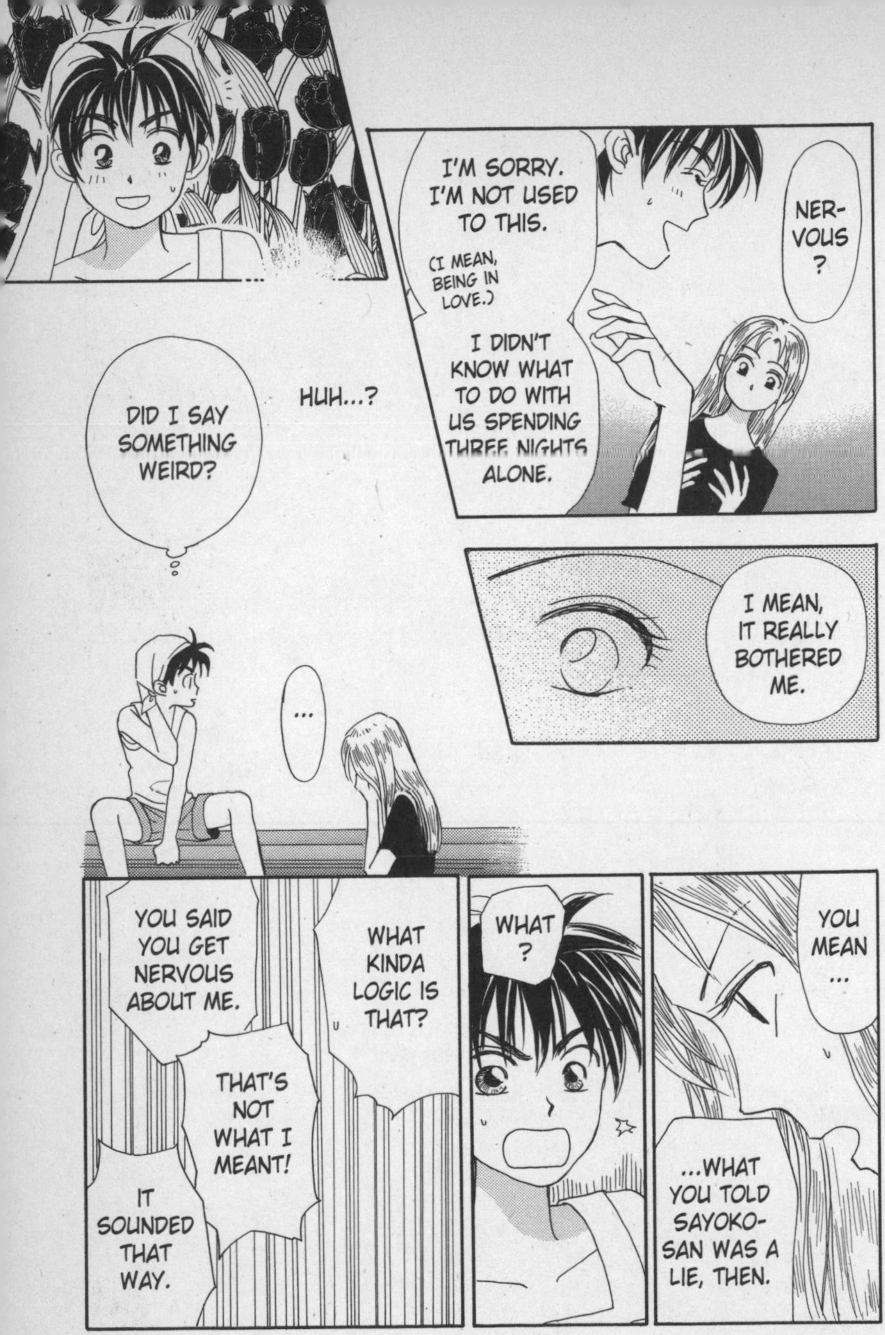
NER-VOUS?
I'M SORRY. I'M NOT USED TO THIS.
(I MEAN, BEING IN LOVE.)
I DIDN'T KNOW WHAT TO DO WITH US SPENDING THREE NIGHTS ALONE.
HUH...?
DID I SAY SOMETHING WEIRD?
I MEAN, IT REALLY BOTHERED ME.
...
YOU MEAN...
...WHAT YOU TOLD SAYOKO-SAN WAS A LIE, THEN.
WHAT?
YOU SAID YOU GET NERVOUS ABOUT ME.
WHAT KINDA LOGIC IS THAT?
THAT'S NOT WHAT I MEANT!
IT SOUNDED THAT WAY.

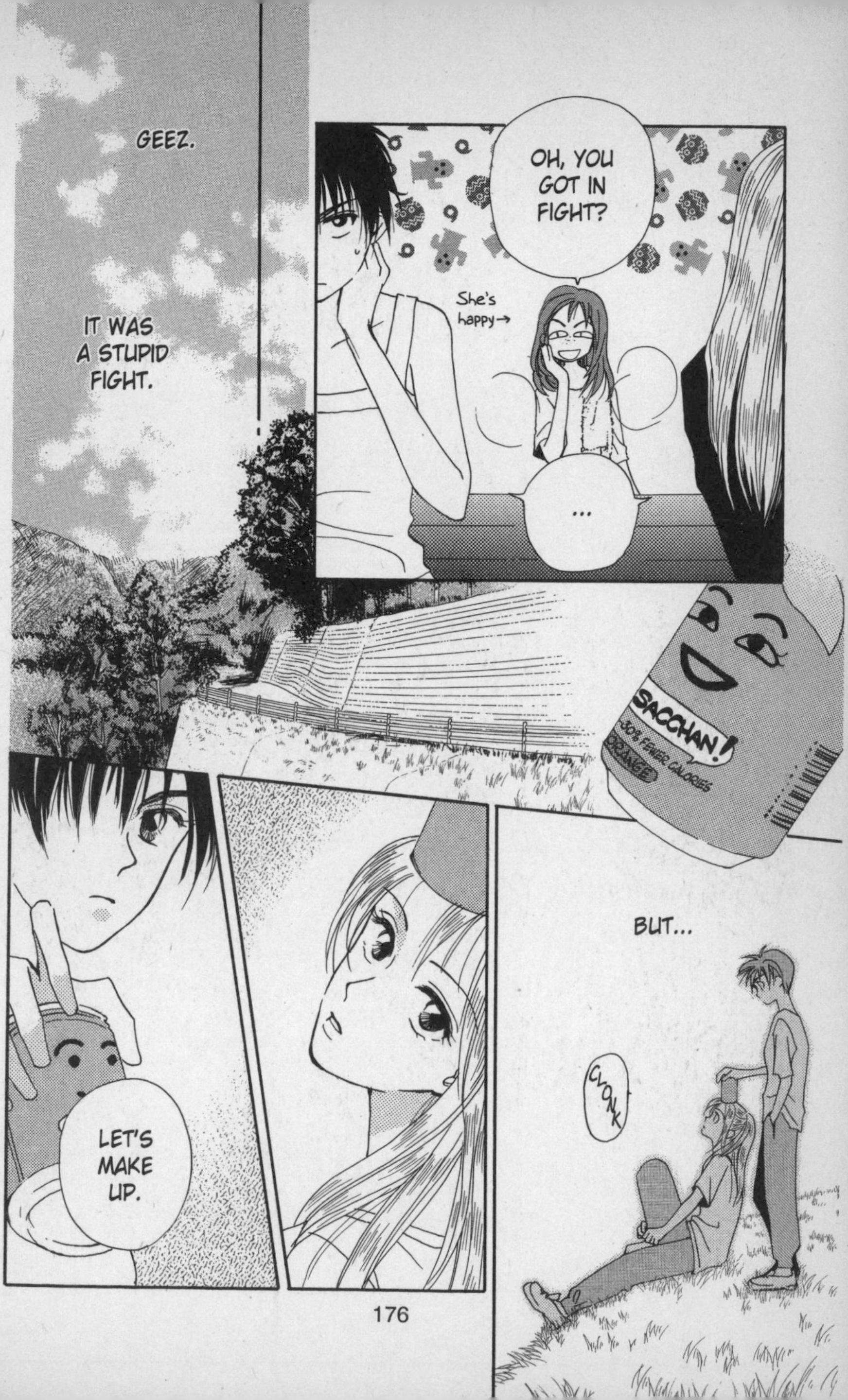
OH, YOU GOT IN FIGHT?
She's happy→
...
GEEZ.
IT WAS A STUPID FIGHT.
SACCHAN!
30% FEWER CALORIES
ORANGE
BUT...
CLONK
LET'S MAKE UP.

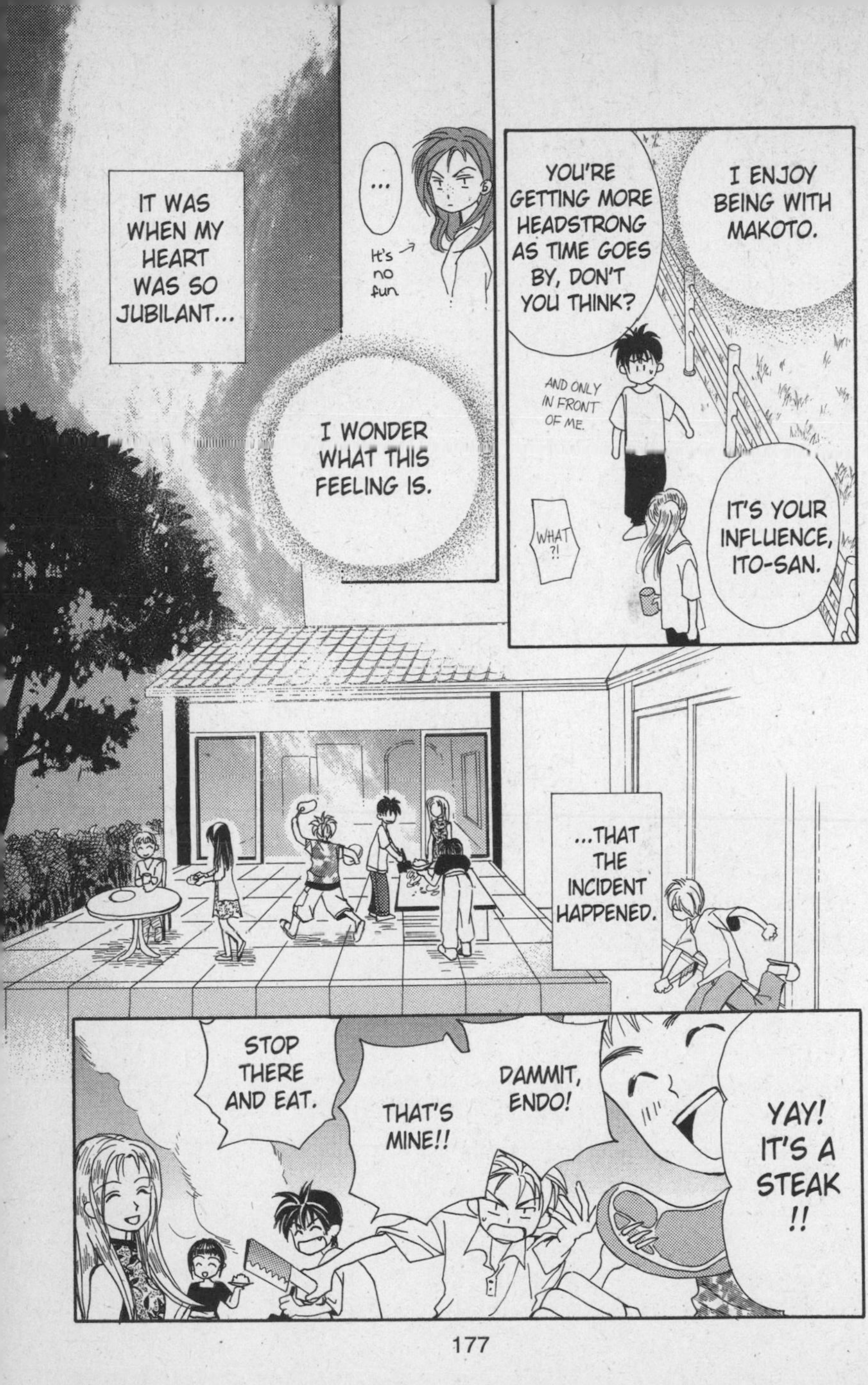
I ENJOY BEING WITH MAKOTO.
YOU'RE GETTING MORE HEADSTRONG AS TIME GOES BY, DON'T YOU THINK?
AND ONLY IN FRONT OF ME.
IT'S YOUR INFLUENCE, ITO-SAN.
WHAT?!
...
It's no fun
I WONDER WHAT THIS FEELING IS.
IT WAS WHEN MY HEART WAS SO JUBILANT...
...THAT THE INCIDENT HAPPENED.
YAY! IT'S A STEAK!!
DAMMIT, ENDO!
THAT'S MINE!!
STOP THERE AND EAT.

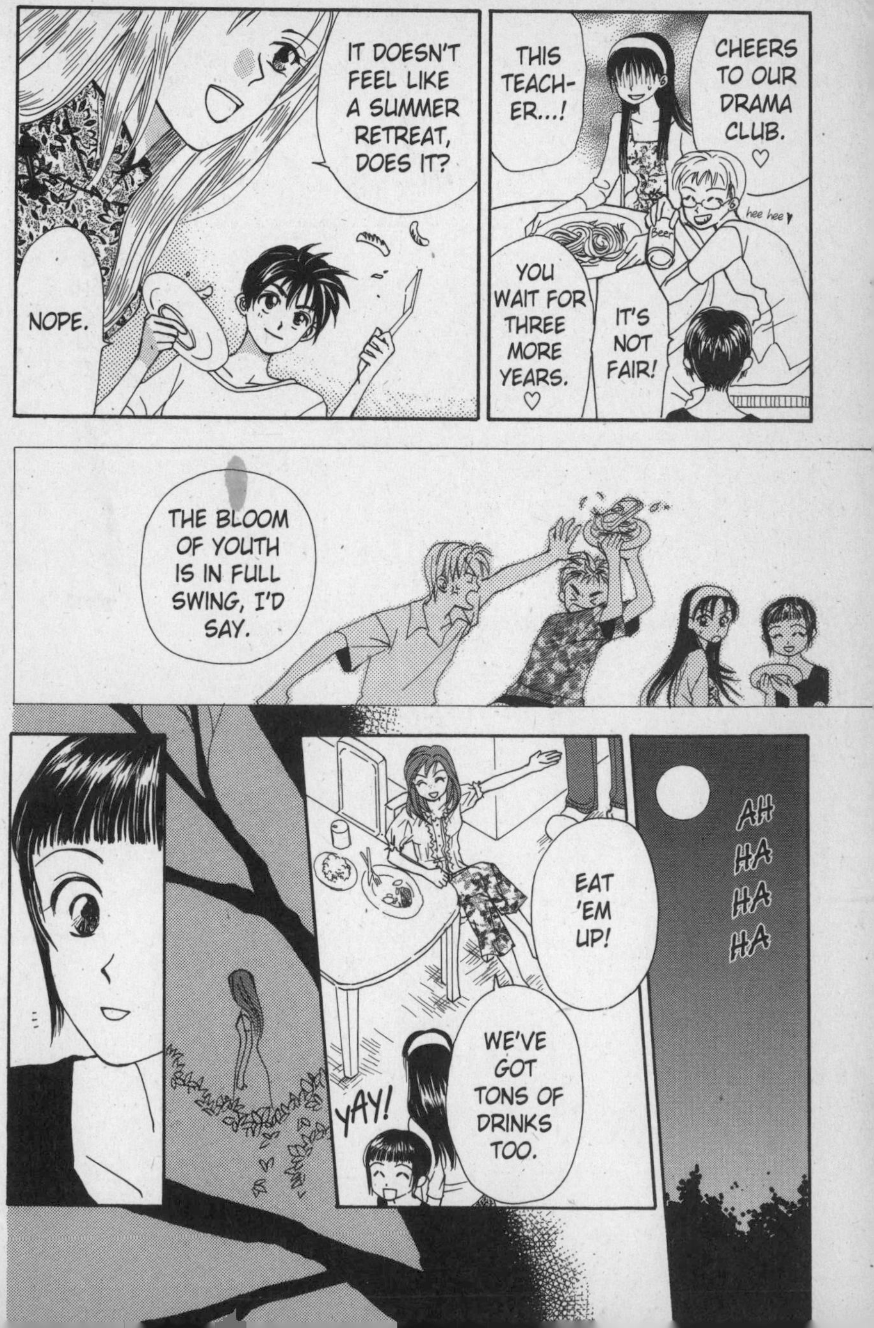
CHEERS TO OUR DRAMA CLUB. ♡
hee hee ♥
Beer
THIS TEACHER...!
IT'S NOT FAIR!
YOU WAIT FOR THREE MORE YEARS. ♡
IT DOESN'T FEEL LIKE A SUMMER RETREAT, DOES IT?
NOPE.
THE BLOOM OF YOUTH IS IN FULL SWING, I'D SAY.
AH HA HA HA
EAT 'EM UP!
WE'VE GOT TONS OF DRINKS TOO.
YAY!

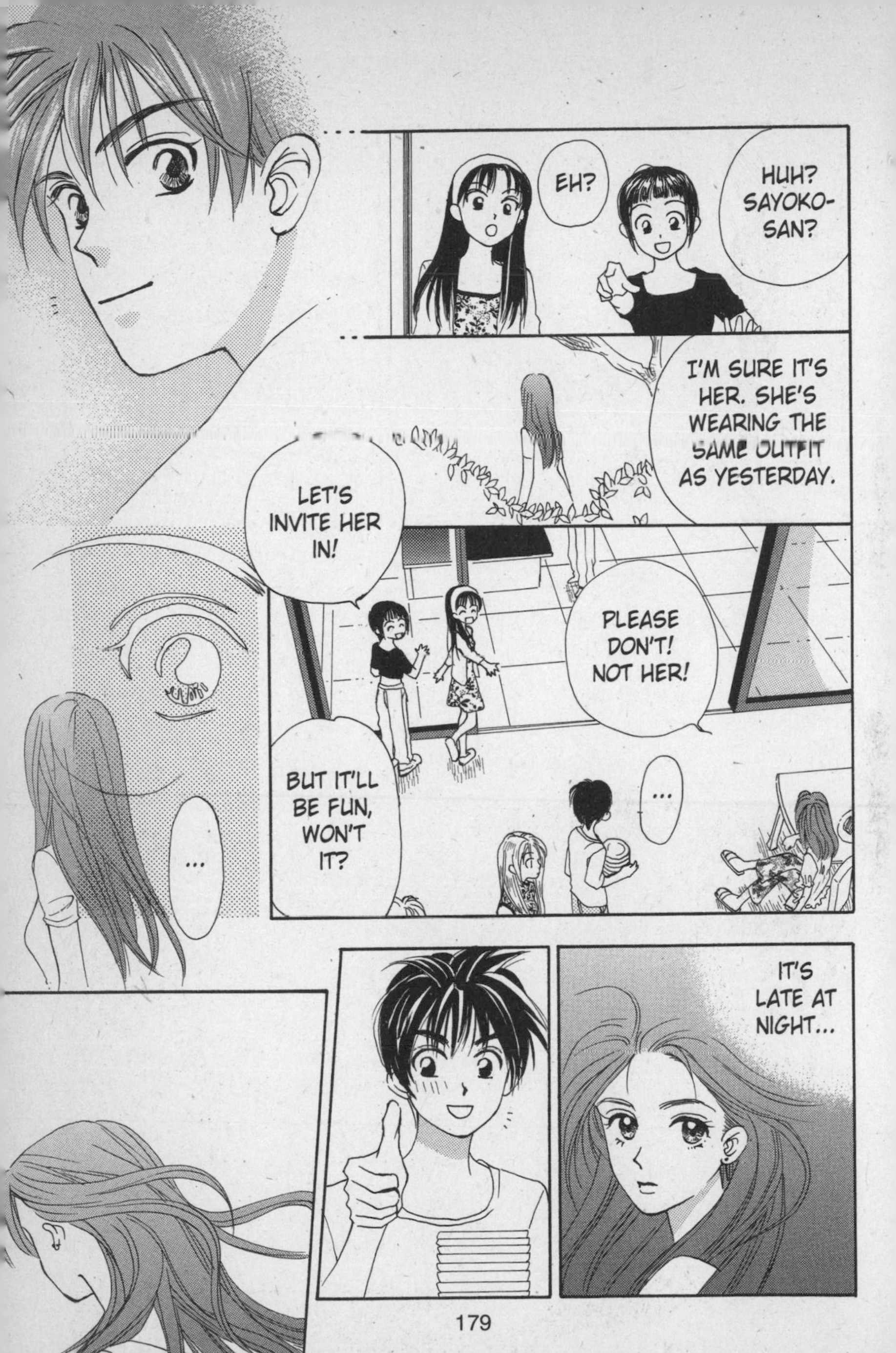
HUH? SAYOKO-SAN?
EH?
I'M SURE IT'S HER. SHE'S WEARING THE SAME OUTFIT AS YESTERDAY.
LET'S INVITE HER IN!
PLEASE DON'T! NOT HER!
BUT IT'LL BE FUN, WON'T IT?
...
...
IT'S LATE AT NIGHT...

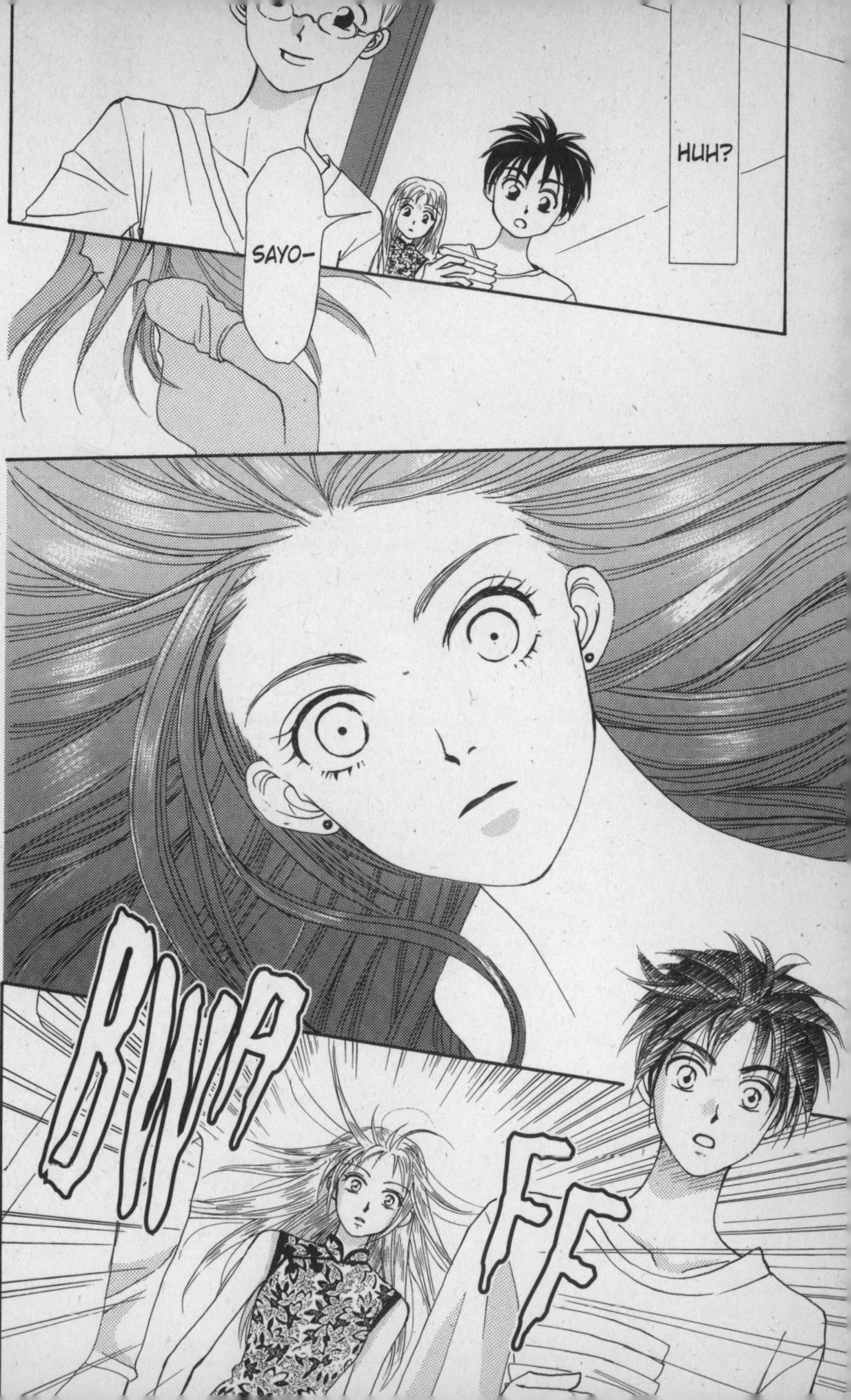
HUH?
SAYO-
BWAFF

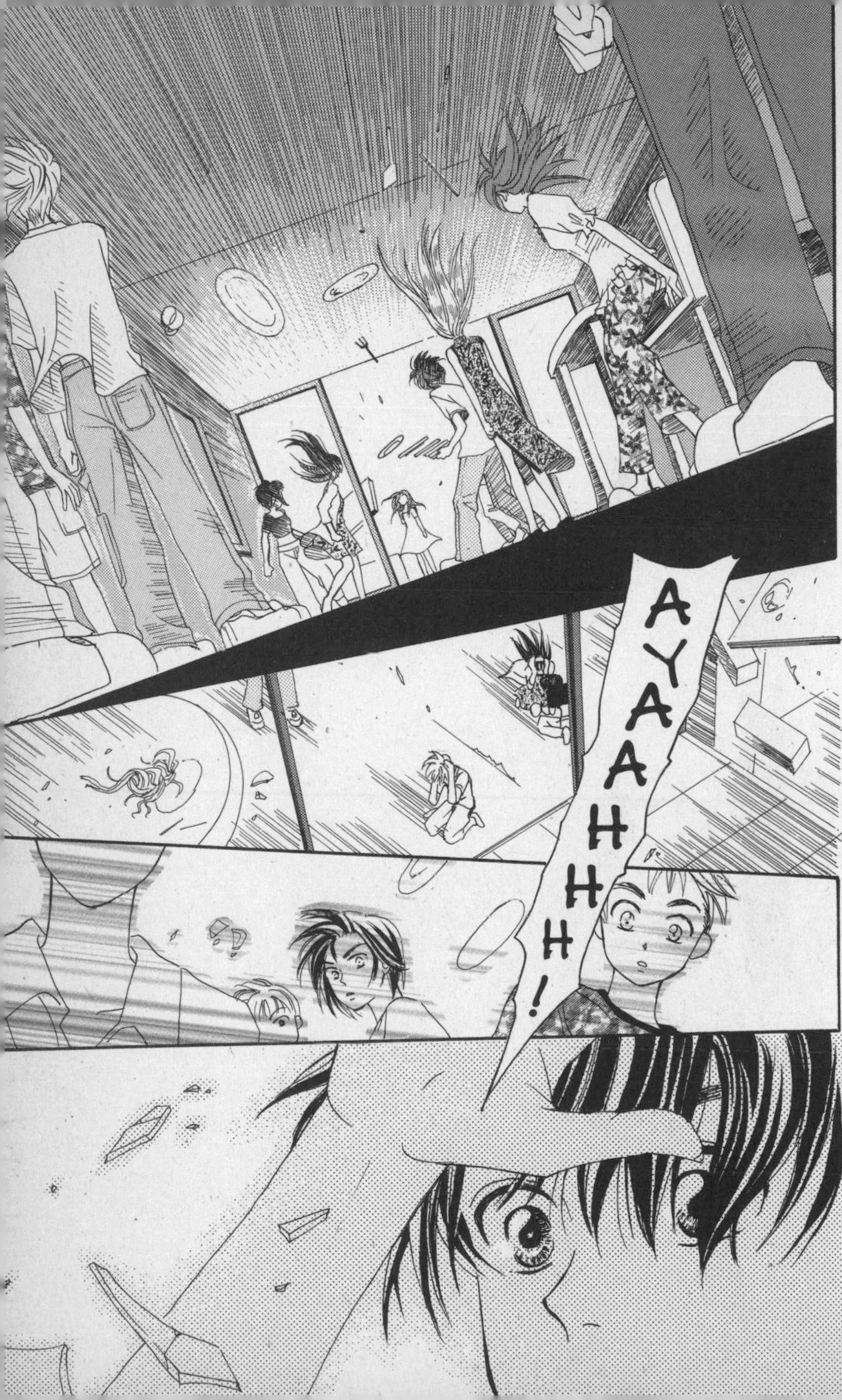
AYAAHHHH!

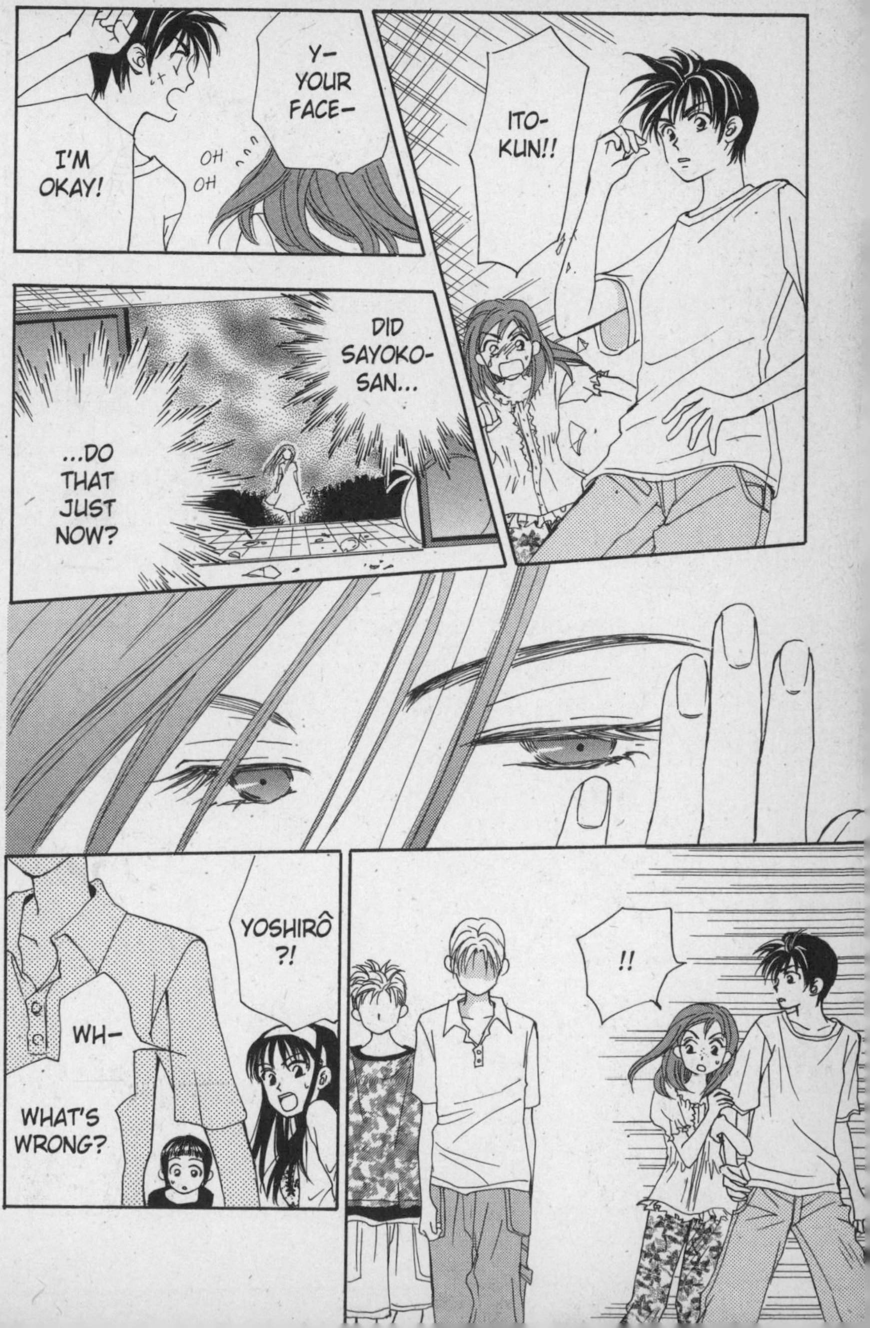
ITO-KUN!!
Y-YOUR FACE-
OH OH
I'M OKAY!
DID SAYOKO-SAN...
...DO THAT JUST NOW?
!!
YOSHIRÔ?!
WH-
WHAT'S WRONG?

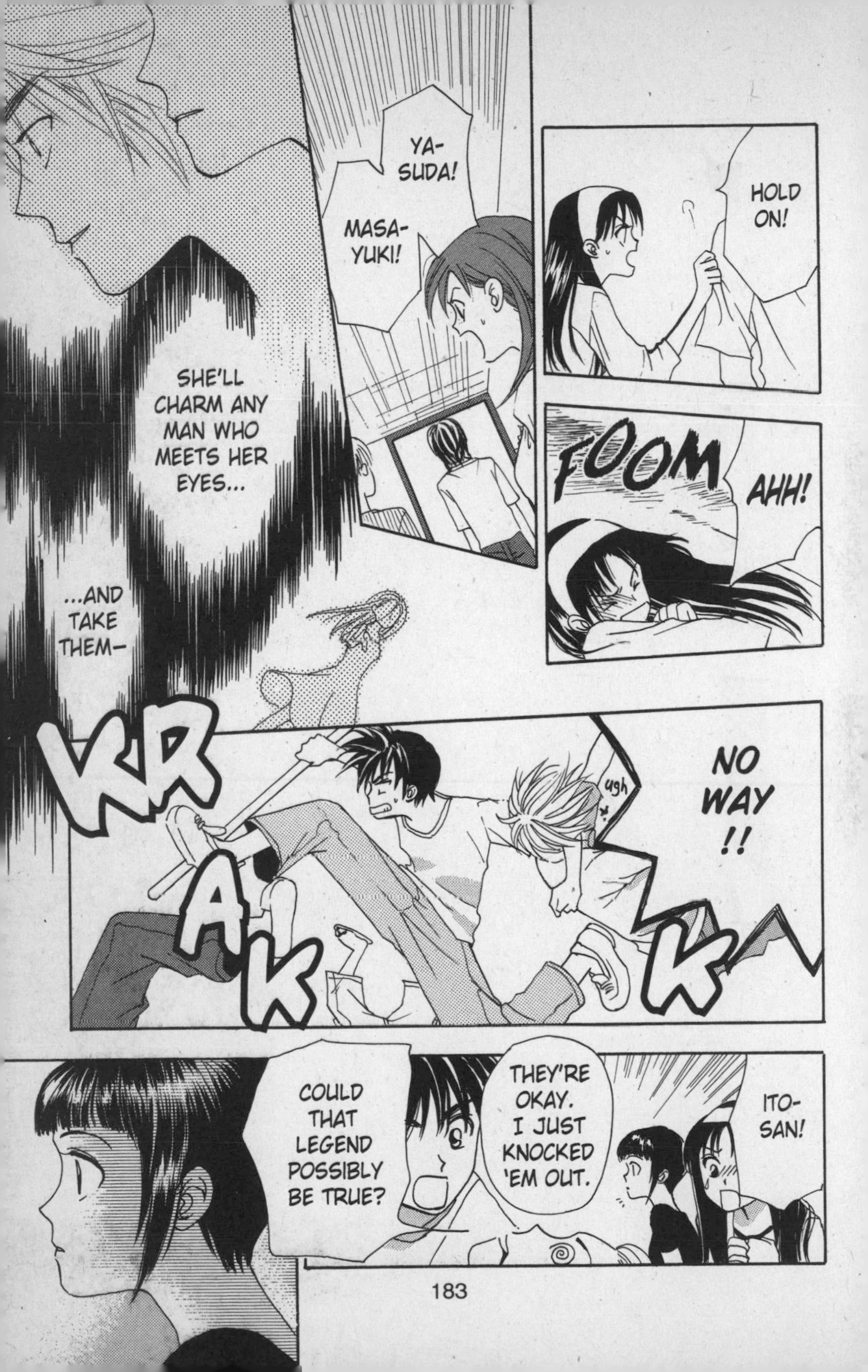
HOLD ON!
FOOM
AHH!
YA-SUDA!
MASA-YUKI!
SHE'LL CHARM ANY MAN WHO MEETS HER EYES...
...AND TAKE THEM-
NO WAY!!
ugh
KRAK
ITO-SAN!
THEY'RE OKAY. I JUST KNOCKED 'EM OUT.
COULD THAT LEGEND POSSIBLY BE TRUE?

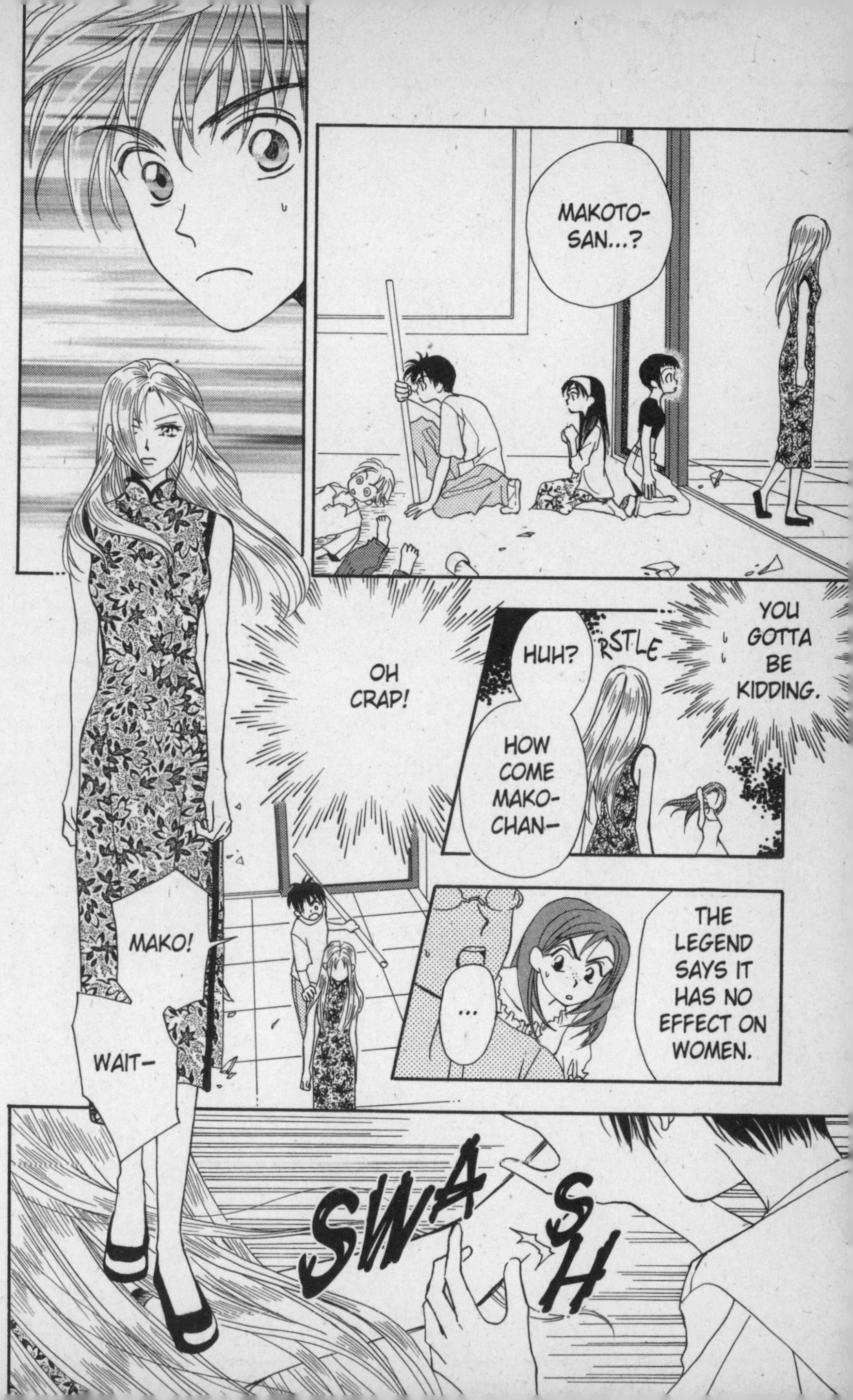
MAKOTO-SAN...?
YOU GOTTA BE KIDDING.
RSTLE
HUH?
HOW COME MAKO-CHAN—
OH CRAP!
THE LEGEND SAYS IT HAS NO EFFECT ON WOMEN.
...
MAKO!
WAIT—
SWASH

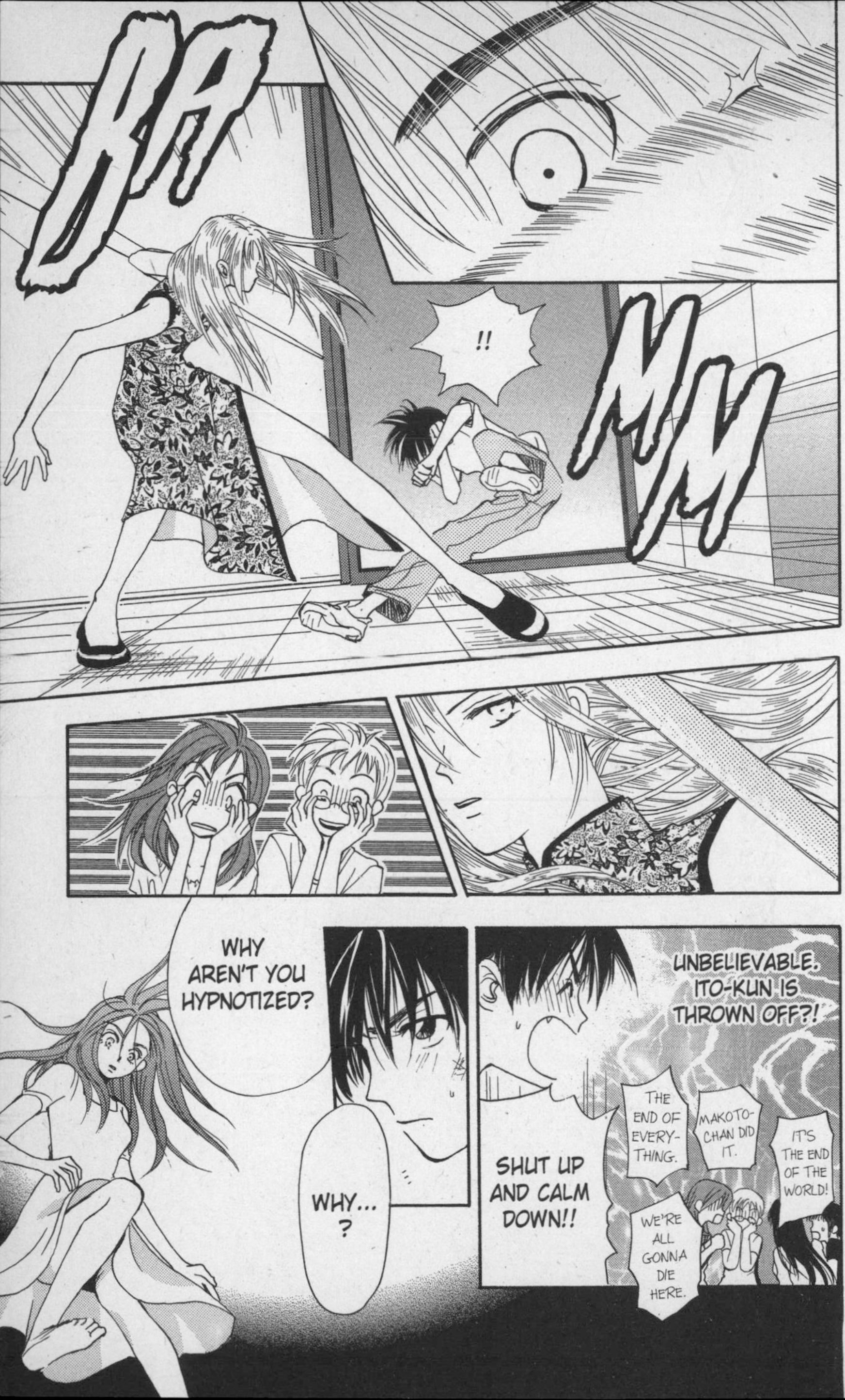
!!
BA
MM
UNBELIEVABLE. ITO-KUN IS THROWN OFF?!
IT'S THE END OF THE WORLD!
MAKOTO-CHAN DID IT.
THE END OF EVERY-THING.
SHUT UP AND CALM DOWN!!
WE'RE ALL GONNA DIE HERE.
WHY AREN'T YOU HYPNOTIZED?
WHY... ?

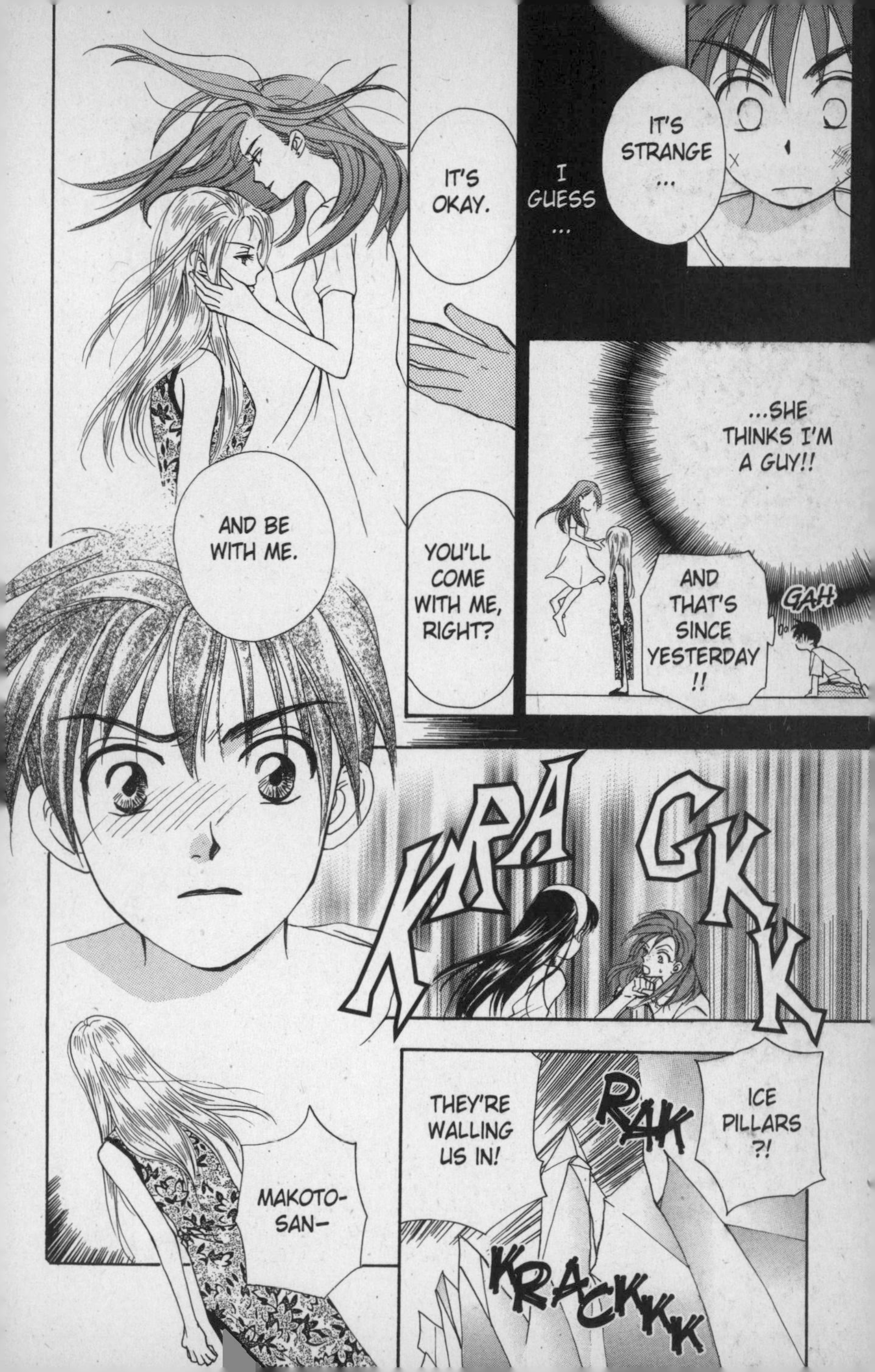

IT'S STRANGE ...
I GUESS ...
...SHE THINKS I'M A GUY!!
AND THAT'S SINCE YESTERDAY!!
GAH
IT'S OKAY.
YOU'LL COME WITH ME, RIGHT?
AND BE WITH ME.
KRAGKK
ICE PILLARS?!
RAK
THEY'RE WALLING US IN!
KRACKKKK
MAKOTO-SAN—

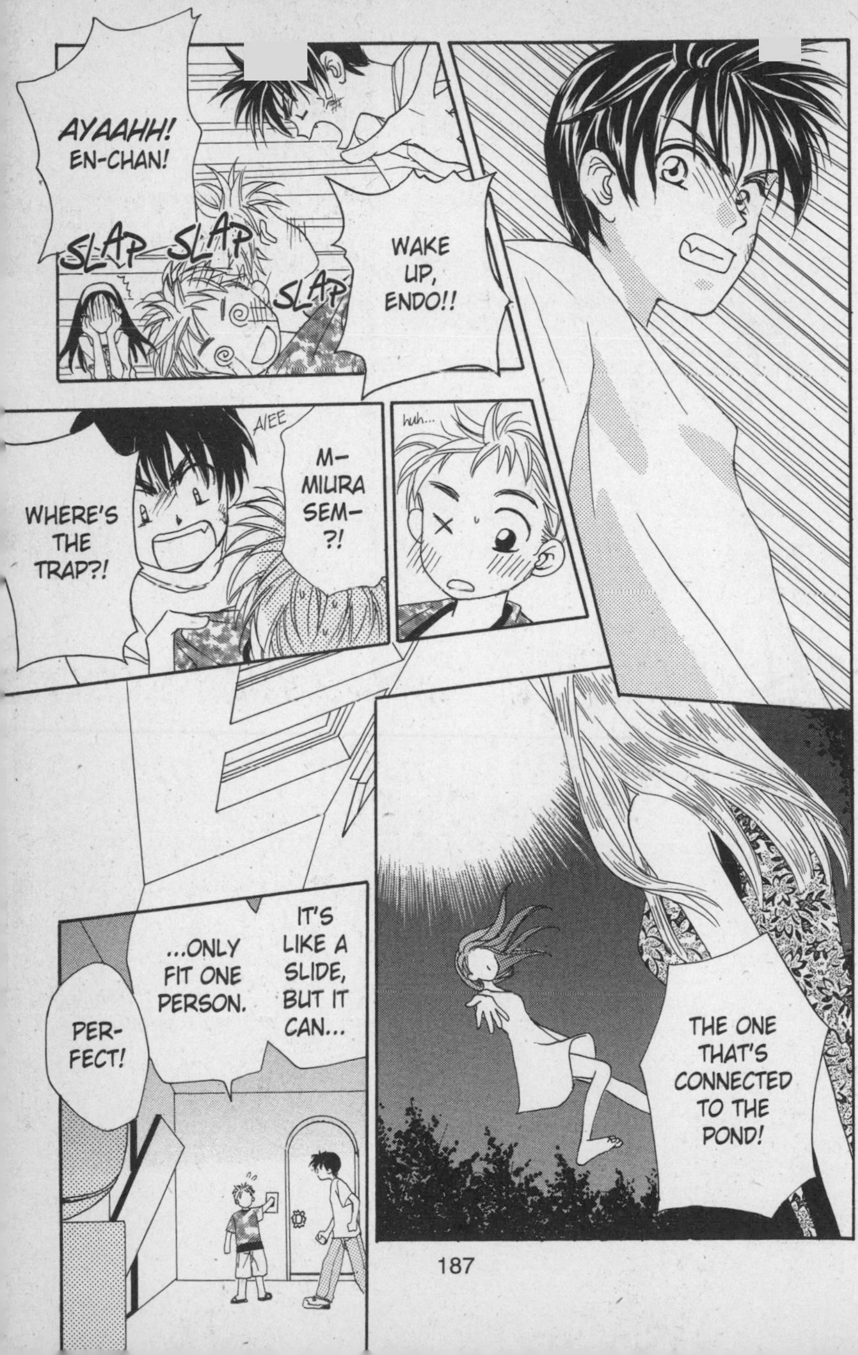

WAKE UP, ENDO!!
AYAAHH! EN-CHAN!
SLAP SLAP SLAP
huh...
M-MIURA SEM-?!
AIEE
WHERE'S THE TRAP?!
THE ONE THAT'S CONNECTED TO THE POND!
IT'S LIKE A SLIDE, BUT IT CAN...
...ONLY FIT ONE PERSON.
PERFECT!

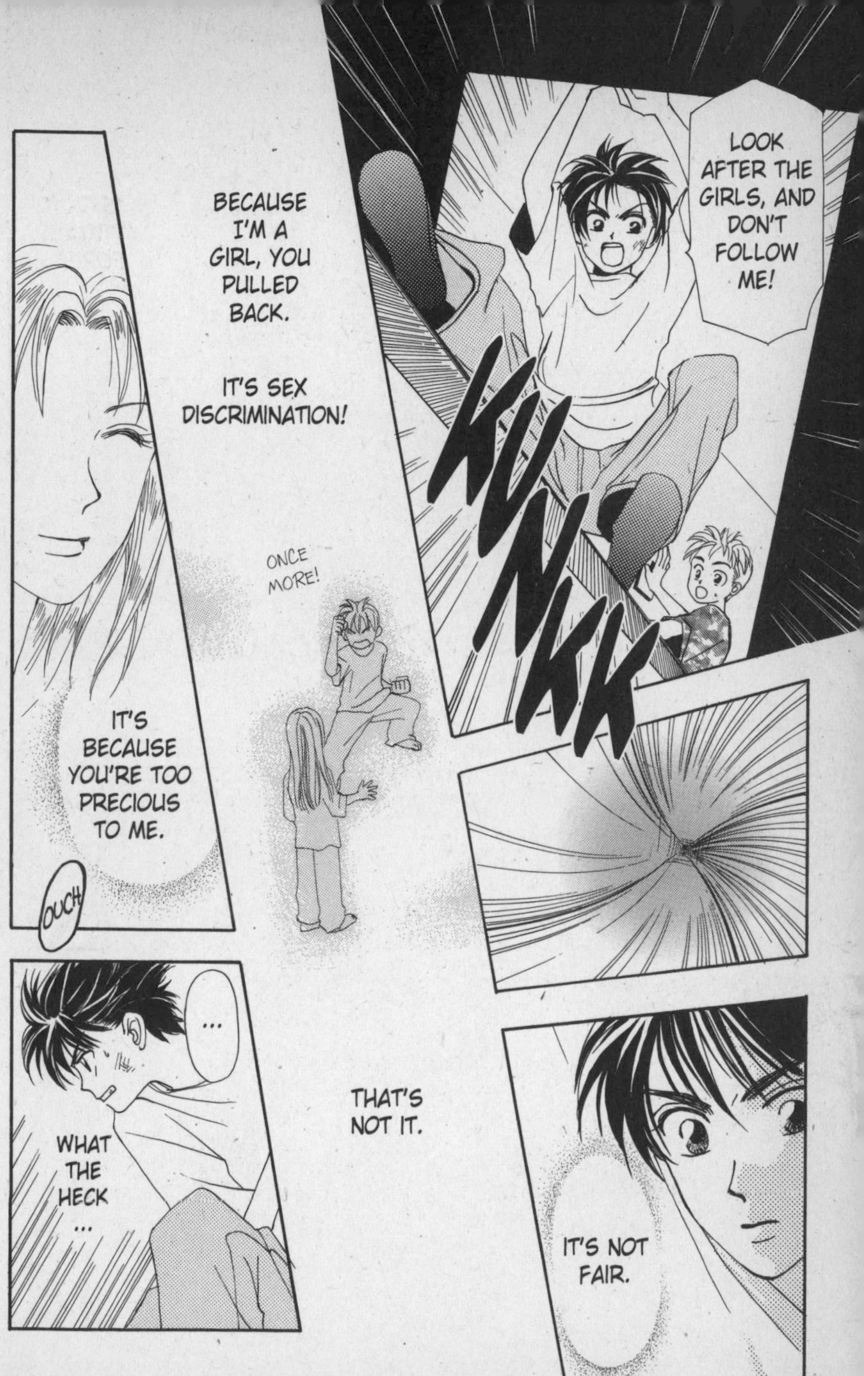
LOOK AFTER THE GIRLS, AND DON'T FOLLOW ME!
BECAUSE I'M A GIRL, YOU PULLED BACK.
IT'S SEX DISCRIMINATION!
ONCE MORE!
IT'S BECAUSE YOU'RE TOO PRECIOUS TO ME.
OUCH
IT'S NOT FAIR.
THAT'S NOT IT.
...
WHAT THE HECK ...

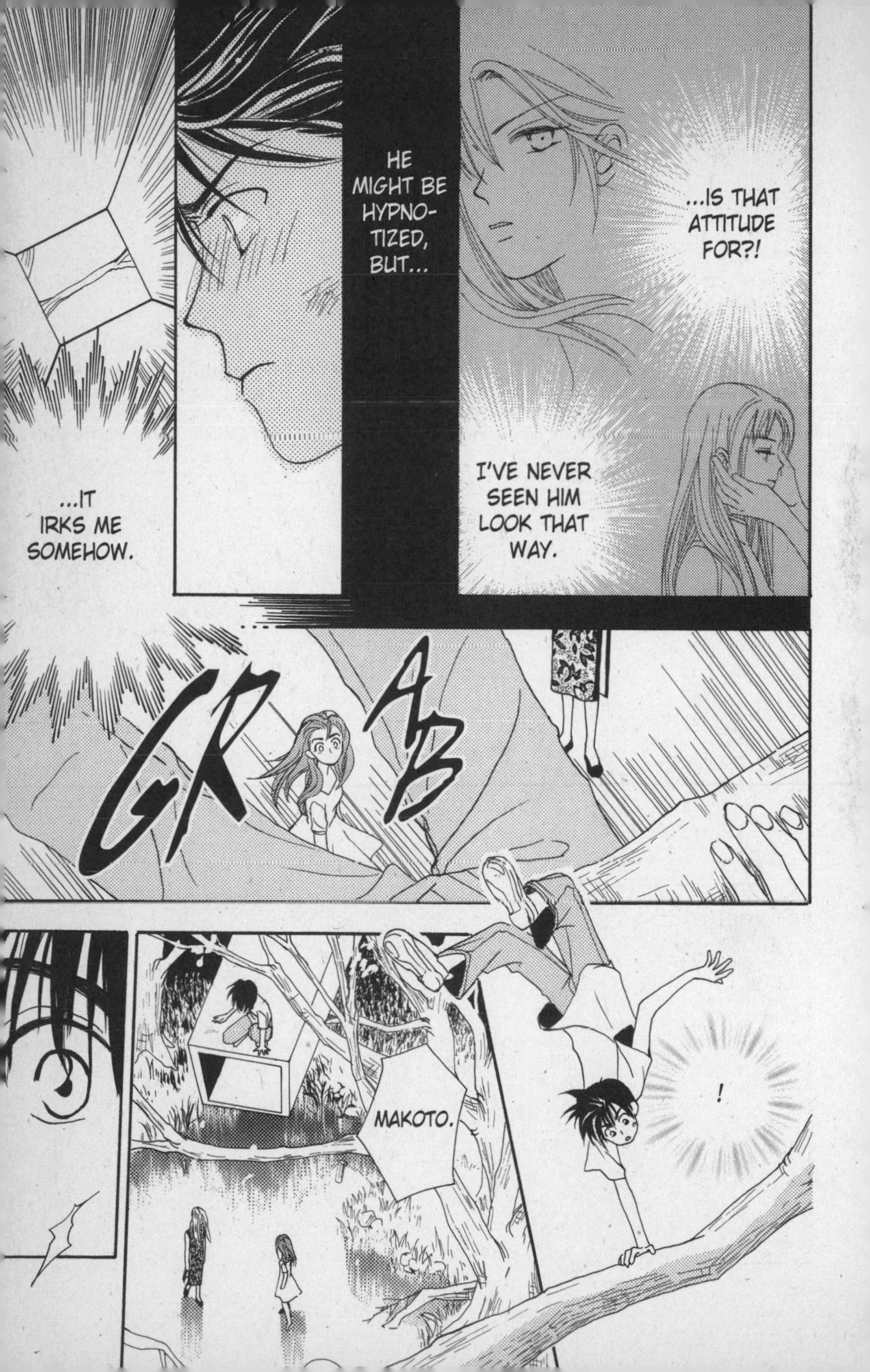
...IS THAT ATTITUDE FOR?!
I'VE NEVER SEEN HIM LOOK THAT WAY.
HE MIGHT BE HYPNO-TIZED, BUT...
...IT IRKS ME SOMEHOW.
GRAB
!
MAKOTO.

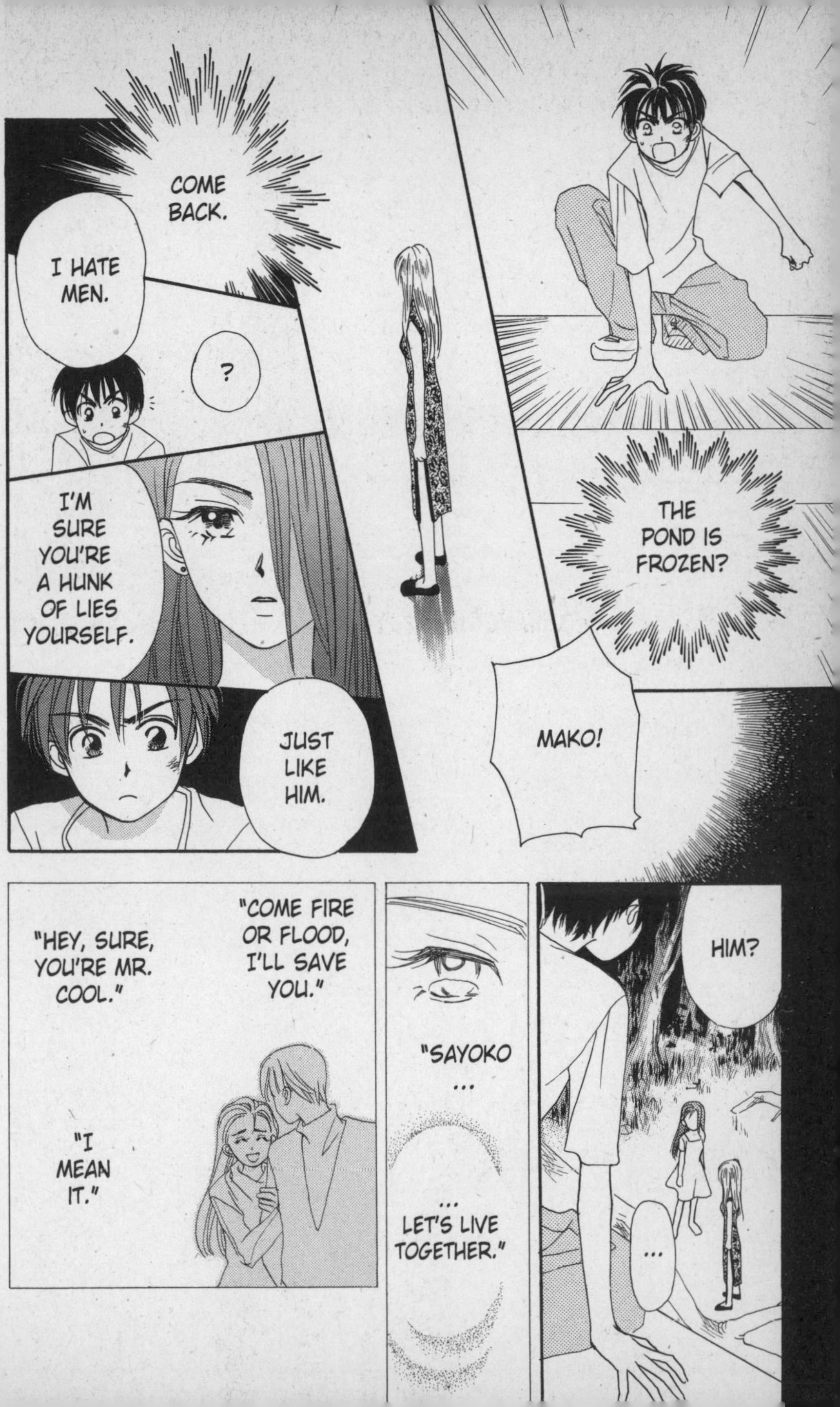
THE POND IS FROZEN?
MAKO!
COME BACK.
I HATE MEN.
?
I'M SURE YOU'RE A HUNK OF LIES YOURSELF.
JUST LIKE HIM.
HIM?
...
"SAYOKO ...
... LET'S LIVE TOGETHER."
"COME FIRE OR FLOOD, I'LL SAVE YOU."
"HEY, SURE, YOU'RE MR. COOL."
"I MEAN IT."

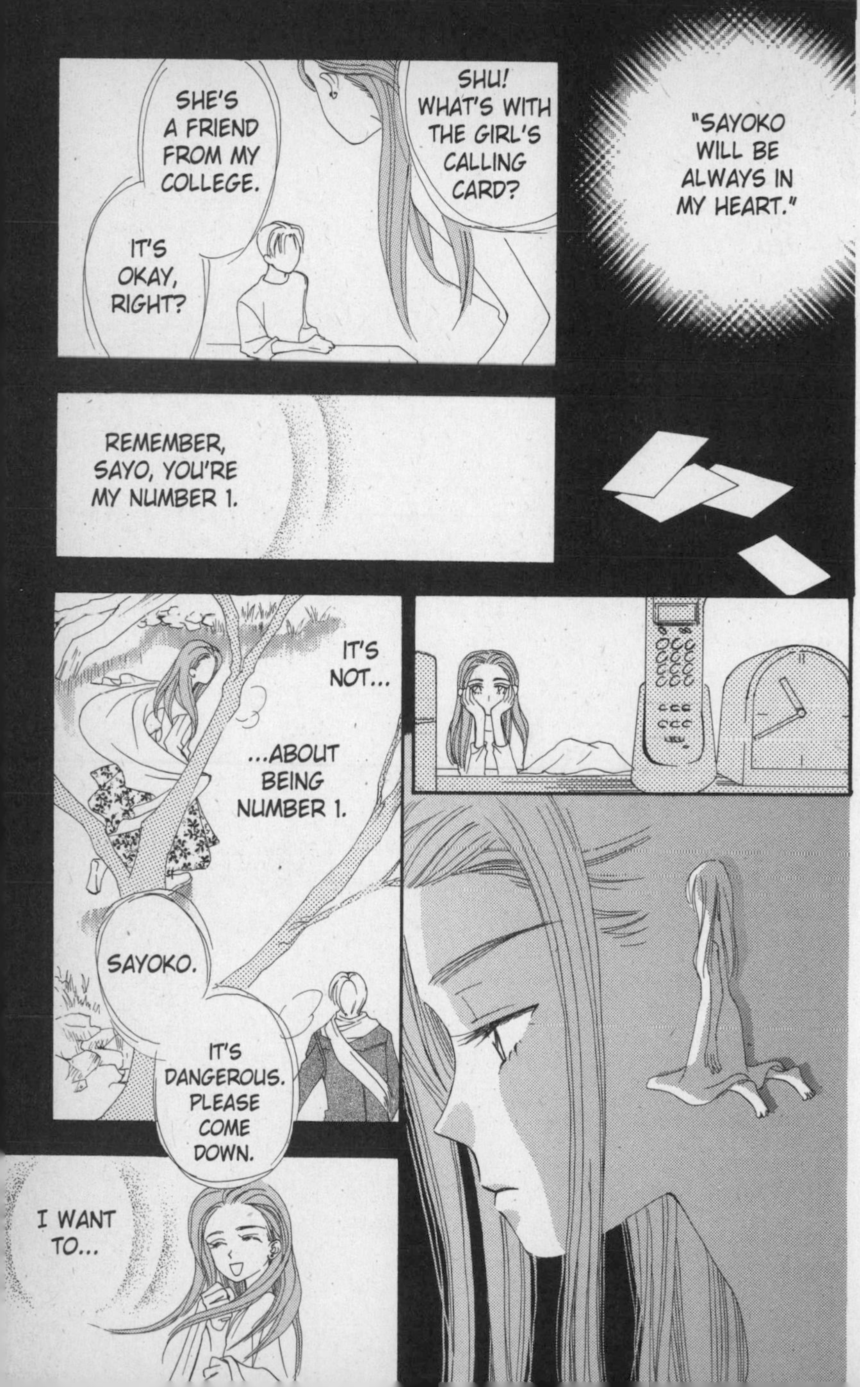
"SAYOKO WILL BE ALWAYS IN MY HEART."
SHU! WHAT'S WITH THE GIRL'S CALLING CARD?
SHE'S A FRIEND FROM MY COLLEGE.
IT'S OKAY, RIGHT?
REMEMBER, SAYO, YOU'RE MY NUMBER 1.
IT'S NOT...
...ABOUT BEING NUMBER 1.
SAYOKO.
IT'S DANGEROUS. PLEASE COME DOWN.
I WANT TO...

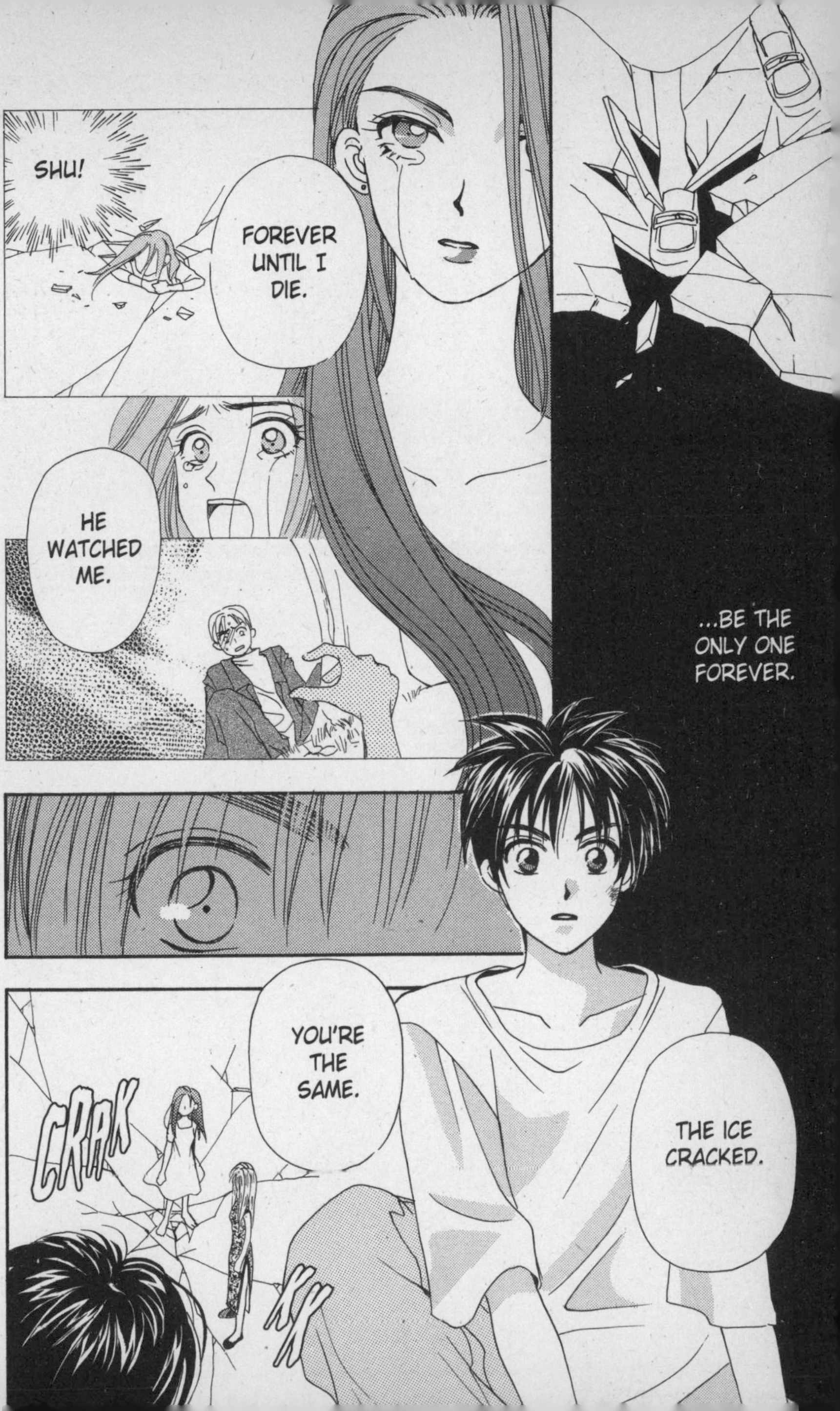
...BE THE ONLY ONE FOREVER.
FOREVER UNTIL I DIE.
SHU!
HE WATCHED ME.
THE ICE CRACKED.
YOU'RE THE SAME.
CRAK

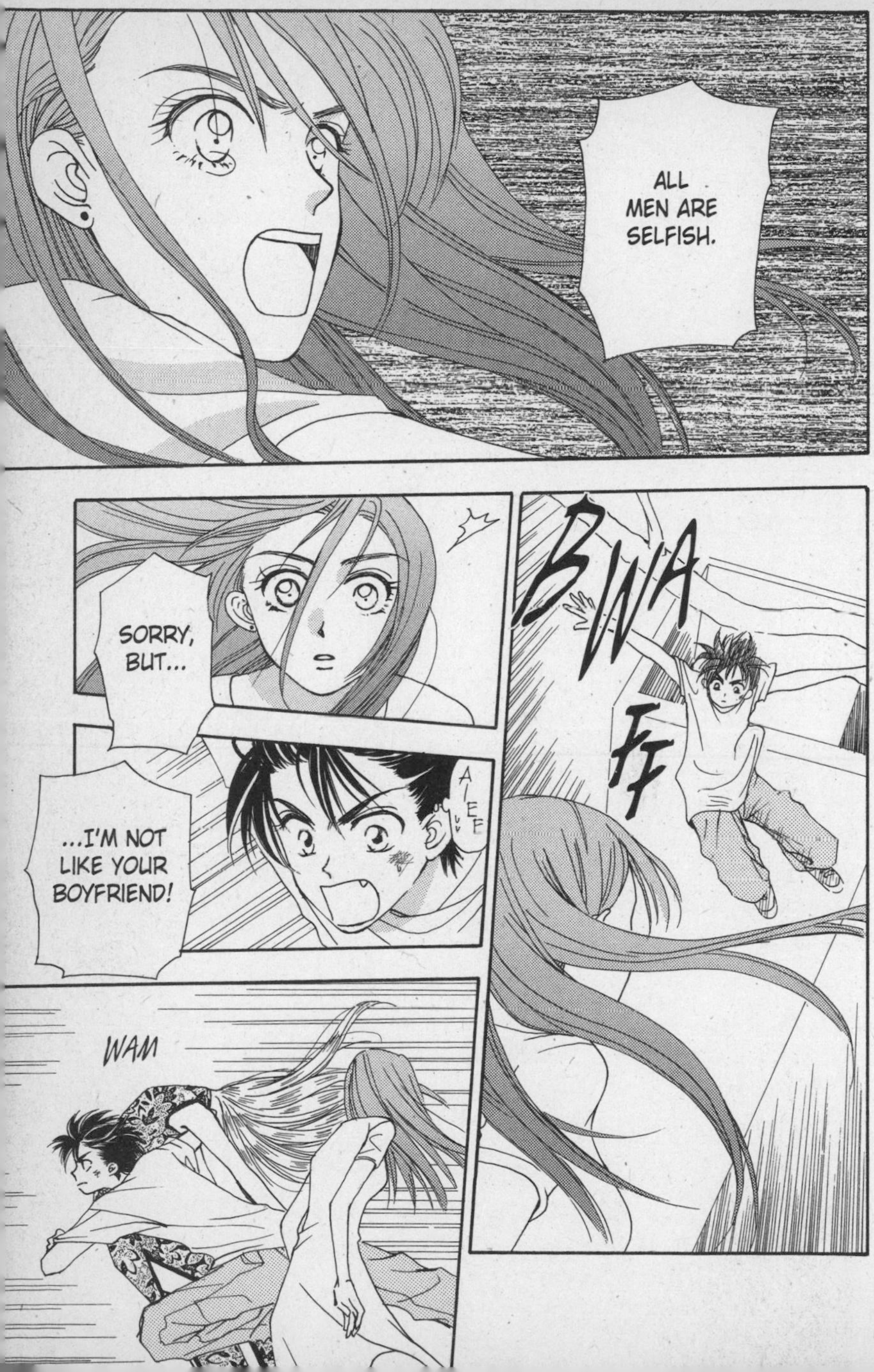
ALL MEN ARE SELFISH.
BWAFF
SORRY, BUT...
...I'M NOT LIKE YOUR BOYFRIEND!
AIEE
WAM

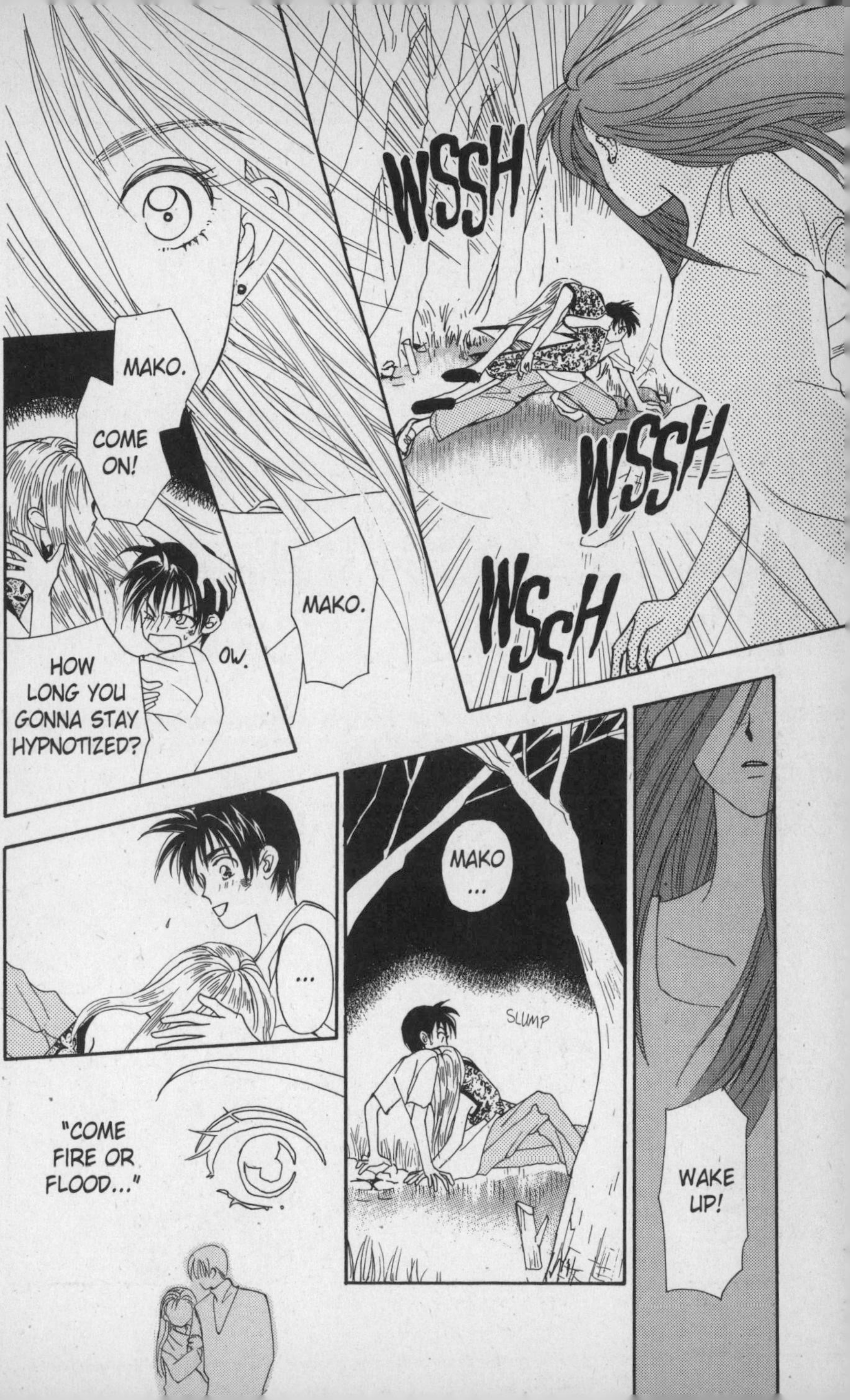
WSSH
WSSH
WSSH
MAKO.
COME ON!
MAKO.
OW.
HOW LONG YOU GONNA STAY HYPNOTIZED?
WAKE UP!
MAKO ...
SLUMP
...
"COME FIRE OR FLOOD..."

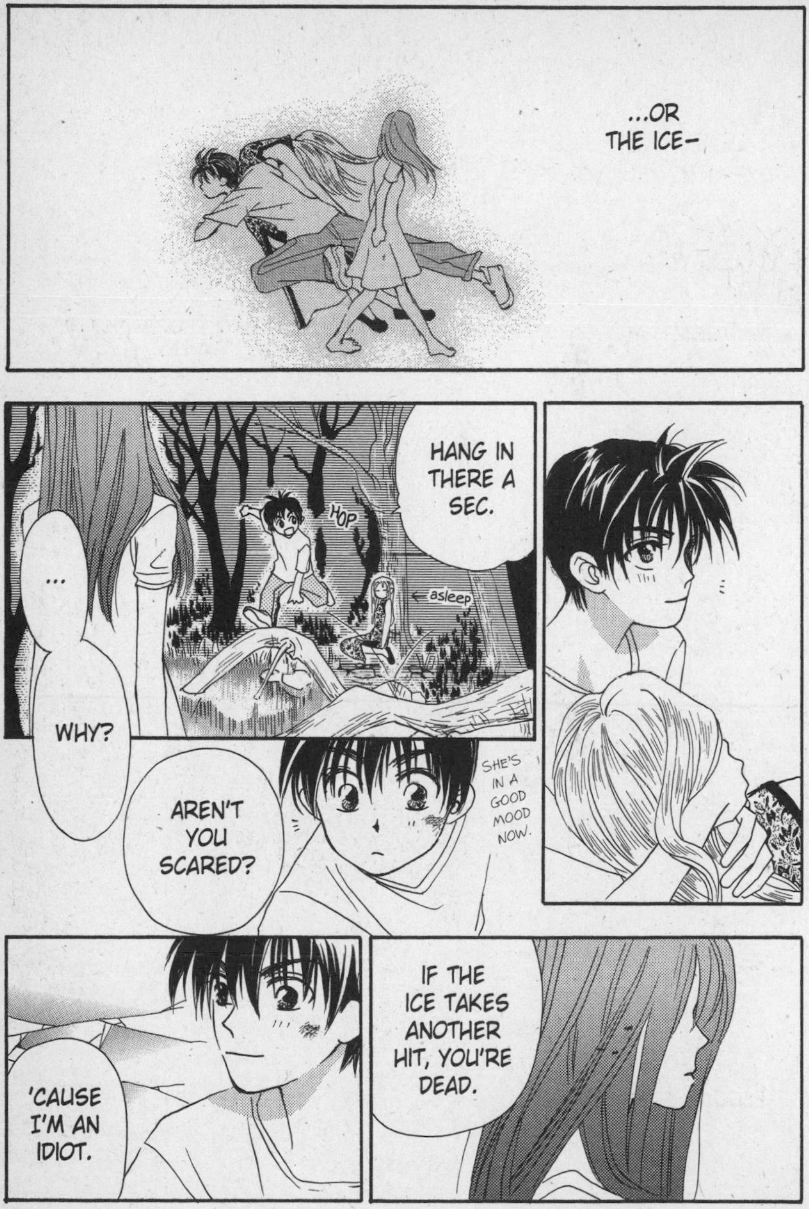
...OR THE ICE-
HANG IN THERE A SEC.
HOP
asleep
...
WHY?
SHE'S IN A GOOD MOOD NOW.
AREN'T YOU SCARED?
IF THE ICE TAKES ANOTHER HIT, YOU'RE DEAD.
'CAUSE I'M AN IDIOT.

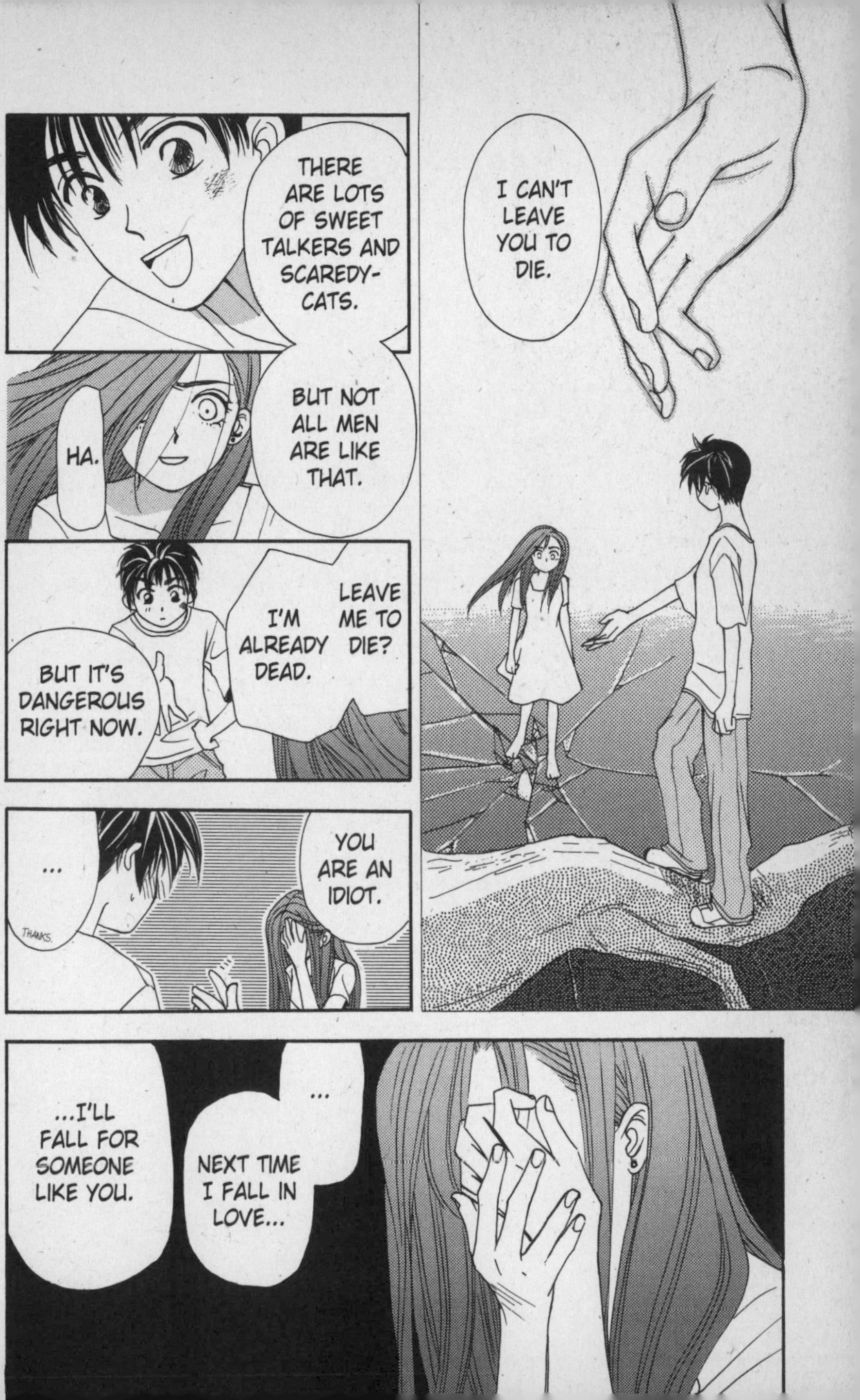
I CAN'T LEAVE YOU TO DIE.
THERE ARE LOTS OF SWEET TALKERS AND SCAREDY-CATS.
BUT NOT ALL MEN ARE LIKE THAT.
HA.
LEAVE ME TO DIE?
I'M ALREADY DEAD.
BUT IT'S DANGEROUS RIGHT NOW.
YOU ARE AN IDIOT.
...
THANKS.
...
NEXT TIME I FALL IN LOVE...
...I'LL FALL FOR SOMEONE LIKE YOU.

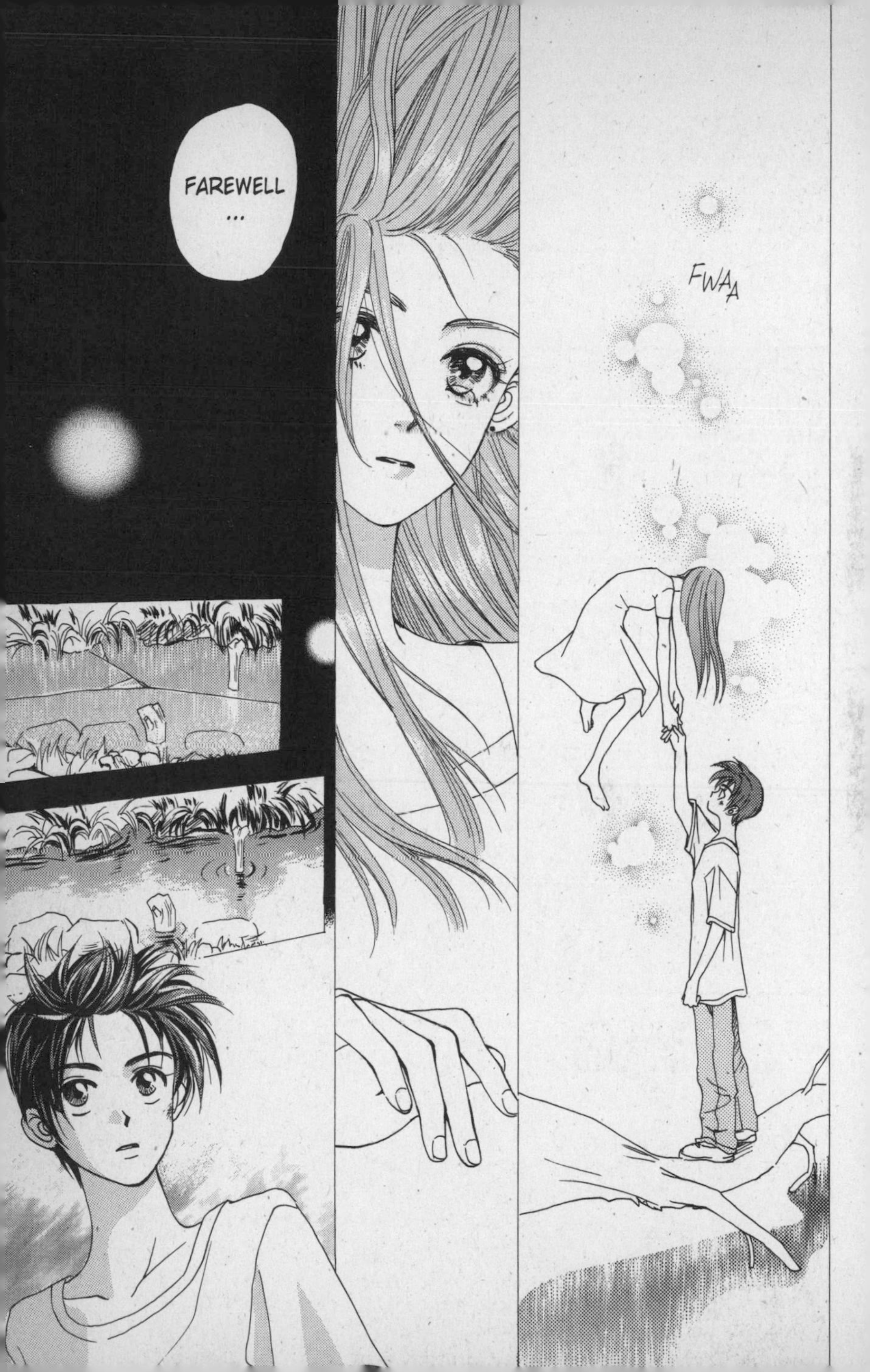
FWAA
FAREWELL ...

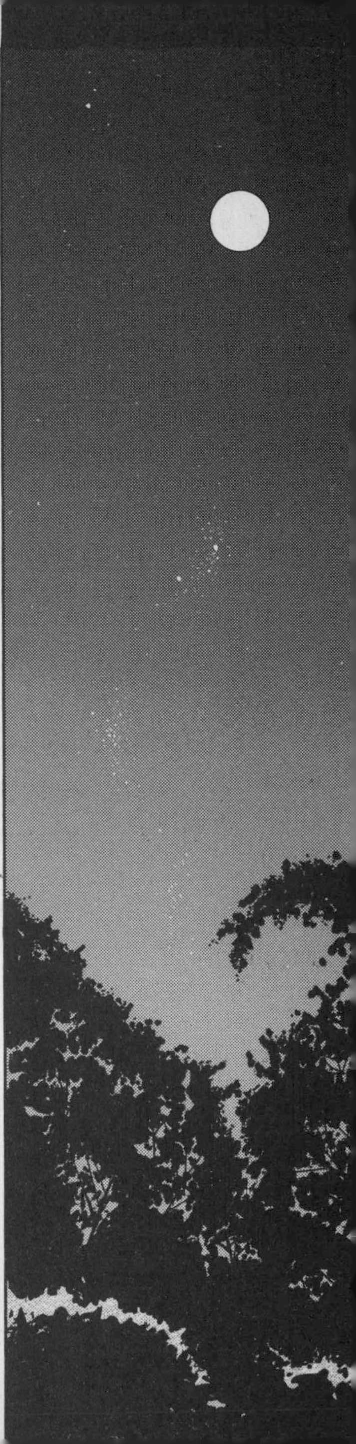

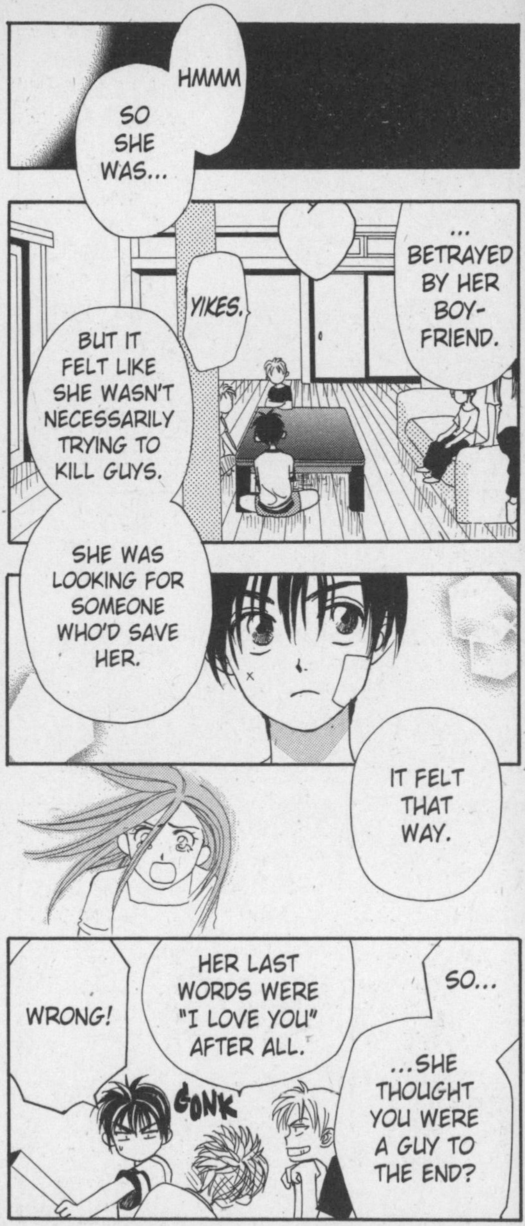
HMMM
SO SHE WAS...
...BETRAYED BY HER BOY-FRIEND.
YIKES.
BUT IT FELT LIKE SHE WASN'T NECESSARILY TRYING TO KILL GUYS.
SHE WAS LOOKING FOR SOMEONE WHO'D SAVE HER.
IT FELT THAT WAY.
SO...
...SHE THOUGHT YOU WERE A GUY TO THE END?
HER LAST WORDS WERE "I LOVE YOU" AFTER ALL.
WRONG!
GONK

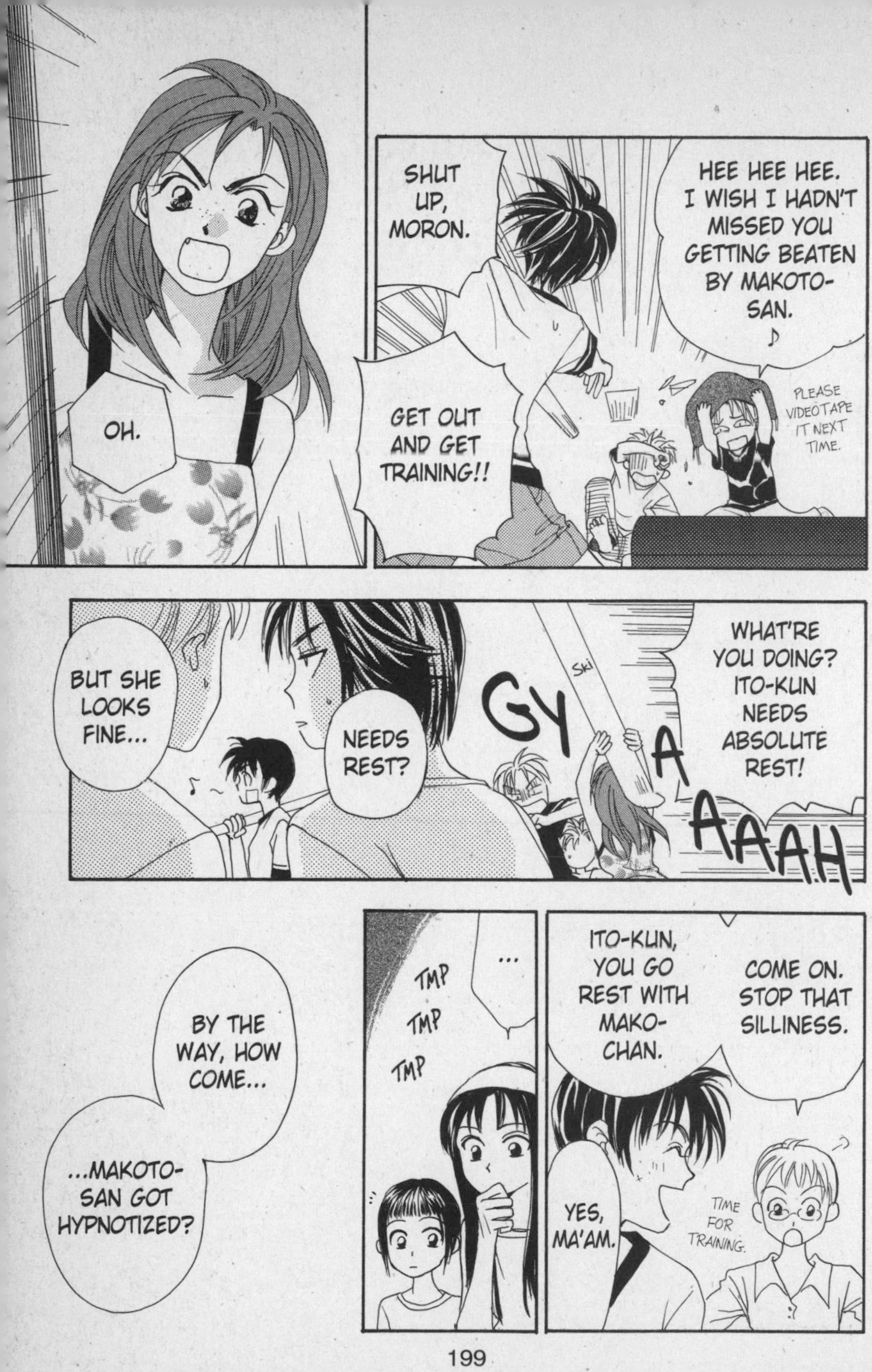
HEE HEE HEE. I WISH I HADN'T MISSED YOU GETTING BEATEN BY MAKOTO-SAN. ♪
SHUT UP, MORON.
PLEASE VIDEOTAPE IT NEXT TIME.
GET OUT AND GET TRAINING!!
OH.
WHAT'RE YOU DOING? ITO-KUN NEEDS ABSOLUTE REST!
GYAAAAH
Ski
NEEDS REST?
BUT SHE LOOKS FINE...
COME ON. STOP THAT SILLINESS.
ITO-KUN, YOU GO REST WITH MAKO-CHAN.
TIME FOR TRAINING.
YES, MA'AM.
...
TMP
TMP
TMP
BY THE WAY, HOW COME...
...MAKOTO-SAN GOT HYPNOTIZED?

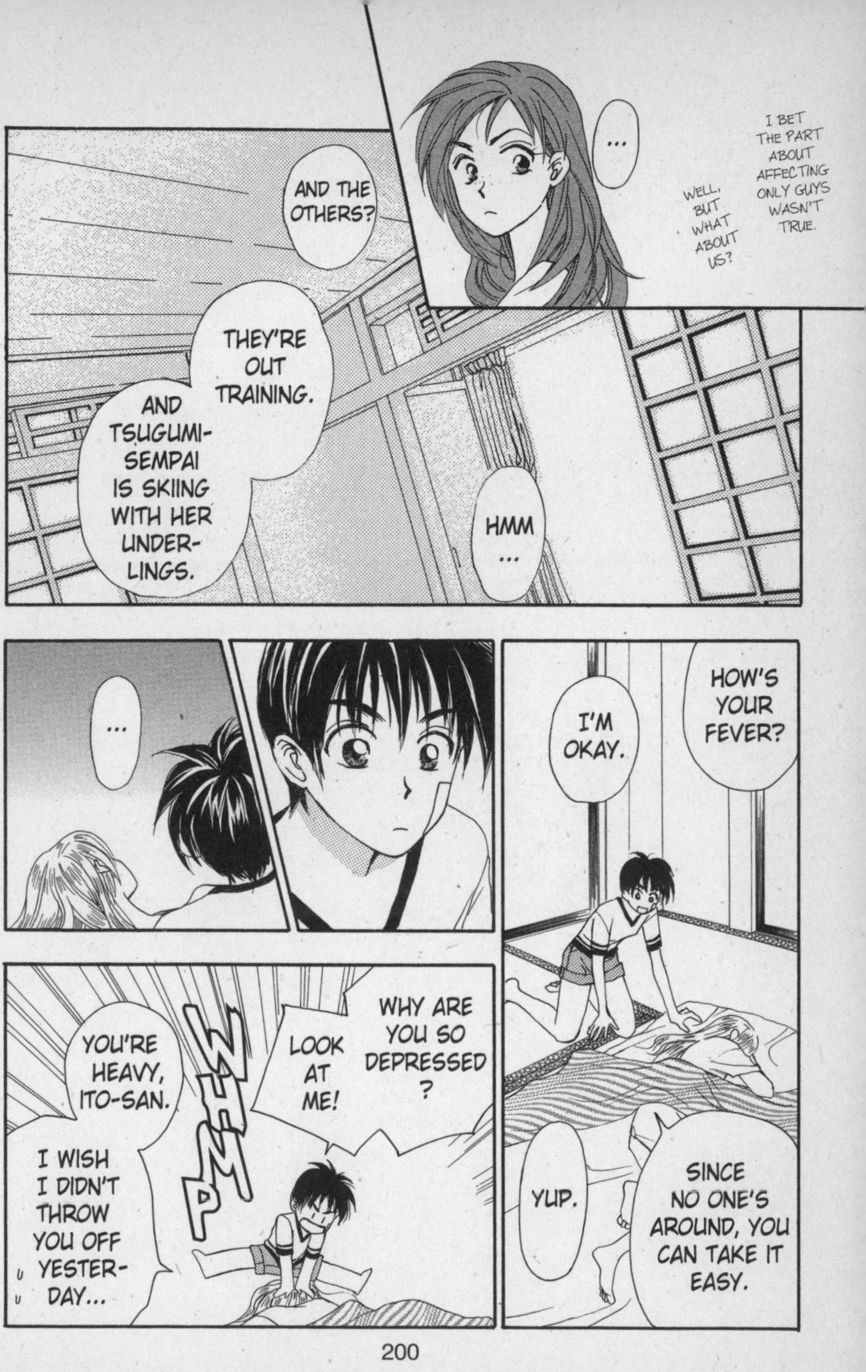
...
I BET THE PART ABOUT AFFECTING ONLY GUYS WASN'T TRUE.
WELL, BUT WHAT ABOUT US?
AND THE OTHERS?
THEY'RE OUT TRAINING.
AND TSUGUMI-SEMPAI IS SKIING WITH HER UNDERLINGS.
HMM...
HOW'S YOUR FEVER?
I'M OKAY.
SINCE NO ONE'S AROUND, YOU CAN TAKE IT EASY.
YUP.
...
WHY ARE YOU SO DEPRESSED?
LOOK AT ME!
WHUMP
YOU'RE HEAVY, ITO-SAN.
I WISH I DIDN'T THROW YOU OFF YESTERDAY...
u u

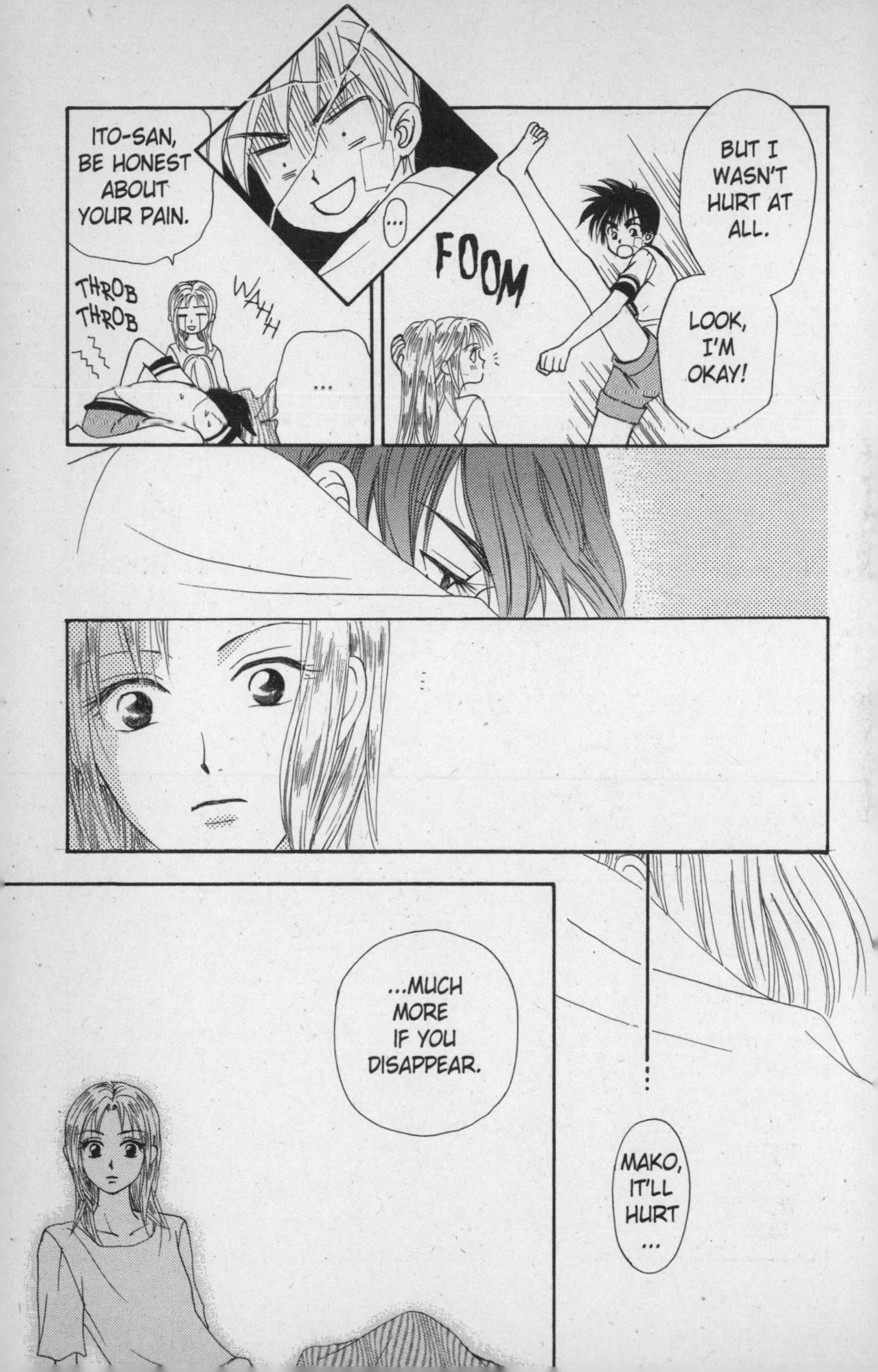
BUT I WASN'T HURT AT ALL.
FOOM
LOOK, I'M OKAY!
ITO-SAN, BE HONEST ABOUT YOUR PAIN.
...
THROB THROB
WAHH
...
...
...
MAKO, IT'LL HURT ...
...MUCH MORE IF YOU DISAPPEAR.

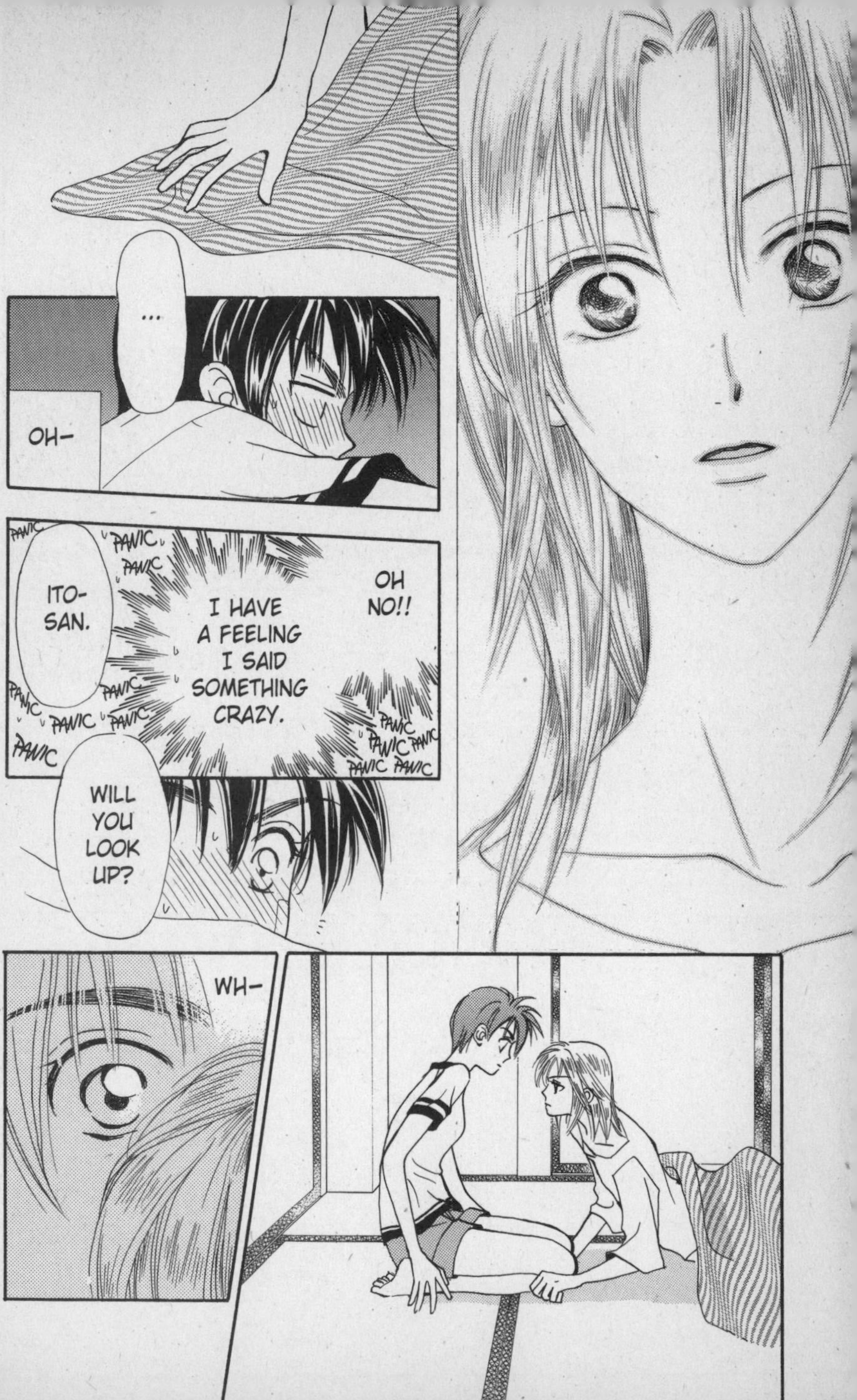
...
OH-
OH NO!!
PANIC PANIC PANIC PANIC PANIC
I HAVE A FEELING I SAID SOMETHING CRAZY.
PANIC PANIC
ITO-SAN.
PANIC PANIC PANIC PANIC PANIC
WILL YOU LOOK UP?
WH-

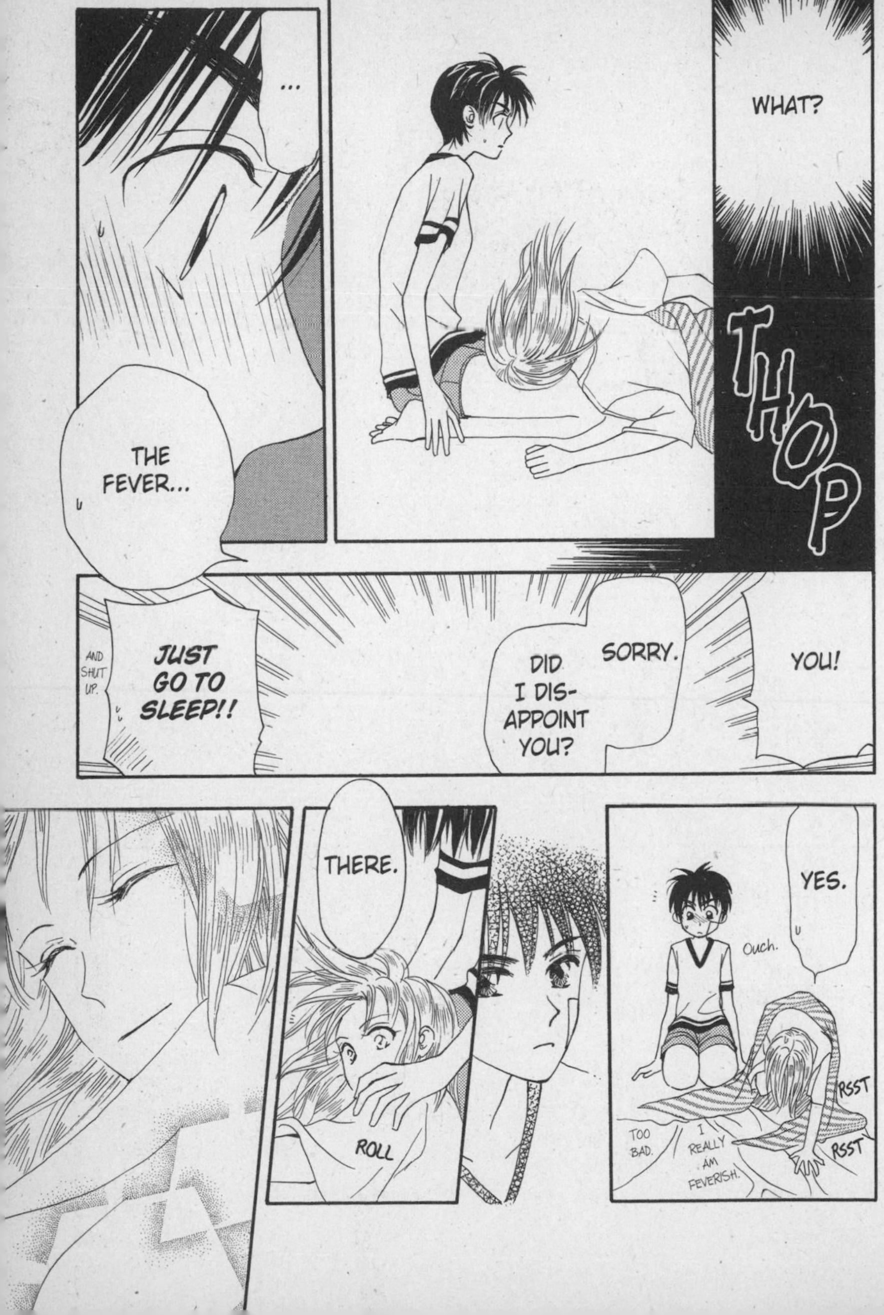
WHAT?
THOP
...
THE FEVER...
YOU!
SORRY.
DID I DIS-APPOINT YOU?
JUST GO TO SLEEP!!
AND SHUT UP.
YES.
Ouch.
RSST
RSST
I REALLY AM FEVERISH.
TOO BAD.
THERE.
ROLL

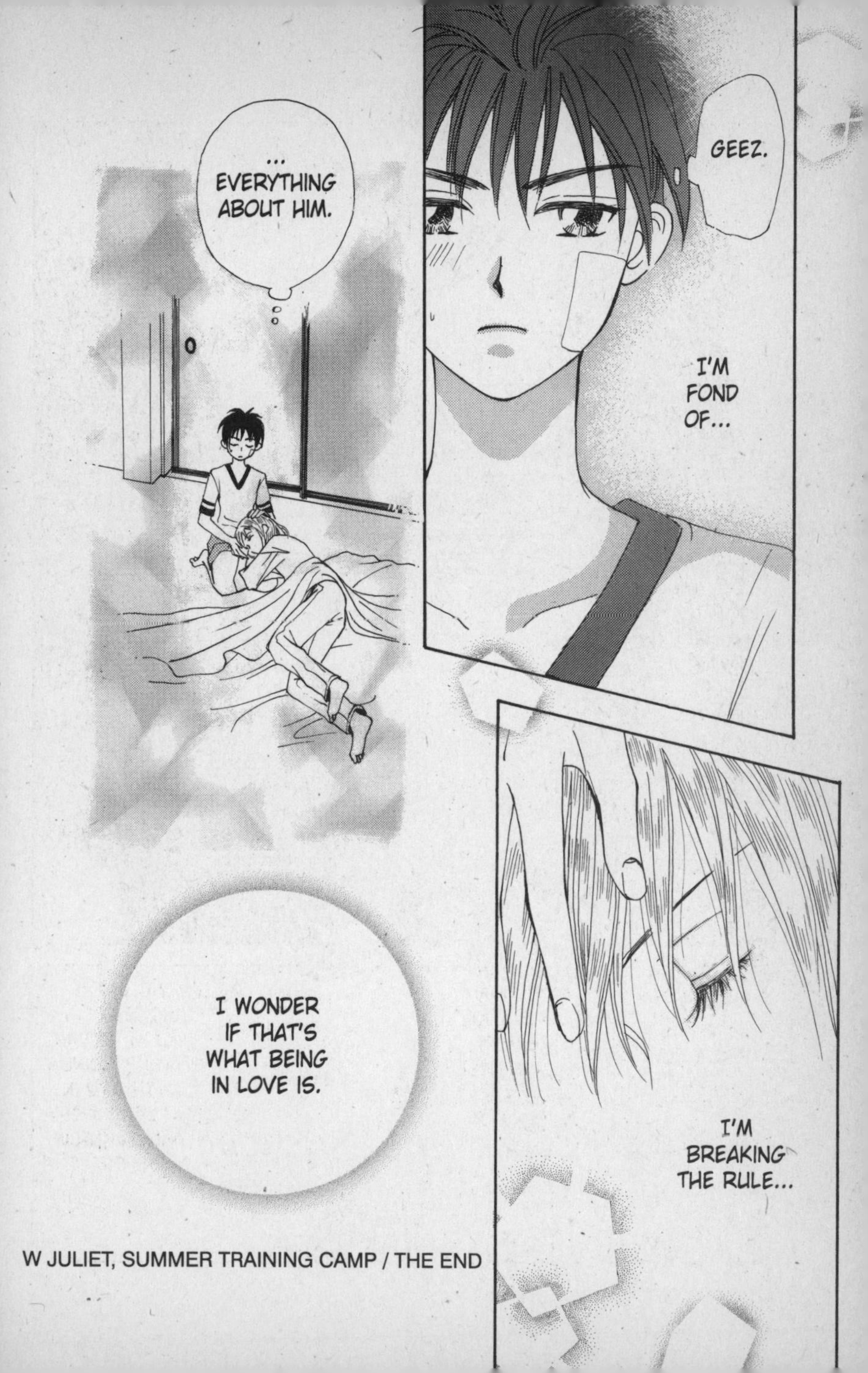
GEEZ.
I'M FOND OF...
I'M BREAKING THE RULE...
... EVERYTHING ABOUT HIM.
I WONDER IF THAT'S WHAT BEING IN LOVE IS.

W JULIET, SUMMER TRAINING CAMP / THE END

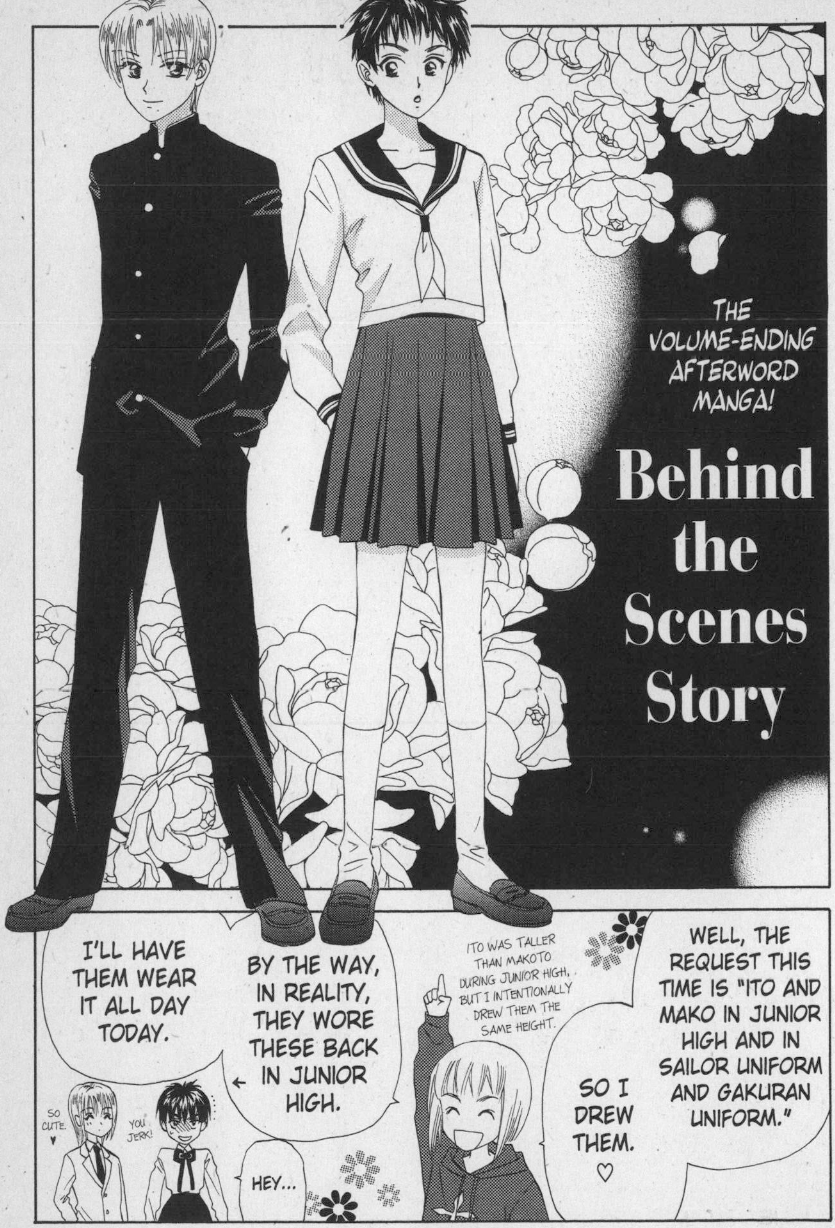
THE VOLUME-ENDING AFTERWORD MANGA!
Behind the Scenes Story
WELL, THE REQUEST THIS TIME IS "ITO AND MAKO IN JUNIOR HIGH AND IN SAILOR UNIFORM AND GAKURAN UNIFORM."
SO I DREW THEM. ♡
ITO WAS TALLER THAN MAKOTO DURING JUNIOR HIGH, BUT I INTENTIONALLY DREW THEM THE SAME HEIGHT.
BY THE WAY, IN REALITY, THEY WORE THESE BACK IN JUNIOR HIGH.
I'LL HAVE THEM WEAR IT ALL DAY TODAY.
HEY...
YOU JERK!
SO CUTE. ♥

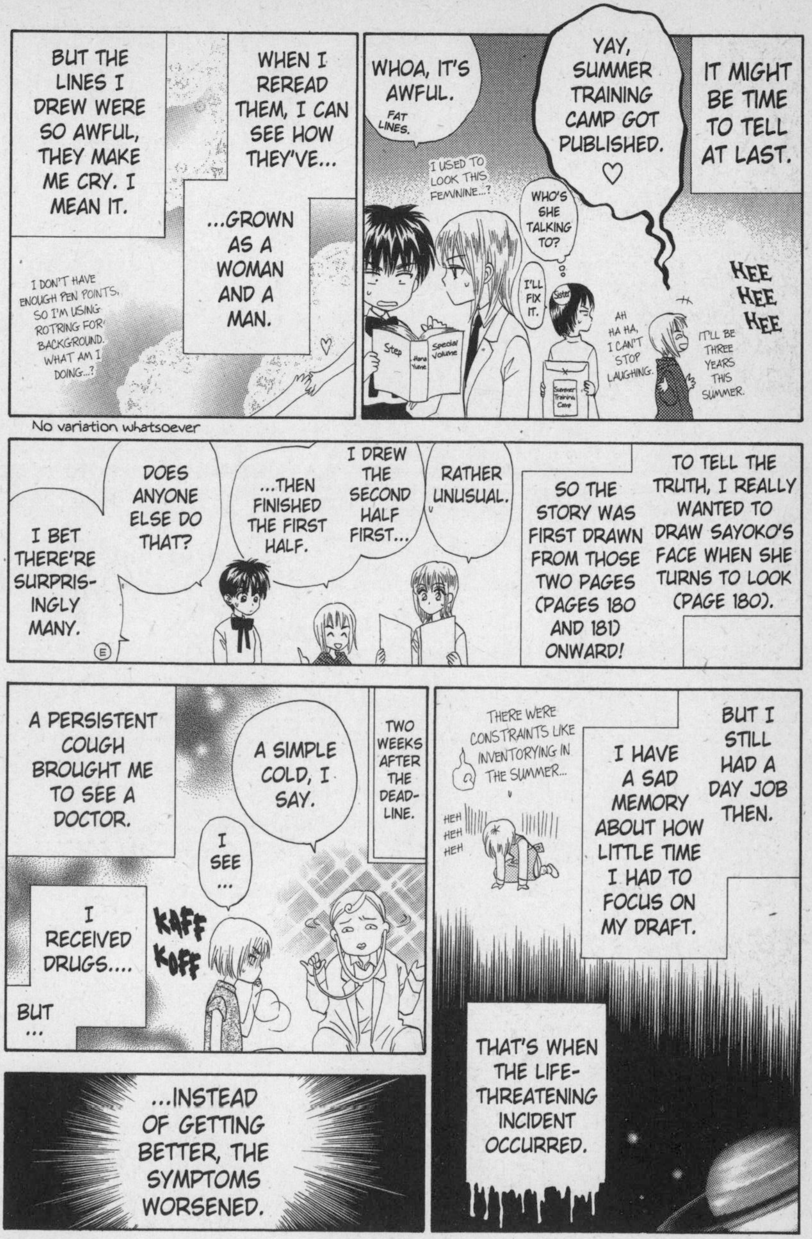
IT MIGHT BE TIME TO TELL AT LAST.
YAY, SUMMER TRAINING CAMP GOT PUBLISHED. ♡
WHOA, IT'S AWFUL.
FAT LINES.
I USED TO LOOK THIS FEMININE...?
WHO'S SHE TALKING TO?
I'LL FIX IT.
Sister
Step
Hana Yume
Special Volume
Summer Training Camp
HEE HEE HEE
AH HA HA, I CAN'T STOP LAUGHING.
IT'LL BE THREE YEARS THIS SUMMER.
WHEN I REREAD THEM, I CAN SEE HOW THEY'VE...
...GROWN AS A WOMAN AND A MAN.
BUT THE LINES I DREW WERE SO AWFUL, THEY MAKE ME CRY. I MEAN IT.
I DON'T HAVE ENOUGH PEN POINTS, SO I'M USING ROTRING FOR BACKGROUND. WHAT AM I DOING...?
No variation whatsoever
TO TELL THE TRUTH, I REALLY WANTED TO DRAW SAYOKO'S FACE WHEN SHE TURNS TO LOOK (PAGE 180).
SO THE STORY WAS FIRST DRAWN FROM THOSE TWO PAGES (PAGES 180 AND 181) ONWARD!
RATHER UNUSUAL.
I DREW THE SECOND HALF FIRST...
...THEN FINISHED THE FIRST HALF.
DOES ANYONE ELSE DO THAT?
I BET THERE'RE SURPRISINGLY MANY.
BUT I STILL HAD A DAY JOB THEN.
I HAVE A SAD MEMORY ABOUT HOW LITTLE TIME I HAD TO FOCUS ON MY DRAFT.
THERE WERE CONSTRAINTS LIKE INVENTORYING IN THE SUMMER...
HEH HEH HEH
THAT'S WHEN THE LIFE-THREATENING INCIDENT OCCURRED.
TWO WEEKS AFTER THE DEAD-LINE.
A PERSISTENT COUGH BROUGHT ME TO SEE A DOCTOR.
A SIMPLE COLD, I SAY.
I SEE...
KAFF KOFF
I RECEIVED DRUGS....
BUT...
...INSTEAD OF GETTING BETTER, THE SYMPTOMS WORSENED.

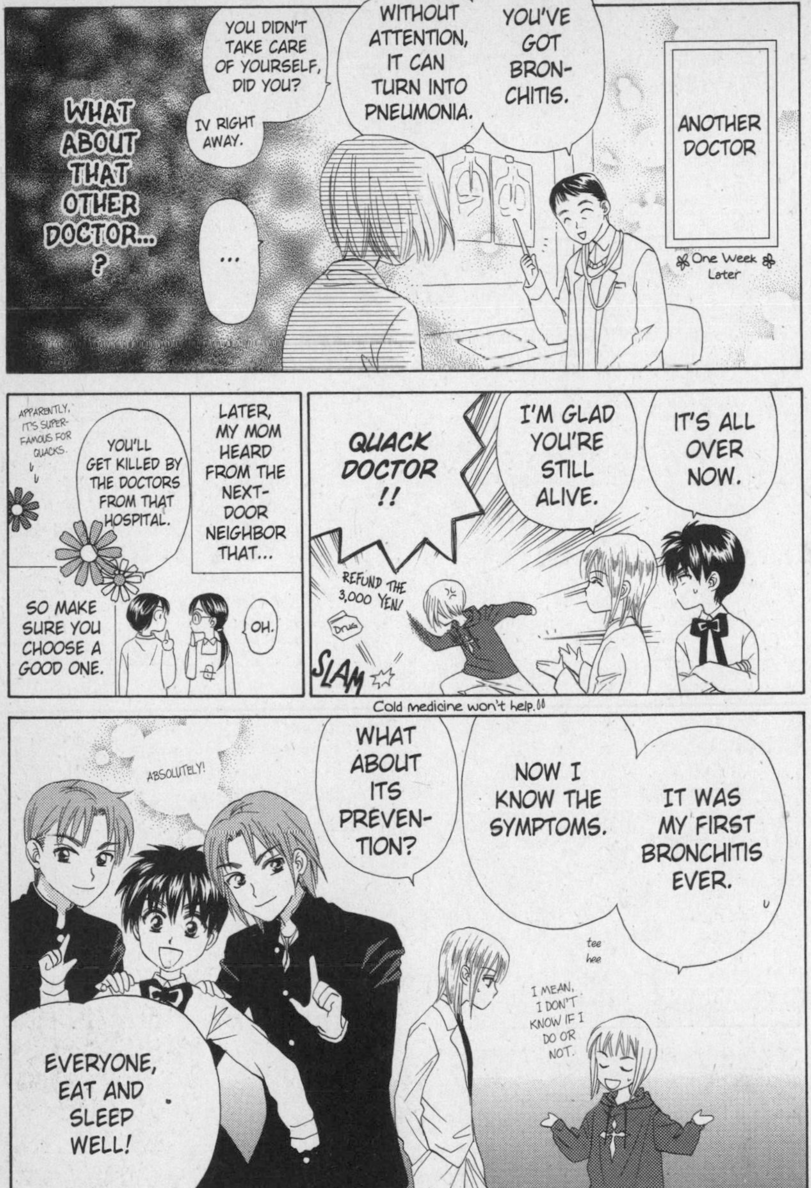
ANOTHER DOCTOR
One Week Later
YOU'VE GOT BRON-CHITIS.
WITHOUT ATTENTION, IT CAN TURN INTO PNEUMONIA.
YOU DIDN'T TAKE CARE OF YOURSELF, DID YOU?
IV RIGHT AWAY.
...
WHAT ABOUT THAT OTHER DOCTOR...?
IT'S ALL OVER NOW.
I'M GLAD YOU'RE STILL ALIVE.
QUACK DOCTOR!!
REFUND THE 3,000 YEN!
Drugs
SLAM
Cold medicine won't help.
LATER, MY MOM HEARD FROM THE NEXT-DOOR NEIGHBOR THAT...
YOU'LL GET KILLED BY THE DOCTORS FROM THAT HOSPITAL.
APPARENTLY, IT'S SUPER-FAMOUS FOR QUACKS.
OH.
SO MAKE SURE YOU CHOOSE A GOOD ONE.
IT WAS MY FIRST BRONCHITIS EVER.
NOW I KNOW THE SYMPTOMS.
tee hee
I MEAN, I DON'T KNOW IF I DO OR NOT.
WHAT ABOUT ITS PREVENTION?
ABSOLUTELY!
EVERYONE, EAT AND SLEEP WELL!

2001. 2. 19 絵夢羅. Emura